The American
Immigration Collection

An Ethnic Survey
of
Woonsocket, Rhode Island

BESSIE BLOOM WESSEL

Arno Press and The New York Times

NEW YORK 1970

Reprint Edition 1970 by Arno Press Inc.

LC# 74-129418
ISBN 0-405-00572-5

The American Immigration Collection—Series II
ISBN for complete set 0-405-00543-1

Manufactured in the United States of America

AN ETHNIC SURVEY
OF
WOONSOCKET, RHODE ISLAND

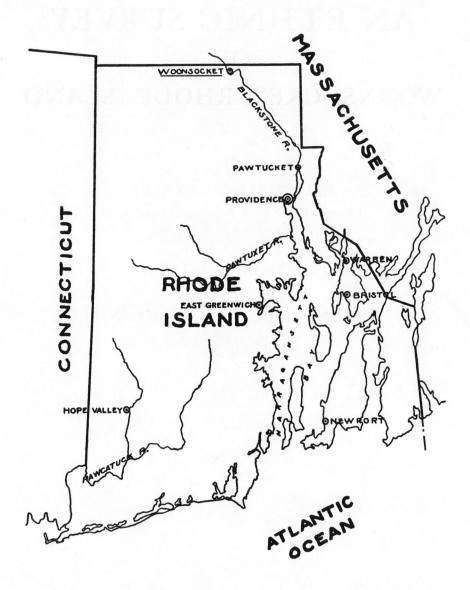

MAP OF WOONSOCKET

AN ETHNIC SURVEY
OF
WOONSOCKET, RHODE ISLAND

By

BESSIE BLOOM WESSEL

Director, Study of Ethnic Factors in Community Life
Associate Professor of Sociology
Connecticut College

THE UNIVERSITY OF CHICAGO PRESS
CHICAGO · ILLINOIS

THE UNIVERSITY OF CHICAGO PRESS
CHICAGO, ILLINOIS
—
THE BAKER & TAYLOR COMPANY
NEW YORK

THE CAMBRIDGE UNIVERSITY PRESS
LONDON

THE MARUZEN-KABUSHIKI-KAISHA
TOKYO, OSAKA, KYOTO, FUKUOKA, SENDAI

THE COMMERCIAL PRESS, LIMITED
SHANGHAI

FOREWORD

The "melting pot" is a popular phrase often regarded as the hope of America. In the minds of many, to question its reality is to flout our national aspirations. Yet everyone agrees that at least some "melting" is in evidence, though few serious attempts have been made to measure in terms of succeeding generations the rate at which this proceeds.

It was as a contribution to this end, in method and in fact, that the author of this book conducted surveys in certain New England urban districts. Further, the study of Woonsocket, as here presented, is not the result of a first attempt, but is based upon experience and insight gained through similar surveys in New London, Stamford, and Providence. As these investigations progressed and confidence was shown to the extent of substantial financial support, the author invited co-operative council in the form of an Advisory Committee mentioned in her Preface. Naturally, the advice given by the members of this Committee was secondary, the author, having conceived the problem, devised the plan of procedure, and carried the study to completion.

The volume speaks for itself. The difficulties to be overcome in such a study are obvious, and concerning these the author labored under no illusions, but faced them persistently. In the end, the data necessary to the measuring of amalgamation are such as relate to what the author of this book chooses to designate as the ethnic descent of succeeding generations. There is often confusion between the nation of one's birth and one's ethnic origin, and students of the social sciences entertain varying opinions as to the relative weight of data for each. Wisely, the author of this volume has amassed data for both national and ethnic origins, using additional checks in language, social ideals, etc., and the tables presented show that people do tend toward loyalty to their ethnic background, even when caught in a maze of mixed marriages. On the other hand, the biological basis to this background tends to vanish in a few generations, since in Woonsocket, at least, 10 per cent of the first-generation parents marry out of their ethnic group, 20 per cent in the second, and 40 per cent in the third. If this rate of increase holds for the fourth and fifth generations, complete biological fusion would result. Yet the author shows us that the case is not so simple, since birth-rates and other variables contribute to the outcome, to evaluate which a pair of racial indices is proposed as a contribution to method.

Finally, this study is an experiment in approaching social surveys through school populations. Psychologists and anthropologists have followed this approach for years, but it seems to have been ignored by others. Further, the data concerning ethnic origins, intermarriage, etc., seem as basic to the study of a modern community as is a genealogical census to field work in cultural anthropology.

CLARK WISSLER

PREFACE

In the ethnic survey which follows there are presented the results of an investigation conducted in the spring of 1926 among the children and the families represented in the public schools of Woonsocket, Rhode Island.

The survey aims to describe the ethnic and regional derivation of the population, ethnic changes which are taking place in the community, and cultural situations which exist there today.

The monograph is presented not only for the light it throws upon these subjects in a given area, but primarily as a study in method, with the hope that the techniques used may give it wider meaning.

The survey of Woonsocket is one of the several conducted, under the direction of the writer, by the Study of Ethnic Factors in Community Life, a temporary organization which functioned under research funds made available for the purpose first to Brown University and more recently to Connecticut College. Other reports have been rendered as specified in the text or are in preparation. This is the only report, however, which contains a full and detailed statement regarding the procedure by which results have been obtained, as well as the basic data from which conclusions have been derived. It has been prepared for publication under an Advisory Committee consisting of Dr. Clark Wissler (chairman), Professor Niles Carpenter of Buffalo University, and Professor Henry P. Fairchild of New York University.

B. B. W.

NEW LONDON, CONN.
AUGUST, 1930

ACKNOWLEDGMENTS

I wish to make full acknowledgment here of the support, financial and otherwise, which has made possible these researches. The nature of this investigation necessitated the collection of first-hand data from thousands of individuals and required some personal contact with them. The gathering of these data would have been impossible without the sincere and intelligent co-operation of many individuals representing strategic positions in their respective communities. Also, the interpretation of data involving race and culture crossing leads to the crossing of scientific boundaries now marked off in academic procedure. In order to disentangle some of the issues involved, I have turned from time to time to scientists who speak with authority in their respective fields. It is difficult to indicate my indebtedness to all persons who have contributed to this investigation. Wherever possible specific indebtedness has been clearly indicated in the text. In addition to the persons so mentioned, my thanks are due:

To Dr. Franklin H. Giddings for early encouragement in this field of research; to Dr. Maurice B. Hexter for his kindly criticism of a first draft of the manuscript; to Miss Alice M. Towsley for her efficient and loyal service as a co-worker; to numerous individuals in the city of Woonsocket —Dr. James F. Rockett, superintendent of schools, to the principals and teachers for their fine co-operation as well as to the leaders among foreign groups who lent us their assistance; to the members who served on the Committee at the Graduate School of Brown University during the year 1927–28 for their hearty indorsement of the project and for their many helpful suggestions. The members of this Committee were drawn from several departments of the university and were Professor James Q. Dealey, chairman; Professors Verner W. Crane, Leland M. Goodrich, Herbert W. Walter, and Dr. Richard D. Allen, the latter representing also the Providence public schools in his capacity as assistant superintendent in charge of research and guidance.

My thanks are especially due to the administration and to my colleagues at Connecticut College for the hospitality and numerous courtesies extended to the Study and to the members of the staff; also to the members of the Advisory Committee more recently appointed to secure publication of this report—whose names I have listed in my Preface and from whom I have received friendly counsel and assistance.

I am deeply indebted to Professor Albert Bennett of Brown University and to Dr. Wissler, both of whom read the manuscript with care and made valuable suggestions which have been incorporated in the text. To Dr. Wissler in particular I owe much for his support and interest in these researches over a period of years.

B. B. W.

TABLE OF CONTENTS

LIST OF TABLES

LIST OF ILLUSTRATIONS

INTRODUCTION

CHAPTER I

THE PROBLEM: NEED OF SCIENTIFIC DATA ON ETHNIC CHANGE IN AMERICAN COMMUNITY LIFE

Anthropologists and students of population have for many years been calling attention to the dearth of adequate data on ethnic origins and on ethnic fusion in the United States; and this in the very country which harbors the most remarkable laboratory in the world for the study of this very problem. Nor can it be said that this dearth is due to lack of interest in races and immigrants. What other problem has commanded so much of our national attention? And over so long a period? The unique position which this country was bound to assume because of the diversity of origins is part of its national history from earliest days. The need of adequately recording these origins, however, has never been met, though it was definitely articulated at least a century and a quarter ago. "A memorial addressed to Congress by Dr. Timothy Dwight just previous to the Federal Census of 1800 contained," says Rossiter, "this rather prophetic suggestion:

> To present and future generations, it will be highly gratifying to observe the progress of population in this country, and to be able to trace the proportions of its increase from native Americans and from foreigners immigrating at successive periods."[1]

Rossiter adds that the Senate unfortunately did not heed the memorial, and we are reminded, as the Fifteenth Census is in progress, that history repeats itself. Splendidly developed as census-taking is in the United States, it still fails to record adequately data on the ethnic origins of our national stock. There has been a constantly increasing number of serious attempts to analyze problems involving migration and racial change, but always the investigator intent upon securing adequate data deplores the meagerness of our records.[2]

[1] Quoted by William S. Rossiter, *Increase of Population in the United States, 1910–1920: Census Monograph 1* (Washington, 1922), p. 95.

[2] The following excerpt is pertinent in this connection (quoted from Harry Jerome, *Migration and Business Cycles*, [National Bureau of Economic Research, 1926], p. 29): "Official annual statistics of immigration are first available with the year ending September 30, 1820; quarterly figures, available with the year ending June 30, 1858; and monthly figures, with the year ending June 30, 1889. However, as noted below, the meaning and comprehensiveness of these statistics have varied from time to time."

3

Official statistics and scattered historical records offer some information. The fact, however, is that our statistics of immigration do not begin
until 1820 when they were first gathered by the Department of State. It
was not until 1850 that foreign-born persons were enumerated by the
Bureau of the Census.[1] The inquiry as to birthplace of foreign parents was
not made until the Census of 1880. Even then only part of the data
secured was tabulated.[2] The chief sources of current information about
immigrants in the country are the statistics published annually by the
commissioner of immigration; those published in the decennial censuses
by the Bureau of the Census, and that contained in various Census monographs.[3] The statistics of emigration compiled by certain foreign countries
constitute another valuable source of information on the subject. These
sources would seem ample, excepting for the fact that the data are not
complete and that the principles of classification are not always uniform.
They are therefore not comparable. The Bureau of Immigration classifies individuals chiefly according to "race or people," although it uses
"countries" also as a basis of classification. The Bureau of the Census
bases all its classifications upon birthplace. When dealing with "race"
Census tables refer only to the primary subdivisions of the human race,
but make no reference to ethnic groupings within these larger divisions.
In addition, "native stock" is not further differentiated as to ethnic origin
in the reports of the Census Bureau.

It is therefore not possible to ascertain from these sources of information the number of individuals actually comprising an ethnic group in the
country at any given time, or to ascertain what the present population of
the United States is by descent. In *Immigrants and Their Children* Professor Niles Carpenter performs a useful service in relating these various
sources of information to each other, and indicates in some measure
significant population changes and types of adjustment not otherwise
clear. But after calling to his aid all the above-mentioned sources, Professor Carpenter, too, finds himself handicapped in drawing conclusions
by the fact that "native stock" always remains further undefined. And

[1] Rossiter, *op. cit.*

[2] "Country of Origin of Foreign White Stock," *Fourteenth Census Reports* (reprint of Vol.
II, chap. ix).

[3] Rossiter, *op. cit.* Also Rossiter, *A Century of Population Growth* (from the first census
of the United States to the twelfth, 1790–1900) (Washington: Government Printing Office,
1909); Niles Carpenter, *Immigrants and Their Children* (Washington: Government Printing
Office, 1920), Census Monograph No. VII.

this native stock, according to the 1920 Census, constitutes over one-half of our population.

The late Professor Drachsler, writing in 1921, opens his discussion of *Intermarriage in New York City*[1] with the following statement:

By common agreement among competent students of American social problems, the proper incorporation of the foreign born and of their immediate descendants into the body politic is considered a question of basic national concern. But although there is much discussion of a controversial nature, both within the narrower circle of scholars and among the public at large, it is based upon comparatively scanty fundamental data. Unrelated, though frequently keen observations alternate with generalizations that are superficial and often flippant, each based on more or less specious race theories.

That monograph was the first significant attempt at the quantitative analysis of a problem which has long continued to be the center of much discussion.

The promulgation of a quota law and the national-origins[2] clause, providing for the control of immigration on a "national" basis, has served to fan the flames of controversy. On the other hand, there has been a steadily increasing scientific interest in ethnic research. The very difficulties which the government experts encountered in an attempt to arrive at a plausible analysis of the national origins of the United States served to call increased attention to the inadequacy of our data on the subject of national composition. Considerable pressure was brought to bear upon the federal government in an effort to bring about changes in the schedule used in the Fifteenth Census of the United States which might improve our record of racial and cultural change. These petitions were not heeded, and yet every year's delay in recording this aspect of the country's history means increased loss of opportunity to locate the basic elements contributing to national stock. Nor does this country have demographic data which can be used as a basis of comparison with the similar data issued by most European countries.[3]

The student who approaches this problem single-handed without comprehensive historical data and without adequate official statistics is thrown upon his own resources in formulating methods for reaching the

[1] Julius Drachsler, *Intermarriage in New York City: A Statistical Study of the Amalgamation of European Peoples.* "Columbia University Studies in History, Economics and Public Law," XCIV, Whole No. 213, (2). See also by the same author, *Democracy and Assimilation: The Blending of Immigrant Heritages in America* (New York: Macmillan & Co., 1920).

[2] See chap. iii for further discussion of these measures.

[3] See, e.g., ethnographic tables and maps contained in Isaiah Bowman, *The New World: Problems in Political Geography* (4th ed.; New York: World Book Co., 1928).

core of the problem. Our national history is relatively short; the migrations represented in any given area are recent. May it not be possible to reconstruct the history of the population within a given area from life-histories of present inhabitants? Can this be done on any extensive basis? *The Ethnic Survey of Woonsocket, Rhode Island*, represents just such an attempt to reconstruct the history of the population in terms of its ethnic descent. The history of such a population unit differs essentially from the history of the community itself.

The data on this score alone may have scientific and historical meaning for us. But the human beings whom we are counting in one way or another are not only bringing about racial changes in the national stock, but they are also effecting changes in the cultural complex of our national life. These adjustments and accommodations offer a wide field for the study of acculturation. The problem of "incorporation" is as much a question of basic national concern as when Professor Drachsler produced his work in 1921, a work which still stands as the outstanding contribution to the literature on the subject of ethnic fusion. Quantitative studies based on factual data gathered for that purpose and dealing more particularly with the subject of ethnic derivation are even more rare. The only recourse left to the investigator is to assemble what techniques he may have for studying a given area, as that area exists, and for resolving a population unit within that area in terms of its ethnic antecedents. Only in this way can we ascertain the essential characteristics of any American community.

We have had numerous surveys in the United States which treat of social conditions or which describe the historical background and industrial aspect of some city. *Middletown*[1] is the most recent contribution to the literature on the study of a given area, and in its approach it incorporates most nearly the methods in use by anthropologists for the study of primitive culture in a given area. More studies of this kind are needed before we may speak with assurance about the nature and content of American life. The emphasis in this volume, however, is more particularly upon those factors which play a basic part in determining the racial and cultural situation. It is therefore more particularly an inquiry into ethnic antecedents and into the nature and extent of ethnic change in Woonsocket, Rhode Island.

[1] Robert S. Lynd and Helen Merrell Lynd, *Middletown: A Study in Contemporary American Culture* (New York: Harcourt, Brace & Co., 1929).

The ethnic survey of the public-school population of Woonsocket, Rhode Island, was inaugurated in the spring of 1926 by the Study of Ethnic Factors in Community Life. Several reasons led to the choice of this particular community as offering an opportunity to conduct such a research. In the first place it is situated close to Brown University, which then served as a base from which this investigation and other similar investigations were being made. It therefore offered a ready opportunity for checking experimental techniques which were being tried out. Woonsocket, too, is unique in that a single foreign group constitutes the dominant ethnic element in the community. It therefore afforded an opportunity to study the adjustment of one ethnic group more intensively. Two-thirds of the population,[1] as determined by this survey, is of French-Canadian descent. The French Canadians not only represent a people which has been coming to this country in appreciable numbers over a long period of years, but one which promises to send us recruits for some time to come, unless Congress extends our restrictive legislation to the Western Hemisphere.

There has been but little research among French Canadians in this country, and this presented itself as an opportune occasion to conduct such an investigation; more so because Mlle Marthe Bossavy,[2] then working on a research grant in this country, had associated herself with the Study, and had chosen as her own special field of investigation French-Canadian adjustments in America.

INVESTIGATIONS BY THE STUDY OF ETHNIC FACTORS IN
COMMUNITY LIFE

As indicated, the Woonsocket survey was one of several similar investigations. In all, surveys were made in four communities, and other experimental work was conducted in a fifth city as follows:

NEW LONDON, CONN. 1921. This survey dealt with 1,819 families then represented in the public schools. It was conducted previous to the formal organization of the Study and was for the most part a student project within the Department of Social

[1] Proportion is reached if both parochial and public school children are included in the estimate.

[2] Mlle Marthe Bossavy herself came from France. She was at that time a research fellow with the Laura Spelman Rockefeller Memorial, and later during her association with this project, professor of romance languages at Vassar College. Mlle Bossavy has since entered the religious life. Previous to her retirement, however, she put on record the material reported in the following pages and that incorporated in Appendix A.

Science at Connecticut College. A report was published under the title, "Ethnic Factors in the Population of New London," in the *American Journal of Sociology*, XXXV, Nos. 1 and 2 (July, 1929, and September, 1929). (Reprinted.)

STAMFORD, CONN. 1925–26. This study was based upon 9,993 racial histories secured from children then in the public, private, and parochial schools of the Stamford school district. (Report pending.)

WOONSOCKET, R.I. 1926. The results of this survey are embodied in the present monograph and cover data obtained in racial histories from 4,978 children in the public schools.

PROVIDENCE, R.I. 1927–28. Several investigations were made under the direction of the author, chiefly by students working for advanced degrees in the Graduate School of Brown University. These students were teachers or supervisors, for the most part, from the Department of Research and Vocational Guidance in the public schools of Providence. Data were gathered for 5,000 children from several school districts. In addition to the ethnic survey made in each school district there were special studies dealing with educational adjustment as related to ethnic history. (Reports pending.)

The following reports in connection with work done in Rhode Island were completed and disposition made as indicated:

An Inquiry into the Relation between Ethnic Origin and School Achievement of Children in the Public Schools of Providence, Rhode Island. By MARGUERITE TULLY, supervisor in charge of achievement tests in the Providence public schools.

This report was filed as a Master's thesis in the Graduate School of Brown University, June, 1928. A copy of it is filed with the Study of Ethnic Factors in Community Life; a summary of it has been prepared for publication.

A Study of Intermarriage in Stamford, Connecticut, and Woonsocket, Rhode Island. By ALICE M. TOWSLEY.

This report is filed as a Master's thesis in the Graduate School of Brown University, June, 1928. A copy of it is filed with the Study of Ethnic Factors in Community Life. See chapter x for an abstract of this investigation.

An Inquiry into the Americanization Theory of French Canadians. By MARTHE L. BOSSAVY.

This statement sets forth and seeks to interpret French attitudes toward the problems of acculturation. A copy is filed with the Study.

Pembroke College, Brown University—an Ethnic Survey.
Report pending.

Anthropometric Measurements of the Students in Pembroke College. By ISABEL GORDON CARTER.
Report in preparation.

Jewish Merchants of Newport in Pre-revolutionary Days. By J. MARK JACOBSON.
This report was filed for reference with the History Department of Brown University. Copies are filed with the Study and with the American Jewish Historical Society.

BUFFALO, N.Y. Under the auspices of the Study and under the direction of Professor Niles Carpenter of the University of Buffalo investigations were conducted among the Poles of that city. Two reports which incorporate findings are: *The Cultural Adjustment of the Polish Group in the City of Buffalo: An Experiment in the Technique of Social Investigation*, by Niles Carpenter and Daniel Katz (reprinted from *Social Forces*, September, 1927); *A Study of Acculturation in the Polish Group of Buffalo, 1926–1928*, by Niles Carpenter and Daniel Katz ("Monographs in Sociology: The University of Buffalo Studies," No. 3).

Each community offered opportunity for experimentation with some phase of the problem. The Stamford survey is the most complete and extensive one. Woonsocket, however, represents one of later investigations conducted by the Study. On the basis of experience gained in the preliminary surveys, certain changes in gathering and presenting data were incorporated into the Woonsocket survey, and it has for this reason been chosen as the subject matter of this report.

SCOPE AND AIM OF THIS INVESTIGATION

In general, the survey of Woonsocket seeks to describe the public-school population in terms of geographic origin, ethnic ancestry, ethnic fusion, and the degree of Americanism.

More specifically, reply is sought to questions such as these: What ethnic groups contribute to the makeup of the present population? In what measure? To what extent do these diverse racial elements fuse, and at what rate is a new population being formed out of these several strains? Do some groups tend to become incorporated in American social life more rapidly than others? What are the conditions that seem to make for more rapid or less rapid amalgamation? Can the survey yield data bearing upon social and cultural factors of fusion such as size of family, language usage, theories of community life, and so on?

In each city the school population was chosen as the unit of investigation because it is the section of the population which must be of greatest interest to those engaged in community planning. It is at the same time that unit in the community which offers the best possible basis for predicting ethnic change. The school children constitute, with some minor exception, the total population of the immediate future. Also, it is in the individual histories of families and children that research cues may be found for the general study of acculturation in American community life.

While the Woonsocket survey deals with only 4,978 cases, these several investigations have covered, in all, the histories of more than 24,000 school children. The history of each child contains information about 6 other members of the family—7 in all: the child, 2 parents, 4 grandparents. This gave the investigators material covering more than 168,000 individuals, a range sufficiently great to test classificatory schemes, and to bring to light the various interrelations which exist between the phenomena under survey.

If, in the face of these data, one enlarged upon the possibilities inherent in a racial and cultural survey, one would be confronted with all the problems inherent in the study of cultural adjustment. This field is covered by the ethnologist in the study of primitive people. Americanization, however, offers parallel data for the study of acculturation in American community life. All the possibilities inherent in a cultural survey of any area await the investigator, who applies that method to modern life with one notable exception, namely, the complications which arise from the very fact that practical issues are involved.

However, the investigator who sees these many possibilities before him must curb his ambition. Humility is ever a sign of good breeding. In this instance it is a necessary condition to achieving perhaps a bare iota in this difficult field. The *Ethnic Survey of Woonsocket* limits itself to a discussion of racial changes which are taking place in the unit under investigation, and to some extent with certain cultural situations which exist there.

ENTRÉE INTO THE COMMUNITY

On the whole, entrée into the community was accomplished without difficulty. It was not possible, however, to secure entrée into the parochial schools. Attention should be called to the fact that inability to obtain returns from Catholic schools was not characteristic of other communities. At one time the writer collected data covering the Catholic schools of New London. In the Stamford survey, made just previous to the Woonsocket one, histories were secured from all the parochial and private schools, as well as from the public schools. Woonsocket is the only instance in which the investigators record inability to get data for Catholic schools. This inability to carry the investigation into the parochial schools of Woonsocket was due to the very serious conflict[1] which then existed between the French-Canadian element and the Catholic hierarchy in Rhode Island, as well as to a standing difference of opinion which exists between those who represent state control of education and the French-Canadian leaders regarding the limits of educational authority. The conflict within the church was at the time so tense that it had its reverberation in the state courts; it was decried in the Senate of the United States,

[1] See chap. xiv.

and was finally carried to the Papal see at Rome. The quarrel has since been adjusted—at least for the time being.

At any rate, the heat of war has given way to conferences about the peace table and to diplomatic parleys. The dramatic events of calling the "Irish" bishop into court on a purely technical charge of faulty administration of church funds, the consequent excommunication of French-Canadian leaders responsible for this procedure, the final repentance and forgiveness—all these are for the most part excrescences due to a small group of insurgents, ardent and radical. At bottom, however, there are very real issues involved relating to the cultural rights of an ethnic minority within a "mother-church" and within a foster-community. These are real issues, recognized as such by the various parties concerned, and are even now the subject of earnest consideration between the groups involved.

Such a conflict is quite properly the subject matter of any inquiry into ethnic adjustment since it is at bottom a conflict between different theories of Americanization. However, no objective analysis was made of this situation, and we can do no more here than to mention the issue and its effect upon the investigation. The controversy was sufficiently tense so that no investigation involving entrée into the parochial schools was possible at the time. Such entrée depended upon the co-operation of the very groups at war with each other. The investigators have retained at all times the frank co-operation of the various leaders as individuals, have had conferences with them which have been helpful in interpreting the conflicts and in securing and understanding data contained in personal histories, but the investigation itself was not carried into the parochial schools.

How does this omission of the parochial schools affect the data? At first glance the omission seems serious since Woonsocket is peculiar in that more than one-half of all its school children are in the parochial schools. The data that have been analyzed, then, deal with one-half of the school population, that half which attends the public schools. On the other hand, the report contains total figures giving the registration for all children in the Irish parochial school and for those in the French-Canadian schools. Our family histories contain information on the size of family. They also contain information regarding those sisters and brothers of public-school children who are in parochial schools. It is therefore possible to measure the discrepancy in estimating the composition of the whole population of children. This is done whenever it seems pertinent. Excepting when reference is to the contrary, however, all analyses are made on the basis of the public-school population from whom individual histories were actually collected.

There were at the time 5,277 children in the parochial schools. Of the parochial school children, 387 were in the Irish school and 4,890 were in French-Canadian schools. More children attend the French-Canadian parochial schools than are registered in the entire public-school system, representing all the other groups in the city combined, namely, 4,978. Only one-fourth of all French-Canadian children attend public school. So large, however, is the French-Canadian element in Woonsocket that in spite of this fact it remains the major ethnic group in the public-school population. Without the parochial school children, the population unit surveyed becomes more typical of other New England communities. Even then in no other community surveyed did any ethnic group attain so high a percentage of the total stock as does the French-Canadian element in the public-school population alone.

Part I of the survey limits itself to the elementary and basic problem of describing the public-school population of Woonsocket in terms of its ethnic and geographic derivation.

Part II is given over to a further analysis of composition and fusion data, with particular reference to intermarriage among parents, and to problems of method.

Part III deals more particularly with the survey in its cultural aspects and with certain "research leads" which seem to merit consideration.

Because of their dominance in the community, the French Canadians call for more intensive treatment. Appendix A has therefore been added; it is a résumé of the data on French Canadians and contains an annotated bibliography dealing with French adjustments on the American continent.

Appendix B is a discussion of method and deals more particularly with the reliability of data and with the feasibility of ethnic surveys. It also contains a selected list of works bearing upon the problems and the technique of this investigation.

CHAPTER II

PROCEDURE

GATHERING OF THE DATA

The findings in this monograph are based upon data contained in histories secured from the 4,978 children who attended the public schools of Woonsocket during the spring of 1926. These histories were secured from questionnaires like the sample one on page 15 which called primarily for information regarding the geographic and ethnic derivation of parents and of grandparents. Other questions dealt with facts of migration, language usage, and size of family. The questionnaires were directed to the parents and were filled out by them; they were carried home by the children.

Previous to the distribution of questionnaires and after entrée into the community had been secured and the necessary steps in organization of the investigation had been completed, the director of the Study addressed the school principals. The investigation had been authorized as a school project by the school administration and was conducted as an official investigation of the school department. At the request of the superintendent, the principals assumed responsibility for securing the data from the children in their respective schools. The purpose of the Study was indicated, the significance of the questions was discussed, more particularly the meaning of the terms "nationality"' and "race." These words have different connotation for the immigrant peoples than they do for individuals educated in our public-school system, and than they do for the American school-teacher. To most teachers, in New England at least, the word "nationality" signifies a political concept. To most immigrant groups the word "nationality" represents an ethnic concept. It was necessary to put this clearly before school-teachers, since in other communities teachers had inadvertently persisted in making children say they were American if the children were native born, or if their fathers were American citizens. The children quite naturally say that their fathers are American citizens but that their "nationality" is German or Italian. This does not mean that immigrant groups do not comprehend political nationality. It simply means that the word "nationality" does not cover that concept for them. Frequently the father would add a note saying that he was a "citizen" of another country from that which he designated as his "nationality," or that he was an American citizen of Italian or German descent. Those terms were used which had, in other investigations by the staff, proved to have definite meaning for parents, quite irrespective of the words by which teachers or investigators label these concepts. The word "descent" and its connotation is equally familiar to all groups. It was used to advantage in other studies, although "nationality" and "race" were the words used in the Woonsocket survey. Every effort was made to evoke the best available information on ethnic derivation in particular.[1]

POPULATION-STUDY
INSTRUCTIONS TO PRINCIPALS AND TEACHERS
[See questionnaire on opposite page]

1. The pink questionnaires are for the girls, the blue ones for the boys.
2. Try for completeness on each questionnaire wherever possible.
3. Discard no sheets because they are incomplete or are not filled out at all. Every child must be accounted for. Turn in the questionnaire even if only the name and address are recorded.
4. Only *one history* is necessary for *each family*. The entire questionnaire is filled out once for each family,—preferably by the oldest child of that family in the school. *Each child* in the family fills out the stub at the top.
5. It would be helpful if each school could have the schedules sorted by families, attaching all the stubs belonging to a family to the history of that family.
6. Teachers please note the letters *C* and *J* in the lower right-hand corner and fill in as follows *after* the slip has been returned by the child.

   If the child is colored, please put a check mark after the *C*. If the child is Jewish, please put a check mark after the *J*.

   [This additional check is necessary in the case of these two groups as otherwise they become erroneously classified according to birthplace, for example, as Russians or Poles in the case of Jews; or as white Americans in the case of Negroes.]
7. The persons making this study will appreciate any suggestions as to how the questionnaire or the procedure may be improved. Ask your principal for further information.

The Woonsocket study benefited by the experience of other surveys in that teachers could be forewarned on this score. They were requested to give the children no instruction bearing upon possible replies. The questions were directed to the parents. Check questions on the questionnaires served to indicate to the investigator how the families interpreted the

---

[1] The word "nationality" reaches the Italian most directly. "Nationality" or "race" both evoke the desired response from Jews, excepting those affiliated with the reform movement in Jewry. French Canadians are familiar with the term "ethnic," and it appears frequently in their daily press. For further discussion of this subject see Appendix B.

questions, or where the history was incomplete. Inconsistent and incomplete histories were later followed up by home visits.

BOYS   RHODE ISLAND   PUT NO WRITING HERE

WOONSOCKET SCHOOLS

School .... Grade.................... Age....................

Name .... Address....................
   (First)   (Last)   (Number)   (Street)

Where were you born?....................
   (Country)   (Province or State)   (City, if in Rhode Island)

If foreign born, at what age did you come to this country? ....

What language other than English do you speak?....................

What is your mother's nationality or race?....................
   (Example: English, French Canadian, Irish, etc.)

Where was your mother born?....................
   (Country)   (Province or State)   (City, if in Rhode Island)

If foreign born in what year did she come to this country?....................At what age?............

Where was your mother's mother born?....................

Where was your mother's father born?....................

When did the first member of your mother's family come to Woonsocket?....................To U. S. A.?............

What is your father's nationality or race?....................

Where was your father born?....................
   (Country)   (Province or State)   (City, if in Rhode Island)

If foreign born, in what year did he come to this country?....................At what age?............

Where was your father's mother born?....................

Where was your father's father born?....................

When did the first member of your father's family come to Woonsocket?....................To U. S. A.?............

In what country were your mother and father married?....................In what year?............

What language is usually spoken in your home?....................

What other languages does your mother speak?....................

What other languages does your father speak?....................

Have you any brothers or sisters in this school?....................

If so, name them, and give grade....................

Have you any brothers or sisters in any other school, or in college? ....

If so, name them and give school they are in....................

Have you any brothers or sisters not in school?....................

If so, name them and give age....................   C.   J.

(Schedule used in population studies in Connecticut and Rhode Island)

The school principals were addressed on a Friday afternoon. The instructions to teachers and questionnaires were distributed through the schools on the following Monday. Most of the replies were returned within the school week. This particular choice of days was found everywhere to bring the best results. No school holiday was permitted to intervene between the day that the child took the questions home and the next day when he was supposed to return them. The latter days of the week gave an opportunity for absentees to be followed up, for stragglers to come in, and for distributing duplicate sheets to children who had lost or destroyed theirs, or to answer any inquiries that might come in from parents. Experience indicates that, given the necessary entrée and with this particular procedure, a school district may be depended upon returning at least 90 per cent of the histories in acceptable form within a school week.[1]

In a survey of Stamford, Connecticut, made the previous year, visits were made to the homes of about a thousand children.[2] This number of visits was larger than was actually necessary to gather the most pertinent data, but in these initial surveys a home visit was made whenever the investigators not only doubted the information, but also when they thought that an interview might throw light upon the possible use of better terminology, the nature of the response which certain questions were evoking, and, in general, upon the technique of gathering the necessary information. The possible sources of error, the relative accuracy of replies, are subjects of discussion later.[3] Perhaps we should say here that all investigators reported that the answers relating to ethnic descent proved to be more frequently correct than any other. The "consciousness of *kin*" is a very definite element in the emotional and thought life of these peoples. This does not necessarily mean that these replies have anthropological validity or that immigrants are aware of their ultimate origin. The replies indicate a consciousness of descent from a certain cultural type or group, which group may or may not represent physically homogeneous types. That remains for the scientist to disentangle, if he can.

Ascertaining "ethnic" derivation was the objective placed above all others. Those terms and those methods which seemed to elicit the best response to questions relating to "ethnic" descent were given precedence over all others. It was on the basis of the home visits in Stamford that

[1] In a subsequent survey where a member of the staff remained at the school during the investigation it was possible to secure full returns within the same period. Children who were uncertain as to the meaning of questions or who needed help were sent to the "home visitor" stationed at the school. No follow-up visits were necessary at this school. Only 5 out of 566 replies were incomplete for the Thomas A. Doyle School, Providence, and these were histories of dependent children who were receiving custodial care in an institution.

[2] This represents, roughly, about 10 per cent of the children in the unit and about 20 per cent of the families.

[3] See Appendix B.

the present terminology, instructions to teachers and parents, even the sequence of questions, was determined. It was found that the very sequence of questions on the blank made considerable difference in replies, and certainly in the efficiency of tabulating and using the data. In all communities the approach, the letters of explanations to individuals who needed them or requested them, and sometimes the forms used were modified in conference with persons in the community under whose auspices and with whose assistance the study was being made.

In Woonsocket visits were made to 841[1] families who returned questionnaires that were incomplete, inconsistent, obviously incorrect, or because the histories contained facts which were in the nature of research cues for specialized investigations. The number of visits made in Woonsocket was increased because of two special investigations. One of these investigations dealt with the descent of "Old American"[2] families. This represents the first attempt in connection with this series of studies[3] to ascertain the ethnic derivation of all "American" stock and to distribute American stock beyond the third generation according to the ethnic elements of which it is composed.

A second investigation dealt with French-Canadian families whose families had been in the United States two or three generations and who were in part or in whole Old American. This investigation was conducted by the French member of the staff. Mlle Bossavy visited 213 French-Canadian families in which one or more grandparents were native born. These visits and her interviews with old settlers gave her insight into the history of French-Canadian migration as it is reflected in the homes of French Canadians in Woonsocket.[4] One of the most interesting features of this investigation was the light it threw upon the various migrations of the family to different places in the United States before settling in any one community, and upon the general thought life of the older French-Canadian settlers.

When the data were complete the questionnaires were coded by staff members and transferred to punch cards for use in Hollerith machines. Since these investigations were frankly experimental in nature, and work was being done in more than one community, if was deemed advisable

---

[1] It required 922 visits to secure the data in full for these 841 families. This represents 29 per cent of all families in the unit—2,876.

[2] I.e., families in which all grandparents were native born (Hrdlička).

[3] I.e., those conducted by the Study of Ethnic Factors in Community Life.

[4] For a report of that investigation see Appendix A.

to bear in mind the possibility of carrying out these studies on a more extensive scale. The validity of data in this field depends upon the careful study of numerous communities and upon the use of an extremely large number of cases. Without these conditions the social processes which are under survey cannot become apparent. The investigators, therefore, bore in mind the utilization of mechanical resources for preparing data of this kind on a much larger scale. Consideration was given both to principles of classification and to the mechanics of tabulation.[1]

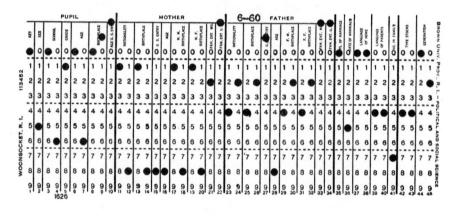

PRINCIPLES OF CLASSIFICATION AND TERMINOLOGY

Early in the course of the researches, of which the Woonsocket survey is one, the investigators were confronted with the need of a classificatory scheme and a definite terminology. In no field is terminology or are classifications more vague and misleading. Nor is this confusion limited to popular usage or to pseudo-scientific writing. Inevitably studies dealing with ethnic phenomena cut across borderlines marked out for themselves by the special social sciences. Here again the same words have different meanings. The writer has therefore chosen to err on the side of too-frequent definition rather than to have moot terms undefined. Whenever current terminology has sufficient precision to fit the data it has been given preference over a possible new term.

The groups under investigation are referred to as ethnic groups or "nationalities," the term "nationality" being used in its ethnic sense. These groups do, for the most part, represent definite types (Boas). It might be said that even these ethnic groups do not offer a sufficient basis for determining truly racial, i.e., hereditary, characteristics. However,

[1] For discussion regarding mechanization and tabulation of data see Appendix B.

we are not at present in a position to disentangle the various racial elements of which these groups are composed. They are generally recognizable and relatively stable "types"[1]—British, French Canadians, Jews, Italians, and so on. They each differ in the degree of homogeneity and purity. The French Canadians are a fairly homogeneous group because of several centuries of inbreeding. The Jews constitute an ethnic group, displaying well-marked cultural cohesion. They are, however, less prone to intermarriage than any other group in the country. On the other hand, they are characterized by physical heterogeneity (Fishberg). The British are in origin a mixed racial group, yet they constitute a definite type not usually mistaken for Armenian or Syrian. In spite of considerable overlapping, these groups do represent definite ethnic entities to the student of population problems. Whatever classification we make must, in the present state of knowledge, be tentative.

In this study a child's place within a group is determined by the ethnic derivation of four grandparents. A child, all four of whose grandparents are Jewish, is classed as Jewish. The birthplaces of parents and grandparents are also recorded. These throw light upon migratory habits of individuals and of groups and in themselves constitute cultural variables for each child. Thus a child who together with his parents was born in Italy of four Italian grandparents may not differ constitutionally from the child also descended from four Italian grandparents but whose parents were born in the United States and who is himself native born. Culturally we may expect a different product. An attempt was made to use symbols which would measure all these factors, or which would at least leave the way open for further cultural analyses.

The ethnic grouping finally determined upon is apparent from the tables. The list given on page 20 may serve as an index.

Since the emphasis throughout the investigation is placed on ascertaining ethnic derivation, the ethnic scheme is primary; the geographic classification is made to conform to this primary scheme. The ethnic and primary grouping is so constituted that in general the same form or list of classes can be used for either an ethnic or a regional distribution, thus obviating the need of two classificatory schemes.[2] The geographic list

[1] The writer is drawing here on a previous statement read before a meeting of the Eugenics Research Association, June, 1929, and published in full in *Eugenics*, II (December, 1929), 12. (Reprinted.)

[2] There are only a few tables in which the actual regions are listed and a dual classification for ethnic and geographic derivation is used. In all other tables one nomenclature is used, that appearing in the first list. See Table 11 entitled "2,876 Fathers by Ethnic versus Regional Derivation" (chap. v).

when used includes regions which are the primary or the secondary home
lands of an appreciable number of immigrants in this particular community. Hence we have several French or British regions. Thus, under
the summary term "British" are included the English, Scotch, and Welsh
for ethnic derivation. Under "British regions" are correspondingly and ob-

DERIVATION*

Albanian	Finnish	b) Norwegian
Armenian	French Canadian	c) Danish
Austrian	French, all others	Slavic§
Belgian (Flemish)	a) French, France	a) Polish
British	b) Walloon	b) Ukrainian
a) English	c) Alsatian	c) Russian
b) Scotch	d) Swiss	d) Lithuanian‖
c) Scotch-Irish	e) French mixed	e) (Galician)
d) Canadian English	German	Spanish
e) Canadian Scotch	Greek	Syrian
f) Canadian unspec.†	Irish	Turkish
g) British mixed	Italian	Mixed ancestry
h) British, others	Jewish	Partly unspecified (n.)¶
Chinese	Portuguese (white)‡	Unspecified (n.)**
Colored	Roumanian	Other unspecified
Czech	Scandinavian	American††
Dutch	a) Swedish	

* "Derivation" signifies either ethnic or regional derivation as indicated in the specific table.

† Probably British.

‡ Includes Portuguese possessions as indicated in the various tables.

§ Only the Slavs from in and about former Russia are placed here. Czechs are grouped independently.

‖ In putting the Lithuanians here we are frankly on controversial soil. They are placed here for convenience because they are a small group (eight parents only), a kindred group culturally, and in Woonsocket they intermarry with the Russian Slavs.

¶ One parent is further unspecified.

** Both parents are unspecified as to ethnic descent. In this and in the preceding instance the information is incomplete for ethnic origin, but the individual is either native born (n.) or of native descent (n.d.). Under "Other unspecified" are included individuals for whom the data on nativity also are lacking.

†† "American" is, for want of a better term, used as an adjective to refer to the United States.

viously Great Britain, Canada, and others as indicated. These are countries from which we expect British immigration. And so with the French.
Only those groups or countries appear on the list which are actually represented in Woonsocket.

In order better to describe the situation it was necessary to make an
overlapping geographic classification. In general an attempt was made
to adhere to a classification based on post-war boundaries. In the course
of the survey it became obvious that the inclusion of certain regions, quite
aside from their political boundaries, served best to interpret the picture

and to suggest causes in explanation of group behavior, migration, inter-marriage, and folk customs. Alsace was retained as such a region, as were also Galicia and the Ukraine, irrespective of their post-war status. Russia, of course, means former Russia, and in this case does not include the Ukraine, which is treated separately because it sends a considerable number of immigrants who claim to be Ukrainian and who constitute a self-conscious group in the community.[1]

The Swiss and Alsatians were included under the French because it was definitely ascertained that in Woonsocket these individuals claim affiliation with the French. In the discussion the several British stocks are frequently discussed as a combined British group, and the Slavic groups as a combined Slavic group. With the French Canadians and the French the treatment is slightly different. The French Canadians are so impor-tant an element in this population that they call for special treatment. The data for this group, therefore, are never actually combined with the data on other French stocks. This separate grouping enables comparisons with other French stocks as well as with non-French stocks. On the other hand, the presentation is such that any conclusions regarding French stocks in general can be easily arrived at.

TERMS[2]

Homogeneous refers to any child, or to a sib, all four of whose grand-parents are of the same ethnic derivation, irrespective of birthplace.

Mixed refers to any child all four of whose grandparents are not of the same ethnic origin and who is therefore the product of fusion. The grand-parents may or may not be of the same geographic origin.

Old American[3] applies to any child all four of whose grandparents were born in this country. Old Americans may be of homogeneous or of mixed descent. Some are homogeneous of British descent; others are homogene-ous of French-Canadian descent, etc. Old American children are those who record the United States as the birthplace for three successive genera-tions: children, parents, and all grandparents are native born.

Partly Old American applies to a child both of whose parents were na-tive born and one or more of whose grandparents, but not all four, were native born.

Intramarriage indicates a marriage between a man and a woman from

---

[1] The author is indebted to Dr. Isaiah Bowman for conference and advice on regional classification before its final adoption. For a list of works which constitute a reference shelf for this and other problems directly connected with the investigation see Appendix B.

[2] See definition given below.   [3] Hrdlička.

the same ethnic group. There is no evidence that more than one stock has entered into the family unit within the generations covered by the investigation. They are both of pure descent and are of the same stock. It is a condition of the study that these individuals are always parents or grandparents of one or more children.

Intermarriage is a term describing any union that results in bringing into the family line more than one racial strain. The individuals uniting in marriage are of different stocks. This definition is subject to further refinement in the chapters dealing specifically with this problem.

Ethnic fusion is a general term to be distinguished from "intermarriage." The union of principals in marriage has only relative significance in a study of population. Population changes are effected not only by rates of intermarriage, but also by differential birth-rates and death-rates, internal migration, and numerous other causes.

Generation is a term currently used in Census publications and by writers on immigration problems to refer to the relation of nativity to migration. A person who is foreign born and a migrant to the United States is said to be of the "first generation."

An individual born in this country of foreign-born parents is of the "second generation." An individual born in this country of native-born parents belongs to at least the "third generation." Some of the families in which the parents are classified as "third generation" are Old American families who have been in this country six, seven, or even ten generations.

Sib denotes all the children of one father and one mother. Sometimes the sib is the unit of enumeration, at other times the child.

Racial is used in this monograph to refer to the stocks which these ethnic groups represent. It is an adjective indicating the hereditary or biologic aspects of the problem. The use of this word does not signify that these groups represent entities or that they may be called races.

Rate is used in general to indicate the pace at which intermarriage or fusion takes place. The mathematical refinements of the time element and the determination of a base cannot be sufficiently indicated at each state in the analysis to give this term its full mathematical significance. The degree of precision which the word carries inevitably varies in different parts of the report and should be clear from the context.

Geographical or regional derivation is determined by birthplace.

Country of origin as used by the United States Bureau of Census "signifies the country of birth of the father of a foreign born person or of the foreign parent or parents of a native."[1]

As a matter of convenience and for purposes of consistency, the father's birthplace is always used in this monograph as the basis for the primary regional classification in this study.

The melting pot, a term derived from Israel Zangwill's play by that name, has come to be applied to the racial situation in the United States and infers that the various racial stocks are in the process of amalgamation. Whenever it is used in this monograph it refers not to the whole unit of population but rather to that part of the stock which is actually in amalgamation, i.e., the product of admixture through intermarriage.

SYMBOLS

The symbols used in this monograph are listed below. The symbol always refers to the generation of parents. The same set of symbols serves to locate children, parents, and grandparents. The child is one generation farther removed from the incident of migration.

The Arabic numeral *1* stands for "first generation." It refers to a parent who is foreign born.

2 stands for "second generation" and refers to a parent who is native born of foreign parentage.

3/2 stands for a parent one of whose parents is in turn native born and one foreign born.

3 stands for a parent who is native born of native parentage.

2x is frequently used to designate a class which includes all native-born individuals, i.e., second generation, 3/2 generation, and third generation.

1–1 refers to a mating or to a home in which both parents are foreign born.

1–1 intramarriage: Both parents belong to the first generation. They are both foreign born, immigrants to the United States, and both of the same ethnic descent.

EXAMPLE: An Italian man of foreign birth is married to an Italian woman also of foreign birth.

1–1 intermarriage: Both parents belong to the first generation. They are both foreign born and immigrants, but are of different stocks. Therefore there is "intermarriage." The birthplaces may or may not be the same.

EXAMPLE: A man of Italian descent is mated with a woman of Irish descent.

[1] *Fourteenth Census Report,* p. 1.

In the second generation we have the same sequence:

2–2: The parents are both native born of foreign parentage.

2–2 intramarriage: Parents are both native born, both of foreign extraction but of the same stock.

EXAMPLE: A man of Italian descent, born in this country, is married to a woman also of Italian descent, born in this country.

2–2 intermarriage: Parents are born in the United States, both of foreign extraction but not of the same stock.

EXAMPLE: A man of Italian descent, born in this country, is married to a woman of Irish descent, also born in this country.

In the third generation we again have the same sequence:

3–3: The parents are both native born of native parentage.

3–3 intramarriage: The parents are native born of native parentage, both of the same ethnic derivation.

EXAMPLE: An Old American man of British descent is married to an Old American woman also of British descent.

3–3 intermarriage: The parents are of native parentage but not of the same ethnic derivation.

EXAMPLE: An Old American man of British descent is married to an Old American woman of French-Canadian descent.[1]

In the illustrations given in the preceding paragraphs both parents are always of the same generation. It frequently happens that one parent belongs to one generation and the other to another generation, as 3–1, 2–3, 2–1, etc. The parents may or may not be of the same ethnic descent. The generation symbol has no reference to stock. In cases where the symbols for generation differ, the one at the left always refers to the father and the one at the right to the mother; thus 3–1 signifies father of native descent and a foreign-born mother.

3–2s represent a combination of several classes.

The number of combinations in which 2 and 3 occur together were so many that it became necessary to create a general class which includes all matings with 2 and 3 factors. The matings designated as *3–2s* include combinations like 3–2; 2–3; 3–(3/2); 3–(2/3); (3/2)–(3/2), etc. No effort

---

[1] In the New London and Stamford studies the procedure in regard to native stock was somewhat different. The data are therefore not strictly comparable. This note is entered here to facilitate comparison with other surveys and to prevent any errors in interpretation. Such changes are inevitable in the use of a technique that is frankly experimental. In previous surveys by the author all 3–3 marriages were called "intramarriages," since all Old Americans were considered as a "native" class.

was made to differentiate between the symbol for the man or the woman
in the 3–2's combination.

ABBREVIATIONS

Fa. = Father	n.p. = Native parentage
Mo. = Mother	n.d. = Native descent
g.p. = Grandparents	Intras. = Intramarriages
n. = Native	Inters. = Intermarriages
n.b. = Native born	Gen. = Generation

In order to make the presentation in each chapter a unit reasonably
complete in itself, a certain amount of repetition has been inevitable. In
several instances this repetition is a matter of form rather than of content
matter, since the quantitative data differ.

PART I

THE SCHOOL POPULATION: A
DESCRIPTIVE ANALYSIS

CHAPTER III

ETHNIC ELEMENTS AND THEIR DIFFUSION: NUMERICAL EQUIVALENTS FOR REGIONAL AND ETHNIC ORIGIN

METHODS IN USE FOR ASCERTAINING ETHNIC COMPOSITION

There are three methods now in use for the analysis of ethnic composition. The Federal Census, for example, uses the living individual as the unit of enumeration and determines derivation by "country of origin."[1] The United States Bureau of Immigration, in recording its data on immigration, also uses the living individual as the unit of enumeration, but it is the only governmental office that tabulates its data according to "race or people," as well as by birthplace. By contrast, the analyses which have been made recently by various experts as a basis for the present national-origins law[2] proceed in a different manner. These estimates of the origins of our national stock are based on historical data and on existing censuses. They deal only with the amount of each stock probably represented in the present composition of the American people. This stock is distributed through individuals of either homogeneous or mixed descent. The purpose is always to estimate the weights or "numerical equivalents" of the different stocks in the present population, quite irrespective of the way in which they are disseminated through the individuals in the population. The "numerical equivalent," or, in other words, the ratio of each national stock to the total composition, constitutes the basis of the present national-origins law. A condition of the law is that "for purposes of this Act, nationality shall be determined by country of birth." The estimates made for the purpose of enforcing this law are therefore geographic in character.[3]

[1] See chap. ii, p. 22.

[2] The national-origins clause is contained in the Immigration Act of 1924 and became effective July 1, 1929. It permits 150,000 immigrants to enter this country each year. "The annual quota of any nationality for the fiscal year . . . . shall be a number which bears the same ratio to 150,000 as the number of inhabitants in continental United States in 1920 having that national origin."

[3] For a copy of the Act of 1924 containing these provisions, and for a discussion of this subject, see the following works: John B. Trevor, *An Analysis of the American Immigration Act of 1924: International Conciliation Bull. 202* (New York: Carnegie Endowment for International Peace, September, 1924); William S. Rossiter, *Increase of Population in the United*

OBJECTIVES OF PRESENT INVESTIGATION

The analysis immediately following seeks to ascertain both the ethnic and the regional derivation of the population. Its aim is to describe the ethnic elements comprising the population, i.e., the numerical equivalents of various stocks, and the living individuals who carry these strains. The study of racial elements that have entered into the population might well be preliminary to the study of individuals derived from this stock. The present chapter, therefore, deals more specifically with the racial elements that have entered into the composition of the Woonsocket public schools. Of what ethnic strains is the population composed? From what European regions have these strains been derived? How have they distributed themselves? What are the "rates" of diffusion for the various stocks? What is the total degree of admixture? In what measure is the population, as a whole, fusing and becoming a new and homogeneous group? These questions pertain to the very genesis of population, and our answers to them require what may be called an inventory of the ethnic elements in the population.

As previously indicated, the analysis is based upon racial histories containing data relative to the regional and ethnic derivation of six immediate ancestors of each child, namely, two parents and four grandparents. Since the birthplace of the father is the method most widely used for determining "nationality," it therefore offers both a common starting-point and a point of departure for the discussion of ethnic composition of any given unit.

DATA ON CHILDREN BY REGIONAL DERIVATION OF FATHER

(Tables 1 and 1a)

The Woonsocket public-school population appears at first glance to be similar to that of numerous other New England communities. As we have seen, there were 4,978 children who attended the public schools of Woonsocket in 1926. These children represented 2,876 homes. As a result of the comparative cessation of immigration due to the World War and to restrictive legislation, the population is comprised mostly of native-born children; 4,612, or 92.7 per cent, are native born, while the remainder, who are foreign-born, number only 366, or 7.3 per cent of the population. When the children are classified by father's birthplace, however, we find

---

States, census monographs; files of the *United States Daily* for current reports on the issue before Congress. See also Bessie Bloom Wessel, "Ethnic Factors in the Population of New London," *op. cit.;* and "The Index of Racial Influence," *Eugenics,* December, 1929.

that 33.5 per cent of the children report fathers native born, while 66.5 per cent report fathers born in 38 foreign regions. French Canada is the major region of origin, while Poland, Italy, and Russia assume appreciable proportions. French Canada alone, however, with 1,034, or 20.8 per cent

TABLE 1

SUMMARY: REGIONAL AND ETHNIC DERIVATION OF PUBLIC-SCHOOL POPULATION
OF WOONSOCKET, RHODE ISLAND: 4,978 CHILDREN
CLASSIFIED BY DERIVATION

DERIVATION	BIRTHPLACE (a)†	FATHER'S			NUMERICAL EQUIVALENTS* FOR	
		Birthplace (b)‡	Ethnic Derivation (c)§	Regional Derivation (d)‖	Ethnic Derivation (e)¶	
British total..................	31	250	521	1,517	2,419
a) From Great Britain.........	5	194	....	1,272	....
b) Canadian British...........	4	56	....	131	....
c) Canadian non-British stock**	22	....	....	114	....
French Canadian..............	205	1,034	1,738	6,417	6,943
French, total all others.........	25	122	129	493	616
Irish........................	1	83	408	1,325	1,853
Italian......................	26	435	439	1,715	1,715
Jewish......................	....	....	191	....	773
Slavic total..................	21	1,071	909	4,343	3,656
a) Polish....................	6	421	511	1,741	2,118
b) Ukrainian.................	1	59	358	206	1,414
c) Russian..................	8	203	34	789	106
d) Lithuanian................	....	11	6	27	18
e) (Galician).................	6	377	....	1,580	....
All others...................	57	315	335	1,425	1,406
Unspecified (n.d.).............	....	....	126	....	521
American (U.S.).............	4,612	1,668	....	2,677	....
Mixed ancestry...............	....	....	182	....	10
GRAND TOTAL.............	4,978	4,978	4,978	19,912	19,912

* Numerical equivalents are obtained by a count of grandparents.
† The figures in this column are derived from Table 19.
‡ The figures in this column are derived from Table 20.
§ The figures in this column are derived from Table 27.
‖ The figures in this column are derived from Table 4.
¶ The figures in this column are derived from Table 3.
** Canada, non-British stock, include 19 Canadian unspecified and 3 Irish Canadian.

of the children reporting that country of origin, approximates the total for these three. The figures for the three countries mentioned are: Poland, 421, or 8.5 per cent of the total number of children; Italy, 435, or 8.7 per cent; and Russia, 203, or 4.1 per cent. British countries including Canada follow with 250, or the low percentage of 5.0 per cent, and the Irish with a still lower figure of 83, or 1.7 per cent.[1] Relatively few of the British im-

[1] The discussions throughout the monograph are limited to major numerical groups. Other groups may be located on detail tables.

migrants in Woonsocket come from Canada as one might expect. By far the largest number come from Great Britain.[1]

But this cursory summary based on father's birthplace is descriptive neither of ethnic composition of the stock as a whole nor of the ethnic derivation of children. It fails us at two points. It fails to distinguish

TABLE 1a

Per Cent Distribution of Table 1: Percentage of 4,978 Children Classified by Their Derivation

Derivation	Birthplace (a)	Father's		Numerical Equivalents* For	
		Birthplace (b)	Ethnic Derivation (c)	Regional Derivation (d)	Ethnic Derivation (e)
British total..................	.7	5.0	10.5	7.7	12.2
a) From Great Britain.........	.1	3.9	....	6.4	....
b) Canadian British...........	.1	.4	....	.7	....
c) Canadian non-British stock..	.5	.7	....	.6	....
French Canadian..............	4.1	20.8	34.9	32.2	34.9
French, total all others........	.5	2.5	2.6	2.5	3.1
Irish........................	†	1.7	8.2	6.6	9.3
Italian......................	.5	8.7	8.8	8.6	8.6
Jewish......................	....	....	3.8	....	3.9
Slavic total..................	.4	21.6	18.3	21.8	18.3
a) Polish....................	.1	8.5	10.3	8.8	10.6
b) Ukrainian.................	†	1.2	7.2	1.0	7.1
c) Russian...................	.2	4.1	.7	4.0	.5
d) Lithuanian................	....	.2	.1	.1	.1
e) (Galician).................	.1	7.6	....	7.9	....
All others...................	1.1	6.2	6.7	7.2	7.0
Unspecified (n.d.)............	....	....	2.5	....	2.6
American (U.S.)	92.7	33.5	....	13.4	....
Mixed ancestry	....	....	3.7	....	.1
Grand total............	100.0	100.0	100.0	100.0	100.0

* Numerical equivalents are obtained by a count of grandparents.
† Less than .1 per cent.   ‡ See note **, Table 1.

between ethnic and geographic derivation, and it fails to account for the maternal line contributing one-half of the stock. We may therefore turn our attention to the correction for these factors. In a later chapter our attention will be focused on the children themselves. In the present chapter the emphasis is placed on the derivation of stock now represented in the population without reference to the manner in which it is carried by

[1] Our restrictive legislation does not apply to Canada, and it would seem that neither that nor the war need have operated to reduce recent immigration. The immigration did fall off both for the British and the French Canadians from Canada, but there is a post-war spurt for the French Canadians not characteristic of the other racial groups. See chap. xiii for discussion relating to date of entry.

the children. The objective is to secure an inventory of the ethnic elements now in the population.

(Summary Tables 1, 1a, Detailed Tables 3, and 4)

A count of grandparents for ethnic origin takes care of the omissions noted, and is an expeditious way of arriving directly at the racial elements in the population.[1] Since each child has four grandparents, 4,978 children have theoretically[2] four times that number of grandparents, namely, 19,912 theoretical grandparents. In this way every grandparent is counted as many times as he or she is actually represented by offspring in the unit of population, and record is made of the two lines of descent, the maternal and the paternal.

The items in column d of Tables 1 and 1a indicate the regional derivation of grandparents, while the items in column e indicate the ethnic derivation of grandparents. These represent the ethnic elements in the present school population. The percentages are in reality numerical equivalents of these stocks.

According to this last analysis, 34.9 per cent of the stock is of French-Canadian origin. North Slavic peoples[3] contribute 18.3 per cent of the total stock; the Italians, 8.6 per cent; and the Jews, 3.9 per cent. The British groups combined constitute 12.2 per cent of the total stock, and the Irish 9.3 per cent.

The "American" group, comprised of those born in the United States, has been resolved into its component elements and therefore does not appear as a unit group in column e, dealing with ethnic derivation. Obviously an attempt to resolve an American population into its component elements leaves no room for a constituent American group.[4]

It will be noted that there are appreciable differences in the weights

[1] This method was suggested to the author by Professor Franz Boas several years ago.

[2] Some of these children have in common the same grandparents. We are however not concerned at this point with the actual number of grandparents.

[3] The Slavic groups are treated as independent units throughout the investigation but combined only in certain summaries for purposes of comparison. The Poles are the largest Slavic group with a numerical equivalent of 10.6. The term "North Slavic" is used to apply to Slavs from in or about former Russia.

[4] Two and six-tenths per cent of the American stock remains unspecified. This figure, however, merely measures the extent to which the study has failed to reach the objective, namely, to analyze an entire population into the ethnic elements from which it is derived.

which the same groups have, dependent upon whether the classification of grandparents is upon a regional or an ethnic basis. This is due in part to the fact that 13.4 per cent of stock which is American according to regional derivation has been assigned to the several ethnic groups from which it is derived by descent. The difference in the last two columns is due also to the fact that numerous migrants claim ethnic derivation that is different from that of the major group in the country in which they were born. They are therefore not counted in the same class in these two tabulations.[1]

The count of grandparents yields, in effect, the numerical equivalents[2] which the government is seeking for the country at large. The emphasis in the foregoing presentation, however, is upon an ethnic rather than upon a geographic definition of "national origins." Also these "numerical equivalents" are based upon histories obtained from individuals now actually present in the population. The present monograph borrows these concepts from national-origins literature, but arrives at them by a different process.

A count of grandparents for ethnic derivation may be adopted as the most direct way of arriving at the numerical equivalents for the ethnic origins of a population. It eliminates the accidental factor of birthplace as a determining factor of nationality and takes into account the maternal line, generally overlooked in studies of ethnic composition. The number of grandparents is theoretical. The data are real in the sense that they represent the stocks from which the actual children in the population are derived and in the numerical measure indicated.

COMPARISON OF FINDINGS BY DIFFERENT METHODS
(Tables 1 and 1a)

A comparison of the several regional distributions offers an opportunity for indicating the extent to which the population as a whole is of American origin. For example, in Table 1a we find that 92.7 per cent of the children are native born and that 33.5 per cent of the children have native-born fathers.

Only 13.4 per cent of the stock, however, is native[3] by virtue of the fact that grandparents are of native origin. We shall discover later that only

[1] The extent to which this affects descriptions of the population is discussed in chaps. v and vii.

[2] Table 3 gives the numerical equivalents for ethnic derivation in detail for grandfathers and for grandmothers. Table 4 gives the numerical equivalents for regional derivation in detail for grandfathers and for grandmothers.

[3] I.e., 13.4 per cent of the theoretical grandparents are native born.

4.5 per cent of the children have four native-born grandparents.[1] These grandparents, representing 13.4 per cent of the total number, are distributed variously through the families in the population. Some families have only one native grandparent; others have two, three, or four.

Since we have taken as our point of departure the classification based upon father's birthplace as the one most generally used, it is interesting to compare the weights assigned to the different stocks on this basis with the numerical equivalents for ethnic derivation obtained by a count of grandparents according to stock. Aside from the radical reduction in the figures for native stock, and of its necessary disappearance in the final column, we find that some stocks change rank, some are increased several fold, and others even appear for the first time as definite groups.

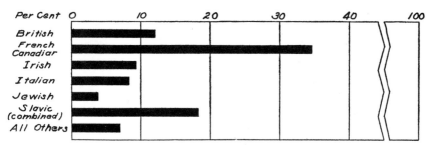

Fig. i.—Ethnic elements in the population: numerical equivalents (derived from a count of grandparents).

The outstanding differences which appear in Table 1a are as follows:[2] the British elements increase from 5.0 to 12.2 per cent;[3] the Irish element increases from 1.7 to 9.3 per cent; the French-Canadian element increases from 20.8 to 34.9 per cent; the Polish element increases from 8.5 to 10.6 per cent; the Russian element decreases from 4.1 to .5 per cent; the Ukrainian element increases from 1.2 to 7.1 per cent; the Jewish element now makes its appearance with 3.9 per cent; the combined Slavic groups change from 21.6 to 18.3 per cent chiefly because the Jews are not now included in this Slavic figure.

Figure 1[4] is a graphic representation of the ethnic elements in the population as determined by a count of grandparents. Figure 4 in a later chap-

[1] Chap. vii, Table 22.

[2] The comparison is always between the items in col. *b* with those in col. *e*.

[3] In the British group the English from Great Britain are the largest constituent element. Further examination of the data indicates that for the English alone the percentage increases from 3.2 for country of origin to 9.3 for ethnic derivation by count of grandparents.

[4] The graphs throughout this monograph were made by Allyn B. Gray.

ter offers a comparison of results obtained by different methods, while the summary in tabular form ("Rank") indicates the differences in rank which are brought about in the realignment of stocks.

There are three reasons which operate to bring about the significant changes in the picture of ethnic composition. In the first place, the analysis has been carried farther back one generation. Second, two lines of descent have been taken into consideration—that of the father and that of the mother. Third, the change in emphasis from a geographic to an ethnic basis brings about appreciable differences for certain groups. How these come about will become apparent from the later and more detailed analyses. The object of the present chapter is merely to describe what is.

RANK

	By Father's Birthplace	By Count of Grandparents (Ethnic)
American	1	*
French stocks, combined	2	1
Slavic, combined	3	2
Italian	4	5
British, combined	5	3
Irish	6	4

* Americans are not given status as an ethnic group, since it is still to be determined to what extent they are an ethnic group.

DIFFUSION FACTS

(Table 2)

The preceding analysis merely indicates the racial elements from which the population is derived. The record does not indicate to what extent these diverse strains have remained homogeneous and to what extent they are distributed through a mixed population. The question is: What proportion of the population is in reality being fused in the "melting pot," and what are the elements in the melting pot?

The evidence is that 17.0 per cent of the stock is in fusion. We have defined a child as homogeneous when all four grandparents are of the same ethnic derivation. It is of mixed ancestry when all four grandparents are not of the same ethnic descent. A count of children according to these definitions indicates that 3,988, or 80.1 per cent, of the children are homogeneous, while 848, or 17.0 per cent, are of mixed ancestry.[1] It follows that this amount of total stock is the product of admixture. In 2.9 per cent of the cases representing for the most part children of native descent, the data are not entirely clear for ethnic descent.

[1] In chap. vii.

TABLE 2
Ethnic Elements and Their Diffusion in the Population of 4,978 Children*

Ethnic Derivation	Numerical Equivalents Per Cent of Total Stock (a)‡	Per Cent of Total Stock and Homogeneous (b)§	Per Cent of Total Stock and Diffused (c) c=(a−b)	Per Cent of Each Stock in Diffusion (d)† d=c/a
Albanian....................				
Armenian....................	.7	.7		
Austrian....................				
Belgian (Flemish)...............	.4	.2	.2	
British total....................	12.2	7.7	4.5	36.9
a) English....................	9.3	5.0	4.3	46.2
b) Scotch....................				
c) Scotch-Irish....................				
d) Canadian English.............				
e) Canadian Scotch.............				
f) Canadian unspec.............				
g) British mixed.............				
h) British, others.............				
Chinese....................	.1	.1		
Colored....................	.2	.2		
Czech....................				
Dutch....................	.2		.2	
Finnish....................	.1		.1	
French Canadian...............	34.9	30.5	4.4	12.6
French, total all others..........	3.1	2.3	.8	25.8
a) French, France....................				
b) Walloon....................				
c) Alsatian....................				
d) Swiss....................				
e) French mixed....................				
German....................	.8	.2	.6	
Greek....................	.4	.4		
Irish....................	9.3	5.5	3.8	40.9
Italian....................	8.6	8.3	.3	3.5
Jewish....................	3.9	3.8	.1	2.6‖
Portuguese (white)...............	.7	.5	.2	
Roumanian................:	.8	.8		
Scandinavian total...............	1.0	.7	.3	30.0
a) Swedish....................	.9	.7	.2	
b) Norwegian....................				
c) Danish....................	.1		.1	
Slavic total....................	18.3	16.8	1.5	8.2
a) Polish....................	10.6	9.9	.7	6.6
b) Ukrainian....................	7.1	6.5	.6	8.5
c) Russian....................	.5	.4	.1	
d) Lithuanian....................	.1		.1	
e) (Galician)....................				
Spanish....................				
Syrian....................	1.4	1.4		
Turkish....................				
Mixed ancestry....................	.1		17.0	
Partly unspecified (n.b.)..........	2.6			
Other unspecified....................	.2			
TOTAL HOMOGENEOUS........		80.1		
TOTAL UNSPECIFIED..........		2.9		
GRAND TOTAL.............	100.0	83.0¶	17.0	

* For diffusion of stock through sibs see similar table in chap. xi, Table 53.

† This per cent is computed only for numerically significant groups.

‡ The figures in this column are derived from Table 3.

§ The figures in this column are derived from Table 21b.

‖ This figure is misleading; there are few cases involved. There are only 2 intermarriages involving 4 children and only 99 Jewish families in all.

¶ This includes the unspecified group with 2.9 per cent.

The diffusion process is described in Table 2, entitled "Ethnic Elements and Their Diffusion, etc." The items in column *a* represent the "numerical equivalents" of the different stocks in the population as obtained by a count of grandparents. The items in column *b* represent that part of each stock which has remained intact, the grandparents[1] of homogeneous children. The items in column *c* represent the per cent of the total stock which each stock contributed to the melting pot. Each item in this column was obtained by subtracting the item in column *b* from the corresponding one in column *a*. Column *c* is therefore a description of the melting pot. Of the total number of children, 17.0 per cent is of mixed ancestry. Seventeen per cent of the theoretical grandparents are diffused in the melting pot. It follows that an equal proportion of the total stock is in the melting pot. The percentage values for these three are always constant.

The melting pot is derived largely from the major groups in the population, French Canadians, British, and Irish, and from an array of minor elements. British and French Canadians contribute equal portions to the melting pot. The Irish are not far below.

It is interesting to note the rôle which French-Canadian stock plays in each distribution. It ranks first in numerical equivalents of total stock, in those for the homogeneous stock, and with the British takes leading rank in its contribution to mixed stock. And this is true even though less than one-fourth of the French-Canadian children are in the public schools and are represented in this unit. The more recent immigrant stocks from Europe are scarcely represented in the melting pot.

But the contribution which each stock makes to the melting pot has no relation to its own "rate"[2] or per cent of diffusion. Thus, the French-Canadian group, with its high numerical weight in the melting pot, has a low per cent of stock which is diffused, while the Irish and British each have a high per cent of diffusion, and have, by comparison, low weights in the melting pot. French Canadians contribute 4.4 per cent toward the 17.0 per cent of the total stock which constitutes the melting pot; the British groups combined contribute 4.5 per cent; the Irish, 3.8 per cent.

---

[1] The number of grandparents is always theoretical. The 3,988 homogeneous children are represented by four times that number of grandparents. This represents the stock that has remained pure. The data are derived from subsequent tables as specified.

[2] This "rate," if used as a basis for comparing the different stocks, is, in a mathematical sense, spurious, since the time element is not always the same for each group. The function of this table is to describe the ethnic elements in the population, and to indicate what they are. A discussion of the implications involved in these percentages and in differential rates is reserved for a later chapter—xi.

But only 12.6 per cent of the French-Canadian stock is diffused while 36.9 per cent of the British stock and 40.9 per cent of the Irish stock is diffused. These three groups are comparable, since they are all old settlers[1] in Woonsocket. For the new groups the percentages of diffusion are: 8.2 per cent for the several Slavic groups combined, 3.5 per cent for the Italians, and 2.6 per cent for the Jews.[2]

Though the foregoing analysis describes the stocks in the population, it does not sufficiently describe the individuals in the group derived from these stocks. As students of society, our interest is in ascertaining how these ethnic elements have assorted themselves through the individuals of the population. What are the ethnic derivations of the children themselves? How many children derived from these strains are of homogeneous descent? How many are the product of admixture? What types of ethnic fusion do the children represent? Who are the children of Woonsocket? Our attention must now be directed to a description of the children themselves rather than of the stocks from which they are derived.[3]

SUMMARY

The analysis in this chapter offers an inventory of the ethnic elements in the population, of those which are carried by homogeneous individuals and of those disseminated through a mixed group. A count of grandparents is offered as the most direct way of arriving at numerical equivalents for regional and ethnic origins in the population.

The population is diverse in origin, the stock being derived from at least 28 ethnic groups emanating from some 38 geographic regions (Tables 3 and 4). In spite of the diversity of origin, 80.1 per cent of the stock is homogeneous in descent, while 17.0 per cent of the stock is diffused through a mixed group. In the case of the remaining children, 2.9 per cent, the data on the score of homogeneity are uncertain.

Only 13.4 per cent of all the stock is Old American by regional derivation, i.e., of native grandparentage. In the ethnic grouping, the Old American stock was redistributed among nationalities from which it is derived.

---

[1] The French Canadians have been coming to Woonsocket for about a century. See historical sketch in chap. xiv.

[2] See Table 2, p. 39, n. †.

[3] The computations in this chapter have been based upon the number of children and theoretical grandparents for 4,978 children. Tables are appended to this chapter in which the computations are based upon the actual number of parents and upon theoretical grandparents for 2,876 families. These yield numerical equivalents for parental stock and serve as a basis for comparisons between the population of parents and that of children. They are also basic for later analyses.

TABLE 3

NUMERICAL EQUIVALENTS FOR ETHNIC DERIVATIONS IN THE POPULATION OF 4,978 CHILDREN

(A Count of Grandparents:* Number and Per Cent Distribution)

ETHNIC DERIVATION	NUMBER			PER CENT		
	Grand-fathers (a)	Grand-mothers (b)	Total Grand-parents (c)	Grand-fathers (a′)	Grand-mothers (b′)	Total Grand-parents (c′)
Albanian................	3	3	6	†	†	†
Armenian...............	68	66	134	.7	.7	.7
Austrian................						
Belgian (Flemish)........	47	41	88	.5	.4	.4
British total............	1,216	1,203	2,419	12.2	12.1	12.2
a) English..............	935	921	1,856	9.4	9.3	9.3
b) Scotch..............	125	117	242	1.2	1.2	1.2
c) Scotch-Irish..........	6	8	14	.1	.1	.1
d) Canadian English......	37	47	84	.4	.5	.4
e) Canadian Scotch.......	21	23	44	.2	.2	.2
f) Canadian unspec.......						
g) British mixed.........	66	62	128	.7	.6	.7
h) British, others........	26	25	51	.2	.2	.3
Chinese................	6	6	12	.1	.1	.1
Colored................	22	22	44	.2	.2	.2
Czech.................	4	4	8	†	†	†
Dutch.................	15	14	29	.2	.1	.2
Finnish................	6	6	12	.1	.1	.1
French Canadian........	3,459	3,484	6,943	34.7	35.0	34.9
French, total all others....	323	293	616	3.2	2.9	3.1
a) French, France........	145	118	263	1.4	1.2	1.3
b) Walloon.............	77	80	157	.8	.8	.8
c) Alsatian.............	33	29	62	.3	.2	.3
d) Swiss................	8	6	14	.1	.1	.1
e) French mixed.........	60	60	120	.6	.6	.6
German................	78	80	158	.8	.8	.8
Greek..................	44	44	88	.4	.4	.4
Irish..................	911	942	1,853	9.2	9.5	9.3
Italian.................	858	857	1,715	8.6	8.6	8.6
Jewish.................	386	387	773	3.9	3.9	3.9
Portuguese (white)........	68	65	133	.7	.7	.7
Roumanian.............	83	83	166	.8	.8	.8
Scandinavian total.......	104	95	199	1.1	1.0	1.0
a) Swedish.............	92	86	178	.9	.9	.9
b) Norwegian...........	5	2	7	.1	†	†
c) Danish..............	7	7	14	.1	.1	.1
Slavic total.............	1,828	1,828	3,656	18.3	18.3	18.3
a) Polish...............	1,059	1,059	2,118	10.6	10.6	10.6
b) Ukrainian............	707	707	1,414	7.1	7.1	7.1
c) Russian.............	53	53	106	.5	.5	.5
d) Lithuanian...........	9	9	18	.1	.1	.1
e) (Galician)...........						
Spanish................	2	1	3	†	†	†
Syrian.................	142	142	284	1.4	1.4	1.4
Turkish................						
Mixed ancestry...........	5	5	10	.1	.1	.1
Partly unspecified (n.b.)...	257	264	521	2.6	2.7	2.6
Other unspecified........	21	21	42	.2	.2	.2
GRAND TOTAL........	9,956	9,956	19,912	100.0	100.0	100.0

* In this table grandparents are weighted by the number of children. Each grandparent is counted as many times as he or she is represented by progeny. Children to the number of 4,978 have theoretically four times as many grandparents, i.e., 19,912.

† Less than .1 per cent.

TABLE 4

NUMERICAL EQUIVALENTS FOR REGIONAL DERIVATIONS IN THE POPULATION OF 4,978 CHILDREN

(A Count of Grandparents:* Number and Per Cent Distribution)

REGIONAL DERIVATION	NUMBER			PER CENT		
	Grand-fathers (a)	Grand-mothers (b)	Total Grand-parents (c)	Grand-fathers (a′)	Grand-mothers (b′)	Total Grand-parents (c′)
Albanian.................	59	56	115	.6	.6	.6
Armenian................	50	48	98	.5	.5	.5
Austrian.................	27	26	53	.3	.2	.3
Belgian (Flemish).........	46	41	87	.5	.4	.4
British total.............	765	752	1,517	7.7	7.6	7.7
a) English..............	539	506	1,045	5.4	5.1	5.3
b) Scotch..............	113	114	227	1.1	1.1	1.1
c) Scotch-Irish..........	....	....	....	....	....	....
d) Canadian English......	33	45	78	.3	.5	.4
e) Canadian Scotch.......	25	28	53	.3	.3	.3
f) Canadian unspec.......						
g) British mixed.........	....	....	....	....	....	....
h) British, others........	55	59	114	.6	.6	.6
Chinese.................	6	6	12	.1	.1	.1
Colored.................						
Czech..................	6	6	12	.1	.1	.1
Dutch..................	9	8	17	.1	.1	.1
Finnish.................	58	58	116	.6	.6	.6
French Canadian........	3,226	3,191	6,417	32.4	32.1	32.2
French, European total....	259	234	493	2.6	2.4	2.5
a) French, France.......	142	118	260	1.4	1.2	1.3
b) Walloon.............	77	79	156	.8	.8	.8
c) Alsatian.............	32	29	61	.3	.3	.3
d) Swiss...............	8	8	16	.1	.1	.1
e) French mixed.........	....	....	....	....	....	....
German.................	60	44	104	.6	.4	.5
Greek..................	49	51	100	.5	.5	.5
Irish...................	669	656	1,325	6.7	6.6	6.6
Italian.................	858	857	1,715	8.6	8.6	8.6
Jewish.................						
Portuguese (white)†.......	74	74	148	.7	.7	.7
Roumanian.............	16	17	33	.1	.2	.2
Scandinavian............	49	42	91	.6	.4	.5
a) Swedish.............	37	33	70	.4	.3	.4
b) Norwegian...........	5	2	7	.1	‡	‡
c) Danish..............	7	7	14	.1	.1	.1
Slavic total.............	2,172	2,172	4,343	21.7	21.7	21.8
a) Polish..............	869	872	1,741	8.7	8.7	8.8
b) Ukrainian...........	103	103	206	1.0	1.0	1.0
c) Russian.............	400	389	789	4.0	3.9	4.0
d) Lithuanian..........	10	17	27	.1	.2	.1
e) (Galician)...........	790	790	1,580	7.9	7.9 '	7.9
Spanish.................	....	....	....	....	....	....
Syrian..................	142	142	284	1.4	1.4	1.4
Turkish.................	24	24	48	.2	.2	.2
Others§.................	4	6	10	‡	.1	‡
Unspecified.............	48	49	97	.5	.5	.5
American (U.S.).........	1,280	1,397	2,677	12.9	14.0	13.4
GRAND TOTAL........	9,956	9,956	19,912	100.0	100.0	100.0

* In this table grandparents are weighted by the number of children. Each grandparent is counted as many times as he or she is represented by progeny. Children to the number of 4,978 have theoretically four times as many grandparents, i.e., 19,912.

† Portuguese includes: Azores and Madeira Islands, 10 cases; Cape de Verde, 60 cases.

‡ Less than .1 per cent.

§ "Others" include the following regional derivations, too small to be listed separately: South America, 1; Latvia, 4; Serbia, 4; and West Indies, 1.

French-Canadian stock is the predominating element in the population. It constitutes 34.9 per cent of the total stock. Northern Slavs, when combined, constitute a second, with 18.3 per cent of the total stock. The British are represented by 12.2 per cent (of which 9.3 per cent is English). The Irish and Italian stocks follow with 9.3 and 8.6 per cent, respectively. There is a wide range in the numerical strength of groups in the total population. The numerical equivalent for French-Canadian stock is almost three times as great as that for the British groups combined, and almost four times as great as that for the Irish. In spite of varying degrees of fusion, each of these contributes similar amounts of stock to the mixed population. This arises from the differences which exist in the numerical strength of each group in the total population.

The melting pot is derived chiefly from strains represented by the older immigration to Woonsocket, namely, British, Irish, and French Canadian, and from a number of scattered elements. The two former groups have the highest percentage of stock diffused, 36.9 and 40.9 respectively. The percentage of diffusion for French-Canadian stock is only 12.6.

The succeeding chapters describe the individuals through whom these strains are distributed.

CHAPTER IV

THE DERIVATION OF GRANDPARENTS

The children in the public schools, 4,978 in number, come from 2,876 families. The ethnic milieu in these families depends upon two factors, the descent of parents and the migratory history of the family which serves to change or vary the cultural content of family life. The ethnic descent of parents is derived directly from that of their parents, the grandparents of children.

It has been possible in this investigation to trace the cultural histories of these families back to the generation of grandparents. Since each of the 5,752 parents brings to the family line two grandparents (and each sib has four grandparents), there are in all 11,504[1] grandparents. These are the immediate ancestors of our population. What was their origin?

(Tables 5 and 6)

An inventory for ethnic and for regional derivation of 11,504 grandparents indicates that these grandparents are descended from at least 28 ethnic groups[2] and were born in 38 different regions. Table 5 indicates that the largest constituent group are the French Canadians with 4,452; the Slavic groups combined form a good second, though not very close, with 1,900. The British groups, combined, rank third with 1,433, followed by the Irish with 1,040. The percentage distributions are 38.7 for the French Canadians, 16.5 for Slavic groups combined, 12.5 for the British groups combined, and 9.0 for the Irish. The Italians and Jews are the only other significant groups numerically, the former with 767 constituting 6.7 per cent of the total number and the latter with 401 constituting 3.5 per cent of the total.

The regional derivations indicated in Table 6 differ somewhat from the distribution for ethnic origin. The British contingent from Canada is rather small, but Galicia appears in the list with 822 as the country of

---

[1] There is some overlapping here. No effort was made to ascertain how many parents in the population are siblings and what the actual number of grandparents is, since it did not serve any end of the study. The number of parents referred to throughout this chapter is always an actual number; grandparents are weighted by the number of actual parents.

[2] Counting the British stocks as one major group and all the European French as another.

TABLE 5

11,504 Grandparents by Ethnic Derivation: Number and Per Cent Distribution

a) Grandfathers, b) Grandmothers, c) Both

ETHNIC DERIVATION	NUMBER			PER CENT		
	Grand-fathers (a)	Grand-mothers (b)	Total Grand-parents (c)	Grand-fathers (a')	Grand-mothers (b')	Total Grand-parents (c')
Albanian..............	3	3	6	.1	.1	.1
Armenian..............	30	28	58	.5	.5	.5
Austrian..............						
Belgian (Flemish)........	41	36	77	.7	.6	.7
British total..............	716	717	1,433	12.5	12.5	12.5
a) English..............	*539*	*535*	*1,074*	*9.4*	*9.3*	*9.3*
b) Scotch..............	*72*	*74*	*146*	*1.2*	*1.3*	*1.3*
c) Scotch-Irish...........	*4*	*5*	*9*	*.1*	*.1*	*.1*
d) Canadian English......	*29*	*36*	*65*	*.5*	*.6*	*.6*
e) Canadian Scotch......	*15*	*19*	*34*	*.3*	*.3*	*.3*
f) Canadian unspec......	*16*	*16*	*32*	*.3*	*.3*	*.3*
g) British mixed.........	*41*	*32*	*73*	*.7*	*.6*	*.6*
h) British, others........						
Chinese..............	6	6	12	.1	.1	.1
Colored..............	8	8	16	.1	.1	.1
Czech..................	2	2	4	*	*	*
Dutch..............	10	8	18	.1	.1	.1
Finnish..............	5	5	10	.1	.1	.1
French Canadian........	2,220	2,232	4,452	38.6	38.8	38.7
French, total all others	206	192	398	3.6	3.3	3.5
a) French, France........	*107*	*95*	*202*	*1.9*	*1.7*	*1.8*
b) Walloon..............	*55*	*58*	*113*	*1.0*	*1.0*	*1.0*
c) Alsatian..............	*21*	*18*	*39*	*.3*	*.3*	*.3*
d) Swiss..............	*4*	*2*	*6*	*.1*	*.0*	*.1*
e) French mixed..........	*19*	*19*	*38*	*.3*	*.3*	*.3*
German..............	49	47	96	.8	.8	.8
Greek..............	21	21	42	.4	.4	.4
Irish..............	512	528	1,040	8.9	9.2	9.0
Italian..............	384	383	767	6.7	6.7	6.7
Jewish..............	200	201	401	3.5	3.5	3.5
Portuguese (white)........	45	43	88	.8	.8	.8
Roumanian..............	48	48	96	.8	.8	.8
Scandinavian total........	67	59	126	1.2	1.0	1.1
a) Swedish..............	*58*	*52*	*110*	*1.0*	*.9*	*.9*
b) Norwegian..........	*4*	*2*	*6*	*.1*	*	*.1*
c) Danish..............	*5*	*5*	*10*	*.1*	*.1*	*.1*
Slavic total..............	950	950	1,900	16.5	16.5	16.5
a) Polish..............	*539*	*539*	*1,078*	*9.4*	*9.4*	*9.4*
b) Ukrainian..............	*375*	*375*	*750*	*6.5*	*6.5*	*6.5*
c) Russian..............	*31*	*31*	*62*	*.5*	*.5*	*.5*
d) Lithuanian..........	*5*	*5*	*10*	*.1*	*.1*	*.1*
e) (Galician)						
Spanish..............	1	1	2	*	*	*
Syrian..................	50	50	100	.9	.9	.9
Turkish..............						
Mixed ancestry..........	5	5	10	.1	.1	.1
Partly unspecified (n.b.)...	153	159	312	2.7	2.8	2.7
Other unspecified........	20	20	40	.3	.3	.3
GRAND TOTAL........	5,752	5,752	11,504	100.0	100.0	100.0

* Less than .1 per cent.

TABLE 6

11,504 GRANDPARENTS BY REGIONAL DERIVATION: NUMBER AND PER CENT DISTRIBUTION
a) Grandfathers, b) Grandmothers, c) Both

REGIONAL DERIVATION	NUMBER			PER CENT		
	Grand-fathers (a)	Grand-mothers (b)	Total Grand-parents (c)	Grand-fathers (a')	Grand-mothers (b')	Total Grand-parents (c')
Albanian..............	33	32	65	.6	.6	.6
Armenian..............	20	18	38	.3	.3	.3
Austrian..............	17	16	33	.3	.3	.3
Belgian (Flemish)........	40	36	76	.7	.6	.7
British total............	447	438	885	7.9	7.6	7.6
a) English..............	298	276	574	5.2	4.8	5.0
b) Scotch..............	68	72	140	1.2	1.3	1.2
c) Scotch-Irish..........	....	....	....	....	....	....
d) Canadian English......	26	34	60	.5	.6	.5
e) Canadian Scotch.......	17	20	37	.3	.3	.3
f) Canadian unspec.......	....	....	....	....	....	....
g) British mixed.........	....	....	....	....	....	....
h) British, others........	38	36	74	.7	.6	.6
Chinese.................	6	6	12	.1	.1	.1
Colored.................	....	....	....	....	....	....
Czech..................	3	3	6	.1	.1	.1
Dutch..................	6	4	10	.1	.1	.1
Finnish.................	31	31	62	.5	.5	.5
French Canadian.........	2,056	2,041	4,097	35.7	35.5	35.6
French, European total....	187	175	362	3.3	3.0	3.2
a) French, France.......	108	96	204	1.9	1.6	1.8
b) Walloon.............	55	57	112	1.0	1.0	1.0
c) Alsatian.............	20	19	39	.3	.3	.3
d) Swiss...............	4	3	7	.1	.1	.1
e) French mixed.........	....	....	....	....	....	....
German.................	35	26	61	.6	.5	.5
Greek..................	22	23	45	.4	.4	.4
Irish...................	364	356	720	6.3	6.1	6.2
Italian.................	384	383	767	6.7	6.7	6.7
Jewish..................	....	....	....	....	....	....
Portuguese (white)*.......	46	46	92	.8	.8	.8
Roumanian..............	13	13	26	.2	.2	.2
Scandinavian total........	39	33	72	.7	.6	.7
a) Swedish..............	30	26	56	.5	.5	.5
b) Norwegian...........	4	2	6	.1	†	.1
c) Danish..............	5	5	10	.1	.1	.1
Slavic total..............	1,127	1,127	2,254	19.5	19.5	19.5
a) Polish...............	451	452	903	7.8	7.8	7.8
b) Ukrainian............	55	55	110	1.0	1.0	1.0
c) Russian..............	204	202	406	3.5	3.5	3.5
d) Lithuanian...........	6	7	13	.1	.1	.1
e) (Galician)............	411	411	822	7.1	7.1	7.1
Spanish.................	....	....	....	....	....	....
Syrian..................	50	50	100	.9	.9	.9
Turkish.................	15	15	30	.3	.3	.3
Others‡.................	3	2	5	†	†	†
Unspecified..............	35	34	69	.6	.6	.6
American (U.S.).........	773	844	1,617	13.4	14.7	14.1
GRAND TOTAL........	5,752	5,752	11,504	100.0	100.0	100.0

* Portuguese includes: Azores and Madeira Islands, 6; Cape de Verde Islands, 30.

† Less than .1 per cent.

‡ "Others" includes the following regional derivations, too small to be listed separately: South American, 1; Serbian, 2; Latvian, 1; and West Indian, 1.

origin for numerous Slavs; Turkey also finds a place, as do one or two other regions with minor figures. The emphasis throughout this study, however, is upon ethnic derivation.

INTRAMARRIAGE AND INTERMARRIAGE AMONG GRANDPARENTS
(Tables 7 and 8)

The ethnic descent of parents depends not only upon the stock of these grandparents,[1] but also upon the ethnic choice in marriage exerted by the grandparents. If the grandparents chose mates from their own ethnic group, the parents of the children are of homogeneous descent. If, however, the grandparents intermarried, the parents are of mixed descent. Ninety-three and one-tenth per cent of the parents, 5,356 in number, are the offspring of matings reported as intramarriages, and they are consequently homogeneous in descent. At least 181 parents, or 3.2 per cent of the total number, are the offspring of intermarriages. (In 215, or 3.7 per cent, of the cases, the data are not entirely clear as to homogeneity. In most of these cases the grandparents are native born and the predominant strain is known, but it is not definitely certain that the strain is pure.[2])

Table 7 describes the matings of all grandparents and at the same time indicates the descent of parents by grandfather and grandmother. Table 8 gives the number and per cent distribution of parents in the present population according to their descent from these grandparents.

THE GENESIS OF THE "MELTING POT"
(Tables 7, 8, and 9)

The marriages of grandparents could not all have taken place in the United States. Only 14.1 per cent of the grandparents were native born. Others came to this country, but since many of the grandparents are the ancestors of immigrant parents and children, it is clear they themselves never came to this country. This in no way affects the description of descent. The facts of descent remain the same, whether or not the grandparents migrated. The data indicate, however, that those matings which fall into our category of intermarriage must have taken place for the most part in this country, if for no other reason than that native Americans

[1] For the purpose of establishing consistent nomenclature, it will be convenient to designate them as grandparents, even though they are being discussed as the parents of parents.

[2] Undoubtedly many of these represent admixture. At least 78 of these cases are later definitely drawn into the fusion class, since they marry persons of mixed and known descent. See chap. vi, p. 78, n. 2; also notes to Tables 28 ff. and 36 ff.

TABLE 8

Ethnic Descent of 5,752 Parents:* Number and
Per Cent Distribution

Ethnic Derivation	Number	Per Cent
Albanian	3	.1
Armenian	28	.5
Austrian		
Belgian (Flemish)	33	.6
British total	642	11.2
a) English	*450*	*7.8*
b) Scotch	*44*	*.8*
c) Scotch-Irish	*3*	*.1*
d) Canadian English	*26*	*.4*
e) Canadian Scotch	*11*	*.2*
f) Canadian unspec.	*11*	*.2*
g) British mixed	*97*	*1.7*
h) British, others		
Chinese	6	.1
Colored	8	.1
Czech	2	†
Dutch	2	†
Finnish	5	.1
French Canadian	2,189	38.1
French, total all others	178	3.1
a) French, France	*77*	*1.3*
b) Walloon	*51*	*.9*
c) Alsatian	*17*	*.3*
d) Swiss	*2*	†
e) French mixed	*31*	*.6*
German	35	.6
Greek	21	.3
Irish	472	8.2
Italian	383	6.7
Jewish	200	3.5
Portuguese (white)	43	.7
Roumanian	48	.8
Scandinavian total	58	1.0
a) Swedish	*51*	*.9*
b) Norwegian	*2*	†
c) Danish	*5*	*.1*
Slavic total	950	16.5
a) Polish	*539*	*9.4*
b) Ukrainian	*375*	*6.5*
c) Russian	*31*	*.5*
d) Lithuanian	*5*	*.1*
e) (Galician)		
Spanish		
Syrian	50	.9
Turkish		
Total homogeneous	5,356	93.1
Partly unspecified (n.d.)	*78*	*1.4*
Unspecified (n.d.)	*117*	*2.0*
Other unspecified	*20*	*.3*
Total unspecified	215	3.7
Mixed ancestry	181	3.2
Grand total	5,752	100.0

* Figures are given in detail for fathers and for mothers in chap. v, Tables 14–15b.

† Less than .1 per cent.

and French Canadians figure so largely in the process.[1] The cases in which parents are the offspring of intermarriage among grandparents in the United States represent the genesis of the melting pot as an American phenomenon.

Certain definite trends in intermarriage which are maintained throughout the study definitely establish themselves at this point. A dozen[2] or more groups contribute to the melting pot, but it is most definitely com-

TABLE 9

RATES OF INTERMARRIAGE AMONG GRANDPARENTS IN MAJOR GROUPS
(Number and Per Cent)

Derivation	No. of G.P.'s Intermarrying	No. of G.P.'s in Population	Per Cent of Intermarriage
British:			
Total	115	1,433	8.0
Men	58	716	8.1
Women	57	717	7.9
Irish:			
Total	78	1,040	7.5
Men	30	512	5.9
Women	48	528	9.1
French Canadians:			
Total	68	4,452	1.5
Men	33	2,220	1.5
Women	35	2,232	1.6
All others:			
Total	101*	4,579	2.2
Men	60	2,304	2.6
Women	41	2,275	1.8
Total	362	11,504	3.2

* This number includes 32 European French and 69 other individuals representing 11 stocks as indicated in Table 7.

posed of three elements, British, Irish, and French Canadians, given in the order of numerical importance, the British contributing 115 persons to the melting pot, the Irish 78, and the French Canadians 68 (European French stocks add 32 to this number). In addition, 69 other persons representing 11 European stocks are drawn into the melting pot here at its inception. Along with certain other strains, Scandinavian, German, and Dutch blood is absorbed into an "American" unit at this point (see Tables 7 and 9).

[1] Discussions relating to intermarriage among parents in chap. viii take into account the place of marriage.

[2] The exact figure depends upon whether British stocks and French stocks are counted each as an ethnic class, or whether the combined groups constitute an ethnic unit.

The British show the greatest tendency to intermarry, the Irish only slightly less. Eight per cent of all British intermarry as against 7.5 per cent of the Irish. Irish women intermarry more freely than Irish men and more freely than any other group—9.1 per cent. These are characteristics which manifest themselves repeatedly in later generations in this unit, and also in other units surveyed by the author.

ETHNIC PREFERENCE IN MATING

(Table 10)

The preferences which the groups have for each other may be indicated by the realignment which takes place as a result of marriage. There are certain preferences which occur so frequently that they may be distinguished as types.

TABLE 10

ETHNIC CHOICE IN MARRIAGE EXERTED IN 5,752 MATINGS
OF 11,504 GRANDPARENTS

Type	Number	Per Cent	Including
Intramarriages......	5,356	93.1	99 Kindred crossings 64 British mixed 35 French mixed
Intermarriages......	181	3.2	51 British×Irish 33 British×French Can. 19 Irish×French Can. 78 All others*
Doubtful..........	215	3.7	
Total..........	5,752	100.0	

* See Table 7.

Table 10 describes the realignment as a result of mating. There is first and foremost the large class of intramarriages, including the numerically significant group of kindred matings.

CROSSING OF KINDRED STRAINS

(Tables 7 and 10)

Before any further conclusions can be drawn about ethnic preference, there should be considered a type of crossing which is numerically significant and which stands halfway between intramarriage and intermarriage as we have strictly defined intermarriage. These are the marriages between members from kindred stocks, namely, matings which unite two British strains or two French strains. There are 99 such matings. This is comparatively a large group, and conclusions regarding fusion depend largely upon how the investigator treats them. There are, for example, 64 matings among grandparents which unite two or more British strains and which are recorded in the British block in Table 7.[1]

This type of cross-marriage obviously is of European origin, as are also the French, Walloon, and Alsatian combinations within the French square. Thirty-five such matings uniting two or more French strains are recorded in the French block in Table 7.[2]

This particular grouping-together of British stocks under one major class, and of French stocks under another major class, was determined upon after considerable experimental work with data. It was possible in this way to give a more accurate picture of what was taking place in Woonsocket, though it did change the numerical measure of fusion seriously at points. Chiefly, it effected radical reductions in the general rate of admixture, but the present method was adopted as indicating more clearly to what extent British groups mingle with non-British groups, French groups with non-French groups, and so on. The figures are always given in detail for each subgroup, and other investigators may determine upon another scheme. This scheme facilitates consistency throughout this investigation. It was made necessary by the very fact that so many cases fall within the squares set aside for these groups in the several intermarriage tables.

SUMMARY OF DATA ON ETHNIC PREFERENCE:
MEN AND WOMEN COMPARED

(Tables 7 and 10)

In summarizing data on preference in marriage we find that the largest proportion of persons—indeed, over 93 per cent—choose mates of their own ethnic variety. Identity of culture is emphatically the desideratum in most cases. Failing to choose a mate from one's very own class, ethnically, a kindred group is called upon. For the British it is some other British stock; for the French, some other French stock. In this manner there is an increasing number of individuals who are of mixed British or mixed French descent.

When we come to the cases which we have defined strictly as intermarriage, we find the most distinctive feature of the situation to be that over

---

[1] At least 73 grandparents are themselves of mixed descent and are in this type of marriage repeating a pattern set by great-grandparents.

[2] Thirty-eight grandparents are themselves of "mixed French" descent. The new "mixed French" matings repeat a precedent set in a previous generation.

one-half of the cases of intermarriage result in admixture of French-Canadian, British, or Irish strains. At least two of these elements are represented in each of these matings. In addition, these stocks are also chosen in marriage by other groups; but the essentially American aspect of the picture and one probably unique to Woonsocket is the admixture established as a result of British–French-Canadian–Irish crossings.

Further examination of the realignment indicates that the British are chosen in marriage frequently both by Irish and by French Canadians. In general, however, the British and Irish show greater preference for each other than for French Canadians. French Canadians prefer British as against the Irish.

The preference differs somewhat for men and women as follows:

Among the British[1] the women marry non-British groups infrequently, but when they do the preference is, first, for French Canadians (19 cases); and, second, for Irish men (18 cases). They also marry into five other groups (20 cases).[2]

The British men are more prone than other men to marry out of their group, preferring in the first place Irish women (33 cases). The second and only other important choice indicated is that for French-Canadian women (14 cases). They also marry into five other groups (11 cases.)

The Irish women, who marry out more frequently than any other class, make as their first choice British men (33 cases), and as their second, French Canadians (10 cases). They also marry into four other groups (5 cases).

Irish men prefer, first, British women (18 cases); and, second, French-Canadian women (9 cases). They marry women of two other groups (3 cases).

Among the French Canadians, relatively few women marry out of the group. Among those who do, the preference is, first, for British men (14 cases); and, second, for Irish men (9 cases). They marry into six other groups (12 cases).

French-Canadian men prefer British women first (19 cases), and Irish second (10 cases). They marry into three other groups (4 cases).

The admixture of these three strains sets a pattern which, as we shall see, is not abandoned in the next generation. It should also be noted, however, that the preferences were determined in large part by the fact that these groups represent the dominant elements present in the popula-

[1] For the per cent of intermarriage in each group refer to Table 9.

[2] The figures given here are derived from Table 7.

tion about the time when grandparents were mating. The French Canadians appear to be a second choice both for British and for Irish persons who intermarry, but British-Irish intermarriages may have been well begun before the French Canadians got a foothold in Woonsocket. At best, the French Canadians must have been an alien and recent group in Woonsocket when the marriages between grandparents were taking place more than a generation ago.

SIGNIFICANCE OF INTERMARRIAGE DATA

It may seem that the number of cases with which we are dealing is too small a figure to account for all the admixture among grandparents.

In reference to the number of cases, any particular class within the population may be small, but the unit includes 5,752 matings and 11,504 grandparents. It is all the evidence on an entire community. While caution is the byword in all preliminary investigations, it is only by recording and interpreting all evidence, however meager at the moment, that we can attain cumulative results, and knowledge about these few cases is basic to the development of this investigation. It might be added, however, that findings in our other surveys corroborate for the most part the trends which manifest themselves here. In Woonsocket, particularly, these cases, though few in number, mark both the genesis and the pattern of the melting pot to which the next generation remains loyal.

As for the small percentage, 3.2, several factors operate to make it small. In the first place, all figures on admixture and intermarriage in this report are minimum figures, since no doubtful cases were included as intermarriage. Even "probable" cases of intermarriage were classed as doubtful. We have, as a result, a relatively large group of doubtful cases—215. Most of these are only part doubtful. The element of doubt is relatively greater in this particular part of the report than elsewhere, as the figures are cumulative for grandparents. It becomes less important as we continue with the history of these families, since proportionately fewer parents and children are affected and the proportion of cases grows smaller. Only 24 Old American families are entirely unspecified for ethnic descent; 65 other families are in some measure doubtful as to ancestry (see Table 16).

One other factor operates to make the per cent of admixture small. This analysis describes intermarriage irrespective of the place. When data are refined for place of marriage, as is done in the case of parents,[1] we

[1] See chap. viii.

find that intermarriage in the United States is five times as frequent as it is among those married in foreign countries. To the extent that the marriages among grandparents did not take place in the United States, we can assume situations which radically reduce the figure for intermarriage. But the relationship between the three groups specified is so distinctly characteristic of Woonsocket that it is fair to assume that the admixture is American in origin and peculiar to that community.

The fact that marriages between kindred groups were taken out of the category of intermarriage served again to reduce the amount of intermarriage about one-third. This, too, was found to be true for the study as a whole, when parents and children are included in the unit.

The figure 3.2 per cent, therefore, describes the proportion of cases in which intermarriage is clear beyond a doubt, and in which it occurs between two very different strains. It was only by strictly limiting in this fashion the class designated as intermarriage that the groundwork could be laid for the study of subsequent admixture in the Woonsocket population.

SUMMARY

The immediate ancestors of these children are 11,504 grandparents: 4 for each sib, 2 for each parent. There are 2,876 sibs, 4,978 children, and 5,752 parents in the population. The derivation of parents in the homes from which children come may be best ascertained by describing the ethnic descent and intermarriage among grandparents.

These grandparents (a number weighted for actual parents) are derived from 28 or more ethnic groups and from 38 different regions. French Canadians are the largest constituent group, contributing 38.7 per cent of the total stock; the Slavic groups combined follow with 16.5 per cent; the British combined, with 12.5 per cent. The Irish contribute 9.0 per cent; the Italians, 6.7 per cent; and the Jews, 3.5 per cent (Table 5).

The regional derivations are somewhat different (Table 6).

Ninety-three and one-tenth per cent of the parents are "offspring" of matings among grandparents which are intramarriages. At least 3.2 per cent of the parents are offspring of matings among grandparents which are intermarriages. Three and seven-tenths per cent, for the most part native born, are in some measure doubtful as to homogeneity (Tables 7 and 8).

The melting pot as an American phenomenon has its genesis in the intermarriage of grandparents. The original elements in the melting pot are most largely British, Irish, and French Canadians, although some ten or twelve other groups each make some contribution.

The British and Irish have the highest per cent of intermarriage with 8.0 and 7.5 per cent to their credit, respectively. Irish women show the highest proportion of intermarriage with 9.1 per cent. These are much higher than the average percentage for the whole group—3.2 per cent.

Grandparents are prone to choose in marriage persons of their own ethnic stock. In addition, numerous matings (99) bring together two kindred strains such as British or French.

When they do intermarry, the evidence is that British are most frequently chosen in marriage by both Irish and French Canadians as well as by others in the community, although the preferences differ somewhat for men and for women. The Irish are more frequently chosen in marriage by the British than by the French Canadians.

These preferences are undoubtedly in large measure determined by the dominance of these groups in Woonsocket of that period.

The percentage of intermarriage, 3.2, is small, because of the restricted meaning assigned to the term, and because certain conditions prevailed which limited the extent of admixture. In spite of these facts, the trends here established are corroborated by those manifest in other communities, where the data include several thousand cases.

As we shall see later, the pattern of admixture established by the grandparents in Woonsocket—a pattern peculiar to that community—holds its own in the next generation, when parents exert their preferences in marriage.

CHAPTER V

THE DERIVATION OF PARENTS

The preceding summaries dealing with the derivation of grandparents and with their ethnic choice in mating describe at the same time the background from which the parental stock has emanated. There is, however, additional information which may be sought for a fuller and more detailed description of parental stock. Tables 7 and 8 in the preceding chapter give the ethnic derivation of parents according to two lines of descent. But these tables give no clue to the regional derivation of parents or to their generation in America. Where were they born? How long have they been here? What differences occur between a classification of the same individuals on a regional basis and one on an ethnic basis? What are the distributions for men and women separately?

The aim of this chapter is to describe more fully the ethnic derivation of parents as individuals, the degree of Americanism as it is measured by generation in America, and the relation which exists between an ethnic and a regional classification. Indeed, it is one of the main objectives in this entire investigation to disentangle in some measure the facts relating to ethnic derivation from those relating to regional origin.

It would be a laborious task that serves no purpose to make each analysis in this monograph on a dual classificatory scheme—one regional and one ethnic. The relationship between these two may be tested for one group. Since father's birthplace is so largely accepted in current usage as the basis for determining nationality, it is especially pertinent to employ the data for fathers for this purpose.

REGIONAL VERSUS ETHNIC DERIVATION: DIFFERENCE TESTED FOR FATHERS

(Tables 11, 12, and 13)

Table 11 indicates both the ethnic and the geographic derivation of the 2,876 men who are the fathers in these families. Of these only 50.8 per cent of the fathers—those appearing in the diagonal, 1,460 in number—claim "nationality," or ethnic descent which is identical with birthplace. Forty-nine and two-tenths per cent of the fathers—those that fall in the scatter on the diagram, 1,416 in number—indicate an ethnic affiliation other than their regional origin. There are two factors which contribute to make the figure for the scatter so large. In the first place, "native" stock has been distributed according to its ethnic derivations. One thousand and eighteen native-born fathers have been distributed among 13 different ethnic groups from which they claim descent.[1] These American-born fathers represent 35.4 per cent of the total. In the second place, the foreign-born themselves contribute to the scatter 13.8 per cent of the total number of fathers.

Put differently, one-half of the total number of fathers change places in the new grouping. More than one-fifth of the immigrant fathers come from geographic regions different from that of their descent. The groups contributing to this result are those emanating primarily from the north Slavic countries, and to a lesser degree, from Finland and from the Balkan Peninsula. While the number of cases is relatively small for these two latter groups, reference is made to them since these groups raise problems which have significant bearing on the general discussion, and also because they might be of greater significance if the area involved in the survey were more extended or represented some other community.

If we are seeking to determine the regional sources of Slavic immigration, we find that the regions of emigration for these particular groups, given in the order of numerical importance, are Poland, former Galicia, Russia, and Ukraine. If, however, we are seeking to determine the ethnic derivation of these same immigrants, we find the three significant groups to be Poles, Ukrainians, and Jews, given again in the order of numerical importance. Jews come from nine different countries, but predominantly from Russia. Ukrainians and a goodly number of Poles come from former Galicia; 105 immigrants come from Russia, but there are only 19 real Russians in our unit, and not more than 10 of these come from Russia. This would bear out the supposition that immigrants come in large measure from countries other than their fatherland.[2]

The Balkans represent a complicated situation sufficiently familiar without need of further discussion. The present classification is a concession to the desire of Roumanians not to be classed as Albanians; Armenians and Greeks are rescued from the designation Turk; Jews are no longer Slavs. The case of the Finns and Swedes brought to light a historical and cultural situation less well known. Of 14 fathers (and families) who claimed Finland as the regional derivation for themselves and all the

---

[1] This includes 71 native-born fathers unspecified for descent.

[2] For a discussion relating to the migration of people who belong to ethnic minorities in European countries see Niles Carpenter, *op. cit.*

Ethnic Derivation of Father	Regional Derivation† of Father	Albanian	Armenian	Austrian	Belgian (Flemish)	British total	a) English	b) Scotch	c) Scotch-Irish	d) Canadian English	e) Canadian Scotch	f) Canadian, others	g) British mixed	h) British, others	Chinese	Colored	Czech	Dutch
Albanian	2																	
Armenian			9															
Austrian																		
Belgian (Flemish)					12													
British total																		
a) English							74											
b) Scotch							1	17										
c) Scotch-Irish																		
d) Canadian English										13								
e) Canadian Scotch											2							
f) Canadian unspec.												6						
g) British mixed							6					1	3					
h) British, others																		
Chinese															2			
Colored																		
Czech																	1	
Dutch																		▮
Finnish																		
French Canadian																		
French, total all others																		
a) French, France																		
b) Walloon																		
c) Alsatian					1													
d) Swiss																		
e) French, mixed					1													
German					1													
Greek																		
Irish								2						5				
Italian																		
Jewish				3										1				
Portuguese (white)																		
Roumanian		15			1													
Scandinavian total																		
a) Swedish																		
b) Norwegian																		
c) Danish																		
Slavic total																		
a) Polish																		
b) Ukrainian																		
c) Russian				2														
d) Lithuanian																		
e) (Galician)																		
Latvian																		
South American																		
Syrian																		
Turkish																		
Mixed ancestry					1			2						9				
Incomplete																		
Unspecified (n.d.)																		
GRAND TOTAL		17	9	6	16	(142)	83	19		13	3	24			2		1	1
PER CENT OF TOTAL																		

* The cases in which ethnic and regional derivation are identical are indicated in boldface. † Meaning bir

NOTE.—Throughout this table the figures in parentheses have reference only to the immediate situation column totals.

TABLE 12

5,752 Parents by Regional Derivation: Number and Per Cent Distribution

a) Fathers, b) Mothers, c) Both

	Number			Per Cent		
Regional Derivation	Fathers (a)	Mothers (b)	Total Parents (c)	Fathers (a')	Mothers (b')	Total Parents (c')
Albanian.................	17	14	31	.6	.5	.5
Armenian...............	9	9	18	.3	.3	.3
Austrian.................	6	10	16	.2	.4	.3
Belgian (Flemish).........	16	16	32	.6	.5	.6
British total.............	142	130	272	4.9	4.5	4.7
a) English..............	83	80	163	2.9	2.8	2.8
b) Scotch..............	19	16	35	.7	.5	.6
c) Scotch-Irish.........	....	....	....	....	....	....
d) Canadian English......	13	11	24	.4	.4	.4
e) Canadian Scotch.......	3	9	12	.1	.3	.2
f) Canadian unspec.......	24	14	38	.8	.5	.7
g) British mixed.........	....	....	....	....	....	....
h) British, others........	....	....	....	....	....	....
Chinese.................	2	3	5	.1	.1	.1
Colored.................	....	....	....	....	....	....
Czech...................	1	2	3	*	.1	.1
Dutch...................	1	....	1	*	*	*
Finnish..................	14	13	27	.5	.4	.5
French Canadian........	660	606	1,266	22.9	21.1	22.0
French, European total....	90	75	165	3.1	2.6	2.9
a) French, France........	56	45	101	1.9	1.6	1.8
b) Walloon.............	23	22	45	.9	.7	.8
c) Alsatian.............	10	8	18	.3	.3	.3
d) Swiss...............	1	....	1	*	*	*
e) French mixed..........	....	....	....	....	....	....
German.................	5	5	10	.2	.2	.2
Greek...................	11	11	22	.4	.4	.4
Irish...................	43	54	97	1.5	1.9	1.7
Italian..................	195	181	376	6.8	6.3	6.5
Jewish..................	....	....	....	....	....	....
Portuguese (white)†.......	25	21	46	.9	.8	.8
Roumanian.............	7	7	14	.2	.2	.2
Scandinavian total.......	13	11	24	.4	.4	.4
a) Swedish.............	10	8	18	.3	.3	.3
b) Norwegian...........	1	1	2	*	*	*
c) Danish..............	2	2	4	.1	.1	.1
Slavic total.............	554	549	1,103	19.3	19.1	19.1
a) Polish..............	219	228	447	7.6	7.9	7.8
b) Ukrainian...........	32	25	57	1.1	.9	1.0
c) Russian.............	105	80	185	3.7	2.8	3.2
d) Lithuanian..........	5	3	8	.2	.1	.1
e) (Galician)...........	193	213	406	6.7	7.4	7.0
Spanish.................	....	....	....	....	....	....
Syrian..................	25	25	50	.9	.9	.9
Turkish.................	8	7	15	.3	.2	.3
Others‡.................	2	2	4	.1	*	.1
Unspecified.............	12	7	19	.4	.2	.3
American (U.S.).........	1,018	1,118	2,136	35.4	38.9	37.1
Grand total........	2,876	2,876	5,752	100.0	100.0	100.0

* Less than .1 per cent.

† Portuguese includes: Azores and Madeira Islands 3; Cape de Verde Islands, 16.

‡ "Others" includes the following regional derivations, too small to be listed separately: Serbian, 1; Latvian, 1; South American, 2.

grandparents in the family, 12 reported their nationality as Swedish. Home visits corroborated this information. Swedes having lived in Finland for two generations still assert cultural loyalty to their Swedish origin. Among grandparents only 56 reported Sweden as their birthplace, while 110 reported Swedish for ethnic descent.

Visits were made to all families who indicated their regional derivation to be Albania, but who claimed to be Roumanian. Field-workers found that all these people came from Koritza, and that the group was essentially Roumanian in its loyalties.

It was definitely the experience of all investigators that the replies to the question involving ethnic descent were answered more readily and were correct with greater frequency than any other. Aside from the conscious and more intimate loyalty which individuals bear to a cultural group than to a political unit the changing boundary lines must inevitably leave a large number of persons uncertain as to whether they or their parents were born in Austria, Poland, or Jugoslavia. Accuracy on this score would indeed involve intimate knowledge of international affairs and current history. There is no such confusion in the mind of the immigrant on the score of ethnic descent or ethnic loyalty. His sense of membership in a certain ethnic group is quite distinct.

It is clear that a regional basis of classification does not adequately define the specific groups for us. Whether the interest in "national origins" is biologic or cultural, the purpose is best served by the ethnic classification. The migratory fortunes which distribute Jews, Roumanians, and Swedes among other countries are indeed variables in the cultural life of these peoples. They do not, however, change the blood and, quite obviously, have not changed the ethnic loyalties. It is apparent that the ends of this study will be best served by adhering primarily to an ethnic grouping. All discussions from this point on, therefore, are based upon ethnic classifications, although data on regional derivations are recorded in full.

INVENTORY OF ALL PARENTS: ETHNIC DERIVATION AND
GENERATION IN AMERICA

(Tables 13, 13a, and 13b; Fig. 2)

Table 8, in the previous chapter, is an inventory of all parents according to ethnic descent, irrespective of generation. Some are foreign born, some are native born; others represent families who have lived in the United States for several generations, but they are classified there only as to descent. The French Canadians lead with 2,189, or 38.1 per cent of all

TABLE 13

5,752 Parents: Ethnic Derivation and Generation in America*

Ethnic Derivation	1st Gen. (a)	2d Gen. (b)	3/2 and 3d Gen. 3/2 Gen. (c)	3d Gen. (d)	Total 3/2 and 3d (e) (e=c+d)	Rejects (f)	Total (g)
Albanian...............	3	......	......	......	......	......	3
Armenian..............	27	1	......	......	......	......	28
Austrian..............	......	......	......	......	......	......	......
Belgian (Flemish).......	33	......	......	......	......	......	33
British total...........	246	64	165	164	329	3	642
a) English............	151	51	111	134	245	3	450
b) Scotch............	29	6	7	2	9	......	44
c) Scotch-Irish........	......	1	2	......	2	......	3
d) Canadian English....	21	1	4	......	4	......	26
e) Canadian Scotch.....	11	......	......	......	......	......	11
f) Canadian unspec.....	10	1	......	......	......	......	11
g) British mixed.......	24	4	41	28	69	......	97
h) British, others......	......	......	......	......	......	......	......
Chinese...............	5	1	......	......	......	......	6
Colored...............	3	......	......	5	5	......	8
Czech................	2	......	......	......	......	......	2
Dutch................	1	1	......	......	......	......	2
Finnish...............	5	......	......	......	......	......	5
French Canadian.......	1,260	555	313	40	353	21	2,189
French, total all others..	156	17	4	1	5	......	178
a) French, France......	71	6	......	......	......	......	77
b) Walloon...........	50	1	......	......	......	......	51
c) Alsatian...........	17	......	......	......	......	......	17
d) Swiss.............	1	1	......	......	......	......	2
e) French mixed.......	17	9	4	1	5	......	31
German...............	15	10	7	3	10	......	35
Greek................	21	......	......	......	......	......	21
Irish.................	110	143	160	59	219	......	472
Italian...............	377	5	1	......	1	......	383
Jewish...............	186	13	......	1	1	......	200
Portuguese (white)......	42	......	......	1	1	......	43
Roumanian............	48	......	......	......	......	......	48
Scandinavian total......	46	10	2	......	2	......	58
a) Swedish...........	40	9	2	......	2	......	51
b) Norwegian.........	2	......	......	......	......	......	2
c) Danish............	4	1	......	......	......	......	5
Slavic total...........	936	10	1	......	1	3	950
a) Polish............	529	7	1	......	1	2	539
b) Ukrainian..........	373	1	......	......	......	1	375
c) Russian...........	29	2	......	......	......	......	31
d) Lithuanian.........	5	......	......	......	......	......	5
e) (Galician)..........	......	......	......	......	......	......	......
Spanish...............	......	......	......	......	......	......	......
Syrian................	50	......	......	......	......	......	50
Turkish...............	......	......	......	......	......	......	......
Total homogeneous......	3,572	830	653	274	927	27	5,356
Partly unspecified.......	1	......	64	13	77	......	78†
Unspecified (n.d.).......	......	......	42	74	116	1	117
Other unspecified.......	......	4	......	......	......	16	20
Mixed ancestry.........	29	31	83	38	121	......	181†
Grand total..........	3,602	865	842	399	1,241	44	5,752

* See Tables 14 and 15 for detailed distribution for fathers and mothers respectively.

† See note to chap. iv, p. 46, and notes to Tables 28 ff. and 36 ff.

TABLE 13a

5,752 PARENTS: PER CENT DISTRIBUTION OF EACH STOCK BY GENERATION

ETHNIC DERIVATION	GENERATION						
	1ST GEN.	2D GEN.	3/2 AND 3D GEN.			REJECTS	TOTAL
			3/2 Gen.	3d Gen.	Total 3/2 and 3d		
	(a)	(b)	(c)	(d)	(e)	(f)	(g)
Albanian....................	100.0	......	......	......	......	......	100.0
Armenian....................	96.4	3.6	......	......	......	......	100.0
Austrian.....	......	......	......	......	......	......	......
Belgian (Flemish).............	100.0	......	......	......	......	......	100.0
British total................	38.3	10.0	25.7	25.6	51.3	.4	100.0
a) English...................	*33.6*	*11.3*	*24.6*	*29.8*	*54.4*	*.7*	*100.0*
b) Scotch...................	*65.9*	*13.6*	*15.9*	*4.6*	*20.5*	......	*100.0*
c) Scotch-Irish..............	......	*33.3*	*66.7*	......	*66.7*	......	*100.0*
d) Canadian English..........	*80.8*	*3.8*	*15.4*	......	*15.4*	......	*100.0*
e) Canadian Scotch...........	*100.0*	......	......	......	......	......	*100.0*
f) Canadian unspec.........	*90.9*	*9.1*	......	......	......	......	*100.0*
g) British mixed.............	*24.7*	*4.1*	*42.3*	*28.9*	*71.2*	......	*100.0*
h) British, others...........	......	......	......	......	......	......	......
Chinese.....................	83.3	16.7	......	......	......	......	100.0
Colored.....................	37.5	......	......	62.5	62.5	......	100.0
Czech.......................	100.0	......	......	......	......	......	100.0
Dutch.......................	50.0	50.0	......	......	......	......	100.0
Finnish......................	100.0	......	......	......	......	......	100.0
French Canadian............	57.5	25.4	14.3	1.8	16.1	1.0	100.0
French, total all others	87.6	9.6	2.2	.6	2.8	......	100.0
a) French, France............	*92.2*	*7.8*	......	......	......	......	*100.0*
b) Walloon..................	*98.0*	*2.0*	......	......	......	......	*100.0*
c) Alsatian..................	*100.0*	......	......	......	......	......	*100.0*
d) Swiss....................	*50.0*	*50.0*	......	......	......	......	*100.0*
e) French mixed.............	*54.9*	*29.0*	*12.9*	*3.2*	*16.1*	......	*100.0*
German.....................	42.8	28.6	20.0	8.6	28.6	......	100.0
Greek.......................	100.0	......	......	......	......	......	100.0
Irish........................	23.3	30.3	33.9	12.5	46.4	......	100.0
Italian......................	98.4	1.3	.3	......	.3	......	100.0
Jewish......................	93.0	6.5	......	.5	.5	......	100.0
Portuguese (white)............	97.7	......	......	2.3	2.3	......	100.0
Roumanian..................	100.0	......	......	......	......	......	100.0
Scandinavian total...........	79.3	17.2	3.5	......	3.5	......	100.0
a) Swedish..................	*78.4*	*17.7*	*3.9*	......	*3.9*	......	*100.0*
b) Norwegian................	*100.0*	......	......	......	......	......	*100.0*
c) Danish...................	*80.0*	*20.0*	......	......	......	......	*100.0*
Slavic total..................	98.6	1.0	.1	......	.1	.3	100.0
a) Polish....................	*98.1*	*1.3*	*.2*	......	*.2*	*.4*	*100.0*
b) Ukrainian.................	*99.4*	*.3*	......	......	......	*.3*	*100.0*
c) Russian...................	*93.5*	*6.5*	......	......	......	......	*100.0*
d) Lithuanian................	*100.0*	......	......	......	......	......	*100.0*
e) (Galician)................	......	......	......	......	......	......	......
Spanish.....................	......	......	......	......	......	......	......
Syrian......................	100.0	......	......	......	......	......	100.0
Turkish.....................	......	......	......	......	......	......	......
TOTAL HOMOGENEOUS......	66.7	15.5	12.2	5.1	17.3	.5	100.0
Partly unspecified.............	1.3	......	82.0	16.7	98.7	......	100.0
Unspecified (n.d.).............	......	......	35.9	63.2	99.1	.9	100.0
Other unspecified.............	......	20.0	......	......	......	80.0	100.0
Mixed ancestry...............	16.0	17.1	45.9	21.0	66.9	......	100.0
GRAND TOTAL..........	62.6	15.0	14.6	6.9	21.5	.9	100.0

TABLE 13b

5,752 Parents: Per Cent Distribution by Stocks within Each Generation

Ethnic Derivation	Generation						
			3/2 and 3d Gen.			Rejects	Total
	1st Gen.	2d Gen.	3/2 Gen.	3d Gen.	Total 3/2 and 3d		
	(a)	(b)	(c)	(d)	(e)	(f)	(g)
Albanian	.1						.1
Armenian	.7	.1					.5
Austrian							
Belgian (Flemish)	.9						.6
British total	6.9	7.4	19.6	41.1	26.5	6.8	11.2
a) English	4.2	5.9	13.2	33.6	19.7	6.8	7.8
b) Scotch	.8	.7	.8	.5	.7		.8
c) Scotch-Irish		.1	.2		.2		.1
d) Canadian English	.6	.1	.5		.3		.4
e) Canadian Scotch	.3						.2
f) Canadian unspec	.3	.1					.2
g) British mixed	.7	.5	4.9	7.0	5.6		1.7
h) British, others							
Chinese	.1	.1					.1
Colored	.1			1.2	.4		.1
Czech	.1						*
Dutch	*	.1					*
Finnish	.1						.1
French Canadian	34.9	64.2	37.2	10.0	28.4	47.7	38.1
French, total all others	4.3	1.9	.5	.3	.4		3.1
a) French, France	1.9	.7					1.3
b) Walloon	1.4	.1					.9
c) Alsatian	.5						.3
d) Swiss	*	.1					*
e) French mixed	.5	1.0	.5	.3	.4		.6
German	.4	1.2	.8	.8	.8		.6
Greek	.6						.3
Irish	3.1	16.5	19.0	14.7	17.6		8.2
Italian	10.5	.6	.1		.1		6.7
Jewish	5.2	1.5		.3	.1		3.5
Portuguese (white)	1.2			.3	.1		.7
Roumanian	1.3						.8
Scandinavian total	1.3	1.2	.2		.2		1.0
a) Swedish	1.1	1.1	.2		.2		.9
b) Norwegian	.1						*
c) Danish	.1	.1					.1
Slavic total	26.0	1.1	.1		.1	6.8	16.5
a) Polish	14.7	.8	.1		.1	4.5	9.4
b) Ukrainian	10.4	.1				2.3	6.5
c) Russian	.8	.2					.5
d) Lithuanian	.1						.1
e) (Galician)							
Spanish							
Syrian	1.4						.9
Turkish							
Total homogeneous	99.2	95.9	77.5	68.7	74.7	61.3	93.1
Partly unspecified	*		7.6	3.3	6.2		1.4
Unspecified (n.d.)			5.0	18.5	9.3	2.3	2.0
Other unspecified		.5				36.4	.3
Mixed ancestry	.8	3.6	9.9	9.5	9.8		3.2
Grand total	100.0	100.0	100.0	100.0	100.0	100.0	100.0

* Less than .1 per cent.

parents. Slavs from the region in and about former Russia constitute together a close second with 950, or 16.5 per cent, the other groups following in order: British, 642 or 11.2 per cent; Irish, 472 or 8.2 per cent; Italian, 383 or 6.7 per cent; and Jews, 200 or 3.5 per cent. These stocks are variously distributed for generation in America.

Tables 13, 13a, and 13b offer an inventory of all parents, both for generation in America and for ethnic derivation. Of the total number of

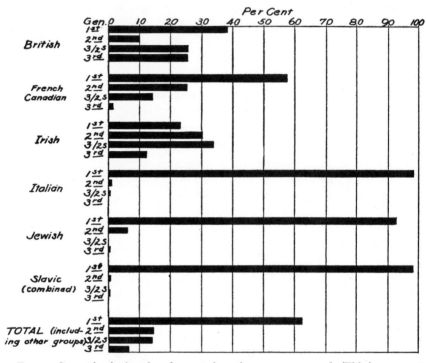

FIG. 2.—Generation in America of parents in major groups compared. (This is a per cent distribution for each group by generation and is based upon the data in Table 13a.)

parents, 62.6 per cent belong to the first generation, i.e., they are immigrants; 15.0 per cent belong to the second generation, i.e., they are native born but of foreign extraction. Only 6.9 per cent are of the third generation, i.e., native born of native parentage. This last group are at least third generation. Included in this class are those who have been here longer than three generations, indeed descendants of the earliest settlers in this country. They are all native varying in the degree of residence in this country. Fourteen and six-tenths per cent of the parents are partly of the third and partly of the second generation (3/2), i.e., at least one grandparent in the family was native born, but not all. Immigrant parents then predominate in the public-school population.

Italians, Slavs, and Jews represent for Woonsocket the major stocks comprising the new immigration. More than 90 per cent of the members in each of these groups are recent immigrants.[1] The British, Irish, and French Canadians are well represented in column *d*. These groups represent the old immigrants, but they represent a continuous stream of immigration, for they are also recent comers, particularly the French Canadians, and to some degree the British. The distribution of these three groups for generation presents an interesting picture. It serves also to establish the sequence in the arrival of these stocks. The Irish, after an initial increase, represent rather an even flow with somewhat of a loss in the first generation. The British, on the other hand, show a decrease in the second generation, but surprisingly enough, like the French Canadians, show a sharp increase for the first generation. The high proportion of British in the first generation indicates that Woonsocket is still recruiting its population from British stock to an appreciable degree. As previously indicated, this stock comes primarily from Great Britain; relatively few British come from Canada.

ETHNIC COMPOSITION OF GENERATIONS COMPARED
(Table 13*b*)

Each generation forms an ethnic mosaic quite distinct in itself. In the first generation only 6.9 per cent of the stock is British, while 93.1 per cent is derived from other European stocks and from the French Canadian; 34.9 per cent of the parents in the first generation are French Canadian. In the third generation, however, 41.1 per cent of the parents are British in origin, 14.7 per cent are Irish, only 10.0 per cent are French Canadian, 18.5 per cent are unspecified, 9.5 per cent are of mixed ancestry.

The second generation shows an equally interesting contrast. Here the French Canadians constitute 64.2 per cent of the total number of parents; the Irish, 16.5 per cent; the British, 7.4 per cent. Several minor elements contribute together the remainder—11.9 per cent.

PARENTS OF MIXED DESCENT

Of the total number of parents, at least 181 are definitely of mixed descent. This admixture is a direct result of the intermarriage of grand-

[1] For further differentiation as to date of entry of first-generation immigrants see Tables 54, 54*a*, and 54*b* and Fig. 5 in chap. xiii.

parents described in the previous chapter as the nucleus of the melting pot.

As a result of the ethnic preference which grandparents exerted in marriage, parents are derived for the most part from French-Canadian, British, and Irish strains, though several other stocks are borne by these parents and their children in the degree indicated in the previous chapter.

The preceding discussion bearing upon the descent of parents provokes the inquiry: How do these parents distribute themselves as heads of families? This is a problem to which we turn in the next chapter.

SUMMARY

The 2,876 fathers and 2,876 mothers, or 5,752 parents, in the population represent largely a recent migratory group to this country. Of the total number 62.6 per cent belong to the first generation, while only 6.9 per cent are Old Americans. The others fall into the intermediate classes (Tables 13, 13a).

Ethnic derivation is not synonymous with regional derivation. Only 50.8 per cent of the fathers claim nationality which coincides with birthplace (Table 11).

An inventory of parents indicates that 38.1 per cent are French Canadian by descent. The Slavic groups combined claim 16.5 per cent; the British, 11.2 per cent; the Irish, 8.2 per cent; the Italians, 6.7 per cent; all others, representing 18 other groups, together constitute 19.3 per cent.

The British, Irish, and French Canadians constitute in Woonsocket the older immigration, an immigration, however, which continues to send recruits. The Italians, Jews, and the Slavic groups constitute the new immigration. Over 90 per cent of these are recent immigrants (Table 13a, Fig. 2).

The ethnic composition of the different generations offers sharp contrasts. Each generation class constitutes ethnic complex unique in itself.

As a direct result of intermarriage between grandparents, at least 181 parents are themselves of mixed descent. These parents are derived in large measure from an admixture of French Canadians, British, and Irish. This latter fact was somewhat to be expected from the analysis of the melting pot in chapter iii.

The parents above described reassort themselves into two major groups: those who marry within the group, and those who marry outside the group. These matings create the immediate background from which the children come.

TABLE 14

Ethnic Derivation	1st Gen. (a)	2d Gen. (b)	3/2 and 3d Gen. 3/2 Gen. (c)	3d Gen. (d)	Total 3/2 and 3d (e) e=c+d	Rejects (f)	Total Excluding e (g)
Albanian	2						2
Armenian	14						14
Austrian							....
Belgian (Flemish)	17						17
British total	126	28	76	86	162	1	317
a) English	76	21	55	71	126	1	224
b) Scotch	18	4	4	2	6		28
c) Scotch-Irish			1		1		1
d) Canadian English	13		2		2		15
e) Canadian Scotch	2						2
f) Canadian unspec.	6						6
g) British mixed	11	3	14	13	27		41
h) British, others							....
Chinese	2	1					3
Colored	2			3	3		5
Czech	1						1
Dutch	1	1					2
Finnish	2						2
French Canadian	654	255	156	20	176	11	1,096
French, total all others	84	9	2		2		95
a) French, France	40	4					44
b) Walloon	26	1					27
c) Alsatian	9						9
d) Swiss	1	1					2
e) French mixed	8	3	2		2		13
German	9	6	3	1	4		19
Greek	11						11
Irish	48	68	76	29	105		221
Italian	195	2	1		1		198
Jewish	95	3		1	1		99
Portuguese (white)	23						23
Roumanian	24						24
Scandinavian total	25	3	1		1		29
a) Swedish	22	3	1		1		26
b) Norwegian	1						1
c) Danish	2						2
Slavic total	468	3				1	472
a) Polish	260	2				1	263
b) Ukrainian	187						187
c) Russian	18	1					19
d) Lithuanian	3						3
e) (Galician)							....
Spanish							
Syrian	25						25
Turkish							....
Total homogeneous	1,828	379	315	140	455	13	2,675
Partly unspecified			31	5	36		36
Unspecified (n.d.)			31	40	71		71
Other unspecified		2				9	11
Mixed ancestry	16	17	36	14	50		83
Grand total	1,844	398	413	199	612	22	2,876

TABLE 14a

2,876 Fathers: Per Cent Distribution of Each Stock by Generation

Ethnic Derivation	Generation						
			3/2 and 3d Gen.				
	1st Gen.	2d Gen.	3/2 Gen.	3d Gen.	Total 3/2 and 3d	Rejects	Total
	(a)	(b)	(c)	(d)	(e)	(f)	(g)
Albanian...................	100.0	......	......	......	......	......	100.0
Armenian..................	100.0	......	......	......	......	......	100.0
Austrian..................							
Belgian (Flemish)...........	100.0	......	......	......	......	......	100.0
British total...............	39.8	8.8	24.0	27.1	51.1	.3	100.0
a) English................	33.9	9.4	24.6	31.7	56.3	.4	100.0
b) Scotch.................	64.3	14.3	14.3	7.1	21.4	......	100.0
c) Scotch-Irish...........	......	......	100.0	......	100.0	......	100.0
d) Canadian English.........	86.7	......	13.3	......	13.3		100.0
e) Canadian Scotch.........	100.0	......	......	......	......		100.0
f) Canadian unspec...........	100.0	......	......	......	......		100.0
g) British mixed...........	26.8	7.3	34.2	31.7	65.9	......	100.0
h) British, others...........							
Chinese....................	66.7	33.3	......	......	......	......	100.0
Colored...................	40.0	......	......	60.0	60.0	......	100.0
Czech....................	100.0	......	......	......	......	......	100.0
Dutch....................	50.0	50.0	......	......	......	......	100.0
Finnish...................	100.0	......	......	......	......	......	100.0
French Canadian..........	59.7	23.3	14.2	1.8	16.0	1.0	100.0
French, total all others.	88.4	9.5	2.1	......	2.1	......	100.0
a) French, France...........	90.9	9.1	......	......	......	......	100.0
b) Walloon................	96.3	3.7	......	......	......	......	100.0
c) Alsatian...............	100.0	......	......	......	......	......	100.0
d) Swiss.................	50.0	50.0	......	......	......	......	100.0
e) French mixed.............	61.5	23.1	15.4	......	15.4	......	100.0
German....................	47.3	31.6	15.8	5.3	21.1	......	100.0
Greek....................	100.0	......	......	......	......	......	100.0
Irish.....................	21.7	30.8	34.4	13.1	47.5	......	100.0
Italian...................	98.5	1.0	.5	......	.5	......	100.0
Jewish....................	96.0	3.0	......	1.0	1.0	......	100.0
Portuguese (white)...........	100.0	......	......	......	......	......	100.0
Roumanian................	100.0	......	......	......	......	......	100.0
Scandinavian total...........	86.2	10.3	3.5	......	3.5	......	100.0
a) Swedish................	84.6	11.6	3.8	......	3.8	......	100.0
b) Norwegian..............	100.0	......	......	......	......	......	100.0
c) Danish................	100.0	......	......	......	......	......	100.0
Slavic total...............	99.2	.6	......	......	......	.2	100.0
a) Polish.................	98.8	.8	......	......	......	.4	100.0
b) Ukrainian..............	100.0	......	......	......	......	......	100.0
c) Russian................	94.7	5.3	......	......	......	......	100.0
d) Lithuanian.............	100.0	......	......	......	......	......	100.0
e) (Galician).............							
Spanish...................							
Syrian....................	100.0	......	......	......	......	......	100.0
Turkish...................							
TOTAL HOMOGENEOUS......	68.3	14.2	11.8	5.2	17.0	.5	100.0
Partly unspecified...........	......	......	86.1	13.9	100.0	......	100.0
Unspecified (n.d.)..........	......	......	43.7	56.3	100.0	......	100.0
Other unspecified............	......	18.2	......	......	......	81.8	100.0
Mixed ancestry.............	19.3	20.5	43.4	16.8	60.2	......	100.0
GRAND TOTAL	64.1	13.8	14.4	6.9	21.3	.8	100.0

Ethnic Derivation	1st Gen.	2d Gen.	3/2 and 3d Gen.			Rejects	Total
			3/2 Gen.	3d Gen.	Total 3/2 and 3d		
	(a)	(b)	(c)	(d)	(e)	(f)	(g)
Albanian....................	.1	......	......	......	......	......	.1
Armenian...................	.8	......	......	......	......	......	.5
Austrian....................							
Belgian (Flemish)............	.9	......	......	......	......	......	.6
British total.................	6.8	7.1	18.4	43.2	26.5	4.5	10.9
a) English...................	4.1	5.3	13.3	35.7	20.6	4.5	7.7
b) Scotch...................	1.0	1.0	1.0	1.0	1.0	......	1.0
c) Scotch-Irish..............	......	......	.2	......	.2	......	*
d) Canadian English.........	.7	......	.5	......	.3	......	.5
e) Canadian Scotch..........	.1	......	......	*	......	......	.1
f) Canadian unspec...........	.3	......	......	......	......	......	.2
g) British mixed.............	.6	.8	3.4	6.5	4.4	......	1.4
h) British, others............	......	......	......	......	......	......	......
Chinese.....................	.1	.2	......	......	......	......	.1
Colored.....................	.1	......	......	1.5	.5	......	.2
Czech......................	.1	......	......	......	......	......	*
Dutch......................	.1	.2	......	......	......	......	.1
Finnish.....................	.1	......	......	......	......	......	.1
French Canadian............	35.4	64.1	37.8	10.1	28.7	50.0	38.1
French, total all others	4.6	2.2	.5	......	.3	......	3.3
a) French, France............	2.2	1.0	......	......	......	......	1.5
b) Walloon..................	1.4	.2	......	......	......	......	.9
c) Alsatian..................	.5	......	......	......	......	......	.3
d) Swiss....................	.1	.2	......	......	......	......	.1
e) French mixed.............	.4	.8	.5	......	.3	......	.5
German.....................	.5	1.5	.8	.5	.7	......	.7
Greek......................	.6	......	......	......	......	......	.4
Irish.......................	2.6	17.1	18.4	14.6	17.1	......	7.7
Italian.....................	10.6	.5	.2	......	.2	......	6.9
Jewish.....................	5.1	.8	......	.5	.2	......	3.4
Portuguese (white)...........	1.1	......	......	......	......	......	.8
Roumanian..................	1.3	......	......	......	......	......	.8
Scandinavian total...........	1.4	.8	.2	......	.2	......	1.0
a) Swedish..................	1.2	.8	.2	......	.2	......	.9
b) Norwegian................	.1	......	......	......	......	......	*
c) Danish...................	.1	......	......	......	......	......	.1
Slavic total.................	25.4	.7	......	......	......	4.5	16.4
a) Polish....................	14.1	.5	......	......	......	4.5	9.1
b) Ukrainian................	10.1	......	......	......	......	......	6.5
c) Russian..................	1.0	.2	......	......	......	......	.7
d) Lithuanian...............	.2	......	......	......	......	......	.1
e) (Galician)................	......	......	......	......	......	......	......
Spanish....................							
Syrian.....................	1.4	......	......	......	......	......	.9
Turkish....................							
Total homogeneous......	99.1	95.2	76.3	70.4	74.4	59.0	93.0
Partly unspecified...........	......	......	7.5	2.5	5.9	......	1.2
Unspecified (n.d.)...........	......	......	7.5	20.1	11.6	......	2.5
Other unspecified............	......	.5	......	......	......	41.0	.4
Mixed ancestry..............	.9	4.3	8.7	7.0	8.1	......	2.9
Grand total..........	100.0	100.0	100.0	100.0	100.0	100.0	100.0

* Less than .1 per cent.

TABLE 15

2,876 Mothers: Ethnic Derivation and Generation in America

ETHNIC DERIVATION	1ST GEN. (a)	2D GEN. (b)	3/2 Gen. (c)	3d Gen. (d)	Total 3/2 and 3d (e) e=c+d	REJECTS (f)	TOTAL (g)
Albanian........................	1	......	......	......	......	......	1
Armenian.....................	13	1	......	......	......	......	14
Austrian.......................							......
Belgian (Flemish).............	16	......	......	......	......	......	16
British total..................	120	36	89	78	167	2	325
a) English....................	75	30	56	63	119	2	226
b) Scotch....................	11	2	3	......	3	......	16
c) Scotch-Irish..............	......	1	1	......	1	......	2
d) Canadian English..........	8	1	2	......	2	......	11
e) Canadian Scotch..........	9	......	......	......	......	......	9
f) Canadian unspec...........	4	1	......	......	......	......	5
g) British mixed.............	13	1	27	15	42	......	56
h) British, others............	......						......
Chinese.......................	3	......	......	......	......	......	3
Colored.......................	1	......	......	2	2	......	3
Czech.........................	1	......	......	......	......	......	1
Dutch.........................	......						......
Finnish.......................	3	......	......	......	......	......	3
French Canadian..............	606	300	157	20	177	10	1,093
French, total all others	72	8	2	1	3	......	83
a) French, France............	31	2	......	......	......	......	33
b) Walloon...................	24	......	......	......	......	......	24
c) Alsatian...................	8	......	......	......	......	......	8
d) Swiss......................	......						......
e) French mixed..............	9	6	2	1	3	......	18
German.......................	6	4	4	2	6	......	16
Greek.........................	10	......	......	......	......	......	10
Irish..........................	62	75	84	30	114	......	251
Italian........................	182	3	......	......	......	......	185
Jewish........................	91	10	......	......	......	......	101
Portuguese (white)............	19	......	......	1	1	......	20
Roumanian....................	24	......	......	......	......	......	24
Scandinavian total............	21	7	1	......	1	......	29
a) Swedish...................	18	6	1	......	1	......	25
b) Norwegian.................	1	......	......	......	......	......	1
c) Danish....................	2	1	......	......	......	......	3
Slavic total...................	468	7	1	......	1	2	478
a) Polish.....................	269	5	1	......	1	1	276
b) Ukrainian.................	186	1	......	......	......	1	188
c) Russian....................	11	1	......	......	......	......	12
d) Lithuanian.................	2	......	......	......	......	......	2
e) (Galician).................	......	......	......	......	......	......	......
Spanish.......................	......						......
Syrian........................	25	......	......	......	......	......	25
Turkish.......................	......						......
TOTAL HOMOGENEOUS......	1,744	451	338	134	472	14	2,681
Partly unspecified.............	1	......	33	8	41	......	42
Unspecified (n.d.).............	......	......	11	34	45	1	46
Other unspecified.............	......	2	......	......	......	7	9
Mixed ancestry...............	13	14	47	24	71	......	98
GRAND TOTAL..........	1,758	467	429	200	629	22	2,876

ETHNIC DERIVATION	GENERATION						
	1ST GEN.	2D GEN.	3/2 AND 3D GEN.			REJECTS	TOTAL
			3/2 Gen.	3d Gen.	Total 3/2 and 3d		
	(a)	(b)	(c)	(d)	(e)	(f)	(g)
Albanian....................	100.0	....	....	....	....	....	100.0
Armenian...................	92.9	7.1	....	....	....	....	100.0
Austrian....................	....	....	....	....	....	....	....
Belgian (Flemish)............	100.0	....	....	....	....	....	100.0
British total................	36.9	11.1	27.4	24.0	51.4	.6	100.0
a) English.................	33.1	13.3	24.8	27.9	52.7	.9	100.0
b) Scotch.................	68.7	12.5	18.8	....	18.8	....	100.0
c) Scotch-Irish.............	....	50.0	50.0	....	50.0	....	100.0
d) Canadian English.........	72.7	9.1	18.2	....	18.2	....	100.0
e) Canadian Scotch..........	100.0	....	....	....	....	....	100.0
f) Canadian unspec..........	80.0	20.0	....	....	....	....	100.0
g) British mixed............	23.2	1.8	48.2	26.8	75.0	....	100.0
h) British, others...........	....	....	....	....	....	....	....
Chinese.....................	100.0	....	....	....	....	....	100.0
Colored....................	33.3	....	....	66.7	66.7	....	100.0
Czech......................	100.0	....	....	....	....	....	100.0
Dutch......................	....	....	....	....	....	....	....
Finnish.....................	100.0	....	....	....	....	....	100.0
French Canadian.............	55.5	27.4	14.4	1.8	16.2	.9	100.0
French, total all others.......	86.8	9.6	2.4	1.2	3.6	....	100.0
a) French, France...........	93.9	6.1	....	....	....	....	100.0
b) Walloon................	100.0	....	....	....	....	....	100.0
c) Alsatian.................	100.0	....	....	....	....	....	100.0
d) Swiss...................	....	....	....	....	....	....	....
e) French mixed............	50.0	33.3	11.1	5.6	16.7	....	100.0
German.....................	37.5	25.0	25.0	12.5	37.5	....	100.0
Greek......................	100.0	....	....	....	....	....	100.0
Irish.......................	24.7	29.9	33.4	12.0	45.4	....	100.0
Italian.....................	98.4	1.6	....	....	....	....	100.0
Jewish.....................	90.0	10.0	....	....	....	....	100.0
Portuguese (white)...........	95.0	....	....	5.0	5.0	....	100.0
Roumanian..................	100.0	....	....	....	....	....	100.0
Scandinavian total...........	72.4	24.1	3.5	....	3.5	....	100.0
a) Swedish................	72.0	24.0	4.0	....	4.0	....	100.0
b) Norwegian..............	100.0	....	....	....	....	....	100.0
c) Danish.................	66.7	33.3	....	....	....	....	100.0
Slavic total.................	97.9	1.5	.2	....	.2	.4	·100.0
a) Polish..................	97.4	1.8	.4	....	.4	.4	100.0
b) Ukrainian..............	98.9	.6	....	....	....	.5	100.0
c) Russian.................	91.7	8.3	....	....	....	....	100.0
d) Lithuanian..............	100.0	....	....	....	....	....	100.0
e) (Galician)...............	....	....	....	....	....	....	....
Spanish.....................	....	....	....	....	....	....	....
Syrian......................	100.0	....	....	....	....	....	100.0
Turkish.....................	....	....	....	....	....	....	....
TOTAL HOMOGENEOUS......	65.1	16.8	12.6	5.0	17.6	.5	100.0
Partly unspecified............	2.4	....	78.6	19.0	97.6	....	100.0
Unspecified (n.d.)............	....	....	23.9	73.9	97.8	2.2	100.0
Other unspecified............	....	22.2	....	....	....	77.8	100.0
Mixed ancestry..............	13.3	14.3	48.0	24.4	72.4	....	100.0
GRAND TOTAL..........	61.1	16.2	14.9	7.0	21.9	.8	100.0

2,876 MOTHERS: PER CENT DISTRIBUTION BY STOCK WITHIN EACH GENERATION

ETHNIC DERIVATION	1ST GEN. (a)	2D GEN. (b)	3/2 Gen. (c)	3d Gen. (d)	Total 3/2 and 3d (e)	REJECTS (f)	TOTAL (g)
Albanian...................	.1	......	....	....	....	....	*
Armenian..................	.7	.2	....	....	....	....	.5
Austrian...................	......	......	....	....	....	....	......
Belgian (Flemish)............	.9	......	....	....	....	....	.6
British total................	6.8	7.6	20.8	39.0	26.6	9.1	11.4
a) English.................	4.3	6.4	13.1	31.5	18.9	9.1	7.9
b) Scotch..................	.6	.4	.7	....	.5	....	.6
c) Scotch-Irish.............	......	.2	.2	....	.2	....	.1
d) Canadian English..........	.5	.2	.5	....	.3	....	.4
e) Canadian Scotch..........	.5	......	....	....	....	....	.3
f) Canadian unspec..........	.2	.2	....	....	....	....	.2
g) British mixed............	.7	.2	6.3	7.5	6.7	....	1.9
h) British, others...........	......	......	....	....	....	....	......
Chinese...................	.2	......	....	....	....	....	.1
Colored...................	.1	......	....	1.0	.3	....	.1
Czech....................	.1	......	....	....	....	....	*
Dutch....................	......	......	....	....	....	....	......
Finnish...................	.2	......	....	....	....	....	.1
French Canadian............	34.4	64.3	36.6	10.0	28.0	45.5	38.0
French, total all others	4.2	1.7	.5	.5	.5	....	2.8
a) French, France...........	1.8	.4	....	....	....	....	1.1
b) Walloon................	1.4	......	....	....	....	....	.8
c) Alsatian................	.5	......	....	....	....	....	.3
d) Swiss..................	......	......	....	....	....	....	......
e) French mixed............	.5	1.3	.5	.5	.5	....	.6
German...................	.3	.9	.9	1.0	1.0	....	.6
Greek....................	.6	......	....	....	....	....	.3
Irish.....................	3.5	16.1	19.6	15.0	18.1	....	8.7
Italian...................	10.2	.6	....	....	....	....	6.4
Jewish...................	5.2	2.2	....	....	....	....	3.5
Portuguese (white)............	1.1	......	....	.5	.2	....	.7
Roumanian................	1.4	......	....	....	....	....	.8
Scandinavian total...........	1.2	1.5	.2	....	.2	....	1.0
a) Swedish................	1.0	1.3	.2	....	.2	....	.9
b) Norwegian..............	.1	......	....	....	....	....	*
c) Danish.................	.1	.2	....	....	....	....	.1
Slavic total................	26.6	1.5	.2	....	.2	9.0	16.7
a) Polish..................	15.3	1.1	.2	....	.2	4.5	9.7
b) Ukrainian...............	10.6	.2	....	....	....	4.5	6.5
c) Russian................	.6	.2	....	....	....	....	.4
d) Lithuanian..............	.1	......	....	....	....	....	.1
e) (Galician)..............	......	......	....	....	....	....	......
Spanish...................	......	......	....	....	....	....	......
Syrian....................	1.4	......	....	....	....	....	.9
Turkish...................	......	......	....	....	....	....	......
TOTAL HOMOGENEOUS......	99.2	96.6	78.8	67.0	75.1	63.6	93.2
Partly unspecified............	.1	......	7.7	4.0	6.5	....	1.5
Unspecified (n.d.)............	......	......	2.6	17.0	7.1	4.6	1.6
Other unspecified............	......	.4	....	....	....	31.8	.3
Mixed ancestry..............	.7	3.0	10.9	12.0	11.3	....	3.4
GRAND TOTAL..........	100.0	100.0	100.0	100.0	100.0	100.0	100.0

* Less than .1 per cent.

CHAPTER VI

THE DERIVATION OF FAMILIES: ETHNIC MILIEU
OF THE HOME AS DETERMINED
BY PARENTAL UNION

The ethnic milieu in a family is determined by the descent and cultural equipment of two parents. As a result of the ethnic choice they made in marriage parents have established in general two racial types of family. By far the largest number have taken mates from their own ethnic group. These parents have established families of homogeneous descent. On the other hand, we learn[1] that 17.8 per cent have chosen mates from some ethnic group other than their own. These have by contrast established families of mixed descent.

This cross-marriage brings about two vital changes in composition: (1) A new class arises, a group of mixed descent. This new group, comprising 513 families, is second in size only to the French Canadians who claim 970 families of homogeneous descent. (2) Since the mixed group is drawn from several other stocks, we find a change in the distribution of stocks as they exist in the parental population. The parental population gave life to these families, but in doing so brought about a realignment of ethnic elements. Only 79.1 per cent of the families claim to be of pure descent. In 3.1 per cent of the families homogeneity was not absolutely established (Table 16b).

ETHNIC DESCENT OF SIBS

(Tables 16 and 16b)

The French Canadians rank first in their contribution to homogeneous stock—970, or 33.7 per cent of all sibs in the population, are homogeneous and French Canadian by descent. The mixed group, as we have seen, intervenes for second place with 513, or 17.8 per cent of the sibs. The Slavic groups combined, with 441 sibs, are a close third, constituting 15.3 per cent of all sibs.[2] The British groups combined now claim only 222, or 7.7 per cent of all sibs, as all British.[3] The Italians are represented by 183, or 6.4 per cent of the homes, while the Irish with 144 claim only 5.0

[1] Chaps. viii and ix.

[2] The Poles alone claim 8.8 per cent of the total number of sibs.

[3] The English here are the largest constituent element, representing 4.9 per cent of all sibs.

71

TABLE 16

2,876 Sibs by Ethnic Derivation and Generation of Parents in America

Ethnic Derivation	1–1	Fa. Mo. 1 – 2x				Fa. Mo. 2x – 1				2–2	3/2 and 3*			Rejects	Total
		1–2	1–3	1–(3/2)	Total Cols. b, c, d	2–1	3–1	(3/2)–1	Total Cols. f, g, h		3/2	3–3	Total Cols. k, l		
	(a)	(b)	(c)	(d)	(e)	(f)	(g)	(h)	(i)	(j)	(k)	(l)	(m)	(n)	(o)
Albanian.............	1	....	....	....	....	....	....	....	....	....	....	....	....	....	1
Armenian............	13	1	....	....	1	....	....	....	....	....	....	....	....	....	14
Austrian.............	....	....	....	....	....	....	....	....	....	....	....	....	....	....	....
Belgian (Flemish)....	8	....	....	....	....	....	....	....	....	....	....	....	....	....	8
British total.........	69	8	8	2	18	7	12	1	20	13	46	55	101	1	222
a) English...........	40	7	3	....	10	3	6	1	10	9	27	44	71	1	141
b) Scotch...........	6	....	....	....	....	....	....	....	....	....	....	....	....	....	6
c) Scotch-Irish......	....	....	....	....	....	....	....	....	....	....	....	....	....	....	....
d) Canadian English..	4	....	....	....	....	....	....	....	....	....	....	....	....	....	4
e) Canadian Scotch...	....	....	....	....	....	....	....	....	....	....	....	....	....	....	....
f) Canadian unspec...	3	....	....	....	....	....	....	....	....	....	....	....	....	....	3
g) British mixed......	16	1	5	2	8	4	6	....	10	4	19	11	30	....	68
h) British, others....	....	....	....	....	....	....	....	....	....	....	....	....	....	....	....
Chinese.............	2	....	....	....	....	1	....	....	1	....	....	....	....	....	3
Colored.............	1	....	....	....	....	....	....	....	....	....	....	2	2	....	3
Czech..............	1	....	....	....	....	....	....	....	....	....	....	....	....	....	1
Dutch..............	....	....	....	....	....	....	....	....	....	....	....	....	....	....	....
Finnish.............	2	....	....	....	....	....	....	....	....	....	....	....	....	....	2
French Canadian.....	424	146	15	30	191	105	10	22	137	121	87	....	87	10	970
French, total all others	60	7	....	1	8	5	....	1	6	6	....	....	....	....	80
a) French, France....	19	....	....	....	....	....	....	....	....	....	....	....	....	....	19
b) Walloon..........	16	....	....	....	....	....	....	....	....	....	....	....	....	....	16
c) Alsatian..........	5	....	....	....	....	....	....	....	....	....	....	....	....	....	5
d) Swiss............	....	....	....	....	....	....	....	....	....	....	....	....	....	....	....
e) French mixed......	20	7	....	1	8	5	....	1	6	6	....	....	....	....	40
German.............	2	....	....	....	....	....	....	....	....	1	1	1	2	....	5
Greek..............	10	....	....	....	....	....	....	....	....	....	....	....	....	....	10
Irish...............	28	8	1	2	11	13	5	1	19	31	42	13	55	....	144
Italian.............	181	1	....	....	1	....	....	....	....	1	....	....	....	....	183
Jewish.............	87	8	....	....	8	1	1	....	2	2	....	....	....	....	99
Portuguese (white)....	18	....	1	....	1	....	....	....	....	....	....	....	....	....	19
Roumanian..........	23	....	....	....	....	....	....	....	....	....	....	....	....	....	23
Scandinavian total....	16	4	....	....	4	1	....	....	1	....	....	....	....	....	21
a) Swedish..........	15	4	....	....	4	1	....	....	1	....	....	....	....	....	20
b) Norwegian........	....	....	....	....	....	....	....	....	....	....	....	....	....	....	....
c) Danish...........	1	....	....	....	....	....	....	....	....	....	....	....	....	....	1
Slavic total.........	432	5	....	....	5	1	....	....	1	2	....	....	....	1	441
a) Polish...........	247	4	....	....	4	1	....	....	1	1	....	....	....	1	254
b) Ukrainian........	174	1	....	....	1	....	....	....	....	....	....	....	....	....	175
c) Russian..........	10	....	....	....	....	....	....	....	....	1	....	....	....	....	11
d) Lithuanian.......	1	....	....	....	....	....	....	....	....	....	....	....	....	....	1
e) (Galician)........	....	....	....	....	....	....	....	....	....	....	....	....	....	....	....
Spanish.............	....	....	....	....	....	....	....	....	....	....	....	....	....	....	....
Syrian..............	25	....	....	....	....	....	....	....	....	....	....	....	....	....	25
Turkish.............	....	....	....	....	....	....	....	....	....	....	....	....	....	....	....
Total Homogeneous...........	1,403	188	25	35	248	134	28	25	187	177	176	71	247	12	2,274
Partly unspecified (n.)†	....	....	8	....	8	....	9	....	9	....	30	4	34	1	52
Unspecified (n.).......	....	....	....	....	....	....	....	....	....	4	....	24	24	9	37
Total Unspecified...........	....	....	8	....	8	....	9	....	9	4	30	28	58	10	89
Mixed ancestry.......	95	42	22	26	90	27	17	20	64	56	162	46	208	....	513
Grand Total.....	1,498	230	55	61	346	161	54	45	260	237	368	145	513	22	2,876

*In cols. *a, j, k, l, m*, it is not necessary to specify which is father and which is mother as both are of the same generation.

† Except in col. *n* it is the native element in each mating that is unspecified.

TABLE 16a

2,876 SIBS: PER CENT DISTRIBUTION OF EACH STOCK BY GENERATION OF PARENTS

ETHNIC DERIVATION	1–1 (a)	FA. MO. 1–2x — 1–2 (b)	1–3 (c)	1–(3/2) (d)	Total Cols. b,c,d (e)	FA. MO. 2x–1 — 2–1 (f)	3–1 (g)	(3/2)–1 (h)	Total Cols. f,g,h (i)	2–2 (j)	3/2 AND 3* — 3/2 (k)	3–3 (l)	Total Cols. k,l (m)	RE-JECTS (n)	TO-TAL (o)
Albanian	100.0														100.0
Armenian	92.9	7.1			7.1										100.0
Austrian															
Belgian (Flemish)	100.0														100.0
British total	31.1	3.6	3.6	.9	8.1	3.2	5.4	.4	9.0	5.9	20.7	24.8	45.5	.4	100.0
a) English	28.4	5.0	2.1		7.1	2.1	4.3	.7	7.1	6.4	19.1	31.2	50.3	.7	100.0
b) Scotch	100.0														100.0
c) Scotch-Irish															
d) Canadian English	100.0														100.0
e) Canadian Scotch															
f) Canadian unspec	100.0														100.0
g) British mixed	23.5	1.5	7.4	2.9	11.8	5.9	8.8		14.7	5.9	27.9	16.2	44.1		100.0
h) British, others															
Chinese	66.7					33.3			33.3						100.0
Colored	33.3										66.7		66.7		100.0
Czech	100.0														100.0
Dutch															
Finnish	100.0														100.0
French Canadian	43.7	15.1	1.5	3.1	19.7	10.8	1.0	2.3	14.1	12.5	9.0		9.0	1.0	100.0
French, total all others	75.0	8.8		1.2	10.0	6.3		1.2	7.5	7.5					100.0
a) French, France	100.0														100.0
b) Walloon	100.0														100.0
c) Alsatian	100.0														100.0
d) Swiss															
e) French mixed	50.0	17.5		2.5	20.0	12.5		2.5	15.0	15.0					100.0
German	40.0									20.0	20.0	20.0	40.0		100.0
Greek	100.0														100.0
Irish	19.4	5.6	.7	1.4	7.7	9.0	3.5	.7	13.2	21.5	29.2	9.0	38.2		100.0
Italian	98.8	.5			.5					.5	.5				100.0
Jewish	87.9	8.1			8.1	1.0	1.0		2.0	2.0					100.0
Portuguese (white)	94.7		5.3		5.3										100.0
Roumanian	100.0														100.0
Scandinavian total	76.2	19.0			19.0	4.8			4.8						100.0
a) Swedish	75.0	20.0			20.0	5.0			5.0						100.0
b) Norwegian															
c) Danish	100.0														100.0
Slavic total	98.0	1.1			1.1	.2			.2	.5				.2	100.0
a) Polish	97.2	1.6			1.6	.4			.4	.4				.4	100.0
b) Ukrainian	99.4	.6			.6										100.0
c) Russian	90.9									9.1					100.0
d) Lithuanian	100.0														100.0
e) (Galician)															
Spanish															
Syrian	100.0														100.0
Turkish															
TOTAL HOMOGENEOUS	61.7	8.3	1.1	1.5	10.9	5.9	1.2	1.1	8.2	7.8	7.8	3.1	10.9	.5	100.0
Partly unspecified (n.)†		15.4			15.4	17.3			17.3		57.7	7.7	65.4	1.9	100.0
Unspecified (n.)†										10.8		64.9	64.9	24.3	100.0
TOTAL UNSPECIFIED		9.0			9.0	10.1			10.1	4.5	33.7	31.5	65.2	11.2	100.0
Mixed ancestry	18.5	8.2	4.3	5.0	17.5	5.3	3.3	3.9	12.5	10.9	31.6	9.0	40.6		100.0
GRAND TOTAL	52.1	8.0	1.9	2.1	12.0	5.6	1.9	1.6	9.1	8.2	12.8	5.0	17.8	.8	100.0

* In cols. a, j, k, l, m, it is not necessary to specify which is father and which is mother as both are of the same generation.

† Except in col. n it is the native element in each mating that is unspecified.

per cent, and the Jews with 99 claim 3.4 per cent. All others constitute 10.7 per cent of the total population (Tables 16 and 16b).

It will be noticed that the British and Irish weights have been appreciably lowered from those which these groups attained in the analyses dealing with ethnic elements or "numerical equivalents" in chapter iii, and from those obtained in an analysis of parental stock in chapter v. This has come about because they have contributed so largely to the mixed group —a fact which may have been anticipated from the high "rates" of diffusion which was indicated for these groups in the primary analysis of the melting pot (chap. iii). In other words, the British and the Irish groups contribute heavily to ethnic composition, but because of their high rates of diffusion rank relatively low in the ratio of families of pure British and pure Irish descent to the total number in the families in the population.

GENERATION IN AMERICA OF ALL SIBS
(Tables 16 and 16a)

In view of the large proportion of immigrants among parents, it is inevitable that the majority of homes should be represented by families in which both parents are immigrants (1–1). Fourteen hundred and ninety-eight, or 52.1 per cent of the total number of sibs, have two foreign-born parents. By contrast, only 145, or 5.0 per cent of the sibs, are definitely known to be Old American, i.e., families in which all four grandparents are native born (3–3). The remainder fall into intermediate classes in which one or more of the ancestors are native born.

The 1–1 sibs are derived largely from French Canadian, Slavic, Italian, and Jewish groups. The British, Irish, and French Canadians are represented in all generations. The 3–2s and 3–3 sibs are largely of mixed ancestry, or homogeneous and of British, French-Canadian, or Irish descent, in the numerical order stated (Table 16b, col. m).

DESCENT OF OLD AMERICANS
(Tables 16, 16a, 16b, and 18)

A certain amount of interest is always attached to the group designated as Old American (3–3). Who are the Old Americans? From what stocks are they derived? Can we arrive at heavier weights for "Americans" if the definition of this class were less restricted? These are pertinent questions and lie at the very heart of any study of Americanization. The definition which limits the category "American" so that it includes only sibs all four of whose grandparents are native born restricts that group to a small proportion of the homes in Woonsocket.

TABLE 17

Ethnic Descent of Both Father and Mother

(... or Sibs of Homogeneous Descent and for Sibs of Mixed Ancestry)*

French, total all others†	a) French, France	b) Walloon	c) Alsatian	d) Swiss	e) French mixed	German	Greek	Irish	Italian	Jewish	Portuguese (white)	Roumanian	Scandinavian total	a) Swedish	b) Norwegian	c) Danish	Slavic total	a) Polish	b) Ukrainian	c) Russian	d) Lithuanian	e) (Galician)	Spanish	Syrian	Turkish	Mixed ancestry	Unspecified (n.d.)‡ Group a	Unspecified (n.d.)‡ Group b	Unspecified	TOTAL UNSPECIFIED	TOTAL HOMOGENEOUS	TOTAL MIXED ANCESTRY	GRAND TOTAL
																															1	1	2
																															14		14
	3				1																					2					8	9	17
																													(8)		(222)	(87)	(317)
						2		15						2		1										30		4	1	5	156	63	224
						1		5						1		1										2		1	1		16	11	28
																															1		1
								2																		2			2		9	4	15
																															2		2
																															4	2	6
								3																		2					34	7	41
								2																							3		3
																															3	2	5
																															1		1
																																2	2
																															2		2
	4	1	1		3	1		43	1	1	1						2									30		9	2	11	979	106	1,096
(80)																															(71)	(24)	(95)
		19	1	2	1			4																		6					30	14	44
		3	16		1			1																		1					22	5	27
			2	5				1																							8	1	9
																																2	2
					8			1																		1					11	2	13
	1				1	5		2	1								1									3					5	14	19
							10																								10	1	11
						2	1	144		1							1									24		2	2		144	75	221
	2	1			1			3	183								2														183	15	198
										99																					99		99
											19																				19	4	23
												23								1											23	1	24
								3						20																	20	6	26
														1																		1	1
																1	(472)														(441)	(31)	(472)
																		254	8	1											254	9	263
																		12	175												175	12	187
																		3	4	11	1										11	8	19
																		2			1										1	2	3
																							25								25		25
	1	3			1	4		19																		24	3					119	119
																										14						14	14
						1		3																				24		57		57	57
												1								1								1	6	11		11	11
						1		3				1											(1)		1		43	9	89				
(66)	26	20	8		12	5	10	144	183	99	19	23		20		1	(441)	254	175	11	1			25							2,274		
(17)	7	4			6	10		104	2	2	1	1		4	1	2	(36)	22	12	1	1					140	3					513	
(83)	33	24	8		18	16	10	251	185	101	20	24		25	1	3	(478)	276	188	12	2			25		140	3	43	9				2,876

(... C)anadian.

(...) to the class of intermarriage. The individuals in Group b, immediately following, are likewise unspecified but they marry persons also of unspecified descent, or of homogeneous and mating remains partly unspecified.

(...) and to the major group indicated—the British, French, or Slavic total as the case may be. They should not be used in computing the individual row or

Ethnic Derivation of Father	Ethnic Derivation of Mother	Albanian	Armenian	Austrian	Belgian (Flemish)	British total	a) English	b) Scotch	c) Scotch-Irish	d) Canadian English	e) Canadian Scotch	f) Canadian unspec.	g) British mixed	h) British, others	Chinese	Colored	Czech	Dutch	Finnish	French Canadian
Albanian		**1**																		
Armenian			**14**																	
Austrian																				
Belgian ((Flemish))					**8**															
British total						(222)														
a) English							**141**	**5**	**1**	**4**	**4**	**1**								
b) Scotch							**10**	**6**												
c) Scotch-Irish							**1**													
d) Canadian English							**4**			**4**	**1**									
e) Canadian Scotch							**2**													
f) Canadian unspec.							**1**					**3**								
g) British mixed													**34**							
h) British, others																				
Chinese															**3**					
Colored																**3**				
Czech																	**1**			
Dutch							1						1							
Finnish																			**2**	
French Canadian					1		18	2			1		5							**97**
French, total all others†																				
a) French, France					3		1													
b) Walloon					4															
c) Alsatian																				
d) Swiss							1													
e) French mixed							1													
German							1						1							
Greek																				
Irish							13		1				6							
Italian									1											
Jewish																				
Portuguese (white)																				
Roumanian																				
Scandinavian total																				
a) Swedish							1						1						1	
b) Norwegian																				
c) Danish																				
Slavic total																				
a) Polish																				
b) Ukrainian																				
c) Russian																				
d) Lithuanian																				
e) (Galician)																				
Spanish																				
Syrian																				
Turkish																				
Mixed ancestry							19	1	1	1	2		6							3
Unspecified (n.d.)‡ Group a																				
Unspecified (n.d.)‡ Group b							10	1			1		3							1
Unspecified							2													
TOTAL UNSPECIFIED						(17)	12	1			1		3							1
TOTAL HOMOGENEOUS		1	14		8	(222)	159	11	1	8	5	4	34		3	3	1		2	98
TOTAL MIXED ANCESTRY					8	(86)	55	4	1	3	3	1	19						1	9
GRAND TOTAL		1	14		16	(325)	226	16	2	11	9	5	56		3	3	1		3	109

* Sibs of homogeneous descent are indicated in boldface and fall in the diagonal; sibs of mixed descent appear in the scatter.

† The figure within the bloc is overlapping; since it includes French-Canadian x European French, i.e., all who are not entirely French-⸱

‡ The unspecified now fall into two groups—those in Group a marry persons who are of mixed and known descent. They therefore fall ⸱ specified descent. We do not know whether this descent is the same or different from that of the individual whom they marry and the entir⸱

Note.—Throughout this table the figures in parentheses have reference only to the immediate situation specified⸱ column totals.

tion of each parent. Sibs with both parents of the same descent fall in the diagonal and are printed in boldface. Sibs with parents not of the same descent fall in the scatter; they make up the melting pot. This table, describing each family by its homogeneity or admixture as the case may be, describes at the same time intermarriage between parents, indicating the preference and the number of matings between members from specific groups.

Further discussion relating to the facts of intermarriage, groups intermarrying, relative frequency of intermarriage, ethnic choice, and ethnic changes effected by intermarriage is reserved for later chapters.[1] Only those data are given here which locate the families and describe the ethnic milieu from which children come.

It will be seen that the melting pot has not only increased in scope, but that numerous new stocks are making their first contribution to it. On the whole, however, the trends initiated by the grandparents are further established. The largest number of families who are of mixed descent draw their stock from the British, Irish, and French-Canadian elements.

The sibs in the melting pot are derived in the following manner (cf. Table 17):

Irish × French Canadian	70
Irish × British	46
British × French Canadian	44
Mixed Slavic	31
All other admixture	87
Repeated admixture (mixed × mixed)	235
Total	513

In addition, 34 sibs are of mixed British descent and 32 are of mixed French descent.

The most significant new feature of the picture is the increasing importance of the rôle which admixture plays in succeeding generations (Tables 16 and 16b). Thus only 6.3 per cent of the sibs in the 1–1 class are of mixed descent, while the percentage rises to 23.6 per cent for sibs from 2–2 homes, and to 44.0 per cent for sibs who are in part Old American. The percentage of admixture is also high in the generation classes where one parent is native born and another foreign born, 25.4 per cent.[2] The decrease in the 3–3 generation (col. l) is undoubtedly due to the small number of cases and is not significant.

[1] Chaps. viii and ix. [2] This figure is for $2x$–1 and 1–$2x$ combined.

REPEATED ADMIXTURE OR MULTIPLE FUSION

Within the group representing admixture the majority of the parents are themselves of pure descent and are initiating the fusion process in their respective family lines.

On the other hand, 235 sibs are listed in the class representing repeated admixture. These represent families in which either the father or the mother or both are of mixed descent, owing to intermarriage among grandparents. These families are for the most part French-Canadian, British, and Irish.[1]

Ordinarily marriages of this kind are not designated as intermarriages. In some cases no new element is added, as when two persons each of the same mixed descent unite in marriage; for example, both the man and the woman may be of French-Canadian–Irish descent. In other cases the union involves three or four racial strains. The investigator believes that this type of intermarriage has less significance culturally than it has racially. Undoubtedly any cultural differences which existed originally have long since been wiped out; but any effort to disentangle the racial facts in the situation requires record of this multiple fusion.

When only the father or mother are of mixed descent we have a second step in the fusion process. When both are of mixed descent (24 cases) we have triple fusion within the span of time covered by the study.[2]

IMPLICATIONS

The leading rank for ethnic dominance which French Canadians maintain throughout the study is challenged by the increasing percentage of admixture which characterizes the older generations. The rapidly changing and increasing proportion of admixture in the population promises to result in a class whose influence as a rival to French Canadians in Woonsocket is more significant than that from any other source. Even now the sibs of mixed descent constitute, next to the French Canadians, the largest constituent element in the entire population. In the combined 3–3 and

---

[1] See Table 7.

[2] Table 17 accounts for 259 parents—140 women and 119 men. The figure for parents of mixed descent given in the previous tables was 181, but 78 additional parents were in part unspecified. A hand count of cards indicated that in practically all cases these individuals married persons of mixed descent different from their own in so far as it was specified. For example, a person of British×American (unspecified) descent married one who was Irish×French. There is no longer any doubt but that this mating falls in the group of mixed descent. Since at least 3 ethnic strains are now represented in each case it must fall into the class of multiple fusion, and the families represented by these 78 parents "partly unspecified" are now transferred to this group. See chap. iv, p. 46, n. 2.

3–2 class they constitute the largest single element; with 40.5 per cent they outrank both French Canadians and British in numerical importance.

An analysis based on sibs constitutes at best only an intermediate step in describing the process which produces the melting pot. In so far as differentials exist in the size of families among different nationalities, a description based upon sibs as the unit of enumeration does not truly indicate the nature of the present population. The admixture which had its origin among grandparents was most emphatically accelerated in the generation of parents. This is obvious from our study of sibs, but the actual results accruing to the population can be indicated more truly by describing all children in accordance with the pattern laid down here for describing the sibs.

SUMMARY

The ethnic milieu of the home is determined by the descent of parents and by the ethnic preference exerted in marriage. The marriage of 5,752 parents resulted in 2,876 matings. In the large majority of families both parents are of the same ethnic descent, and the sibs are of homogeneous descent. In 17.8 per cent of the cases the parents married out of their specific groups. An equal number of sibs are consequently of mixed ancestry.

The realignment of stocks as a result of marriage and cross-marriage changes the distribution of stocks and their respective ranks. The French Canadians of homogeneous descent still hold first rank with 33.7 per cent of the total number of sibs. There has emerged a group of mixed descent which, with 17.8 per cent of the sibs, is now the second largest group in the community. The Slavic groups of homogeneous descent follow in third place with 15.3 per cent; the British, with 7.7 per cent; the Italians, with 6.4 per cent, the Irish, with 5.0 per cent; and the Jews, with 3.4 per cent. These figures refer only to families of homogeneous descent as specified.

The fusion process initiated by grandparents has been greatly accelerated in the generation of parents, but the same trends there established have been corroborated. The melting pot is derived largely from British, Irish, and French-Canadian elements, but with an increasing number of other and new racial elements.

Within the group of mixed descent there are 235 sibs, 8.2 per cent of the total (2,876), who are the product of multiple fusion, i.e., grandparents intermarried first, and parents continued the diffusion of strains.

There is a rapid and steady increase in the ratio of mixed stock to total

population with increasing generation in America. Only 6.3 per cent of
1–1 sibs are of mixed descent, while among those in the third and 3–2
generations combined 40.5 per cent are of mixed descent (Table 16*b*,
col. *m*).

Sibs in the third and 3–2 generations are mostly of mixed descent, those
of British descent rank next, French Canadians third. The Irish are the
next most important constituent element, but their contribution is considerably less than that of the others.

CHAPTER VII

THE DERIVATION OF CHILDREN

We have now arrived at a consideration of the ethnic derivation of the children themselves, the group which compels our main interest in this investigation. The symbols used here are made consistent with those used in the previous chapters to describe grandparents, parents, parental unions, and sibs; but they may be used independently of this chapter. The presentation made here, therefore, is complete, so that it may stand alone. It does not necessarily depend upon the previous analyses, although the previous analyses describe the antecedent conditions from which this group of children has emerged.

Once again we are concerned primarily with the following problems: (1) the regional derivation of children; (2) the ethnic derivation of each child in terms of both ancestral lines; (3) the generation in America, whatever the ethnic derivation of each child, also the ethnic derivation of Old American children; (4) the degree of homogeneity and the degree of admixture in the population at large; (5) the types of admixture.

It may seem at first that these factors have already been analyzed in the previous sections. This would be so if we could assume that children and parents constitute a like group. But the population of children now in Woonsocket is the product of intermarriage between men and women of different stocks, of differential birth-rates and death-rates, of internal migration, and of numerous other social processes. In the case of the children we are dealing with a population which has emanated from the racial stocks hitherto described and from the ancestors previously enumerated, but the children constitute a population unit unique in itself.

REGIONAL DERIVATION OF ALL CHILDREN

(Tables 19 and 20)

The 4,978 children in the public schools were for the most part native born, only 366, or 7.3 per cent, having been born in foreign countries—the only large contingent in this group having come from French Canada, namely, 205, or 4.1 per cent. The others represent some 26 or more birthplaces. A more significant approach to the problem of regional derivation might be that which indicates the regional origin of parents, since it more truly describes the milieu from which the families were recently derived.

81

TABLE 19

4,978 CHILDREN: DERIVATION BY BIRTHPLACE AND ETHNIC DESCENT

DERIVATION	BIRTHPLACE Number (a)	BIRTHPLACE Per Cent (b)	ETHNIC DESCENT* Number (c)	ETHNIC DESCENT* Per Cent (d)
Albanian	11	.2	1	†
Armenian	1	†	33	.7
Austrian	2	†	....	....
Belgian (Flemish)	4	.1	9	.2
British total	31	.7	385	7.7
a) English	4	.1	251	5.0
b) Scotch	1	†	12	.2
c) Scotch-Irish	....	....	....	....
d) Canadian English	4	.1	4	.1
e) Canadian Scotch	....	....	....	....
f) Canadian non-British	22‡	.5	5	.1
g) British mixed	....	....	113	2.3
h) British, others	....	....	....	....
Chinese	3	.1	3	.1
Colored	....	....	9	.2
Czech	....	....	2	†
Dutch	....	....	....	....
Finnish	....	....	2	†
French Canadian	205	4.1	1,516	30.5
French, total all others	25	.5	112	2.3
a) French, France	18	.4	21	.4
b) Walloon	7	.1	24	.5
c) Alsatian	....	....	9	.2
d) Swiss	....	....	....	....
e) French mixed	....	....	58	1.2
German	2	†	7	.2
Greek	3	.1	21	.4
Irish	1	†	272	5.5
Italian	26	.5	414	8.3
Jewish	1	....	191	3.8
Portuguese (white)§	10	.2	27	.5
Roumanian	....	....	40	.8
Scandinavian total	....	....	35	.7
a) Swedish	....	....	34	.7
b) Norwegian	....	....	....	....
c) Danish	....	....	1	†
Slavic total	21	.4	838	16.8
a) Polish	6	.1	493	9.9
b) Ukrainian	1	†	325	6.5
c) Russian	8	.2	18	.4
d) Lithuanian	....	....	2	†
e) (Galician)	6	.1	....	....
Spanish	....	....	....	....
Syrian	7	.1	71	1.4
Others‖	13	.3	....	....
TOTAL HOMOGENEOUS	....	....	3,988	80.1
Partly unspecified (n.d.)	....	....	99	2.0
Unspecified (n.d.)	....	....	37	.8
Other unspecified	....	....	6	.1
TOTAL UNSPECIFIED	....	....	142	2.9
American (U.S.)	4,612¶	92.7¶	....	....
Mixed ancestry	....	....	848	17.0
GRAND TOTAL	4,978	100.0	4,978	100.0

* The derivation of each child is determined by the stock of 4 grandparents (see Table 21, col. *o*).

† Less than .1 per cent.

‡ These 22 are derived as follows: 19, Canadian unspecified; 3, Irish Canadian.

§ Portuguese includes: 1, Cape de Verde.

‖ "Others" includes: Serbian, 5; South American, 4; West Indian, 3; and unspecified, 2.

¶ The foreign-born total is 366 and constitutes 7.3 per cent of the whole.

TABLE 20

4,978 Children by Regional Derivation of Each Parent: Number and Per Cent Distribution

a) Fathers, b) Mothers, c) Both

REGIONAL DERIVATION	NUMBER			PER CENT		
	Fathers (a)	Mothers (b)	Total Parents* (c)	Fathers (a')	Mothers (b')	Total Parents† (c')
Albanian................	30	25	55	.6	.5	.5
Armenian................	24	24	48	.5	.5	.5
Austrian................	8	17	25	.2	.4	.3
Belgian (Flemish).........	18	17	35	.4	.4	.4
British total.............	250	234	484	5.0	4.7	4.9
a) English..............	*160*	*150*	*310*	*3.2*	*3.0*	*3.1*
b) Scotch..............	*34*	*29*	*63*	*.7*	*.6*	*.6*
c) Scotch-Irish.........						
d) Canadian English......	*16*	*13*	*29*	*.3*	*.3*	*.3*
e) Canadian Scotch.......	*3*	*14*	*17*	*.1*	*.3*	*.2*
f) Canadian others.......	*37*	*28*	*65*	*.7*	*.5*	*.7*
g) British mixed..........						
h) British, others........						
Chinese................	2	3	5	†	*	.1
Colored................						
Czech................	2	4	6	‡	.1	.1
Dutch................	4		4	.1		†
Finnish................	27	27	54	.5	.5	.5
French Canadian.........	1,034	928	1,962	20.8	18.6	19.7
French, European total....	122	99	221	2.5	2.0	2.2
a) French, France........	*71*	*53*	*124*	*1.4*	*1.1*	*1.2*
b) Walloon..............	*32*	*33*	*65*	*.7*	*.6*	*.7*
c) Alsatian..............	*17*	*13*	*30*	*.4*	*.3*	*.3*
d) Swiss................	*2*		*2*	†		†
e) French mixed..........						
German	6	6	12	.1	.1	.1
Greek..................	22	24	46	.4	.5	.4
Irish..................	83	105	188	1.7	2.1	1.9
Italian................	435	412	847	8.7	8.3	8.5
Jewish................						
Portuguese (white)§.......	41	25	66	.9	.5	.7
Roumanian.............	9	9	18	.2	.2	.2
Scandinavian total........	15	13	28	.2	.3	.2
a) Swedish..............	*12*	*10*	*22*	*.2*	*.2*	*.2*
b) Norwegian...........	*1*	*1*	*2*	†	†	†
c) Danish..............	*2*	*2*	*4*	†	†	†
Slavic total.............	1,071	1,067	2,138	21.6	21.4	21.5
a) Polish...............	*421*	*448*	*869*	*8.5*	*9.0*	*8.7*
b) Ukrainian............	*59*	*46*	*105*	*1.2*	*.9*	*1.1*
c) Russian.............	*203*	*159*	*362*	*4.1*	*3.2*	*3.6*
d) Lithuanian...........	*11*	*7*	*18*	*.2*	*.1*	*.2*
e) (Galician)............	*377*	*407*	*784*	*7.6*	*8.2*	*7.9*
Spanish................						
Syrian................	71	71	142	1.4	1.4	1.4
Turkish................	15	13	28	.3	.3	.3
Others‖................	5	5	10	.1	.1	.1
Unspecified.............	16	12	28	.3	.2	.3
American (U.S.).........	1,668	1,838	3,506	33.5	36.9	35.2
GRAND TOTAL........	4,978	4,978	9,956	100.0	100.0	.100.0

* Throughout this table the parents are weighted by the number of children. This column gives the regional derivation of 9,956 theoretical parents (4978 ✕ 2). For regional derivation of actual parents see chap. v, Table 12.

† See end of this chapter for similar table (No. 27) on ethnic derivation of parents, weighted as to children.

‡ Less than .1 per cent.

§ Portuguese includes: Azores and Madeira Islands, 5; Cape de Verde Islands, 33.

‖ "Others" includes the following regional derivations too small to be listed separately: Latvian, 4; Serbian, 2; and South American, 4.

Table 20 classifies children by the birthplace of parents. Though some rearrangement takes place in the various distributions, owing to differential fecundity, in general the distributions are those which might be expected from the distributions of parents (chap. v, Table 12). Only 35.2 per cent of the parentage is native born, while French Canada with 19.7 per cent outranks all other single groups unless it is the combined Slavic group which together outranks all others with 21.5 per cent. Italy is the third most important region of origin with 8.5 per cent of the parentage coming from that country. Only 4.9 per cent of the parentage has its geographic origin in British regions, and not more than 1.9 per cent are claimed by the Irish. The children claim 30 or more regions of the world as birthplaces for parents. But we have come to see that regional derivation is merely indicative of recent derivation, and is only in part indicative of ethnic origin.[1] What are really the ethnic origins of the public-school children in Woonsocket?

ETHNIC DERIVATION OF ALL CHILDREN

(Table 19, cols. c and d)

Of the 4,978 children enumerated in the public schools, 3,988, or 80.1 per cent, report four grandparents of the same ethnic stock, and are, by our definition, of homogeneous descent; 848, or 17.0 per cent, are of mixed descent, i.e., all four grandparents are not of the same stock. The distribution of children on this basis is given in Table 19, columns c and d. Here we have all the children as they themselves are by racial descent. (Two and nine-tenths per cent returned histories partially incomplete, so that homogeneity was not absolutely established. These are for the most part the Old American children whose ancestry is in part unspecified.)

As might be expected from our previous knowledge of the community, the French Canadians contribute the heaviest strain. Fifteen hundred and sixteen, or 30.5 per cent of the total number of children, are of pure French-Canadian descent. Children of mixed ancestry, representing 848, or 17.0 per cent of the total, are next to the French Canadians, the most important group numerically.

If the Slavic groups are combined (these groups really represent cultural entities and are combined merely as kindred groups), we find that they number 838, or 16.8 per cent of the total, a group competing for numerical importance with the group of mixed descent. More than one-half of the

[1] See Table 26 for a description indicating the difference between a classification of children by regional and one by ethnic derivation of fathers.

Slavic children are of Polish descent; 493, or 9.9 per cent of all children in the schools, report Polish origin. The other groups as indicated in Table 19 follow in order: Italian, 414 or 8.3 per cent; British, 385 or 7.7 per cent; Irish, 272 or 5.5 per cent; and Jews, 191 or 3.8 per cent. It was noted in the preceding chapter where the sib was the unit of enumeration that the British and Irish contribute relatively few families of pure descent as compared with the "numerical equivalents" of stock assigned these groups in ethnic composition. Also, few children are of pure British or pure Irish descent. Considerable British and Irish blood, however, is diffused through the mixed population.

The children carrying these diverse strains are dissimilar, however, for length of residence in America. A few are Old Americans by virtue of long-continued residence of the family in this country; some of these children are themselves immigrants; the majority fall into intermediate classes.

GENERATION IN AMERICA OF ALL CHILDREN

(Tables 21, 21a, and 21b; Fig. 3)

In Table 21 all children are described according to the generation of their parents. Since the generation symbol always refers to parents, the children themselves are in reality one generation farther removed than the symbol would indicate. While only 366, or 7.3 per cent, of the children, are themselves foreign born, 2,696, or 54.2 per cent, are children from 1–1 families, i.e., families in which both parents are immigrants. By contrast we find only 224, or 4.5 per cent, of the children, coming from Old American homes (3–3).

The children who come from immigrant or first generation homes are predominantly of French-Canadian, Italian, Slavic, and Jewish descent, 75.4 per cent of all the 1–1 children being derived from these strains (Table 21b, col. a). The French Canadians contribute 23.3 per cent[1] of all 1–1 cases; Italians, 15.3 per cent; Slavs, 30.5 per cent; Jews, 6.3 per cent; British, 4.5 per cent; and the Irish, only 2.2 per cent. French-Canadian, British, and Irish children are represented in practically all generation groupings, since these are the old settlers, but the French Canadians are more largely represented in the first generation than either of the others. A goodly proportion of the British children come from immigrant homes,[2] but relatively few Irish children are from immigrant families.

---

[1] European French contribute an additional 2.9 per cent.

[2] Thirty-one and seven-tenths per cent of all British children fall in the 1–1 group.

AN ETHNIC SURVEY

TABLE 21

4,978 Children by Ethnic Derivation and Generation of Parents in America

Column groups under **Generation of Father and Mother**: **FA. Mo. 1-2x** = cols (b)(c)(d)(e); **FA. Mo. 2x-1** = cols (f)(g)(h)(i); **2-2** = col (j); **(3-2) and (3-3)*** = cols (k)(l)(m).

Ethnic Derivation	1-1 (a)	1-2 (b)	1-3 (c)	1-(3/2) (d)	Total Cols. b,c,d (e)	2-1 (f)	3-1 (g)	(3/2)-1 (h)	Total Cols. f,g,h (i)	2-2 (j)	3-2 (k)	3-3 (l)	Total Cols. k,l (m)	Rejects (n)	Total (o)
Albanian	1														1
Armenian	32	1			1										33
Austrian															
Belgian (Flemish)	9														9
British total	122	19	14	5	38	9	19	1	29	17	86	92	178	1	385
a) English	72	16	8		24	4	10	1	15	13	54	72	126	1	251
b) Scotch	12														12
c) Scotch-Irish															
d) Canadian English	4														4
e) Canadian Scotch															
f) Canadian unspec.	5														5
g) British mixed	29	3	6	5	14	5	9		14	4	32	20	52		113
h) British, others															
Chinese	2					1			1						3
Colored	3											6	6		9
Czech	2														2
Dutch															
Finnish	2														2
French Canadian	629	231	24	54	309	171	20	31	222	199	142		142	15	1,516
French, total all others	77	15		3	18	9		1	10	7					112
a) French, France	21														21
b) Walloon	24														24
c) Alsatian	9														9
d) Swiss															
e) French mixed	23	15		3	18	9		1	10	7					58
German	2									1	3	1	4		7
Greek	21														21
Irish	59	17	1	2	20	24	7	1	32	65	77	19	96		272
Italian	412	1			1					1					414
Jewish	171	13			13	2	1		3	4					191
Portuguese (white)	26		1		1										27
Roumanian	40														40
Scandinavian total	28	6			6	1			1						35
a) Swedish	27	6			6	1			1						34
b) Norwegian															
c) Danish	1														1
Slavic total	822	8			8	2			2	2				4	838
a) Polish	480	6			6	2			2	1				4	493
b) Ukrainian	323	2			2										325
c) Russian	17									1					18
d) Lithuanian	2														2
e) (Galician)															
Spanish															
Syrian	71														71
Turkish															
Total homogeneous	2,531	311	40	64	415	219	47	34	300	296	308	118	426	20	3,988
Partly unspecified (n.)†			15		15		18		18		51	6	57	1	91
Unspecified (n.)†										5		37	37	9	51
Total unspecified			15		15		18		18	5	51	43	94	10	142
Mixed ancestry	165	59	47	48	154	43	22	31	96	97	273	63	336		848
Grand total	2,696	370	102	112	584	262	87	65	414	398	632	224	856	30	4,978

* In columns *a, j, k, l, m,* it is not necessary to specify which is father and which is mother as both are of the same generation.

† Except in col. *n* it is the native element in each mating that is unspecified.

TABLE 21a

4,978 CHILDREN: PER CENT DISTRIBUTION BY GENERATION WITHIN EACH STOCK

ETHNIC DERIVATION	1–1 (a)	Fa. Mo. 1–2x 1–2 (b)	1–3 (c)	1–(3/2) (d)	Total Cols. b, c, d (e)	Fa. Mo. 2x–1 2–1 (f)	3–1 (g)	(3/2)–1 (h)	Total Cols. f, g, h (i)	2–2 (j)	(3–2) AND (3–3)* 3–2 (k)	3–3 (l)	Total Cols. k, l (m)	RE-JECTS (n)	TO-TAL (o)
Albanian	100.0														100.0
Armenian	97.0	3.0			3.0										100.0
Austrian															
Belgian (Flemish)	100.0														100.0
British total	31.7	4.9	3.7	1.3	9.9	2.3	4.9	.3	7.5	4.4	22.3	23.9	46.2	.3	100.0
a) English	28.7	6.4	3.2		9.6	1.6	4.0	.4	6.0	5.1	21.5	28.7	50.2	.4	100.0
b) Scotch	100.0														100.0
c) Scotch-Irish															100.0
d) Canadian English	100.0														100.0
e) Canadian Scotch															
f) Canadian unspec	100.0														100.0
g) British mixed	25.7	2.7	5.3	4.4	12.4	4.4	8.0		12.4	3.5	28.3	17.7	46.0		100.0
h) British, others															
Chinese	66.7					33.3			33.3						100.0
Colored	33.3										66.7		66.7		100.0
Czech	100.0														100.0
Dutch															
Finnish	100.0														100.0
French Canadian	41.5	15.2	1.6	3.6	20.4	11.3	1.3	2.0	14.6	13.1	9.4		9.4	1.0	100.0
French, total all others	68.7	13.4		2.7	16.1	8.0		.9	8.9	6.3					100.0
a) French, France	100.0														100.0
b) Walloon	100.0														100.0
c) Alsatian	100.0														100.0
d) Swiss															
e) French mixed	39.7	25.9		5.1	31.0	15.5		1.7	17.2	12.1					100.0
German	28.6									14.3	42.8	14.3	57.1		100.0
Greek	100.0														100.0
Irish	21.7	6.2	.4	.7	7.3	8.8	2.6	.4	11.8	23.9	28.3	7.0	35.3		100.0
Italian	99.6	.2			.2		.2		.2						100.0
Jewish	89.5	6.8			6.8	1.1	.5		1.6	2.1					100.0
Portuguese (white)	96.3		3.7		3.7										100.0
Roumanian	100.0														
Scandinavian total															
a) Swedish	79.4	17.7			17.7	2.9			2.9						100.0
b) Norwegian															
c) Danish	100.0														100.0
Slavic total	98.1	1.0			1.0	.2			.2	.2				.5	100.0
a) Polish	97.4	1.2			1.2	.4			.4	.2				.8	100.0
b) Ukrainian	99.4	.6			.6										100.0
c) Russian	94.4									5.6					100.0
d) Lithuanian	100.0														100.0
e) (Galician)															
Spanish															
Syrian	100.0														100.0
Turkish															
TOTAL HOMOGENEOUS	63.5	7.8	1.0	1.6	10.4	5.5	1.2	.8	7.5	7.4	7.7	3.0	10.7	.5	100.0
Partly unspecified (n.)†			16.5		16.5		19.8		19.8		56.0	6.6	62.6	1.1	100.0
Unspecified (n.)										9.8		72.5	72.5	17.7	100.0
TOTAL UNSPECIFIED			10.6		10.6		12.7		12.7	3.5	35.9	30.3	66.2	7.0	100.0
Mixed ancestry	19.5	7.0	5.5	5.7	18.2	5.1	2.6	3.6	11.3	11.4	32.2	7.4	39.6		100.0
GRAND TOTAL	54.2	7.4	2.0	2.3	11.7	5.3	1.7	1.3	8.3	8.0	12.7	4.5	17.2	.6	100.0

* In columns a, j, k, l, m, it is not necessary to specify which is father and which is mother as both are of the same generation.

† Except in col. n it is the native element in each mating that is unspecified.

TABLE 21b

4,978 CHILDREN: PER CENT DISTRIBUTION OF STOCKS WITHIN EACH GENERATION

ETHNIC DERIVATION	1-1	FA. MO. 1 – 2x				FA. MO. 2x – 1				2-2	(3-2) AND (3-3)*			RE-JECTS	TO-TAL
		1-2	1-3	1-(3/2)	Total Cols. b, c, d	2-1	3-1	(3/2)-1	Total Cols. f, g, h		3-2	3-3	Total Cols. k, l		
	(a)	(b)	(c)	(d)	(e)	(f)	(g)	(h)	(i)	(j)	(k)	(l)	(m)	(n)	(o)
Albanian	†														
Armenian	1.2	.3			.2										†
Austrian															.7
Belgian (Flemish)	.3														.2
British total	4.5	5.1	13.7	4.4	6.5	3.4	21.8	1.5	7.0	4.3	13.6	41.1	20.8	3.3	7.7
a) English	2.7	4.3	7.8		4.1	1.5	11.5	1.5	3.6	3.3	8.5	32.2	14.7	3.3	5.0
b) Scotch	.4														.2
c) Scotch-Irish															
d) Canadian English	.1														.1
e) Canadian Scotch															.1
f) Canadian unspec.	.2														.1
g) British mixed	1.1	.8	5.9	4.4	2.4	1.9	10.3		3.4	1.0	5.1	8.9	6.1		2.3
h) British, others															
Chinese	.1					.4			.3						.1
Colored	.1											2.7	.7		.2
Czech	.1														†
Dutch															†
Finnish	.1														†
French Canadian	23.3	62.4	23.5	48.2	52.9	65.3	23.0	47.7	53.6	50.0	22.4		16.6	50.0	30.5
French, total all others	2.9	4.1		2.7	3.1	3.4		1.5	2.4	1.7					2.3
a) French, France	.8														.4
b) Walloon	.9														.4
c) Alsatian	.3														.5
d) Swiss															.2
e) French mixed	.9	4.1		2.7	3.1	3.4		1.5	2.4	1.7					1.2
German	.1									.3	.5	.4	.5		.2
Greek	.8														.4
Irish	2.2	4.6	1.0	1.8	3.4	9.1	8.0	1.5	7.7	16.3	12.2	8.5	11.2		5.5
Italian	15.3	.3			.2					.3					8.3
Jewish	6.3	3.5			2.2	.8	1.2		.7	1.0					3.8
Portuguese (white)	1.0		1.0		.2										.5
Roumanian	1.5														.8
Scandinavian total	1.0	1.6			1.0	.4			.3						.7
a) Swedish	1.0	1.6			1.0	.4			.3						.7
b) Norwegian															.7
c) Danish	†														†
Slavic total	30.5	2.2			1.3	.8			.5	.5				13.4	16.8
a) Polish	17.8	1.6			1.0	.8			.5	.3				13.4	9.9
b) Ukrainian	12.0	.6			.3										6.5
c) Russian	.6									.2					.4
d) Lithuanian	.1														†
e) (Galician)															
Spanish															
Syrian	2.6														1.4
Turkish															
TOTAL HOMOGENEOUS	93.9	84.1	39.2	57.1	71.0	83.6	54.0	52.2	72.5	74.4	48.7	52.7	49.8	66.7	80.1
Partly unspecified (n.)‡			14.7		2.6		20.7		4.3		8.1	2.7	6.7	3.3	1.9
Unspecified (n.)										1.2		16.5	4.3	30.0	1.0
TOTAL UNSPECIFIED			14.7		2.6		20.7		4.3	1.2	8.1	19.2	11.0	33.3	2.9
Mixed ancestry	6.1	15.9	46.1	42.9	26.4	16.4	25.3	47.8	23.2	24.4	43.2	28.1	39.2		17.0
GRAND TOTAL	100.0	100.0	100.0	100.0	100.0	100.0	100.0	100.0	100.0	100.0	100.0	100.0	100.0	100.0	100.0

* In columns a, j, k, l, m, it is not necessary to specify which is father and which is mother as both are of the same generation.

† Less than .1 per cent.

‡ Except in col. n it is the native element in each mating that is unspecified.

The country of origin, interestingly enough, for British children is Great Britain rather than Canada as one might expect. European French stocks also are represented only in the immigrant column. This may be

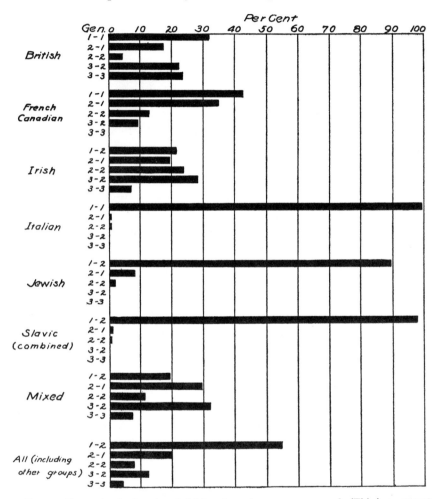

FIG. 3.—Generation in America of children in major groups compared. (This is a per cent distribution for each group by generation of parents and is based upon the data in Table 21a.)

due in part to the fact that the earlier French comers are absorbed in the group designated as "French mixed"; but there are 25 European French children who are themselves foreign born. Foreign-born children are few in number (Table 19, col. a), and these 25 represent the fourth largest contingent of foreign-born children: 26 children are born in Canada in addition to the 205 who are French Canadian; 26 are born in Italy. The actual descent of children is more accurately indicated in column c of Table 19.

In general, the children from immigrant homes are heterogeneous and diverse in origin. Who, on the other hand, are the Old American children? Are they similarly diverse in origin?

ETHNIC DERIVATION OF OLD AMERICAN CHILDREN
(Tables 21 and 21a, col. l)

Only 224, or 4.5 per cent of the children (those appearing in the 3–3 col. [l] of Tables 21 and 21a), are Old American. Among these the largest constituent class is the British with 92[1] children. The group of mixed descent ranks next in importance with 63 children, while the Irish children constitute the only other competing group, but with only 19 children is not a close competitor. These, then, are the Old Americans in Woonsocket, less diverse than the first-generation population to begin with, and with one-fourth of the group already of mixed descent. In other words, in the Old Americans we have a group less diverse in origin than the immigrant class, and as a result of time more thoroughly intermixed.

It may be argued that the percentage of children designated as Old American is so small owing to the restricted meaning assigned the term "American." It is therefore interesting to note that by the same criterion 22.0 per cent of the families were found to be Old American in New London. In Stamford, Connecticut, 21.8 per cent of the families and 18.0 per cent of the children were Old American. Woonsocket is again unique in the small percentage that is indicated to be Old American. Can the group designated as American be increased appreciably by making the term "American" more inclusive?

OTHER AMERICANS
(Tables 21, 21a, and 21b, col. m)

The 3–3 column sets apart Old American children as a single class. Were we to provide a separate category for an American ethnic group, as distinct from any other, these children would constitute such a unit. The present arrangement has the advantage of measuring this unit for two aspects at the same time, for Americanism and for descent.

There are, however, various measures of Americanism as a term which

[1] Twenty of these are British mixed; 72, English.

refers to origin. Their proper use depends upon the objective in mind. Thus, the term "American" might be variously applied, as follows:

92.7 per cent of the children are native born [Table 19]

45.2 per cent have one or both parents who are native born[1]

25.2 per cent have two native-born parents

20.0 per cent have only one native-born parent

17.2 per cent have two native-born parents and one or more but not all grandparents are native born[2]

4.5 per cent have four native-born grandparents, plus two native-born parents

These measures of American origin may be useful for various purposes. Certainly Woonsocket cannot lay claim to a population that has been

TABLE 22

4,978 CHILDREN BY NUMBER OF GRANDPARENTS NATIVE BORN: NUMBER AND PER CENT DISTRIBUTION

Number of Native-born Grandparents	Number of Cases	Per Cent	Number of Foreign-born Grandparents
4..........................	224	4.5	0
3..........................	135	2.7	1
2..........................	423	8.5	2
1..........................	441	8.9	3
0..........................	3,726	74.8	4
Incomplete histories........	29	.6	....
Total...............	4,978	100.0	

subjected long to an American environment, unless it chooses to use one of the more inclusive measures of Americanism to indicate American derivation. By far the largest proportion of children come from homes predominantly foreign in their ethnic milieu. Fifty-four and two-tenths per cent of the children (the 1–1 group) have all six of their immediate ancestors foreign born, and no ancestor native born, and 74.8 per cent of the children have four foreign-born grandparents (Table 22). This is in contrast to the 4.5 per cent of 3–3 children who have all four grandparents native born.

In seeking the derivation of American children it may be well not to limit our discussion to those who are entirely Old American, but to in-

[1] This and the following figures are all derived from Table 21a.

[2] There are still other classes. The 3–1 children claim native parents and native grandparents on one side; on the other, foreign parents and foreign grandparents. These bring the number of children who claim foreign grandparents up to 24.6 per cent. See Table 22 for distribution of children according to the number of grandparents who are native born.

clude also those who are in some degree Old American, i.e., children who
have at least one or more native grandparents, and who have native
parents.[1] This increases our American group threefold, since 856, or 17.2
per cent of the children, now fall in this new category. The composition
of this group is different both from the immigrant, or 1–1, group and from
that of the Old American, or 3–3 group.

The largest single group of children in this newly created American
class is that of mixed ancestry (Table 21b): 336, or 39.2 per cent. After
that the British lead with 178, or 20.8 per cent. French Canadians follow
with 142, or 16.6 per cent, and Irish with 96, or 11.2 per cent.[2] The French
Canadians, who do not appear at all in the 3–3 column, take third rank
after the group of mixed descent and the group of British descent in the
3–3 and 3–2 class combined. This is due largely to the tendency already
noted among the French-Canadian parents to choose in marriage one who
is of French-Canadian descent, whether or not the mate is of the same
generation.

In Table 21 we have before us a fairly complete picture of school population for ethnic derivation and for generation in America. The data on
the mixed group, however, which now constitutes the second largest class
in the community, are not sufficiently descriptive of the melting pot for
those whose curiosity impels them to ask: What is the nature of admixture? Who are the children of mixed ancestry?

As one traces ethnic composition from generation to generation and
compares the constituent elements in each generation, one finds not only
that leadership shifts from one ethnic class to another but that the group
of mixed descent is of ever increasing importance. It emerges in the 1–1
generation with 6.1 per cent of stock in admixture. In the 1–2x[3] groups
some 25 per cent of the children are of mixed descent; in the 2–2 class,
24.4 per cent; and in the "American" classes, i.e., the 3–3 and 3–2 combined, 39.2 per cent of all children are of mixed descent.

THE CHILDREN OF MIXED DESCENT

(Table 23)

Table 23 gives the tory of fusion. All children are classified here according to the ethnic escent of father and of mother. The children rep-

[1] See Tables 21 and 21a, col. m, which give totals for 3–3 and 3–2 children combined.

[2] The percentage distribution is somewhat different from that for sibs given in the last
chapter, owing to differential rates of increase and other similar influences. See discussion in
chap. xi.

[3] Including 2x–1 groups.

resented in the diagonal and in boldface have two parents of the same ethnic descent and are those children whom we have designated as "homogeneous." The children represented in the scatter are of mixed parentage and are derived from the strains described ethnically and numerically in chapter iii, Table 2, as constituting the melting pot. There we find a description of the elements in the melting pot, an inventory of the "numerical equivalents" of these strains. Here are the living children derived from these strains.

The children of mixed descent are the direct product of intermarriage among parents.[1] They are derived alike from new and from old strains in the population. As we might well expect from our previous analysis of the elements in the melting pot, the largest number of children of mixed descent are derived from an admixture of "old" strains. Thus, the 848 children of mixed ancestry represent the following types of admixture:

116 children are of Irish×French-Canadian descent
73 children are of Irish×British descent
72 children are of British×French-Canadian descent
71 children are the product of cross-Slavic amalgamation
380 children are the product of repeated admixture, one or both parents are of mixed descent; i.e., grandparents as well as parents intermarried
136, the remainder, represent all other types of fusion

The children listed above are in each case the product of marriages which we have called "intermarriages." In addition there are 171 children, whom we have not included among the cases of admixture, who are the product of kindred crossings. One hundred and thirteen children are of mixed British descent, and 58 children are of mixed French descent.

CHILDREN AS OFFSPRING OF REPEATED ADMIXTURE
(Table 23)

The summary just preceding based upon Table 23 describes in general the nature of the melting pot and the children of mixed descent, excepting the 380[2] children who are the offspring of repeated admixture. Here the strains represented by each child are not fully indicated, nor are the vari-

---

[1] It should be noted, however, that while 17.8 per cent of the parents have intermarried, and while 17.8 per cent of all families are of mixed descent, only 17.0 per cent of all children are of mixed descent. The families of mixed descent are represented by relatively fewer children in the population. For further differences regarding comparative size of family among different nationalities see chaps. xi and xiii.

[2] These 380 children are derived as follows: 182 report fathers with mixed ancestry, 236 have mothers of mixed ancestry, 38 of these overlap since both father and mother are of mixed descent (Table 23).

ous stocks designated that have been injected into the melting pot as a result of intermarriage of grandparents in distant lands. Thus, some of the parents of these children carry Dutch, Scandinavian, Spanish, and Flemish strains—strains which are not otherwise, or only inappreciably, represented in the population. The intermarriage of grandparents, we may recall, depicts an entirely different intermingling of isolated stocks from that of parents. What these strains are can be ascertained by glancing at the table dealing with the intermarriage of grandparents.[1] The weight of these strains is indicated in the tables dealing with "numerical equivalents" of the various stocks.[2] In what degree or manner they flow through the veins of these children is designated in still another analysis (chap. xi), where the children are listed according to each strain they carry. It is therefore possible to locate more specifically the origins for these children who are the product of repeated admixture.

These children, who represent repeated admixture, constitute a significant group in the population; 7.6 per cent of all children in the population represent repeated admixture. This means that only 9.4 per cent of the children represent initial admixture, those whose parents were the first to intermarry, within the span covered by this history of intermarriage. Together these 17.0 per cent of the children constitute the melting pot in Woonsocket.

FINDINGS BY DIFFERENT METHODS COMPARED
(Tables 24, 25, 26; Fig. 4)

The preceding pages give us a picture of the school population as it now exists—the regional derivations, the ethnic descent, the generation in America. The question may well be asked: What essential differences, if any, are there between the various classifications we have made? More particularly, how do the ethnic classifications differ from the usual one based upon father's birthplace?

There are three basic classifications: father's birthplace, "numerical equivalents" for ethnic composition, and ethnic descent of children themselves. These are compared in the next two tables and in the accompanying diagram.

The most significant comparison is between ethnic elements represented in the population and the children derived from those ethnic elements. The difference in this case is due only secondarily to the method em-

[1] See chap. iv, Table 7.
[2] See chap. iii, Tables 1 and 1a.

ployed; the method serves only to call attention to the actual transformation of stocks into children.

TABLE 24

COMPARISON OF FINDINGS BY DIFFERENT METHODS; 4,978 CHILDREN
(Per Cent Distribution)

Derivation	Father's Birthplace* (a)	Numerical Equiv. (Ethnic)† (b)	Ethnic Descent (Stock of 4 G.P.) (c)
American (U.S.)	33.5	. . . .	. . . .
Slavic	21.6	18.3	16.8
Polish	8.5	10.6	9.9
Galician	7.6	. . . .	. . . .
Russian	4.1	.5	.4
Ukrainian	1.2	7.1	6.5
Lithuanian	.2	.1	. . . .
French Canadian	20.8	34.9	30.5
Italian	8.7	8.6	8.3
British	5.0	12.2	7.7
Irish	1.7	9.3	5.5
Jews‡	. . . .	3.9	3.8
Mixed	. . . .	.1	17.0

* Arranged in order of rank.
† Ethnic elements as represented by a count of 19,912 theoretical grandparents.
‡ In most cases Slavic by regional derivation of fathers, i.e., birthplace.

The outstanding feature in column *c* of Tables 24 and 25 is the emergence of a group of children of mixed descent, representing 17.0 per cent

TABLE 25

COMPARISON OF RANK BY DIFFERENT METHODS; 4,978 CHILDREN

Derivation	Father's Birthplace* (a)	Numerical Equiv. (Ethnic)† (b)	Ethnic Descent (Stock of 4 G.P.) (c)
Slavic	1	2	3
French Canadian	2	1	1
Italian	3	5	4
British	4	3	5
Irish	5	4	6
Jews	. . . .	6	7
Mixed	. . . .	. . . .	2

* Arranged in order of rank.
† Ethnic elements as represented by a count of 19,912 theoretical grandparents.

of the total number of children, and taking second rank in the population. Since these children have been derived largely from British, Irish, and French-Canadian elements, the percentages for these groups have decreased correspondingly.

Similarly we find significant differences when we compare the findings on the ethnic descent of children with those for regional derivation of children, as determined by birthplace of father. In the latter classification, Slavic countries, when combined, have a slight precedence over

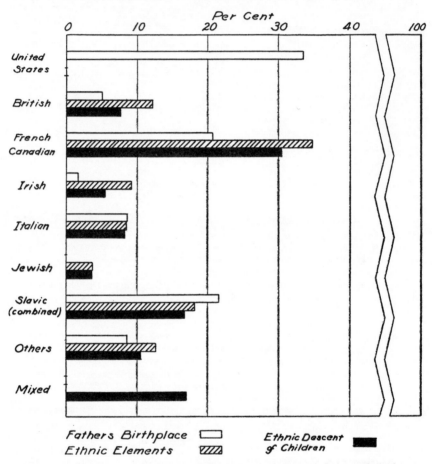

Fig. 4.—Findings on composition compared: children by father's birthplace, ethnic elements in population, and ethnic descent of children. (This graph is based upon the data in Table 24.)

French Canadians, but only because they are combined. If the European French were similarly grouped with the French Canadians, the French stocks would rank with the Slavic in importance. These two classes represent the most significant contributions to the population in all classifications. But the values for most groups change when the classification is on an ethnic basis. Chiefly, Jewish children and children of mixed descent are given a place in the sun. Russia almost disappears, since most families derived from Russia are Jewish or of some Slavic descent. The children who in column *a* are counted as of American origin are allocated in column *c* to various ethnic groups, thus swelling the figures for several stocks.

Father's birthplace indicates the residence at one time in one of the family lines; it is obviously most fallacious as an indication of the ethnic origins of our national stock.

In chapter v, dealing with parents, the relation of a regional to an ethnic classification was tested out for the actual fathers in the population. We saw there that ethnic derivation of fathers was identical with regional derivation in only 50.8 per cent[1] of the cases. This discrepancy repeats itself at this point and is of especial significance in its bearing upon children. Throughout the investigation the point of departure in our discussions has been that classification which is most widely used for determining composition, and for designating the nationality of a child, namely, father's birthplace. In Table 26, where the children are classified both by father's birthplace and by ethnic origin of father, we find that only 51.5 per cent of the children report geographic origin identical with that of ethnic derivation. This is a significant discrepancy in view of the extent to which the former is used to indicate ethnic origin. It is to be noted that 1,668, or 33.5 per cent, of all children report fathers native born and that these contribute to the total number who shift places in the new classification. In addition 746 or 15.0 per cent of the total number of children claim a regional origin for fathers not identical with ethnic origin. These constitute about one-fifth of all children of foreign origin. These differences are sufficient to challenge regional derivation of father or country of origin as a sufficient guide even to ethnic descent of fathers alone. It surely is no guide to nationality as determined by the stock of four grandparents.

SUMMARY

The 4,978 children in the public schools of Woonsocket are for the most part native born, only 7.3 per cent having been born in foreign countries. Among those born in foreign countries, the largest number and only significant group numerically are the 205 children born in French Canada. The other foreign-born children report birthplaces in some 26 or more foreign countries (Table 19).

The evidence on regional derivation of parents (Table 20, col. *c'*) in-

[1] See chap. v, p. 55, also Table 11.

dicates that 35.2 per cent of the parentage is native in origin; 64.8 per cent is foreign born, representing origins in 30 or more different regions. French Canada with 19.7 per cent of the total population outranks all other regional derivations, unless we treat the groups from Slavic countries as a combined group, in which case the Slavic contribution is 21.5 per cent. Italy ranks third as a region of origin for parents with 8.5 per cent; British countries fourth with 4.9 per cent; Ireland claims only 1.9 per cent.

The evidence on ethnic derivation, Table 19, column d, indicates that 3,988 or 80.1 per cent of the children are homogeneous by descent; 17.0 per cent are of mixed descent (2.9 per cent are in some measure doubtful; they are for the most part Old American children who could not be allocated definitely to any one group).

The children of mixed descent are the second largest group in the population and are outranked only by the children of homogeneous French-Canadian descent, who are represented by 1,516 children, or 30.5 per cent of the total number. The Slavic groups combined contribute 838, or 16.8 per cent of the total; the Italians, 8.3 per cent; the British, 7.7 per cent; the Irish, 5.5 per cent; and the Jews, 3.8 per cent. There are in addition 15 other ethnic groups represented in the population.

These children of various descents fall into different generation classes (Tables 21, 21a and 21b). Twenty-six hundred and ninety-six, or 54.2 per cent, come from 1–1 (immigrant) homes; only 224, or 4.5 per cent, come from 3–3 homes, namely, Old American.

A comparison of generations for ethnic origin indicates an entirely different ethnic set-up for different generations in the community. Children from immigrant (1–1) homes are predominantly Slavic and Italian in origin; the French Canadians standing halfway. The alignment is, as follows: Slavic, 30.5 per cent; French Canadians, 23.3 per cent; Italians, 15.3 per cent; Jews, 6.3 per cent; British, 4.5 per cent; and the Irish, only 2.2 per cent. The children of mixed ancestry represent 6.1 per cent of the 1–1 generation, and 14 other groups together contribute only 11.8 per cent.

The Old Americans (3–3) show an entirely different makeup. They are less diverse in origin, British representing the dominant element and the Irish contributing the only other significant number. Twenty-eight and one-tenth per cent of all Old American children are of mixed descent.

As we change our definition of "American" the ethnic composition of the class changes (Table 21, col. m; see text for full data).

TABLE 27

4,978 CHILDREN BY ETHNIC DESCENT OF EACH PARENT:
NUMBER AND PER CENT DISTRIBUTION

a) Fathers, *b*) Mothers, *c*) Both

ETHNIC DERIVATION	NUMBER			PER CENT		
	Fathers (a)	Mothers (b)	Total Parents* (c)	Fathers (a′)	Mothers (b′)	Total Parents (c′)
Albanian................	2	1	3	†	†	†
Armenian..............	33	33	66	.7	.7	.7
Austrian................	....	....	....	....	....	....
Belgian (Flemish)........	20	17	37	.4	.3	.4
British total............	521	569	1,090	10.5	11.4	10.9
a) English..............	374	405	779	7.5	8.1	7.8
b) Scotch..............	43	25	68	.9	.5	.7
c) Scotch-Irish..........	1	2	3	†	†	†
d) Canadian English......	19	14	33	.4	.3	.3
e) Canadian Scotch.......	2	13	15	†	.3	.1
f) Canadian unspec.......	....	....	....	....	....	....
g) British mixed.........	73	102	175	1.5	2.0	1.8
h) British, others........	9	8	17	.2	.2	.2
Chinese................	3	3	6	.1	.1	.1
Colored................	13	9	22	.3	.2	.2
Czech.................	2	2	4	†	†	†
Dutch.................	5	....	5	.1	....	.1
Finnish................	2	4	6	†	.1	.1
French Canadian........	1,738	1,704	3,442	34.9	34.2	34.6
French, total all others....	129	115	244	2.6	2.3	2.5
a) French, France.......	56	37	93	1.2	.7	.9
b) Walloon.............	36	35	71	.7	.7	.7
c) Alsatian.............	15	12	27	.3	.3	.3
d) Swiss...............	6	....	6	.1	....	.1
e) French mixed.........	16	31	47	.3	.6	.5
German................	29	27	56	.6	.6	.6
Greek.................	23	21	44	.5	.4	.4
Irish..................	408	435	843	8.2	8.7	8.5
Italian.................	439	418	857	8.8	8.4	8.6
Jewish................	191	195	386	3.8	3.9	3.9
Portuguese (white)........	35	30	65	.7	.6	.6
Roumanian.............	41	42	83	.8	.9	.8
Scandinavian total.......	45	46	91	.9	.9	.9
a) Swedish.............	42	40	82	.9	.8	.8
b) Norwegian...........	1	1	2	†	†	†
c) Danish..............	2	5	7	†	.1	.1
Slavic total............	909	919	1,828	18.3	18.5	18.3
a) Polish..............	511	548	1,059	10.3	11.0	10.6
b) Ukrainian...........	358	349	707	7.2	7.0	7.1
c) Russian.............	34	19	53	.7	.4	.5
d) Lithuanian..........	6	3	9	.1	.1	.1
e) (Galician)...........	....	....	....	....	....	....
Spanish................	....	....	....	....	....	....
Syrian................	71	71	142	1.4	1.4	1.4
Turkish................	....	....	....	....	....	....
Unspecified (n.d.)........	126	71	197	2.5	1.4	2.0
Other unspecified........	11	10	21	.2	.2	.2
Mixed ancestry..........	182	236	418	3.7	4.8	4.2
GRAND TOTAL.......	4,978	4,978	9,956	100.0	100.0	100.0

* Throughout this table the parents are weighted by children. This column gives the ethnic derivation of 9,956 theoretical parents (4978×2). See Table 20 for similar data on regional derivation. For derivation of actual parents see Tables 12 and 13.

† Less than .1 per cent.

A group of children of mixed descent emerges in the first generation and assumes constantly increasing numerical importance, rising from 6.1 per cent in the 1–1 class to 39.2 per cent in the 3–2 and 3–3 class combined.

The children in the melting pot represent a realignment of stocks, of new strains and old strains, in admixture. Some 32 strains have been brought together in fusion but certain types of admixture predominate, chiefly those involving French-Canadian, British, and Irish elements. In addition, numerous children are of mixed British, or of mixed French descent (Table 23).

Of the 17.0 per cent of children who are of mixed descent, 9.4 per cent represent initial admixture and 7.6 per cent represent repeated admixture.

A comparison of findings by different methods indicates significant differences between analyses for derivation based upon father's birthplace, ethnic derivation of father, ethnic elements (numerical equivalents of stocks), and ethnic descent of children. Over 50 per cent of the cases are classified differently in the first two instances.

Table 21 appears to offer the best description of the ethnic descent of children and indicates the disposition made of the stock in the population.

PART II

INTERMARRIAGE AMONG PARENTS: FURTHER
ANALYSIS OF COMPOSITION AND
FUSION DATA

CHAPTER VIII

INTERMARRIAGE TRENDS: FIRST ANALYSIS OF INTERMARRIAGE BASED UPON THE NUMBER OF INDIVIDUALS WHO MARRY OUT OF EACH GROUP

THE PROBLEM

Up to this point our effort in this investigation has been directed toward describing the school population and tracing its origin. Admixture was the subject of discussion because it was a characteristic of the population, but admixture and fusion were described only in so far as these effected actual change in composition. Our attention in this part of the volume is directed toward an inquiry into intermarriage among parents.

Do certain stocks tend to intermarry more frequently than others? What is the relation of generation in America to "rates" of intermarriage? Do certain groups attract each other in marriage? To what extent do culture similarity, proximity, and communal institutions contribute to fusion?

The study of intermarriage may be approached in two ways:

1. We may make an inventory of the parents, indicating the number and per cent marrying out of each stock in each generation, thus establishing rates of intermarriage for each group. These rates measure to what extent the cohesion of each group is breaking down and the pace at which group disintegration is setting in. Or we may attack the problem from another angle:

2. We may describe the mixed matings. This has the advantage of bringing before us the result of intermarriage and of describing the families which are represented by these unions. If the former method indicates the disintegration which each ethnic group is suffering, the latter, by contrast, describes the integration of diverse elements. It is not enough to know at what rate groups are intermarrying. Our concern is with the realignment as it affects the population. Both these problems are therefore treated in the order stated, since each serves its purpose in describing a different phase of the picture. The present chapter is given over to the first problem and concerns itself with intermarriage trends among the peoples of Woonsocket. The following chapter is devoted to the second form of analysis in which the marriage is the unit of enumeration, and in which ethnic preference is the basic fact.

Since we have been seeking merely to describe the composition of the population, no distinction has been made between intermarriages which have taken place in the United States and those which have taken place elsewhere. If the children were here the derivation of stock, however it came about, was the matter of concern. Now, however, the problem is somewhat different. Facts relating to intermarriage in the United States are to be treated independently of facts of fusion. The questions no longer are: Who are the people of Woonsocket? How are they derived? The questions are rather: What is the nature and extent of intermarriage as a phenomenon which takes place in the United States? Do the findings differ significantly when refinement is made for place of marriage?

It develops that refinement of the data on this score brings about considerable change in the rates of intermarriage. It is chiefly for this reason that the study of intermarriage as a process which takes place in the United States was reserved for independent and comparative treatment.

DATA FOR ALL MARRIAGES

For purposes of comparison the total figures might well be reviewed (Tables 28 and 28a).

The 5,752 men and women representing the parental stock have formed 2,876 unions. Since 513 of these matings are intermarriages, it follows that 513 men and 513 women, 1,026 parents in all, have intermarried: in each case 17.8 per cent of the total number. The percentage of intermarriage in each generation for the entire population, irrespective of the country in which marriage occurred, is as follows:

9.6 per cent of all first-generation individuals have intermarried
20.9 per cent of all second-generation individuals have intermarried
40.4 per cent of all 3/2- and third-generation individuals have intermarried
17.8 per cent of all parents in the population have intermarried

It was necessary to re-examine only 1–1 matings for information regarding the place of marriage, i.e., only those cases where both parties to the marriage are foreign born, on the assumption that the United States was logically the place of marriage where one or both parties are native born. If, in the latter case, the marriage does not take place in the United States, the fact is not significant for our purpose. In many instances, for example, French Canadians born in the United States go to Canada to be married. The occasion offers an opportunity for a family reunion and wedding trip combined. But the place of marriage in this case is of no importance from our point of view.

TABLE 28

5,752 Parents: Number Who Marry within Each Stock and Number Who Marry out of Each Stock by Generation*

	GENERATION											GRAND TOTALS	
	1ST GEN.		2D GEN.		3/2 AND 3D GEN.						RE-JECTS		
					3/2 Gen.		3d Gen.		Total 3/2 and 3d				
ETHNIC DERIVATION	Total No. (a)	No. Inter. (b)	Total No. (c)	No. Inter. (d)	Total No. (e)	No. Inter. (f)	Total No. (g)	No. Inter. (h)	Total No. (i)	No. Inter. (j)	(k)	Total No. (l)	No. Inter. (m)
Albanian..........	3	1										3	1
Armenian.........	27		1									28	
Austrian..........													
Belgian (Flemish)..	33	17										33	17
British total......	246	61	64	21	165	60	164	31	329	91	3	642	173
a) English........	151	37	51	15	111	41	134	25	245	66	3	450	118
b) Scotch........	29	9	6	3	7	3	2		9	3		44	15
c) Scotch-Irish.....			1		2	1			2	1		3	1
d) Canadian English	21	7	1		4				4			26	7
e) Canadian Scotch	11	3										11	3
f) Canadian unspec.	10	2	1	1								11	3
g) British mixed...	24	3	4	2	41	15	28	6	69	21		97	26
h) British others...													
Chinese..........	5		1									6	
Colored..........	3	1					5	1	5	1		8	2
Czech............	2											2	
Dutch............	1	1	1	1								2	2
Finnish...........	5	1										5	1
French Canadian...	1,260	68	555	49	313	70	40	14	353	84	21	2,189	201
French, total all others	156	32	17	5	4	3	1	1	5	4		178	41
a) French, France..	71	19	6	2								77	21
b) Walloon........	50	8	1	1								51	9
c) Alsatian........	17	1										17	1
d) Swiss..........	1	1	1	1								2	2
e) French mixed...	17	3	9	1	4	3	1	1	5	4		31	8
German	15	10	10	8	7	5	3	1	10	6		35	24
Greek............	21	1										21	1
Irish.............	110	23	143	60	160	69	59	27	219	96		472	179
Italian...........	377	14	5	2	1	1			1	1		383	17
Jewish...........	186	2	13				1		1			200	2
Portuguese (white) .	42	5					1		1			43	5
Roumanian........	48	2										48	2
Scandinavian total..	46	9	10	4	2	2			2	2		58	15
a) Swedish........	40	5	9	3	2	2			2	2		51	10
b) Norwegian......	2	2										2	2
c) Danish.........	4	2	1	1								5	3
Slavic total........	936	66	10		1	1			1	1	3	950	67
a) Polish.........	529	30	7		1	1			1	1	2	539	31
b) Ukrainian......	373	24	1								1	375	24
c) Russian........	29	9	2									31	9
d) Lithuanian.....	5	3										5	3
e) (Galician)......													
Spanish...........													
Syrian............	50											50	
Turkish...........													
Partly unspecified ..	1	1			64	64†	13	13†	77	77†		78	78†
Unspecified (n.b.)..					42	12†	74	5†	116	17†	1	117	17†
Other unspecified...			4								16	20	
Mixed ancestry....	29	29	31	31	83	83	38	38	121	121		181	181
GRAND TOTAL..	3,602	344	865	181	842	370	399	131	1,241	501	44	5,752	1,026

* See Tables 33 and 34 for detailed distribution for fathers and mothers, respectively.

† These individuals are themselves "Partly Unspecified" or "Unspecified (n.b.)" but marry individuals of mixed descent whose ancestry is specified. Admixture is therefore definitely established.

5,752 Parents: Per Cent Who Marry out of Each Stock by Generation

ETHNIC DERIVATION	1ST GEN. (a)	2D GEN. (b)	GENERATION 3/2 AND 3D GEN. 3/2 Gen. (c)	3d Gen. (d)	Total 3/2 and 3d (e)	GRAND TOTAL (f)
Albanian.................	33.3	....	....	....	....	33.3
Armenian.................	....	....	....	....	....	....
Austrian.................	....	....	....	....	....	....
Belgian (Flemish).........	51.5	....	....	....	....	51.5
British total..............	24.8	31.7	36.4	18.9	27.7	26.9
a) English...............	24.5	29.4	36.9	18.6	26.9	26.2
b) Scotch...............	31.0	50.0	42.8	....	33.3	34.1
c) Scotch-Irish...........	....	....	50.0	....	50.0	33.3
d) Canadian English......	33.3	....	....	....	....	26.9
e) Canadian Scotch.......	27.3	....	....	....	....	27.3
f) Canadian unspec.......	20.0	100.0	....	....	....	27.3
g) British mixed..........	12.5	50.0	36.6	21.4	30.4	26.8
h) British, others........	....	....	....	....	....	....
Chinese..................	....	....	....	....	....	....
Colored.................	33.3	....	....	20.0	20.0	25.0
Czech...................	....	....	....	....	....	....
Dutch...................	100.0	100.0	....	....	....	100.0
Finnish..................	20.0	....	....	....	....	20.0
French Canadian.........	5.4	8.8	22.4	35.0	23.9	9.1
French, total all others....	20.5	25.0	75.0	100.0	80.0	23.0
a) French, France........	26.8	33.3	....	....	....	27.3
b) Walloon..............	16.0	100.0	....	....	....	17.6
c) Alsatian..............	5.9	....	....	....	....	5.9
d) Swiss.................	100.0	100.0	....	....	....	100.0
e) French mixed..........	17.6	11.1	75.0	100.0	80.0	25.8
German.................	66.6	80.0	71.4	33.3	60.0	68.6
Greek...................	4.8	....	....	....	....	4.8
Irish....................	20.9	41.9	43.1	45.7	44.2	37.9
Italian..................	3.7	40.0	100.0	....	100.0	4.4
Jewish..................	1.1	....	....	....	....	1.0
Portuguese (white)........	11.9	....	....	....	....	11.6
Roumanian..............	4.2	....	....	....	....	4.2
Scandinavian total.......	19.6	40.0	100.0	....	100.0	25.9
a) Swedish..............	12.5	33.3	100.0	....	100.0	19.6
b) Norwegian............	100.0	....	....	....	....	100.0
c) Danish...............	50.0	100.0	....	....	....	60.0
Slavic total..............	7.0	....	100.0	....	100.0	7.0
a) Polish................	5.7	....	100.0	....	100.0	5.8
b) Ukrainian.............	6.4	....	....	....	....	6.4
c) Russian...............	31.0	....	....	....	....	29.0
d) Lithuanian............	60.0	....	....	....	....	60.0
e) (Galician).............	....	....	....	....	....	....
Spanish.................	....	....	....	....	....	....
Syrian..................	....	....	....	....	....	....
Turkish.................	....	....	....	....	....	....
Partly unspecified........	100.0	....	100.0	100.0	100.0	100.0
Unspecified (n.b.).........	....	....	28.6	6.8	14.7	14.5
Other unspecified........	....	....	....	....	....	....
Mixed ancestry...........	100.0	100.0	100.0	100.0	100.0	100.0
PER CENT OF TOTAL ..	9.6	20.9	43.9	32.8	40.4	17.8

Table 29 gives the picture for place of marriage.

Only 4.3 per cent of the intermarriages did not take place in the United States; 95.7 per cent of all intermarriages took place in the United States. Our concern is now more particularly with the latter, involving 4,638 parents and 2,319 matings. Five times as many intermarriages took place in this group as among those who married elsewhere than in the United States. Furthermore, the rates of intermarriage change appreciably, for some groups more so than for others.

The per cent of intermarriage for the total population rises from 17.8 to 21.2 per cent when the data cover only the United States. That for the

TABLE 29

2,876 MATINGS BY PLACE OF MARRIAGE

Class	Total Number	Number of Intram.	Number of Interm.	Number Unspec.	Per Cent of Interm. in Each Class	Per Cent of Total Interm.
Matings consummated in foreign countries........	557	535	22	....	3.9	4.3
Matings consummated in the U.S...............	2,319	1,739	491	89	21.2	95.7
Total number of matings..............	2,876	2,274	513	89	17.0	100.0

first generation rises from 9.6 to 12.1 per cent. The rates for the other generations remain constant. Corrected, the rates of intermarriage for the United States by generation are as follows (see Table 30a):

12.1 per cent of all first-generation individuals marrying in the United States have intermarried
20.9 per cent of all second-generation individuals have intermarried
40.4 per cent of all 3/2- and third-generation individuals have intermarried
21.2 per cent of all marriages consummated in the United States are intermarriages[1]

PER CENT OF PARENTS INTERMARRYING IN EACH STOCK
IN THE UNITED STATES

(Tables 30–32a)

Table 30 gives the number of men and women marrying out of each ethnic group by generation when these marriages took place in the United States. Table 30a is a percentage distribution for the same data.

[1] This is still a gross rate for the United States. For further refinement see discussion on initial versus multiple fusion (pp. 118–20).

TABLE 30

4,638 PARENTS: NUMBER MARRYING OUT OF EACH ETHNIC GROUP BY GENERATION WHEN MARRIAGES TAKE PLACE IN THE UNITED STATES*

ETHNIC DERIVATION	1ST GEN. Total No. (a)	1ST GEN. No. Inter. (b)	2D GEN. Total No. (c)	2D GEN. No. Inter. (d)	3/2 Gen. Total No. (e)	3/2 Gen. No. Inter. (f)	3d Gen. Total No. (g)	3d Gen. No. Inter. (h)	Total 3/2 and 3d Total No. (i)	Total 3/2 and 3d No. Inter. (j)	REJECTS (k)	GRAND TOTALS Total No. (l)	GRAND TOTALS No. Inter. (m)
Albanian	1	1										1	1
Armenian	21		1									22	
Austrian													
Belgian (Flemish)	15	9										15	9
British total	188	61	64	21	165	60	164	31	329	91	3	584	173
a) English	107	37	51	15	111	41	134	25	245	66	3	406	118
b) Scotch	21	9	6	3	7	3	2		9	3		36	15
c) Scotch-Irish			1		2	1			2	1		3	1
d) Canadian English	21	7	1		4				4			26	7
e) Canadian Scotch	11	3										11	3
f) Canadian unspec.	8	2	1	1								9	3
g) British mixed	20	3	4	2	41	15	28	6	69	21		93	26
h) British, others													
Chinese	1		1									2	
Colored	3	1					5	1	5	1		8	2
Czech													
Dutch	1	1	1	1								2	2
Finnish	4											4	
French Canadian	850	66	555	49	313	70	40	14	353	84	21	1,779	199
French, total all others	69	21	17	5	4	3	1	1	5	4		91	30
a) French, France	33	14	6	2								39	16
b) Walloon	22	5	1	1								23	6
c) Alsatian	4											4	
d) Swiss	1	1	1	1								2	2
e) French mixed	9	1	9	1	4	3	1	1	5	4		23	6
German	10	9	10	8	7	5	3	1	10	6		30	23
Greek	7	1										7	1
Irish	101	22	143	60	160	69	59	27	219	96		463	178
Italian	197	14	5	2	1	1			1	1		203	17
Jewish	112	2	13				1		1			126	2
Portuguese (white)	21	4					1		1			22	4
Roumanian	8	2										8	2
Scandinavian total	43	8	10	4	2	2			2	2		55	14
a) Swedish	39	4	9	3	2	2			2	2		50	9
b) Norwegian	2	2										2	2
c) Danish	2	2	1	1								3	3
Slavic total	782	56	10		1	1			1	1	3	796	57
a) Polish	450	25	7		1	1			1	1	2	460	26
b) Ukrainian	300	19	1								1	302	19
c) Russian	27	9	2									29	9
d) Lithuanian	5	3										5	3
e) (Galician)													
Spanish													
Syrian	32											32	
Turkish													
Partly unspecified	1	1†			64	64†	13	13†	77	77†		78	78†
Unspecified (n.b.)					42	12†	74	5†	116	17†	1	117	17†
Other unspecified			4								16	20	
Mixed ancestry	21	21	31	31	83	83	38	38	121	121		173	173
GRAND TOTAL	2,488	300	865	181	842	370	399	131	1,241	501	44	4,638	982

* See Tables 31 and 32 for detailed distribution for fathers and mothers respectively.

† These individuals are themselves "Partly Unspecified" or "Unspecified (n.b.)" but marry individuals of mixed descent whose ancestry is specified. Admixture is therefore definitely established.

The extent to which any group has suffered disintegration by inter-marriage is indicated by the total number of intermarriages in that group for all generations combined. The following percentages indicate the ratio of intermarriage in each case:

For the old immigrant groups:[1]

	Per Cent
Irish	38.4
British	29.6
French Canadians	11.2

For the new immigrant groups:

Italians	8.4
Slavs	7.2*
Jews	1.6

* Per cent for the combined Slavic groups.

The Irish and British rank first in marrying out of their group. By comparison with these, French Canadians are slow to intermarry. Jews seldom intermarry.

These measures of intermarriage, however, are gross values. Rates of intermarriage are comparable only when the data are further refined for generation. The comparison can be made only for similar generation groups. The last three groups are comparable, since these are all recent im-migrants. But the British, French Canadians, and Irish, on the other hand, have been coming to this country for three generations or more, and may be compared with one another but not with recent immigrants. How do these same stocks behave in the first generation when they, too, are recent immigrants? The evidence is available; all three of these nationali-ties are well represented in the first generation. None has less than 100 cases, although the French Canadians constitute a disproportionate class with 850 cases. Comparing the rates for the first generation only for all groups (Table 30a, col. a), the rank attained by each does not change significantly. They are:

	Per Cent
1. British	32.4
2. Irish	21.8
3. French Canadians	7.8
4. Slavs	7.2
5. Italians	7.1
6. Jews	1.8
7. Per cent, all groups in the population combined	12.1

[1] Tables 33a and 34a give similar distributions for men and women separately.

TABLE 30a

4,638 Parents: Per Cent Marrying out of Each Ethnic Group by Generation
When Marriages Take Place in the United States

Ethnic Derivation	1st Gen. (a)	2d Gen. (b)	3/2 Gen. (c)	3d Gen. (d)	Total 3/2 and 3d (e)	Grand Total (f)
Albanian................	100.0	....	....	....	....	100.0
Armenian................	....	....	....	....	....	....
Austrian................	....	....	....	....	....	....
Belgian (Flemish)........	60.0	....	....	....	....	60.0
British total............	32.4	31.7	36.4	18.9	27.7	29.6
a) English..............	34.6	29.4	36.9	18.6	26.9	29.1
b) Scotch..............	42.9	50.0	42.8	....	33.3	41.7
c) Scotch-Irish.........	....	....	50.0	....	50.0	33.3
d) Canadian English......	33.3	....	....	....	....	26.9
e) Canadian Scotch.......	27.3	....	....	....	....	27.3
f) Canadian unspec.......	....	....	....	....	....	....
g) British mixed.........	15.0	50.0	36.6	21.4	30.4	28.0
h) British, others........	25.0	100.0	....	....	....	33.3
Chinese................	....	....	....	....	....	....
Colored................	33.3	....	....	20.0	20.0	25.0
Czech................	....	....	....	....	....	....
Dutch................	100.0	100.0	....	....	....	100.0
Finnish................	....	....	....	....	....	....
French Canadian........	7.8	8.8	22.4	35.0	23.9	11.2
French, total all others....	30.4	25.0	75.0	100.0	80.0	33.0
a) French, France........	42.4	33.3	....	....	....	41.0
b) Walloon............	22.7	100.0	....	....	....	26.1
c) Alsatian............	....	....	....	....	....	....
d) Swiss..............	100.0	100.0	....	....	....	100.0
e) French mixed..........	11.1	11.1	75.0	100.0	80.0	26.1
German................	90.0	80.0	71.4	33.3	60.0	76.7
Greek................	14.3	....	....	....	....	14.3
Irish................	21.8	41.9	43.1	45.7	44.2	38.4
Italian................	7.1	40.0	100.0	....	100.0	8.4
Jewish................	1.8	....	....	....	....	1.6
Portuguese (white)........	19.0	....	....	....	....	18.2
Roumanian............	25.0	....	....	....	....	25.0
Scandinavian total........	18.6	40.0	100.0	....	100.0	25.5
a) Swedish............	10.3	33.3	100.0	....	100.0	18.0
b) Norwegian...........	100.0	....	....	....	....	100.0
c) Danish..............	100.0	100.0	....	....	....	100.0
Slavic total............	7.2	....	100.0	....	100.0	7.2
a) Polish..............	5.6	....	100.0	....	100.0	5.7
b) Ukrainian............	6.3	....	....	....	....	6.3
c) Russian............	33.3	....	....	....	....	31.0
d) Lithuanian...........	60.0	....	....	....	....	60.0
e) (Galician)............	....	....	....	....	....	....
Spanish................	....	....	....	....	....	....
Syrian................	....	....	....	....	....	....
Turkish................	....	....	....	....	....	....
Partly unspecified........	100.0	....	100.0	100.0	100.0	100.0
Unspecified (n.b.)........	....	....	28.6	6.8	14.7	14.5
Other unspecified.........	....	....	....	....	....	....
Mixed ancestry..........	100.0	100.0	100.0	100.0	100.0	100.0
Per Cent of Total ...	12.1	20.9	43.9	32.8	40.4	21.2

TABLE 31

2,319 Fathers: Number Marrying out of Each Ethnic Group by Generation When Marriages Take Place in the United States

ETHNIC DERIVATION	1ST GEN. Total No. (a)	1ST GEN. No. Inter. (b)	2D GEN. Total No. (c)	2D GEN. No. Inter. (d)	3/2 Gen. Total No. (e)	3/2 Gen. No. Inter. (f)	3d Gen. Total No. (g)	3d Gen. No. Inter. (h)	Total 3/2 and 3d Total No. (i)	Total 3/2 and 3d No. Inter. (j)	RE-JECTS (k)	GRAND TOTAL Total No. (l)	GRAND TOTAL No. Inter. (m)
Albanian	1	1										1	1
Armenian	11											11	
Austrian													
Belgian (Flemish)	8	5										8	5
British total	97	36	28	7	76	26	86	18	162	44	1	288	87
a) English	54	21	21	5	55	21	71	16	126	37	1	202	63
b) Scotch	14	8	4	1	4	2	2		6	2		24	11
c) Scotch-Irish					1				1			1	
d) Canadian English	13	4			2				2			15	4
e) Canadian Scotch	2											2	
f) Canadian unspec	5	2										5	2
g) British mixed	9	1	3	1	14	3	13	2	27	5		39	7
h) British, others													
Chinese			1									1	
Colored	2	1					3	1	3	1		5	2
Czech													
Dutch	1	1	1	1								2	2
Finnish	2											2	
French Canadian	450	31	255	23	156	42	20	10	176	52	11	892	106
French, total all others	39	13	9	3	2	1			2	1		50	17
a) French, France	20	10	4	1								24	11
b) Walloon	12	2	1	1								13	3
c) Alsatian	2											2	
d) Swiss	1	1	1	1								2	2
e) French mixed	4		3		2	1			2	1		9	1
German	6	6	6	5	3	2	1		4	2		16	13
Greek	4	1										4	1
Irish	43	7	68	24	76	32	29	11	105	43		216	74
Italian	105	13	2	1	1	1			1	1		108	15
Jewish	58		3				1		1			62	
Portuguese (white)	12	3										12	3
Roumanian	4	1										4	1
Scandinavian total	23	4	3	2	1	1			1	1		27	7
a) Swedish	21	2	3	2	1	1			1	1		25	5
b) Norwegian	1	1										1	1
c) Danish	1	1										1	1
Slavic total	391	26	3								1	395	26
a) Polish	221	7	2								1	224	7
b) Ukrainian	150	9										150	9
c) Russian	17	8	1									18	8
d) Lithuanian	3	2										3	2
e) (Galician)													
Spanish													
Syrian	16											16	
Turkish													
Partly unspecified					31	31*	5	5*	36	36*		36	36*
Unspecified (n.b.)					31	10*	40	4*	71	14*		71	14*
Other unspecified			2								9	11	
Mixed ancestry	14	14	17	17	36	36	14	14	50	50		81	81
GRAND TOTAL	1,287	163	398	83	413	182	199	63	612	245	22	2,319	491

* These individuals are themselves "Partly Unspecified" or "Unspecified (n.b.)" but marry individuals of mixed descent whose ancestry is specified. Admixture is therefore definitely established.

TABLE 31a

2,319 Fathers: Per Cent Who Intermarry in the United States

Ethnic Derivation	1st Gen. (a)	2d Gen. (b)	3/2 and 3d Gen. 3/2 Gen. (c)	3d Gen. (d)	Total 3/2 and 3d (e)	Grand Total (f)
Albanian................	100.0	....	....	....	....	100.0
Armenian...............	....	....	....	....	....	....
Austrian................	....	....	....	....	....	....
Belgian (Flemish)........	62.5	....	....	....	....	62.5
British total.............	37.1	25.0	34.2	20.9	27.1	30.2
a) English..............	38.9	23.8	38.2	22.5	29.3	31.2
b) Scotch..............	57.1	25.0	50.0	....	33.3	45.8
c) Scotch-Irish.........	....	....	....	....	....	....
d) Canadian English......	30.8	....	....	....	....	26.7
e) Canadian Scotch......	....	....	....	....	....	....
f) Canadian unspec......	40.0	....	....	....	....	40.0
g) British mixed.........	11.1	33.3	21.4	15.4	18.5	17.9
h) British, others........	....	....	....	....	....	....
Chinese................	....	....	....	....	....	....
Colored................	50.0	....	....	33.3	33.3	40.0
Czech.................	....	....	....	....	....	....
Dutch.................	100.0	100.0	....	....	....	100.0
Finnish................	....	....	....	....	....	....
French Canadian.........	6.9	9.0	26.9	50.0	29.5	11.9
French, total all others....	33.3	33.3	50.0	....	50.0	34.0
a) French, France........	50.0	25.0	....	....	....	45.8
b) Walloon.............	16.7	100.0	....	....	....	23.1
c) Alsatian.............	....	....	....	....	....	....
d) Swiss...............	100.0	100.0	....	....	....	100.0
e) French mixed.........	....	....	50.0	....	50.0	11.1
German................	100.0	83.3	66.7	....	50.0	81.3
Greek.................	25.0	....	....	....	....	25.0
Irish..................	16.3	35.3	42.1	37.9	40.9	34.3
Italian.................	12.4	50.0	100.0	....	100.0	13.9
Jewish................	....	....	....	....	....	....
Portuguese (white)........	25.0	....	....	....	....	25.0
Roumanian.............	25.0	....	....	....	....	25.0
Scandinavian total........	17.4	66.7	100.0	....	100.0	25.9
a) Swedish.............	9.5	66.7	100.0	....	100.0	20.0
b) Norwegian...........	100.0	....	....	....	....	100.0
c) Danish..............	100.0	....	....	....	....	100.0
Slavic total.............	6.6	....	....	....	....	6.6
a) Polish...............	3.2	....	....	....	....	3.1
b) Ukrainian............	6.0	....	....	....	....	6.0
c) Russian..............	47.1	....	....	....	....	44.4
d) Lithuanian...........	66.7	....	....	....	....	66.7
e) (Galician)............	....	....	....	....	....	....
Spanish................	....	....	....	....	....	....
Syrian.................	....	....	....	....	....	....
Turkish................	....	....	....	....	....	....
Partly unspecified........	....	....	100.0	100.0	100.0	100.0
Unspecified (n.b.)........	....	....	32.2	10.0	19.7	19.7
Other unspecified........	....	....	....	....	....	....
Mixed ancestry..........	100.0	100.0	100.0	100.0	100.0	100.0
Per cent of total...	12.7	20.9	44.1	31.7	40.0	21.2

TABLE 32

2,319 MOTHERS: NUMBER MARRYING OUT OF EACH ETHNIC GROUP BY GENERATION
WHEN MARRIAGES TAKE PLACE IN THE UNITED STATES

ETHNIC DERIVATION	1ST GEN.		2D. GEN.		3/2 AND 3D GEN.						RE-JECTS	GRAND TOTAL	
					3/2 Gen.		3d Gen.		Total 3/2 and 3d				
	Total No. (a)	No. Inter. (b)	Total No. (c)	No. Inter. (d)	Total No. (e)	No. Inter. (f)	Total No. (g)	No. Inter. (h)	Total No. (i)	No. Inter. (j)	(k)	Total No. (l)	No. Inter. (m)
Albanian													
Armenian	10		1									11	
Austrian													
Belgian (Flemish)	7	4										7	4
British total	91	25	36	14	89	34	78	13	167	47	2	296	86
a) English	53	16	30	10	56	20	63	9	119	29	2	204	55
b) Scotch	7	1	2	2	3	1			3	1		12	4
c) Scotch-Irish			1		1	1			1	1		2	1
d) Canadian English	8	3	1		2				2			11	3
e) Canadian Scotch	9	3										9	3
f) Canadian unspec	3		1	1								4	1
g) British mixed	11	2	1	1	27	12	15	4	42	16		54	19
h) British, others													
Chinese	1											1	
Colored	1						2		2			3	
Czech													
Dutch													
Finnish	2											2	
French Canadian	400	35	300	26	157	28	20	4	177	32	10	887	93
French, total all others	30	8	8	2	2	2	1	1	3	3		41	13
a) French, France	13	4	2	1								15	5
b) Walloon	10	3										10	3
c) Alsatian	2											2	
d) Swiss													
e) French mixed	5	1	6	1	2	2	1	1	3	3		14	5
German	4	3	4	3	4	3	2	1	6	4		14	10
Greek	3											3	
Irish	58	15	75	36	84	37	30	16	114	53		247	104
Italian	92	1	3	1								95	2
Jewish	54	2	10									64	2
Portuguese (white)	9	1					1		1			10	1
Roumanian	4	1										4	1
Scandinavian total	20	4	7	2	1	1			1	1		28	7
a) Swedish	18	2	6	1	1	1			1	1		25	4
b) Norwegian	1	1										1	1
c) Danish	1	1	1	1								2	2
Slavic total	391	30	7		1	1			1	1	2	401	31
a) Polish	229	18	5		1	1			1	1	1	236	19
b) Ukrainian	150	10	1								1	152	10
c) Russian	10	1	1									11	1
d) Lithuanian	2	1										2	1
e) (Galician)													
Spanish													
Syrian	16											16	
Turkish													
Partly unspecified	1	1*			33	33*	8	8*	41	41*		42	42*
Unspecified (n.b.)					11	2*	34	1*	45	3*	1	46	3*
Other unspecified			2								7	9	
Mixed ancestry	7	7	14	14	47	47	24	24	71	71		92	92
GRAND TOTAL	1,201	137	467	98	429	188	200	68	629	256	22	2,319	491

* These individuals are themselves "Partly Unspecified" or "Unspecified (n.b.)" but marry individuals of mixed descent whose ancestry is specified. Admixture is therefore definitely established.

TABLE 32a

2,319 Mothers: Per Cent Who Intermarry in the United States

Ethnic Derivation	1st Gen. (a)	2d Gen. (b)	Generation 3/2 and 3d Gen. 3/2 Gen. (c)	3d Gen. (d)	Total 3/2 and 3d (e)	Grand Total (f)
Albanian................	....	....	....	....	....	....
Armenian................	....	....	....	....	....	....
Austrian................	....	....	....	....	....	....
Belgian (Flemish).........	57.1	....	....	....	....	57.1
British total.............	27.5	38.9	38.2	16.7	28.1	29.1
a) English.............	30.2	33.3	38.9	14.3	24.3	27.0
b) Scotch..............	14.3	100.0	33.3	....	33.3	33.3
c) Scotch-Irish.........	....	....	100.0	....	100.0	50.0
d) Canadian English......	37.5	....	....	....	....	27.3
e) Canadian Scotch......	33.3	....	....	....	....	33.3
f) Canadian unspec........	....	100.0	....	....	....	25.0
g) British mixed..........	18.2	100.0	44.5	26.7	38.1	35.2
h) British, others.........	....	....	....	....	....	....
Chinese..................	....	....	....	....	....	....
Colored.................	....	....	....	....	....	....
Czech...................	....	....	....	....	....	....
Dutch...................	....	....	....	....	....	....
Finnish..................	....	....	....	....	....	....
French Canadian.........	8.8	8.7	17.8	20.0	18.0	10.5
French, total all others....	26.7	25.0	100.0	100.0	100.0	31.7
a) French, France........	30.8	50.0	....	....	....	33.3
b) Walloon..............	30.0	....	....	....	....	30.0
c) Alsatian.............	....	....	....	....	....	....
d) Swiss...............	....	....	....	....	....	....
e) French mixed..........	20.0	16.7	100.0	100.0	100.0	35.7
German..................	75.0	75.0	75.0	50.0	66.7	71.4
Greek...................	....	....	....	....	....	....
Irish....................	25.9	48.0	44.6	53.3	46.6	42.1
Italian..................	1.1	33.3	....	....	....	2.1
Jewish..................	3.7	....	....	....	....	3.1
Portuguese (white)........	11.1	....	....	....	....	10.0
Roumanian..............	25.0	....	....	....	....	25.0
Scandinavian total........	20.0	28.6	100.0	....	100.0	25.0
a) Swedish.............	11.1	16.7	100.0	....	100.0	16.0
b) Norwegian...........	100.0	....	....	....	....	100.0
c) Danish.............	100.0	100.0	....	....	....	100.0
Slavic total..............	7.7	....	100.0	....	100.0	7.7
a) Polish..............	7.9	....	100.0	....	100.0	8.1
b) Ukrainian...........	6.7	....	....	....	....	6.6
c) Russian.............	10.0	....	....	....	....	9.1
d) Lithuanian..........	50.0	....	....	....	....	50.0
e) (Galician)...........	....	....	....	....	....	....
Spanish.................	....	....	....	....	....	....
Syrian..................	....	....	....	....	....	....
Turkish.................	....	....	....	....	....	....
Partly unspecified.........	100.0	....	100.0	100.0	100.0	100.0
Unspecified (n.b.).........	....	....	18.2	2.9	6.6	6.5
Other unspecified.........	....	....	....	....	....	....
Mixed ancestry...........	100.0	100.0	100.0	100.0	100.0	100.0
Per Cent of Total ...	11.4	21.0	43.8	34.0	40.7	21.2

In general, these figures corroborate the trends indicated in the previous ones. British and Irish tend to have the highest rates of intermarriage, even in the first generation.

INCREASING RATES OF INTERMARRIAGE WITH GENERATION
(Table 30a)

While the foregoing figures indicate definite trends on the part of certain groups to intermarry more readily than others, even in the first generation, the rates for most groups in the second and third generations are considerably greater than those for the first generation. The British rate, which is an exception, is 32.4 per cent in the first generation, 31.7 per cent in the second generation, and only 18.9 per cent for the third generation. It is 27.7 per cent for the third and 3/2 generations combined. The decrease for the third generation is probably a matter of chance and is insignificant, as we are dealing here with the smallest class, numerically. The French-Canadian rate is 7.8 per cent in the first generation, 8.8 per cent in the second, 35.0 per cent for the third generation. The Irish rate rises from 21.8 per cent in the first generation to 41.9 per cent in the second generation, and 45.7 per cent for those belonging to the third generation.[1]

As has been indicated, the rates for the whole community show similar increases by generation: 12.1 per cent of all first-generation individuals married in the United States marry out of their group; the rate is 43.9 per cent for the 3/2 generation and 32.8 per cent for the third generation. The most significant fact, it seems to the author, is the high rate of intermarriage for the French Canadians who belong in whole or in part to the third generation. This increase is especially significant in view of the very low rates of intermarriage for French Canadians in the first and second generations, and in view of the reputation which the group has for its tenacity of cultural values. Intermarriage surely is the most basic challenge to group cohesion. This tenacity, even among the most tenacious, is undermined by long-continued residence in this country.

CROSSING OF KINDRED STRAINS
Attention should be called again to the procedure in this monograph regarding the treatment of kindred peoples. It was previously[2] indicated

---

[1] The rates here are in all cases higher for the United States matings than they are when all marriages are taken into account, irrespective of place of marriage. In the latter instance the rates for the first generation are: British, 24.8 per cent; Irish, 20.9 per cent; French Canadians, 5.4 per cent (see Table 28a).

[2] See p. 49 in chap. iv for treatment of same kind of data for grandparents.

that cross-marriage involving two British strains and cross-marriage involving two French strains was not defined as intermarriage. This was made necessary by the fact that numerous families are of mixed British and of mixed French descent. By treating the data in this way it is easier to indicate to what extent the amalgamation of British strains and of French strains into a general British and into a general French stock is taking place; also to what extent British and French stocks mix with non-British and with non-French stocks. This treatment serves to reduce the percentages of intermarriage for these groups and for the community at large.[1] One hundred and eighty-four individuals were involved in such matings. There are 64 cross-British marriages and 28 cross-French marriages, 92 matings in all, as recorded in Table 36.[2]

By contrast, marriage between Slavic peoples was defined as intermarriage, owing to differences in language, culture, and regional derivation which characterize the specific groups. They have been treated at times as a combined unit only because they readily fall into a larger grouping whose behavior may be compared with that of British stocks, French stocks, and so on. However, the Slavic groups do represent cultural entities. A Ukrainian-Polish marriage was therefore called an intermarriage. Though unlike in language and culture, there is, on the other hand, a greater community of interest between these groups than there is between any one of these groups and other non-Slavic groups. In all, 7.2 per cent of the Slavs intermarry, but these intermarriages are almost entirely within the Slavic groups.

Ethnological judgment on grouping is not sufficiently consistent to be of much avail, and, frankly, the measures of admixture obtained by several different methods are so far apart as seriously to tax the investigator's ingenuity in creating parallel groups. There is, undoubtedly, room for a difference of opinion as to method at this point. However, the data are clear on this score and are presented in full. Rates based upon other interpretations can therefore be reconstituted. The net result of the procedure adopted is that rates of intermarriage for British and French stocks are reduced as is also the total figure of admixture for the population as a whole.

[1] The per cent of admixture was 23.0 per cent in a preliminary layout of the study instead of 17.0 per cent when this type of marriage was defined as intermarriage.

[2] These figures are obtained by counting the number of matings with more than one British strain recorded in the British bloc and those with more than one French strain in the French bloc.

INTERMARRIAGE OF MEN AND WOMEN COMPARED

(Tables 31–32a)

The figures thus far have dealt with combined groups of men and women. In general, no great differences are found between the behavior of men and women in this respect, although the specific groups vary considerably.

In Woonsocket, as elsewhere, Irish women are most assertive of their marital freedom to marry out of the group. Seven and eight-tenths per cent more Irish women intermarry than men. This difference is even greater for the very first generation, where 9.6 per cent more women than men marry out. Among the Slavic groups, 1.1 per cent more women intermarry than men. British men exceed the percentage for women only by the slight margin of 1.1 per cent; the French Canadians by 1.4 per cent. Italian men exceed Italian women by 11.8 per cent. These are practically all first-generation matings. As a matter of fact, only two Italian women have married out of the group.

It would be erroneous to gather from the foregoing paragraphs that any discrepancy in the number of men and women marrying out of any group is determined by a disproportion in the number of each sex available as possible mates in the community, although such an explanation is plausible. It is impossible to determine the distribution of the sexes for each group in each community in which a marriage took place. Individuals uniting in marriage very often come from different communities. More frequently, the bride is the one brought into the community. On the whole, however, there are compensating changes. Individuals leave the community, others come in. In this case, undoubtedly the Old Americans of pure British descent have been steadily leaving the community for social and economic ventures more promising than Woonsocket offers. Perhaps the men have done so to a greater extent than the women, since there are more native-born women than men in the community.

While French Canadians are steadily coming in and there is plenty of opportunity to secure a French-Canadian mate in Woonsocket, there are other French-Canadian colonies in Rhode Island among whom there are relatives, friends, acquaintances. Cultural kin are not far to seek.

Similarly with the Irish, one intent upon finding an Irish mate does not find Providence, a half-hour by train, with its large Irish population beyond reach. In view of the fact that Irish women persistently have the highest rank in intermarriage in different communities,[1] it is probably correct to assume a preponderance of Irish women available for intermarriage. In the first generation, Irish and French-Canadian women are chosen more frequently than others in marriage by members of other ethnic groups.[2]

INITIAL VERSUS MULTIPLE FUSION

In every investigation the findings depend largely upon the definition of categories. In the field of ethnic research, definitions are amazingly inconsistent and contradictory, and yet it is inevitable that conclusions regarding ethnic phenomena should be based upon methods in current use. Comparisons are all too frequently made between findings based upon classificatory schemes not comparable. The rates just established have been refined for place of marriage. In addition, they depend upon a definition of intermarriage not strictly comparable with that in use by other investigators, chiefly Drachsler, with whose findings in general comparison may be made.

Included among the intermarriages just described are marriages between men and women themselves of mixed descent. The rates of intermarriage therefore are not initial but cumulative. If an individual is of mixed descent, he inevitably intermarries as a result of our definition of intermarriage. For example, when a man whose father is French Canadian and whose mother is Irish marries a woman whose father is French Canadian and whose mother is Irish, Drachsler and other investigators do not call this an intermarriage, since the father of the man and the father of the woman are of the same nationality.[3] In this study such a situation has been recorded as intermarriage three times, once for each set of grandparents, and once again for the parents. The children are not only half-French-Canadian and half-Irish, but they represent a second filial generation in admixture. They are the result of triple intermarriage. Quite possibly this is not truly an intermarriage on social grounds, since no new element has been introduced either racially or culturally. Yet the procedure here adopted seems to be demanded on biologic grounds in an investigation seeking to disentangle the facts of origin.[4]

The foregoing illustration, too, is excessively simple. There are mar-

---

[1] I.e., in New London, Stamford, and Providence.

[2] Ethnic preference in marriage is discussed further in the next chapter.

[3] Drachsler determines nationality by birthplace in most cases.

[4] The writer is indebted to Dr. Charles B. Davenport for advice which finally determined this procedure.

riages in which the alliance is between a man whose father is Irish and whose mother is French Canadian, and a woman whose father is French Canadian and whose mother is Irish. According to current practice this is illogically described as an intermarriage because the fathers of the principals are different. But the admixture is biologically exactly like the preceding one, which is usually called an intramarriage because the fathers claim identical origin. Any one of the following conditions may exist: (French Canadian)×(French Canadian–Irish), or (French Canadian–British)×(Irish–British), and so on without end. Two hundred and fifty-one[1] of the marriages in the United States have been predestined to be intermarriages in this study because either the father or the mother, or both, had parents who had intermarried.

If we were seeking to establish initial rates of intermarriage in the United States, and if we wish to make the present findings comparable with those of other investigators, all cases of this type which represent repeated admixture should be subtracted from the total number. When this is done, rates of initial intermarriage in the United States are reduced as follows:[2]

First generation—11.2 per cent as against 12.1 per cent, the gross rate
Second generation—17.3 per cent as against 20.9 per cent, the gross rate
Third and 3/2 generations—24.4 per cent as against 40.4 per cent, the gross rate
Total net rate—15.8 per cent as against 21.2 per cent, the gross rate

The rates of the last two generations suffer most, because it is in these generations that there are proportionately so many individuals of mixed descent. But again we fail to find the last word. To what extent do these marriages constitute merely a reassortment of identical strains, and to what extent do they bring new blood into admixture? In a large proportion of cases representing second and triple fusion, individuals of mixed descent mate with someone who has a similar strain. In other words, they "marry back" into one of the stocks from which they claim descent.

For example, there is a strong tendency for a person of French-Canadian and Irish descent to marry a person who is either of French-Canadian or of Irish descent. Of the 21 individuals of mixed descent in the first generation, 20 married back.[3] In the second generation fully one-

[1] According to Table 28 there are 259 cases, but only 251 of these were consummated in the United States.

[2] The initial rates are derived from Tables 30, 31, and 32, and are obtained in the following manner: The parents of "mixed ancestry" are subtracted from the total number of intermarriages. This leaves only the number of initial intermarriages.

[3] These statements are based on a hand count of cards.

half of the individuals married back. In the 3/2 and third generations about one-half married back. Even after fusion is once initiated in a family line the pull as a result of ethnic similarity is strong. Of all the intermarriages which took place in the United States, about 30 per cent are second or third steps in fusion, but over one-half of these merely bring about another reassortment of the same ethnic strains. No new strains are added in over 90 per cent of the cases. This situation is undoubtedly due in large measure to the limitations upon choice due to the ethnic makeup of the community.

The gross rates of fusion measure the total amount of admixture which has taken place in the United States; the net rates of fusion measure the initial fusion. The actual degree in which fusion takes place and in which there is always some new strain is measured by a figure in between these rates—initial fusion plus those cases of double or triple fusion which involve only new racial elements when the parents intermarry. It would be fruitless to invoke further statistical refinements with so few cases. The issues are as follows:

The net rates of intermarriage measuring initial fusion constitute minimum measures of fusion and are useful chiefly for purposes of comparison with findings of other investigators. They indicate the point of departure from strict intramarriage. The gross rates of fusion more truly describe actual racial and ethnic change as it depends upon intermarriage in the United States. They take into account repeated admixture. There seems to be no good reason why, when we are studying admixture in the United States, we should exclude individuals of mixed descent who are carrying that admixture farther.

SUMMARY

The data on intermarriage indicate that 9.6 per cent of all first-generation parents have married out of their group, 20.9 per cent of second generation parents, and 40.4 per cent of those who belong to the third and 3/2 generations; 17.8 per cent of all parents have intermarried. These percentages are based on the total number of intermarriages, irrespective of the place where they occurred. They, therefore, describe the admixture in the population, but not intermarriages taking place in the United States as a distinctly American phenomenon (Table 28a).

Only 2,319, or 80.6 per cent of the marriages involving 4,638 individuals, took place in the United States. When the findings deal only with United States marriages, the rates of intermarriage show significant increases. They are 12.1 per cent for the first generation, 20.9 per cent for the second generation, and 40.4 per cent for the third and 3/2 generations; the per cent of intermarriage for the entire population rises to 21.2 per cent (Table 30a).

The rates of intermarriage for all groups in the first generation are much higher for the 4,638 parents marrying in the United States than they are when the rate is based on the total number of 5,752 parents.

The tendency to intermarry makes itself felt in the very first generation. The percentage of intermarriage in each nationality among the foreign born is: British, 32.4; Irish, 21.8; French Canadians, 7.8; Slavs, 7.2; Italians, 7.1; Jews, 1.8, as compared with the general average of 12.1.

Among the more recent immigrants the Jews show the least tendency to intermarry. The Italians and Slavs are on a par with a rate around 7 per cent. Slavs marry into other Slavic groups almost entirely.

Among the three groups which constitute our old immigrants, the following trends appear in the several generations:

The French Canadians with the lowest rate begin in the first generation with 7.8 per cent, rise to 8.8 per cent in the second generation, and to 35.0 per cent in the third generation.

The Irish begin with 21.8 per cent in the first generation, much above the average for the community at large, increase to 41.9 per cent in the second generation, and to 45.7 per cent in the third generation.

The British begin with the extremely high rate of 32.4 per cent, and while they maintain some increase, the group never rises above 36.4 per cent.

The rates of intermarriage indicate definite trends characteristic of different national groups in Woonsocket and of different generations within these groups. The tendency to cohesion among all ethnic groups is great. Of all individuals in the community who marry in the United States, only 21.2 per cent marry out of their own stock.

However, in spite of the powerful attraction which ethnic identity assumes in marital choice, intermarriage early begins to undermine the integrity of practically all groups in varying degrees. Increased generation in America is a powerful force in accelerating assimilation. The rate of intermarriage in the third generation, all groups combined, is more than three times as great as in the first.

There are no very great differences in the percentage of men and of women who intermarry for each group when the total figures are compared. The case is somewhat different if we compare the generation classes from each group separately. Eleven and eight-tenths per cent more Italian men intermarry than women. Seven and eight-tenths per cent more Irish women intermarry. It is impossible to indicate to what extent a discrepancy in numbers between the sexes has acted as a causative factor in intermarriage, as the data do not give us the necessary information about the number of available mates at the time and place of marriage.

The percentages of admixture are reduced considerably by the fact that kindred matings, i.e., crossings between two British strains and crossings between two French strains, are not defined as intermarriage. There were 184 individuals involved in such matings.

The percentages given represent cumulative rates of admixture, since the marriages of parents who were themselves of mixed descent are included in the class of intermarriages, whether or not both parents are of the same mixed descent or of different descent. The objective is to record all admixture as it affects children. Rates of initial intermarriage are lower and are also recorded.

The manner in which these intermarriages affect the population depends upon the preferences exerted by those who marry out of the group, since the family milieu and, in the long run, the racial and cultural complex of the community are determined by the two ethnic lines that are brought together through admixture. In this chapter the individual has been the unit of enumeration. In the next chapter the mating is the unit of enumeration.

TABLE 33

2,876 Fathers: Number Who Marry within Each Stock and Number Who Marry out of Each Stock by Generation

Ethnic Derivation	1st Gen. Total No. (a)	No. Inter. (b)	2d Gen. Total No. (c)	No. Inter. (d)	3/2 Gen. Total No. (e)	No. Inter. (f)	3d Gen. Total No. (g)	No. Inter. (h)	Total 3/2 and 3d Total No. (i)	No. Inter. (j)	Rejects (k)	Grand Total Total No. (l)	No. Inter. (m)
Albanian	2	1										2	1
Armenian	14											14	
Austrian													
Belgian (Flemish)	17	9										17	9
British total	126	36	28	7	76	26	86	18	162	44	1	317	87
a) English	76	21	21	5	55	21	71	16	126	37	1	224	63
b) Scotch	18	8	4	1	4	2	2		6	2		28	11
c) Scotch-Irish					1				1			1	
d) Canadian English	13	4			2				2			15	4
e) Canadian Scotch	2											2	
f) Canadian unspec	6	2										6	2
g) British mixed	11	1	3	1	14	3	13	2	27	5		41	7
h) British, others													
Chinese	2		1									3	
Colored	2	1					3	1	3	1		5	2
Czech	1											1	
Dutch	1	1	1	1								2	2
Finnish	2											2	
French Canadian	654	31	255	23	156	42	20	10	176	52	11	1,096	106
French, total all others	84	20	9	3	2	1			2	1		95	24
a) French, France	40	13	4	1								44	14
b) Walloon	26	4	1	1								27	5
c) Alsatian	9	1										9	1
d) Swiss	1	1	1	1								2	2
e) French mixed	8	1	3		2	1			2	1		13	2
German	9	7	6	5	3	2	1		4	2		19	14
Greek	11	1										11	1
Irish	48	8	68	24	76	32	29	11	105	43		221	75
Italian	195	13	2	1	1	1			1	1		198	15
Jewish	95		3				1		1			99	
Portuguese (white)	23	4										23	4
Roumanian	24	1										24	1
Scandinavian total	25	5	3	2	1	1			1	1		29	8
a) Swedish	22	3	3	2	1	1			1	1		26	6
b) Norwegian	1	1										1	1
c) Danish	2	1										2	1
Slavic total	468	31	3								1	472	31
a) Polish	260	9	2								1	263	9
b) Ukrainian	187	12										187	12
c) Russian	18	8	1									19	8
d) Lithuanian	3	2										3	2
e) (Galician)													
Spanish													
Syrian	25											25	
Turkish													
Partly unspecified					31	31*	5	5*	36	36*		36	36*
Unspecified (n.b.)					31	10*	40	4*	71	14*		71	14*
Other unspecified			2								9	11	
Mixed ancestry	16	16	17	17	36	36	14	14	50	50		83	83
Grand total	1,844	185	398	83	413	182	199	63	612	245	22	2,876	513

* These individuals are themselves "Partly Unspecified" or "Unspecified (n.b.)" but marry individuals of mixed descent whose ancestry is specified. Admixture is therefore definitely established.

TABLE 33a

2,876 Fathers: Per Cent Who Marry out of Each Stock by Generation

ETHNIC DERIVATION	GENERATION					
	1ST GEN.	2D GEN.	3/2 AND 3D GEN.			GRAND TOTAL
			3/2 Gen.	3d Gen.	Total 3/2 and 3d	
	(a)	(b)	(c)	(d)	(e)	(f)
Albanian..............	50.0	....	....	....	....	50.0
Armenian..............	....	....	....	....	....	....
Austrian..............	....	....	....	....	....	....
Belgian (Flemish).........	53.0	....	....	....	....	53.0
British total..............	28.6	25.0	34.2	20.9	27.1	27.4
a) English..............	27.6	23.8	38.2	22.5	29.3	28.1
b) Scotch..............	44.4	25.0	50.0	....	33.3	39.3
c) Scotch-Irish..........	....	....	....	....	....	....
d) Canadian English......	30.8	....	....	....	....	26.7
e) Canadian Scotch.......	....	....	....	....	....	....
f) Canadian unspec......	33.3	....	....	....	....	33.3
g) British mixed..........	9.1	33.3	21.4	15.4	18.5	17.0
h) British, others........	....	....	....	....	....	....
Chinese..............	....	....	....	....	....	....
Colored..............	50.0	....	....	33.3	33.3	40.0
Czech..............	....	....	....	....	....	....
Dutch..............	100.0	100.0	....	....	....	100.0
Finnish..............	....	....	....	....	....	....
French Canadian........	4.7	9.0	26.9	50.0	29.5	9.6
French, total all others....	23.8	33.3	50.0	....	....	25.2
a) French, France........	32.5	25.0	....	....	....	31.8
b) Walloon..............	15.4	100.0	....	....	....	18.5
c) Alsatian..............	11.1	....	....	....	....	11.1
d) Swiss..............	100.0	100.0	....	....	....	100.0
e) French mixed..........	12.5	....	50.0	....	50.0	15.4
German..............	77.7	83.3	66.7	....	50.0	73.6
Greek..............	9.1	....	....	....	....	9.1
Irish..............	16.7	35.3	42.1	37.9	40.9	33.9
Italian..............	6.7	50.0	100.0	....	100.0	7.5
Jewish..............	....	....	....	....	....	....
Portuguese (white)........	17.3	....	....	....	....	17.3
Roumanian..............	4.1	....	....	....	....	4.1
Scandinavian total........	20.0	66.7	100.0	....	100.0	27.5
a) Swedish..............	13.6	66.7	100.0	....	100.0	23.0
b) Norwegian............	100.0	....	....	....	....	100.0
c) Danish..............	50.0	....	....	....	....	50.0
Slavic total..............	6.6	....	....	....	....	6.5
a) Polish..............	3.5	....	....	....	....	3.4
b) Ukrainian..............	6.3	....	....	....	....	6.3
c) Russian..............	44.4	....	....	....	....	42.1
d) Lithuanian..............	66.7	....	....	....	....	66.7
e) (Galician)..............	....	....	....	....	....	....
Spanish..............	....	....	....	....	....	....
Syrian..............	....	....	....	....	....	....
Turkish..............	....	....	....	....	....	....
Partly unspecified........	....	....	100.0	100.0	100.0	100.0
Unspecified (n.b.)........	....	....	32.2	10.0	19.7	19.7
Other unspecified........	....	....	....	....	....	....
Mixed ancestry..........	100.0	100.0	100.0	100.0	100.0	100.0
PER CENT OF TOTAL ..	10.3	20.9	44.1	31.7	40.0	17.8

TABLE 34

2,876 Mothers: Number Who Marry within Each Stock and Number Who Marry out of Each Stock by Generation

Ethnic Derivation	1st Gen.		2d Gen.		3/2 and 3d Gen.							Grand Totals	
					3/2 Gen.		3d Gen.		Total 3/2 and 3d		Re-jects		
	Total No. (a)	No. Inter. (b)	Total No. (c)	No. Inter. (d)	Total No. (e)	No. Inter. (f)	Total No. (g)	No. Inter. (h)	Total No. (i)	No. Inter. (j)	(k)	Total No. (l)	No. Inter. (m)
Albanian............	1	....	....	....	....	....	....	....	....	....	....	1	....
Armenian...........	13	....	1	....	....	....	....	....	....	....	....	14	....
Austrian............	....	....	....	....	....	....	....	....	....	....	....	....	....
Belgian (Flemish)....	16	8	....	....	....	....	....	....	....	....	....	16	8
British total........	120	25	36	14	89	34	78	13	167	47	2	325	86
a) English..........	75	16	30	10	56	20	63	9	119	29	2	226	55
b) Scotch..........	11	1	2	2	3	1	....	....	3	1	....	16	4
c) Scotch-Irish......	....	....	1	....	1	1	....	....	1	1	....	2	1
d) Canadian English .	8	3	1	....	2	....	....	....	2	....	....	11	3
e) Canadian Scotch..	9	3	....	....	....	....	....	....	....	....	....	9	3
f) Canadian unspec...	4	....	1	1	....	....	....	....	....	....	....	5	1
g) British mixed.....	13	2	1	1	27	12	15	4	42	16	....	56	19
h) British, others....	....	....	....	....	....	....	....	....	....	....	....	....	....
Chinese............	3	....	....	....	....	....	....	....	....	....	....	3	....
Colored............	1	....	....	....	....	....	2	....	2	....	....	3	....
Czech.............	1	....	....	....	....	....	....	....	....	....	....	1	....
Dutch..............	....	....	....	....	....	....	....	....	....	....	....	....	....
Finnish............	3	1	....	....	....	....	....	....	....	....	....	3	1
French Canadian.....	606	37	300	26	157	28	20	4	177	32	10	1,093	95
French, total all others	72	12	8	2	2	2	1	1	3	3	....	83	17
a) French, France....	31	6	2	1	....	....	....	....	....	....	....	33	7
b) Walloon..........	24	4	....	....	....	....	....	....	....	....	....	24	4
c) Alsatian..........	8	....	....	....	....	....	....	....	....	....	....	8	....
d) Swiss............	....	....	....	....	....	....	....	....	....	....	....	....	....
e) French mixed.....	9	2	6	1	2	2	1	1	3	3	....	18	6
German............	6	3	4	3	4	3	2	1	6	4	....	16	10
Greek..............	10	....	....	....	....	....	....	....	....	....	....	10	....
Irish...............	62	15	75	36	84	37	30	16	114	53	....	251	104
Italian.............	182	1	3	1	....	....	....	....	....	....	....	185	2
Jewish.............	91	2	10	....	....	....	....	....	....	....	....	101	2
Portuguese (white)...	19	1	....	....	....	....	1	....	1	....	....	20	1
Roumanian.........	24	1	....	....	....	....	....	....	....	....	....	24	1
Scandinavian total....	21	4	7	2	1	1	....	....	1	1	....	29	7
a) Swedish.........	18	2	6	1	1	1	....	....	1	1	....	25	4
b) Norwegian.......	1	1	....	....	....	....	....	....	....	....	....	1	1
c) Danish..........	2	1	1	1	....	....	....	....	....	....	....	3	2
Slavic total.........	468	35	7	....	1	1	....	....	1	1	2	478	36
a) Polish...........	269	21	5	....	1	1	....	....	1	1	1	276	22
b) Ukrainian........	186	12	1	....	....	....	....	....	....	....	1	188	12
c) Russian..........	11	1	1	....	....	....	....	....	....	....	....	12	1
d) Lithuanian........	2	1	....	....	....	....	....	....	....	....	....	2	1
e) (Galician)........	....	....	....	....	....	....	....	....	....	....	....	....	....
Spanish............	....	....	....	....	....	....	....	....	....	....	....	....	....
Syrian.............	25	....	....	....	....	....	....	....	....	....	....	25	....
Turkish............	....	....	....	....	....	....	....	....	....	....	....	....	....
Partly unspecified....	1	1*	....	....	33	33*	8	8*	41	41*	....	42	42*
Unspecified (n.b.)....	....	....	....	....	11	2*	34	1*	45	3*	1	46	3*
Other unspecified.....	....	....	2	....	....	....	....	....	....	....	7	9	....
Mixed ancestry......	13	13	14	14	47	47	24	24	71	71	....	98	98
Grand total....	1,758	159	467	98	429	188	200	68	629	256	22	2,876	513

* These individuals are themselves "Partly Unspecified" or "Unspecified (n.b.)" but marry individuals of mixed descent whose ancestry is specified. Admixture is therefore definitely established.

TABLE 34a

2,876 Mothers: Per Cent Who Marry out of Each Stock by Generation

Ethnic Derivation	1st Gen. (a)	2d Gen. (b)	3/2 and 3d Gen.			Grand Total (f)
			3/2 Gen. (c)	3d Gen. (d)	Total 3/2 and 3d (e)	
Albanian...............	....	....	....	....	....	....
Armenian...............	....	....	....	....	....	....
Austrian...............	....	....	....	....	....	....
Belgian (Flemish).........	50.0	....	....	....	....	50.0
British Total............	20.8	38.9	38.2	16.7	28.1	26.5
a) English..............	21.4	33.3	38.9	14.3	24.3	24.3
b) Scotch..............	9.1	100.0	33.3	....	33.3	25.0
c) Scotch-Irish.........	....	....	100.0	....	100.0	50.0
d) Canadian English......	37.5	....	....	....	....	27.3
e) Canadian Scotch......	33.3	....	....	....	....	33.3
f) Canadian unspec......	....	100.0	....	....	....	20.0
g) British mixed.........	15.4	100.0	44.5	26.7	38.1	33.9
h) British, others........	....	....	....	....	....	....
Chinese..............	....	....	....	....	....	....
Colored..............	....	....	....	....	....	....
Czech...............	....	....	....	....	....	....
Dutch...............	....	....	....	....	....	....
Finnish..............	33.3	....	....	....	....	33.3
French Canadian........	6.1	8.7	17.8	20.0	18.0	8.6
French, total all others	16.7	25.0	100.0	100.0	100.0	20.5
a) French, France........	19.3	50.0	....	....	....	21.2
b) Walloon.............	16.7	....	....	....	....	16.7
c) Alsatian............	....	....	....	....	....	....
d) Swiss..............	....	....	....	....	....	....
e) French mixed.........	22.2	16.7	100.0	100.0	100.0	33.3
German...............	50.0	75.0	75.0	50.0	66.7	62.5
Greek...............	....	....	....	....	....	....
Irish..................	24.2	48.0	44.6	53.3	46.6	41.4
Italian...............	.5	33.3	....	....	....	1.1
Jewish...............	2.2	....	....	....	....	2.0
Portuguese (white).......	5.3	....	....	....	....	5.0
Roumanian............	4.2	....	....	....	....	4.2
Scandinavian total.......	19.0	28.6	100.0	....	100.0	24.1
a) Swedish.............	11.1	16.7	100.0	....	100.0	16.0
b) Norwegian...........	100.0	....	....	....	....	100.0
c) Danish.............	50.0	100.0	....	....	....	66.7
Slavic total............	7.5	....	100.0	....	100.0	7.5
a) Polish.............	7.8	....	100.0	....	100.0	7.9
b) Ukrainian...........	6.4	....	....	....	....	6.4
c) Russian............	9.1	....	....	....	....	8.3
d) Lithuanian...........	50.0	....	....	....	....	50.0
e) (Galician)..........	....	....	....	....	....	....
Spanish..............	....	....	....	....	....	....
Syrian...............	....	....	....	....	....	....
Turkish..............	....	....	....	....	....	....
Partly unspecified.........	100.0	....	100.0	100.0	100.0	100.0
Unspecified (n.b.)........	....	....	18.2	2.9	6.6	6.5
Other unspecified........	....	....	....	....	....	....
Mixed ancestry..........	100.0	100.0	100.0	100.0	100.0	100.0
Per Cent of Total ...	9.0	21.0	43.8	34.0	40.7	17.8

CHAPTER IX

ETHNIC PREFERENCE IN MARRIAGE: A SECOND ANALYSIS OF INTERMARRIAGE IN WHICH THE MATING IS THE UNIT OF INVESTIGATION

In this chapter the discussion of intermarriage is based upon the mating as the unit of enumeration. Such a procedure allows for a description of ethnic choice in mating and for a description of the realignment of stocks which occur as a result of intermarriage. Only the 2,319 matings which took place in the United States constitute the subject matter of this chapter; 491 of these are intermarriages.

In some instances these intermarriages are between individuals of the same generation (1–1) or (3–3). In other cases they are between individuals from different generation groups (3–1), etc. The latter is an intermarriage only if the stocks are different. For example, if a third-generation person of French-Canadian descent is married to an immigrant of French-Canadian descent, we have an intramarriage (3–1). If, however, a third-generation person of British descent marries an immigrant of French-Canadian descent, we have, according to the terms of this study, an intermarriage (3–1) since two different racial strains are united.

Table 35 is a summary of all intermarriages which actually took place in the United States, according to the generation of each parent.

SUMMARY OF MATINGS BY GENERATION IRRESPECTIVE OF PREFERENCE

(Table 35)

The largest number of cases, 368, fall into the 3–2 generation group, which is a combination of several classes.[1] There are 73 intermarriages between two foreign-born individuals, 154 cases in which one parent is native born and the other foreign born; and 264 intermarriages between two native-born individuals.

The rate of admixture increases rapidly with each generation; intermarriage is three times as frequent in the 2–2 generation as it is in the 1–1 generation, and over five times as frequent in the 3–2 combinations. The evidence seems to indicate that no American population, however foreign in its composition, and no group, however confessedly "resistant" to Americanization, is immune to assimilation. The mere fact of long-continued residence in America becomes *ipso facto* a disintegrating factor in

[1] See note to Table 35.

group cohesion. This same condition, on the other hand, is the most powerful factor in fusing the stocks in this country into a single homogeneous unit, however heterogeneous in origin.

But what stocks are being absorbed into this new unit? The answer to this question may be found by studying the intermarriage tables here appended, which indicate the descent of each party to the mating. Table

TABLE 35
SUMMARY OF ALL INTERMARRIAGES IN THE UNITED STATES ACCORDING TO GENERATION OF EACH PARENT
(2,319 Matings)

Generation Father—Mother	Total No. of Matings in Each Generation Class (a)	No. of Intermarriages in Each Generation Class (b)	Rate of Intermarriage in Each Generation (c)	Per Cent of Intermarriage in Total No. of Matings (d)
1–1.................	941	73	7.8	3.2
Total both foreign born.............	941	73	7.8	3.2
2–1.................	230	42	28.3	1.8
3–1.................	55	22	40.0	.9
(3/2)–1.................	61	26	42.6	1.1
1–2.................	161	27	16.8	1.2
1–3.................	54	17	31.5	.7
1–(3/2).............	45	20	44.4	.9
Total one foreign born..	606	154	25.4	6.6
2–2.................	237	56	23.6	2.4
3–2*.................	368	162	44.0	7.0
3–3.................	145	46	31.7	2.0
Rejects.................	22	....	....	....
Total both native born	772	264	34.2	11.4
TOTALS.........	2,319	491	....	21.2

* All 3–2 generations combined. See "Procedure," p. 24.

17, in chapter vi, which described the 2,876 matings, describes the population as it now is as a result of intramarriage and intermarriage whenever it occurred. Table 36 following describes only the 2,319 marriages which took place in the United States. It therefore gives a picture of admixture which is the result of ethnic preference expressed in this country.

ETHNIC PREFERENCE: SUMMARY OF DATA ON 2,319 MATINGS TAKING PLACE IN THE UNITED STATES

(Tables 36 and 37)

In all, 982 individuals were drawn into the melting pot as a result of the 491 intermarriages which took place in the United States.

Ethnic Derivation of Father	Albanian	Armenian	Austrian	Belgian (Flemish)	British total	a) English	b) Scotch	c) Scotch-Irish	d) Canadian English	e) Canadian Scotch	f) Canadian unspec	g) British mixed	h) British, others	Chinese	Colored	Czech	Dutch	Finnish	French Canadian	French, total all
Albanian																			1	
Armenian		1																		
Austrian																				
Belgian (Flemish)																			1	
British total					(18)															
a) English						10													1	
b) Scotch						1													1	
c) Scotch-Irish																				
d) Canadian English						2													2	
e) Canadian Scotch						1														
f) Canadian unspec																				
g) British mixed												4							1	
h) British, others																				
Chinese																				
Colored																				
Czech																				
Dutch																1				
Finnish																				
French Canadian						4	1					3							191	(
French, total all others†																				
a) French, France						1													2	
b) Walloon																			1	
c) Alsatian																			1	
d) Swiss																				
e) French mixed																			1	
German														1						
Greek																				
Irish						2													1	
Italian																			4	
Jewish																				
Portuguese (white)																			1	
Roumanian																				
Scandinavian total																				
a) Swedish																				
b) Norwegian																				
c) Danish																			1	
Slavic total																				
a) Polish																				
b) Ukrainian																				
c) Russian																				
d) Lithuanian																				
e) (Galician)																				
Spanish																				
Syrian																				
Turkish																				
Mixed ancestry						1													2	
Partly unspecified																				
Unspecified (n.d.)†																				
Unspecified																				
TOTAL UNSPECIFIED																				
TOTAL INTRAMARRIAGE		1			(18)	14						4							196	
TOTAL INTERMARRIAGE					(14)	8	1					5							16	
GRAND TOTAL		1			(32)	22	1					9							212	

* Intramarriages are indicated in boldface and appear in the diagonal; intermarriages are represented in the scatter.
† The figure within the bloc is overlapping; since it includes French-Canadian x European French, i.e., all who are not entirely French Can[...]

NOTE.—Throughout this table the figures in parentheses have reference only to the immediate situation specified a[nd] column totals.

Born)

Irish	Italian	Jewish	Portuguese (white)	Roumanian	Scandinavian total	a) Swedish	b) Norwegian	c) Danish	Slavic total	a) Polish	b) Ukrainian	c) Russian	d) Lithuanian	e) (Galician)	Spanish	Syrian	Turkish	Mixed ancestry	Partly unspecified	Unspecified (n.d.)‡	Other unspecified	TOTAL UNSPECIFIED	TOTAL INTRA-MARRIAGE	TOTAL INTER-MARRIAGE	GRAND TOTAL
1								1															(20)	(7)	(27)
																							15	6	21
																							1		1
																							4	1	5
																							1		1
																								1	1
8		1								1								2					141	17	158
																							(2)	(1)	(3)
																							2	1	1
1	1																							2	2
19		1																					19	13	32
																								1	1
		2																					2		2
						1																	1		1
									(1)														(1)		(1)
										1													1		1
1																								21	21
																		1						1	1
																						9			9
																						9			
19		2				1			(1)	1													187		
11	1	2						1	(1)	1												3		64	
30	1	4				1		1	(2)	2												3			260

duals in Group b, immediately following, are likewise unspecified but they marry persons also of unspecified descent, or of homogeneous and

—the British, French, or Slavic total as the case may be. They should not be used in computing the individual row or

Every reassortment of the data gives emphasis to the initial conclusions: British and Irish intermarry most frequently, now one, now the other leads in the proportion who intermarry. In absolute numbers, however, more French Canadians have been absorbed into the melting pot than any other group.[1]

DATA ON PREFERENCE REFINED FOR GENERATION
(Tables 38–44)

The foregoing summary was based on the evidence for all generations combined. Does ethnic choice differ from generation to generation? Are the intermarriages between foreign-born individuals different in kind from those between native-born individuals, or from those which are consummated between a person who is native born and one who is foreign born? The evidence is that such differences do exist, and may be obtained by reclassifying the data for four major generation types: (1) matings between two foreign-born persons (1–1); (2) matings between two native-born persons (2–2, 3–3, 3–2, etc.); (3) matings between one foreign-born person and one native-born person (1–2).

Careful scrutiny of the tables in this chapter giving the detail figures for these combinations indicate surprising fidelity to certain types of crossing, and interesting changes from generation to generation.

In the 1–1 generation Slavs are well started on the road to amalgamation into a larger Slavic unit; but the British and the French show, on the chart, but slight deviation from strict adherence to the diagonal which records strict intramarriage. Each British and each French group remains loyal to its specific subgroup, and this in spite of the fact that marriage takes place in the United States (Table 38).

The 1–1 intermarriage may be classed as follows:

British × Irish	5
British × French Canadian	3
Irish × French Canadian	2
Belgian × French stocks*	7
Cross-Slavic	26
All others, involving ten new strains	30
Total	73

* Including one mixed.

The outstanding characteristic of the 1–1 matings is that 26 out of the total 73 intermarriages are crosses between Slavic strains. There are only ten

[1] Within the French-Canadian–Irish–British alliance, however, the Irish are chosen most frequently by both French Canadians and British (see Table 37).

TABLE 41
All 2–2 Generation Matings*

Ethnic Derivation of Father	British total	a) English	b) Scotch	c) Scotch-Irish	d) Canadian English	e) Canadian unspec.	f) British mixed	French Canadian	French, total all others†	a) French, France	b) Walloon	c) French mixed	German	Irish	Italian	Jewish	Swedish	Slavic total	a) Polish	b) Russian	Mixed ancestry	Unspecified	Total Unspecified	Total Intra-marriage	Total Inter-marriage	Grand Total
British total	(13)																				1	1	(1)	(13)	(5)	(19)
a) English		9											1	1									1	11	3	15
b) Scotch		2											1											2	1	3
c) Scotch-Irish					1																					
d) Canadian English			1																							
e) Canadian unspec.																										
f) British mixed	2									1				9							3	1			1	1
French Canadian								121				2												124		139
French, total all others								3	(6)					1	1									(3)	(3)	(7)
a) French, France										1				1										1	1	4
b) Walloon														1											1	1
c) French mixed												2			1									2		2
German		1	1					1					1								2			1	2	5
Irish		2						11						31							2			31	16	47
Italian															1									1		1
Jewish																2								2		2
Swedish					1	1											1				1				2	2
Slavic total																		(2)						(2)		(2)
a) Polish																				1				1		1
b) Russian																			1	1				1		1
Mixed ancestry								5						5			1								11	11
Unspecified	1																				1		2			2
Total Unspecified	(1)	1															1				2	2	4			
Total Intramarriage	(13)	11	1	1	1	1		124	(3)	1		2	1	31	1	2		(2)	1	1				177		
Total Intermarriage	(8)	5					1	17	(3)		1		2	18	1		1				10	2			56	
Grand Total	(22)	17	1	1	1	1	1	141	(3)	1		2	3	49	2	2	1	(2)	1	1	10	2				237

* Intramarriages are indicated in boldface and appear on the diagonal; intermarriages appear in the scatter.

† The figure within the bloc is overlapping; since it includes French-Canadian × European French, i.e., all who are not entirely French Canadian.

Note.—Throughout this table the figures in parentheses have reference only to the immediate situation specified and to the major group indicated—the British, French, or Slavic total as the case may be. They should not be used in computing the individual row or column totals.

TABLE 42

All 3–2 Generation Matings*

Ethnic Derivation of Father	British total	a) English	b) Scotch	c) Scotch-Irish	d) Canadian English	e) British mixed	French Canadian	French, total all others †	a) French mixed	German	Irish	Italian	Swedish	Slavic total	a) Polish	Mixed ancestry	Unspecified (n.d.)† Group a	Unspecified (n.d.)† Group b	Total unspecified	Total intra-marriage	Total inter-marriage	Grand total
British total	(46)																		(3)	(46)	(25)	(74)
a) English		27	2		2		6			1	6					7		2	2	31	20	53
b) Scotch		2														1		1	1	2	1	4
c) Scotch Irish				1																1		1
d) Canadian English		2																		2		2
e) British mixed						11					2					1				11	3	14
French Canadian		6					87	(1)			12					17		5	5	87	36	128
French, total all others †																					(1)	(1)
a) French mixed											1										1	1
German									1	1										1	1	2
Irish		4	1				5		1		42	1	1			16		1	1	42	30	73
Italian											1										1	1
Swedish			1																		1	1
Slavic total																						
a) Polish																1						1
Mixed ancestry		7					13			3	8				1	18	2				57	57
Unspecified (n.d.)† Group a																10					10	10
Unspecified (n.d.)† Group b		5				2	11				3								21			21
Total unspecified	(7)	2	1				5				1							21	30			30
Total intramarriage	(46)	31	2		2	11	87			1	42									176		176
Total intermarriage	(29)	19	1	1		8	24 (2)	(2)	2	3	30	1	1		1	70	2	9			162	162
Grand total	(82)	55	3	1	2	21	122 (2)	(2)	2	4	75		1		1	70	2	9		176	162	368

* Intramarriages are indicated in boldface and appear in the diagonal; intermarriages appear in the scatter.

† The unspecified now fall into two groups—those in Group a marry persons who are of mixed and known descent. They therefore fall into the class of intermarriage. The individuals in Group b, immediately following, are likewise unspecified but they marry persons also of unspecified descent, or of homogeneous and specified descent. We do not know whether this descent is the same or different from that of the individual whom they marry and the entire mating remains partly unspecified.

Note.—Throughout this table the figures in parentheses have reference only to the immediate situation specified and to the major group indicated—the British, French, or Slavic total as the case may be. They should not be used in computing the individual row or column totals.

matings which represent the crossings of British, French-Canadian, and Irish strains. These are less significant numerically than other matings and lead to the conclusion that the reassortment of these three racial strains so dominant in the melting pot results most largely from inter-

TABLE 43

ALL 3–3 GENERATION MATINGS*

Ethnic Derivation of Father	British (Ethnic Derivation of Mother)	a) English	b) Scotch	c) British mixed	Colored	French Canadian	French, total all others	a) French mixed	German	Irish	Mixed ancestry	Unspecified (n.d.)† Group a	Unspecified (n.d.)† Group b	Total Unspecified	Total Intra-marriage	Total Inter-marriage	Grand Total
British total	(55)													(1)	(55)	(14)	(70)
a) English		44							3	10			1	1	44	13	58
b) Scotch		2													2		2
c) British mixed				9					1						9	1	10
Colored					2				1						2	1	3
French Canadian		3		1							2					6	6
French, total all others																	
a) French mixed																	
German									1						1		1
Irish				1				1	1	13	5				13	8	21
Mixed ancestry		4		1		1				3	4	1				14	14
Unspecified (n.d.)† Group a											3					3	3
Unspecified (n.d.)† Group b		2				1							24	27			27
TOTAL UNSPECIFIED	(2)	2				1							25	28			
TOTAL INTRAMARRIAGE	(55)	46		9	2					1	13				71		
TOTAL INTERMARRIAGE	(10)	7		3		1		1	1	8	24	1				46	
GRAND TOTAL	(67)	55		12	2	2		1	2	21	24	1	25				145

* Intramarriages are indicated in boldface and appear in the diagonal; intermarriages are represented in the scatter.

† The unspecified now fall into two groups—those in Group *a* marry persons who are of mixed and known descent. They therefore fall into the class of intermarriage. The individuals in Group *b*, immediately following, are likewise unspecified but they marry persons also of unspecified descent, or of homogeneous and specified descent. We do not know whether this descent is the same or different from that of the individual whom they marry and the entire mating remains partly unspecified.

NOTE.—Throughout this table the figures in parentheses have reference only to the immediate situation specified and to the major group indicated—the British, French, or Slavic total as the case may be. They should not be used in computing the individual row or column totals.

marriages in which one or both parties are native born. Residence in the United States seems to be a necessary contributory element to the fusion of these three stocks.

The 1–1 class offers the greatest variety of new elements in the melting pot because there are more immigrant types to choose from (Table 38).[1]

[1] Table 38 includes only the 1–1 marriages which occurred in the United States. Table 38*a* is presented for purposes of comparison. It includes all 1–1 marriages, those taking place in the United States and those consummated elsewhere.

There are certain conditions involving cultural traits which seem to affect choice. These are the subject of further treatment in the next chapter. It may be well to note in passing that only 8 intermarriages occur between individuals one of whom is derived from an English-speaking group and one of whom claims a foreign language as mother-tongue. Foreigners have in common a sense of aloofness from English-speaking peoples—they have their foreignness in common.

In Tables 38–43 inclusive all marriages are accounted for according to the generation combination in which they fall, excepting 22 cases which were "reject" for generation. These 22 distribute themselves as follows for ethnic descent:

INTRAS
Both Parents

English	1
French Canadian	10
Polish	1
Total	12

DOUBTFUL

Father	Mother	
French Canadian	Unspecified	1
Unspecified	English	1
Unspecified	Ukrainian	1
Unspecified	Unspecified (n.d.)	1
Unspecified	Unspecified	6
Total		10
GRAND TOTAL		22

Table 38 should be used in reconstructing the total of 2,319 matings consummated in the United States. Table 38a should be used in reconstructing the total of 2,876 matings, consummated in either the United States or elsewhere.

ETHNIC PREFERENCE OF MEN AND WOMEN COMPARED[1]

(Tables 44, 45, and 46)

Examination of the data contained in the detailed intermarriage tables seems to warrant the following conclusions regarding any differences which may appear between men and women in the rates of intermarriage and in the preferences which they exert when marrying out of their own groups.

Irish men intermarry freely—34.3 per cent of all Irish men[2] intermarry

[1] See Tables 44, 45, and 46 which summarize all matings among British, French Canadians, and Irish for generation and for ethnic choice.

[2] The intermarriage rates are taken from Tables 31a and 32a in chap. viii.

—but less frequently than Irish women. Irish men, particularly those who are native born, choose first, when they marry out, French-Canadian women (26 cases). Women of mixed descent are a close second (24 cases), but many of these have Irish blood, and these marriages are largely between individuals both of whom are native born. British women are a third choice (20 cases). Three other groups are chosen in marriage (4 cases).

Irish women intermarry freely; 42.1 per cent of all Irish women intermarry. When foreign born their first choice in intermarriage is French Canadian (9 cases), preferably native born. Some of the cultural differences are evidently counteracted by the native origin of the French-Canadian husband. They marry into three other groups (6 cases). When native born, Irish women who marry out choose first and emphatically French-Canadian men (34 cases), with a preference for those who are native born. Their next choice is British (22 cases). The third choice is for men of mixed descent, native born (18 cases), but many of these undoubtedly have Irish blood; five other groups are chosen in marriage (15 cases).

French-Canadian men[1] intermarry infrequently—only 11.9 per cent of all men intermarry—but when they do their first choice is Irish (43 cases); women of mixed descent are second choice (30 cases) and women of British descent third choice (26 cases). They marry into seven other groups (15 cases). The choice does not differ greatly between native-born or foreign-born.

French-Canadian women marry out least frequently—only 10.5 per cent of all French-Canadian women intermarry. Among the foreign-born who intermarry the preference is first for men of mixed descent, probably in part French (13 cases); Irish men constitute a second choice (9 cases) and British a third (7 cases); all others combined (6 cases) represent four nationalities. French-Canadian women who are native born prefer when intermarrying, first, men of mixed descent, probably in part French Canadian (21 cases); second, Irish men (17); third, British men (11). They also marry into six other groups (9 cases). The range of choice is wider than that for foreign-born French-Canadian women, but the most favored stocks do not change rank.

British men, whether foreign or native born, when they intermarry—as 30.2 per cent do—prefer, first, women of mixed descent (34 cases); second, Irish (26); and third, French Canadian (18); three other nationalities are chosen (9 cases).

[1] For further discussion of intermarriage among French Canadians see Appendix A.

TABLE 44

Summary of Ethnic Preference Exerted by British Men and British Women Marrying in the United States*

(Intramarriages Designated in Boldface)

Ethnic Derivation	British Men Of 1st Generation — Marry Women Of 1st Gen.	2x Gen.	Total	British Men Of 2x Generation — Marry Women Of 1st Gen.	2x Gen.	Total	Grand Total	British Women Of 1st Generation — Marry Men Of 1st Gen.	2x Gen.	Total	British Women Of 2x Generation — Marry Men Of 1st Gen.	2x Gen.	Total	Grand Total
Albanian														
Armenian														
Austrian														
Belgian (Flemish)														
British total	**40**	**18**	**58**	**20**	**114**	**134**	**192**	**40**	**20**	**60**	**18**	**114**	**132**	**192**
a) English														
b) Scotch														
c) Scotch-Irish														
d) Canadian English														
e) Canadian Scotch														
f) Canadian unspec.														
g) British mixed														
h) British, others														
Chinese														
Colored														
Czech														
Dutch								1	1	1			1	2
Finnish														
French Canadian	2	5	7	5	6	11	18	1	4	5	8	13	21	26
French, total all others								1	1	1		1	2	3
a) French, France														
b) Walloon														
c) Alsatian														
d) Swiss														
e) French mixed														
German	2		2		2	2	4				1	1	2	2
Greek														
Irish	3	8	11	1	14	15	26	2	4	6	2	12	14	20
Italian									1	1				1
Jewish														
Portuguese (white)														
Roumanian														
Scandinavian total														
a) Swedish	1	1	2		1	1	3					2	2	2
b) Norwegian														
c) Danish		1	1	1		1	2							
Slavic total														
a) Polish														
b) Ukrainian														
c) Russian														
d) Lithuanian														
e) (Galician)														
Spanish														
Syrian														
Turkish														
Mixed ancestry		13	13		21	21	34	2	9	11	1	18	19	30
Unspecified (n.)		3	3		4	4	7		6	6		9	9	15
Other unspecified					1	1	1					1	1	1
TOTAL UNSPECIFIED		3	3		5	5	8		6	6		10	10	16
TOTAL INTRAS	40	18	58	20	114	134	192	40	20	60	18	114	132	192
TOTAL INTERS	8	28	36	7	44	51	87	5	20	25	14	47	61	86
GRAND TOTAL	48	49	97	27	163	190	287	45	46	91	32	171	203	294

* One hundred and seventy-three, or 29.6 per cent, of all British men and women marrying in the United States have intermarried: Eighty-seven, or 30.2 per cent, of the men intermarried; 86, or 29.1 per cent, of the women intermarried. See Tables 30-32a.

TABLE 45

Summary of Ethnic Preference Exerted by French-Canadian Men and Women Marrying in the United States*

(Intramarriages Designated in Boldface)

Ethnic Derivation	French-Canadian Men Of							French-Canadian Women Of						
	1st Generation			2x Generation			Grand Total	1st Generation			2x Generation			Grand Total
	Marry Women Of							Marry Men Of						
	1st Gen.	2x Gen.	Total	1st Gen.	2x Gen.	Total		1st Gen.	2x Gen.	Total	1st Gen.	2x Gen.	Total	
Albanian											1		1	1
Armenian														
Austrian														
Belgian (Flemish)				1		1	1	2		2	1		1	3
British total	1	8	9	4	13	17	26	2	5	7	5	6	11	18
a) English														
b) Scotch														
c) Scotch-Irish														
d) Canadian English														
e) Canadian Scotch														
f) Canadian unspec.														
g) British mixed														
h) British, others														
Chinese														
Colored														
Czech														
Dutch														
Finnish														
French Canadian	221	191	412	137	208	345	757	221	137	358	191	208	399	757
French, total all others	1	2	3	4	1	5	8	3	2	5	5	3	8	13
a) French, France														
b) Walloon														
c) Alsatian														
d) Swiss														
e) French mixed														
German		1	1				1	1		1		1	1	2
Greek														
Irish	1	13	14	8	21	29	43	1	8	9	1	16	17	26
Italian					1	1	1	1		1	4		4	5
Jewish				1		1	1							
Portuguese (white)	1		1				1	2		2	1		1	3
Roumanian														
Scandinavian total														
a) Swedish														
b) Norwegian														
c) Danish											1		1	1
Slavic total														
a) Polish				1	1	2	2							
b) Ukrainian														
c) Russian														
d) Lithuanian														
e) (Galician)														
Spanish														
Syrian														
Turkish														
Mixed ancestry	1	5	6	2	22	24	30	4	9	13	2	19	21	34
Unspecified (n.)		4	4		5	5	9		2	2		12	12	14
Other unspecified					1	1	1							
Total unspecified		4	4		6	6	10		2	2		12	12	14
Total intras	222	193	415	141	209	350	765	224	139	363	196	211	407	770
Total inters	4	27	31	17	58	75	106	13	22	35	16	42	58	93
Grand total	226	224	450	158	273	431	881	237	163	400	212	265	477	877

*One hundred and ninety-nine, or 11.2 per cent, of all French-Canadian men and women marrying in the United States have intermarried: 106, or 11.9 per cent, of the men intermarried; 93, or 10.5 per cent, of the women intermarried. See Tables 30–32a.

TABLE 46

SUMMARY OF ETHNIC PREFERENCE EXERTED BY IRISH MEN AND IRISH WOMEN MARRYING IN THE UNITED STATES*

(Intramarriages Designated in Boldface)

Ethnic Derivation	Irish Men Of 1st Generation — Marry Women Of 1st Gen.	2x Gen.	Total	2x Generation — Marry Women Of 1st Gen.	2x Gen.	Total	Grand Total	Irish Women Of 1st Generation — Marry Men Of 1st Gen.	2x Gen.	Total	2x Generation — Marry Men Of 1st Gen.	2x Gen.	Total	Grand Total
Albanian														
Armenian														
Austrian														
Belgian (Flemish)														
British total	2	2	4	4	12	16	20	3	1	4	8	14	22	26
a) English														
b) Scotch														
c) Scotch-Irish														
d) Canadian English														
e) Canadian Scotch														
f) Canadian unspec.														
g) British mixed														
h) British, others														
Chinese														
Colored												1	1	2	2
Czech														
Dutch														
Finnish														
French Canadian	1	1	2	8	16	24	26	1	8	9	13	21	34	43
French, total all others					2	2	2				4	2	6	6
a) French, France														
b) Walloon														
c) Alsatian														
d) Swiss														
e) French mixed														
German					1	1	1		1	1	1		1	2
Greek														
Irish	24	11	35	19	86	105	140	24	19	43	11	86	97	140
Italian											2	1	3	3
Jewish				1		1	1							
Portuguese (white)														
Roumanian														
Scandinavian total														
a) Swedish											2	1	3	3
b) Norwegian														
c) Danish														
Slavic total														
a) Polish														
b) Ukrainian														
c) Russian														
d) Lithuanian														
e) (Galician)														
Spanish														
Syrian														
Turkish														
Mixed ancestry		1	1		23	23	24		1	1	2	16	18	19
Unspecified (n.)		1	1		1	1	2						3	3
Other unspecified														
TOTAL UNSPECIFIED		1	1		1	1	2						3	3
TOTAL INTRAS	24	11	35	19	86	105	140	24	19	43	11	86	97	140
TOTAL INTERS	3	4	7	13	54	67	74	4	11	15	33	56	89	104
GRAND TOTAL	27	16	43	32	141	173	216	28	30	58	44	145	189	247

* One hundred and seventy-eight, or 38.4 per cent, of all Irish men and women marrying in the United States intermarried: 74, or 34.3 per cent, of the men intermarried; 104, or 42.1 per cent, of the women intermarried. See Tables 30–32a.

British women marry out of their respective groups less frequently than Irish women, but still the per cent of intermarriage is high, 29.1 per cent. Even when foreign born, British women rarely take a foreign-born husband; the first preference is for men of mixed descent, probably Old American in part British (11 cases); Irish (6); French Canadian (5); three others (3). Among native-born women of British descent who marry out, men of mixed descent are again first choice (19 cases); men of French-Canadian descent, second choice (21); and men of Irish descent, third choice (14); four other nationalities are chosen (7 cases).

British men and British women both prefer Americans of mixed descent. But when they marry into Catholic groups they give preference to Irish over against French Catholics. Similarity in religion seems to be an attractive force, and Irish and French Canadians intermarry freely. But when British men marry out of their ethnic group and out of their religion,[1] the Irish are chosen in greater number than are the French Canadians, i.e., language similarity is given preference. Historic conflicts between groups do not seem to deter intermarriage. When it comes to choosing mates in marriage, the Irish in Woonsocket seem quite ready to forgive the French Canadians their antagonism to the hierarchy in Rhode Island, nor are they deterred by British-Irish conflicts in recent history.

IMPLICATIONS

We have previously indicated that the intermarriage of grandparents represented the genesis of the melting pot.[2] The precedent established in that generation has been most emphatically followed and the process accelerated in this generation. With but one exception exactly the same summary paragraph describes the new situation:

"The melting pot as an American phenomenon has its genesis in the intermarriage of grandparents. The original elements in the melting pot are most largely British, Irish, and French Canadian, although some ten or twelve other groups each make some contribution. The British are most frequently preferred as mates by both Irish and French Canadians, although the preferences differ somewhat for men and for women. The Irish are more frequently chosen by the British than by the French Canadians. These preferences are undoubtedly in large measure determined by the dominance of these groups in the Woonsocket of that period."

[1] This is an assumption. No evidence was secured on the faith of individuals mating. For further discussion of the religious factor see chap. x.

[2] Chap. iv, p. 46.

The exception refers to the fact that the order of choice has changed within these classes. Among the parents Irish are chosen most frequently, French Canadians next, and British least frequently.

But here again the situation as regards choice may well have been limited by the peculiar conditions governing choice in Woonsocket. One thing is certain, that when the British and Irish were the major stocks they chose each other in marriage. When the French Canadians came in large numbers these three groups chose mates from among each other. As the French Canadians increased in number, intermarriage with them also increased. With the coming of other and more recent immigrants there is an increasing number of intermarriages which account for new strains in the melting pot—Italian, Portuguese, Polish. In the older generations the minor contributions were Dutch and Scandinavian. In addition, the amalgamation of several Slavic stocks into a general Slavic stock is distinctly characteristic of the parental generation.

The number of cases with which we are dealing is frequently small, and should serve as a caution against too hasty generalization about group tendencies. On the other hand, this is all the evidence for the entire community—the families of all children in the public schools.

The end-results are due to two interacting sets of causes: on the one hand, racial idiosyncrasies or customs, and, on the other, the environmental factors within the given community which play upon these tendencies. Final judgment as to how individual groups behave must await other community studies which will indicate whether this behavior varies, if it does, from community to community. On the whole, the behavior of these groups in Woonsocket seems to corroborate, in general, tendencies observed elsewhere for these same groups—with some modification usually imposed by the community. As we have noted, the Irish and British, for example, intermarry freely in every one of the several communities surveyed by the author. But ethnic preference which these groups could exert was necessarily limited in Woonsocket. In Stamford, Connecticut, each of these groups exerts a much wider range of choice, though every community offers cumulative evidence that there are many individuals in this country of British-Irish descent. As a check upon any too hasty generalization which may be drawn on the face of the Woonsocket data, it is helpful to have for comparison the figures obtained from the parallel study made in Stamford.

The data for both cities were examined for comparative purposes, and the evidence on trends and preference for the two communities was compared.[1] There is striking similarity in the behavior of specific groups in different communities. Not only are the tendencies to intermarry corroborated, but certain social factors seem to function with equal potency in different situations. A special study was made of the conditions which seem to accompany intermarriage with particular reference to 1–1 matings in both Woonsocket and Stamford, covering in all 319 cases of 1–1 intermarriage. These intermarriages were examined for place of marriage, length of residence in the United States at time of marriage, mother-tongue, and language usage.

The findings are useful in further interpreting the conditions which make for amalgamation and are the subject matter of the following chapter.

SUMMARY

The purpose of this chapter has been to discover the preferences which are exerted in ethnic crossing. The unit of enumeration is the mating. In this way a picture is obtained of strains which unite in marriage.

Four hundred and ninety-one intermarriages took place in the United States. The first and emphatic choice is for a mate from one's very own stock and background. Failing to obtain a mate from one's own origin, the choice is frequently for one from a kindred group. A member of one British stock chooses a mate from another British stock. A member derived from one French stock chooses a mate from another French stock. In at least 75.0 per cent of the cases men and women have chosen mates from their own ethnic derivation. In 21.2 per cent of the cases intermarriage was definitely established. (In 3.8 per cent of the cases the data included grandparents of native descent further unspecified and therefore doubtful as to homogeneity.)

An increased percentage of admixture is characteristic of the older generations. Intermarriage is over three times as frequent in the 2–2 generation as it is in the 1–1 generation, and over five times as frequent in the 3–2 combinations as it is in the 1–1 generation. Forty-four per cent of all 3–2 combinations are cases of intermarriage.

As a result of the 491 intermarriages, 982 individuals have been brought into the melting pot—199 French Canadians, 178 Irish, 173 British, and 432 others representing 22 different European stocks.

The preferences exerted in cross-marriage serve to bring into the melting pot, in large measure, the same racial elements and the same type of

---

[1] See chap. i, p. 8, for reference to investigation by Alice M. Towsley, also chap. x for further discussion of findings.

admixture initiated by the grandparents at the inception of the "melting pot" in Woonsocket. There is a slight shift in numerical emphasis. The French Canadians and Irish supersede the British in importance, but on the whole these three groups choose one another freely in marriage. Within the French-Canadian–British–Irish alliance the Irish are chosen more frequently both by British and by French Canadians. Slavs prefer other Slavs when marrying out.

Refinement of the data on the basis of a generation grouping throws light on ethnic preferences in the 1–1 group, as compared with those of older groups. The outstanding characteristic of 1–1 matings is that 26 out of a total of 73 intermarriages are intermarriages between individuals of different Slavic strains. Only 10 marriages are of the French-Canadian–British–Irish variety. The admixture of these three elements is largely the result of matings in which one or both parties are native born. They prefer each other after some Americanization has wiped out the initial differences.

Preferences differ somewhat for men and women and from generation to generation. Data are recorded in full. Irish women intermarry freely and into several groups. British men are first choice; French Canadians, second choice, preferably when native born. British men and women prefer Old Americans of mixed descent, but when they marry into Catholic groups Irish are given preference over French Canadians.

Men or women of mixed descent most frequently choose a mate who bears some similar strain.

Individuals from foreign-language groups who intermarry in the first generation favor another foreign-language group rather than an English-speaking group.

Undoubtedly the "preferences" are determined by the situation in the community which governs availability, but there are, in addition, tendencies and preferences among nationalities which exert themselves over and above these conditions.

CHAPTER X

SOCIAL FACTORS IN INTERMARRIAGE

Further interpretation of the data on intermarriage requires additional information regarding cultural factors which are associated with assimilation. Much more cumulative evidence is needed before any generalizations can be made regarding those factors which seem to determine or accelerate ethnic fusion. The summary given in the next few pages represents certain conditions which are associated with the intermarriages under discussion. The conclusions are derived in large measure from a report on a special investigation[1] by Alice M. Towsley, formerly a member of the staff. Histories covering all 1–1 intermarriages in Woonsocket and Stamford were examined for the social traits noted. In each community Poles and Irish constitute numerically important groups. The investigation was therefore not limited to 1–1 cases in these nationalities, but included all intermarriages, those among native as well as among foreign-born individuals. The data given here deal more particularly with Woonsocket,[2] reference being made to any outstanding differences between these and the Stamford data whenever such exist.

PLACE, AGE, AND LENGTH OF RESIDENCE IN THE UNITED STATES

In Woonsocket 76.8 per cent of all the admixture in the 1–1 generation is due to intermarriage which took place in this country; while only 23.2 per cent of the intermarriages took place elsewhere. By comparison with Stamford this is a higher per cent of foreign intermarriage, since only 18.0 per cent of the 1–1 intermarriages in that city took place outside of the United States. This higher percentage of foreign intermarriage in Woonsocket is due in part to the proximity of Canada, and in part to the fact, previously indicated, that cross-Slavic, French-Flemish, and British-Irish intermarriages have their origin in Europe. These types form a good proportion of the cases in Woonsocket.

[1] *Op. cit.* See chap. i, p. 8.

[2] In order to make the materials in Miss Towsley's report strictly comparable with the procedure in the present monograph, I have had to interpret her figures and results, and on the basis of my own knowledge of the data have translated them into terms strictly comparable with the rest of the presentation. In several instances the figures, therefore, are different from those given in her report.

Length of residence in the United States and age at the time of marriage might well constitute important factors in the amount of intermarriage which takes place. The longer the residence in this country, the greater, presumably, the degree of Americanization. Since languages are acquired readily in youth, it might be supposed that the ability to speak English has been acquired and that it offers one point of contact at least. It is not expedient to give the detailed distributions for these data, but the foregoing assumption is supported by the facts at hand. The median age of the foreign-born women in Woonsocket who intermarried with foreign-born men was twenty-two years at the time of marriage, and the median age for foreign-born men who intermarried with foreign-born women was twenty-seven years. The average length of residence in the United States was four years for the women and five years for the men. The data for Stamford were similar.

REGIONAL DERIVATION OF CONTRACTING PARTIES

The evidence on birthplace as well as that on language usage among those who intermarry throws light on cultural factors which may possibly have led to intermarriage. An examination of all 1–1 histories indicates that even when the contracting parties are of different ethnic origins, and even when the marriage takes place in the United States, the contracting parties were in many instances born in the same European country.[1] An even larger number were born in neighboring countries. This indicates the strong rôle played in intermarriage by the community of interests arising from common background. It also calls attention to the fact that migration back and forth between European countries must be taken into consideration in interpreting our data. Peoples of diverse nationality inhabit the same political territory; many of the intermarriages in this country are really between men and women who have been brought up in the same country and who have in consequence a host of common ties.

One region which illustrates this situation is former Galicia, a territory which has been apportioned among several nations since the war. Coming from this territory we find Ukrainians, Poles, Jews, Russians, and other stocks. First examination of the data indicates a decided tendency for Polish and Ukrainian people to intermarry. Upon detailed examination of the family histories it develops that the persons mating were brought up in the same community or in neighboring communities in

---

[1] This has significance for methodological procedure. If birthplace were used as a criterion of nationality these marriages would fall in the category of intramarriage.

Galicia. There are in Woonsocket 20 Polish-Ukrainian marriages. In 13 cases both of the contracting parties were born in Galicia. It is for this reason that Galicia and other regions presenting similar situations were retained in the list for geographic derivation, even though our classification is based primarily upon post-war boundaries.[1] This seemed advisable not only because a number of individuals who claim Galicia as their birth-place are unable to give the post-war name of the region in which they were born, but more so because it permits a record of this type of situation. The migration back and forth in the Slavic states of Russia, Poland, and the Ukraine, and the general similarity of cultural background, offer an explanation of intermarriage among these groups. France, Belgium, and the Alsace constitute another group of countries which may be mentioned in this same category. Alsace, like Galicia, was retained in our classification on the same principle. The frequency with which Belgians give France as their birthplace indicates that there is a considerable migration back and forth in these countries, and that common residence in some foreign country is one of the conditions antecedent to intermarriage in this country. Ethnic groups who have had contact in Europe find this contact a bond in the United States.

The part that identical or adjacent birthplace plays in the intermarriage question is obvious from the fact that in 78 per cent of the 1–1 intermarriages the contracting parties report birthplace either in the same country or in adjacent[2] countries. And this figure is exclusive of kindred[3] matings in which the contracting parties almost invariably claim similar regional derivation.

LANGUAGE SIMILARITY

Language similarity is closely allied with regional proximity, and indeed flows from it. The evidence on this score indicates that language similarity plays an important part in marital choice. Persons having similar culture and using similar languages marry each other more readily than do those speaking entirely different languages.

[1] See chapter on "Procedure."

[2] The following regions were classed by Miss Towsley as adjacent countries:
> British Isles
> Scandinavia and Finland
> Alsace, Belgium, France
> Slavic countries:
>> Russia, Galicia, the Ukraine, and Lithuania;
>> Czecho-Slovakia and Jugoslavia

[3] British mixed, French mixed, etc. Similarly it was found that in several instances two Irish persons marrying in this country claim Canada as birthplace.

Common knowledge of the same language or of a kindred language on the part of contracting parties occurs in the large majority of cases; English and Irish have in common the English language (at least); Belgians of Flemish descent are familiar with French and marry freely into French stocks—Walloon, Alsatian, and "France French." For example, in every case in which a Belgian of Flemish descent has married out of his Flemish group, either in the United States or elsewhere, the other party to the marriage is of some French descent. In all, 7 such marriages took place in the United States and 8 elsewhere.

Examination of the data on language usage indicates that among the 92 cases of 1–1 intermarriage in Woonsocket the language origin of parents is as follows: in 8 cases one person is derived from an English-speaking group and the other from a foreign-language group; in 14 cases both are derived from the same language group. The 26 Slavic cases might be grouped together as a kindred language group. Only 14 cases are derived from two different language groups. In 10 other cases one parent is of mixed-descent mating with a German-speaking person in 1 case and with French-speaking persons in 9 other cases. There probably was language similarity in these 9 cases at the time of marriage. It seems logical to assume also that in the first group of 8 cases English is a learned language on the part of the individual who claims descent from a foreign-language group.

The detailed distribution is given below:

One person is derived from an English-speaking group and the other from a foreign language; 8 cases as follows:

Irish × French Canadian.................	2
English × French Canadian...............	3
English × German......................	2
English × Swedish......................	1

Both are derived from the same language group; 14 cases as follows:

English × Irish.........................	5
French × Belgian.......................	7
British × Mixed........................	2

Both are derived from a kindred language group—multilingualism occurs frequently and both parties are familiar with one or more languages in common. In this respect the Slavs constitute a class all by themselves—26 cases.

Each person is derived from a different language group; 14 cases as follows:

3 Portuguese×French Canadian	1 German ×French
4 Italian×French or French Canadian	1 Greek×Roumanian
2 Italian×Polish	1 Norwegian×Roumanian
1 German×Polish	1 Norwegian×Swedish

One parent is of mixed descent, with evidence on language origin uncertain; 10 cases as follows:

$$\text{Mixed×French.................} \quad 9$$
$$\text{Mixed×German.................} \quad 1$$

We find only 14 cases of intermarriage between individuals derived from two different foreign-language groups. In at least 9 of these cases Catholicism may offer a common bond of interest, since the individuals involved are French Canadian, Portuguese, Italian, and Polish. Only 5 cases are left which are not explained in terms of cultural similarity having its origin in religion or language. Even here at least 3 cases can be attributed to cultural intimacy between the two groups antecedent to American life. The German-Polish marriage and the Norwegian-Swedish marriage undoubtedly have their roots in such cultural contact. The Greek-Roumanian marriage falls in the same category, when we recall the scattered geographic origin of our Roumanians, and the fact that in several instances their geographic derivation is Greece. These common experiences in the life-history of individuals offer a bond of union even when the marriage takes place in the United States. The Norwegian-Roumanian marriage is the single one which cannot be explained in terms of cultural similarity, or previous cultural contact. There might be some difference of opinion as to the German-French marriage, but on the whole the evidence is preponderant for common cultural experience somewhere in the family.

The question arises, What happens so far as language usage is concerned in homes of mixed descent when neither parent claims English as an ancestral language? In following up this problem Miss Towsley finds that over 60 per cent of such families report the daily use of some foreign language. In Woonsocket French-speaking and Slavic-speaking peoples together are responsible for the high proportion of homes which retain the use of a foreign language even when the parents are not identical in ethnic derivation. Families in which one parent is of French descent have an additional inducement to retain French, since in Woonsocket they do not need to learn English in order to get along. They can use their own language in their own colony, and they can use French as well, or even better, than English in their trade relations. Clerks almost without exception speak French as well as English, sometimes French being the only language spoken or the language in which a prospective purchaser is addressed. It has been noted elsewhere that many public-school children who are not themselves of French descent report the use of French.

There is no evidence that either the father's or the mother's language is given preference. As many cases report the adoption of the mother's language as of the father's language. Frequently the mother never learns to speak English, but since the children speak it she learns to comprehend what is said. The father, as a rule, learns to speak English more quickly than the mother, since he has wider contact outside the home. In the cases where one parent is of Polish descent and one of Ukrainian descent there seems to be a decided tendency for the Ukrainian tongue to replace the Polish. Out of the 20 Polish-Ukrainian marriages in Woonsocket, Ukrainian was retained as the language of common use in 17 cases; Polish in only 3. Only one of these families reports also the use of English.

RELIGIOUS PREFERENCE

Religious preference[1] in intermarriage must be largely conjectured, since the investigation did not ask for information on religious affiliation. It would seem inconsistent, therefore, to discuss this phase of the problem in a monograph otherwise based upon inductive procedure, except for the fact that empirical observation, and some of the data on hand, open up leads for possible further discussion. Record is here made of what positive data we do have.

In the communities in which these investigations were conducted, it may be taken for granted that certain language groups are loyally Catholic. We recall that in Woonsocket the Irish and French Canadians intermarried most frequently. Such marriages are consummated as a rule in Catholic churches but they were, nevertheless, regarded with apprehension by some of the French Catholic priests with whom the investigators discussed the matter.

Curiously enough the Italians, a like religious group, are chosen but in-

[1] The pages just preceding dealt, necessarily, only with 1–1 intermarriages. The references from here on are to all persons who intermarry in the given unit, whether they are foreign born, native born, or of native descent.

frequently in marriage by the Irish, and less frequently in Stamford where they constitute the major ethnic group. There are as many Irish-Italian marriages in Woonsocket as there are in Stamford, even though the Italian population is more than six times as large in the latter city.[1] The only possible interpretation of this situation is that in Stamford the Italians are a first-generation group, while the Irish are largely native born, so that in general the Italians are a lower-prestige group. We find elsewhere that continued residence in America is necessary to wipe out cultural difference. It may indeed wipe out religious differences too. The Germans constitute a significant group in Stamford, and we find that 12.9 per cent of the Irish who intermarry marry Germans and Scandinavians, a fact which would call attention to the ethnic set-up of the community and generation in the country as a conditioning factor in choice.

THE RELATION OF MIGRATION TO INTERMARRIAGE[2]

The relation of migration to intermarriage is a subject alluring in the extreme. Examination of the data relating to regions of origin brings into perspective a continual shifting of population. So many and so numerous are the migrations even within family lines that an attempt to arrange families into some sort of orderly grouping seems at first well-nigh impossible: We have 2,876 families each recording 7 birthplaces—1 for the child, 2 for the parents, and 4 for the grandparents. The relationship of these birthplaces to one another, within each family, constitutes cultural variables of utmost significance in the cultural adjustment of the family. Research problems present themselves here in quick succession. As the data are put into some orderly array, a panorama of migration presents itself which brings to light the movement of whole ethnic groups from one habitat to another—at one time assuming cultural traits, at another time sloughing them off, as the occasion or the environment demands.

Only one of these problems was followed up in this investigation, namely, the relation of migration to intermarriage. The number of birthplaces recorded for each family is a minimum record of migration, particularly if all members claim the same descent. Thus an Irish family may

[1] The total number of parents in Stamford is 10,204 as against 5,752 in Woonsocket. There are 883 Irish parents in Stamford, 2,363 Italian parents, and 421 German parents. There are 3 Irish-Italian intermarriages in Woonsocket and only 4 in Stamford.

[2] This subject was not covered in the Towsley report.

report birthplaces in England, Ireland, Canada, and the United States. A Jewish family may report birthplaces for its members in the Ukraine, Austria, Poland, and Germany. Ethnic groups vary in mobility.

Almost one-half of the families record derivation from two or more places, as that is determined by birthplace. The distribution is as follows:[1]

1,458 families report the same birthplace for parents and grandparents
1,091 families report 2 or more birthplaces
264 families report 3 birthplaces
40 families report 4 birthplaces
1 family reports 5 birthplaces

These data undoubtedly have significant bearing upon cultural traits discussed elsewhere. At the present moment our inquiry is limited to facts of intermarriage. When the same foreign birthplace is recorded for all six ancestors the rate of intermarriage is 1.4 per cent. When the United States is recorded as the birthplace for all six ancestors the rate of intermarriage is 40.5 per cent. When 2 birthplaces are recorded for the family the per cent of intermarriage rises to 27. When 3 or more birthplaces are recorded the per cent of intermarriage is from 95 to 100.

It does not seem feasible to present the raw material and tabulations from which these conclusions are derived. It requires a record of all families on a geographic basis in the same manner as it has been made upon an ethnic basis throughout the monograph, a procedure which is obviously not practicable. The histories were individually examined by the investigator and the results as summarized are derived from the work sheets.

In the following list we have merely a summary which may indicate the multiplicity of migratory types which exist in this population. More detailed tabulation would indicate that there is a constant relationship between the number of birthplaces and the number of intermarriages. The percentage of intermarriage rises directly with the number of birthplaces. For example, in the 2–1 generation no intermarriage was recorded in Class I with 285 cases—all 4 grandparents having been born in the same country. However, in the next two classes, II and III, 60 cases of intermarriage are reported out of a total number of 76 cases—in these classes grandparents report 3 birthplaces. All the marriages in Classes IV and V were intermarriages; here the grandparents report 4 and 5 birthplaces. This situation repeats itself in the other generation groupings.

[1] The histories of 22 families are incomplete on this score.

AN ETHNIC SURVEY

LIST GIVING MIGRATORY HISTORY OF FAMILIES

(See p. 156 for List of Symbols Used in Table)

MIGRATORY TYPE		NUMBER OF BIRTH- PLACES	GENERATION OF PARENTS	NUMBER OF CASES	NUMBER OF INTERM.*	PER CENT OF INTERM.
Regional Origin Of	Parents					
Grandparents	Fa.-Mo.					
		1–1				
I. B-B-B-B..........	b-b	1	....	1,313	....	....
	c-c	2	....	5	....	....
	c-b	2	....	8	....	....
II. B-B-C-C..........	b-b	2	....	5	....	....
	c-c	2	....	6	....	....
	c-b	2	....	102	....	....
	d-b	3	....	9	....	....
III.† B-B-B-C..........	b-b	2	....	10	....	....
	b-c	2	....	9	....	....
	c-c	2	....	2	....	....
	d-b	3	....	1	....	....
IV. B-B-C-D..........	b-b	3	....	3	....	....
	c-b	3	....	3	....	....
	d-b	3	....	3	....	....
	d-d	3	....	1	....	....
	d-c	3	....	2	....	....
	c-c	3	....	1	....	....
V. B-C-B-C..........	c-c	2	....	1	....	....
VI. B-C-B-D..........	d-d	3	....	1	....	....
VII.† A-B-B-B..........	b-b(M)‡	2	....	12	....	....
VIII. A-A-B-B..........	b-b(M)	2	....	1	....	....
Total.............	....	....	....	1,498	95	6.3

* See Tables 16 and 16b.

† This is a summary group made up of four smaller groups. In each of these groups three grandparents were born in one country and the fourth in another country. But the sequence is not always the same. The C or A represents any one grandparent who does not claim the same birthplace as the others. Actually there are four possibilities for the position of C or A. All possibilities were represented in the data. This procedure was adopted throughout the list for grandparents. In the case of parents it is indicated to which one of the parents the symbol refers.

‡ These cases marked M represent a migratory type in a special sense; parents are foreign born in spite of the fact that grandparents are native born. The grandparents emigrated from the United States; the parents migrated back again. The grandparents, however, were of foreign descent. If the grandparents are of native origin and the residence elsewhere temporary in the list of family, as in the case of missionaries, government officials, etc., the family is classed as native.

LIST GIVING MIGRATORY HISTORY OF FAMILIES—*Continued*

Migratory Type Regional Origin Of		Number of Birth-places	Generation of Parents	Number of Cases	Number of Interm.*	Per Cent of Interm.
Grandparents	Parents Fa.-Mo.					
			2-1			
I. *B-B-B-B*	*b-a*	2	....	169	....	....
	a-b	2	....	115	....	....
	a-c	3	....	1	....	....
II. *B-B-C-C*	*a-b*	3	....	22	....	....
	c-a	3	....	34	....	....
	c-a	3	....	2	....	....
	a-d	4	....	1	....	....
III.† *B-B-B-C*	*b-a*	3	....	... 5	....	....
	a-b	3	....	7	....	....
	c-a	3	....	4	....	....
	a-c	3	....	1	....	....
IV. *B-C-D-D*	*a-b*	4	....	3	....	....
	d-a	4	....	3	....	....
	c-a	4	....	1	....	....
V. *B-C-D-E*	*e-a*	5	....	1	....	....
VI.† *A-B-B-B(M)‡*	*b-a*	2	....	1	....	....
VII.† *A-B-B-B(M)*	*c-a*	3	....	1	....	....
VIII. *A-B-B-C(M)*	*c-a*	3	....	1	....	....
Partly incomplete	*a-b*	2	....	11	....	....
	b-a	2	....	8	....	....
Total	....	....	....	391	69	17.6

LIST GIVING MIGRATORY HISTORY OF FAMILIES—*Continued*

Migratory Type — Regional Origin Of Grandparents	Parents Fa.-Mo.	Number of Birth-places	Generation of Parents	Number of Cases	Number of Interm.*	Per Cent of Interm.
3–1						
I. A-A-B-B..........	b-a	2	....	51	....	....
	a-b	2	....	48	....	....
	c-a	3	....	1	....	....
II. A-A-B-C..........	b-a	3	....	2	....	....
	c-a	3	....	1	....	....
	a-c	3	....	3	....	....
	a-d	4	....	3	....	....
Total..............	....	....	....	109	39	35.8
(3/2)–1						
I. A-B-B-B..........	b-a	2	....	19	....	....
	a-b	2	....	14	....	....
II. A-B-B-C..........	d-a	4	....	1	....	....
	a-d	4	....	1	....	....
	c-a	3	....	1	....	....
	a-b	3	....	13	....	....
III. B-A-B-B..........	b-a	2	....	18	....	....
	a-b	2	....	16	....	....
	c-a	3	....	1	....	....
IV. A-B-C-C..........	b-a	3	....	1	....	....
	c-a	3	....	18	....	....
V. B-A-C-D..........	c-a	4	....	1	....	....
	a-c	4	....	1	....	....
	d-a	4	....	1	....	....
Total..............	....	....	(3/2)–1	106	46	43.3
2–2						
I. B-B-B-B..........	a-a	2	....	162	....	....
II. B-B-C-C..........	a-a	3	....	41	....	....
III. B-B-B-C..........	a-a	3	....	14	....	....
IV. B-C-B-C..........	a-a	3	....	7	....	....
V. B-B-C-D..........	a-a	4	....	11	....	....
VI. B-C-B-D..........	a-a	4	....	2	....	....
Total..............	....	....	....	237	56	23.6

LIST GIVING MIGRATORY HISTORY OF FAMILIES—*Continued*

MIGRATORY TYPE		NUMBER OF BIRTH-PLACES	GENERATION OF PARENTS	NUMBER OF CASES	NUMBER OF INTERM.*	PER CENT OF INTERM.
Regional Origin Of						
Parents						
Grandparents	Fa.-Mo.					
All 3–2 Combinations:						
3–2						
I. *A-A-B-B*.........	*a-a*	2	....	106	....	....
II. *A-A-B-C*.........	*a-a*	3	....	12	....	....
(3/2)–2						
I. *A-B-B-B*.........	*a-a*	2	....	94	....	....
II. *A-B-C-B*.........	*a-a*	3	....	15	....	....
III. *A-B-C-C*.........	*a-a*	3	....	26	....	....
IV. *A-B-C-D*.........	*a-a*	4	....	11	....	....
3–(3/2)						
I. *A-A-A-B*.........	*a-a*	2	....	79	....	....
(3/2)–(3/2)						
I. *A-B-B-A*.........	*a-a*	2	....	19	....	....
II. *A-B-A-C*.........	*a-a*	3	....	6	....	....
Grand total for 3–2....	....	....	....	368	162	44.0
3–3						
I. *A-A-A-A*.........	*a-a*	1	....	145	46	40.5
Incomplete.............	....	....	....	22	....	....
GRAND TOTAL........	....	....	....	2,876	513	17.8

LIST OF SYMBOLS USED IN TABLE PERTAINING TO BIRTHPLACE OR REGIONAL
ORIGIN OF PARENTS AND GRANDPARENTS

a, b, c, etc.—Small letters refer to the birthplace of parents

A, B, C, etc.—Capital letters refer to birthplace of grandparents

a or *A*.—Signifies native origin (All other letters indicate foreign origin. Each new letter indicates a different birthplace from the preceding ones.)

ILLUSTRATIONS

A-A-A-A aa.—Signifies that all six immediate ancestors of the child are native born

B-B-B-B bb.—Signifies that all six immediate ancestors of the child are foreign born and that all were born in the same region

B-B-C-C bc.—Signifies that two grandparents and one parent were born in one country and two grandparents and the other parent were born in another country

CONCLUSION

Contact and proximity are necessarily conditions of intermarriage, but frequent migration undoubtedly stimulates intermarriage even when mates are available from one's own group. In addition, common residence in a new country helps to bring about that cultural similarity which we found to be a factor in determining intermarriage. Cultural similarity based upon common ethnic descent accounts for the large degree of intramarriage; but intermarriage proceeds rapidly as cultural similarity is established through migration and contact. Persons who have lived in the same country and who speak the same language join frequently in marriage. The country may be Galicia, Canada, Alsace, or, with increasing frequency, the United States. When intermarriage occurs in this country between two foreign-born persons, it is usually between persons who report cultural similarity of some kind.

CHAPTER XI[1]

INDICES OF RACIAL INFLUENCE: THE BEHAVIOR OF STOCKS IN DIFFUSION; MANNER OF DIFFUSION

We have now traveled with some twenty-two thousand people[2] over the face of the globe through three generations in the attempt to study the relationships which may account for the present population in Woonsocket—more particularly in reference to those factors and conditions which lead to ethnic fusion.

In the course of our investigation we have established several measures of change. We know that these peoples are fusing slowly but surely into an American population at certain "rates" and in accordance with definite and varied tendencies on the part of specific groups. To be able to arrive at quantitative measures for these trends and for population changes which they effect may be deemed laudable by those who insist upon quantitative symbols by way of explanation. But does the ardor for such quantitative measures cool when we discover that any one of several measures, each apparently at variance with the other, may be used to describe the same general process?

Thus far several different measures have been used to describe the general fusion process. In chapter iii we established measures of diffusion descriptive of what had already taken place. Later in chapters vi and vii we discussed percentages of admixture characteristic of the population. Still later in chapter ix we spoke of rates of intermarriage—of the trends among specific groups and of the general trend to homogeneity in the community at large as a result of cross-marriage. And now we are about to propose two other measures of population change. But why? Since the various measures of change already presented corroborate one another, what end is served by these many and complicated analyses? The fact is that no single figure may be taken entirely to indicate ethnic change or fusion. Any one of these might be said to measure change. There are, however, several processes at work which make for differential rates of

---

[1] This chapter, in so far as it deals with the A index, is a revision of a former statement on the subject entitled "The Index of Racial Influence," presented at a meeting of the Eugenics Research Association, June, 1929, and published in *Eugenics*, II (December, 1929), 12. The B index was not discussed in the earlier paper.

[2] There are 4,978 children, 5,752 parents, and 11,504 grandparents.

fusion, and the picture is incomplete unless the several indices descriptive of all these processes are called into use.

Each of these measures applies only to some specific phase of the subject, and while they contribute to the picture as a whole, no one symbol may be said to describe the whole situation. Some are sensitive to one set of changes, and some to others. If we make an array of these measures, we find some apparent discrepancies which provoke further inquiry and demand explanation. For example, the data for French Canadians derived from Table 2 are as follows:

34.9 per cent is the numerical equivalent for French-Canadian stock in the population of children

30.5 per cent is the numerical equivalent for French-Canadian homogeneous stock in the population of children

4.4 per cent is the numerical equivalent for French-Canadian stock in the melting pot

12.6 per cent is the measure of the diffusion of French-Canadian elements

9.1 per cent, however, represents the amount of intermarriage among French Canadians, all generations combined (Table 28a)

Which of these figures is more significant? Moreover, the numerical equivalent of French-Canadian stock in the melting pot is only 4.4 per cent. This amount of French-Canadian stock, however, is distributed through 8.7 per cent of the children—the number who are part French Canadian and part something else.[1]

If we examine the data for other groups, we find similar differences. But these differences are not constant. The extent to which a given amount of stock affects the population varies for the different groups. The indication is that the rates of intermarriage and the percentages of admixture do not tell the whole story. One differential influence is piled upon another, and together these effect changes in the population. Can we locate the factors which serve to create such differentials?

The percentages of diffusion and the rates of intermarriage describe the amount of admixture. Ethnic choice in marriage determines the nature of admixture, but these two do not altogether account for the resultant population. Natural rates of increase, migration, and long-time influences in general all contribute to the final result in composition. The problem is to find a tool which will indicate the relative strength which various groups have in the genetic process of stock formation. The "Index of Racial Influence" represents an attempt to formulate such a tool.

[1] See Table 48. Of the total number of children in public school, 1,950, or 39.2 per cent, report some French-Canadian blood; 1,516, or 30.5 per cent, are homogeneous French Canadians. The remainder, 8.7 per cent, are in the melting pot.

THE "A" INDEX OF RACIAL INFLUENCE

(Tables 47, 48, and 48a)

In order to test the thesis which the author has in mind, and to indicate what it is, it will be necessary to reverse the whole process of analysis which has hitherto been adopted. In the early part of this investigation we began with the grandparents and traced the advent of our school population through the matings of grandparents and then of parents. In this chapter we shall begin with the children, classifying them in a way which will describe the manner in which each stock has diffused itself through the population. In this instance we shall locate the grandparents

TABLE 47

A INDICES FOR MAJOR GROUPS

	Num. Equiv. of Each Stock in Population* (a)	Per Cent of 4,978 Children Carrying Given Strain† (b)	Index A =100b/a‡ (c)
British...................	12.2	17.5	143
French Canadians..........	34.9	39.2	112
Irish....................	9.3	13.8	148
Italians..................	8.6	8.9	103
Jewish..................	3.9	3.9	100
Slavic groups combined.....	18.3	19.9	108

* Data are derived from Table 48a, col. f.
† Data are derived from Table 48, col. f.
‡ Or the formula indicated on p. 170 may be used to derive this index.

via the children. If our techniques have been correct, we must arrive ultimately at the numerical equivalents previously established and incidentally make some discoveries en route.

The chief problem is, In what manner, other than that previously described, have the racial strains been diffused to account for the results we have indicated? How does it happen that 4.4 per cent of the stock which is French Canadian becomes diffused through 8.7 per cent of the children, and that 4.5 per cent of the stock that is British and in diffusion is carried, as we shall see, by 9.8 per cent of the children?

The process by which a stock spreads itself over the population may be made clear by counting the number of children who carry that strain, according to the degree in which they carry the strain. If a child bears two or more strains he is counted two or more times according to the number of grandparents he has of each strain. Thus a child may have four British grandparents, or he may have only three British grandparents, two, or

TABLE 48

4,978 Children Classified by Number of Grandparents of Given Strain

Ethnic Derivation	Four Grand-parents (a)	Three Grand-parents (b)	Two Grand-parents (c)	One Grand-parent (d)	Total Number of Children Bearing Given Strain (e)	Per Cent of 4,978 Children Bearing Given Strain (f)
Albanian................	1	....	1	....	2	*
Armenian...............	33	....	....	2	35	.7
Austrian...............	....	....	....	....	....	....
Belgian (Flemish)........	9	4	16	8	37	.7
British total..........	385	62	269	155	871	17.5
a) English............	....	....	....	....	....	....
b) Scotch.............	....	....	....	....	....	....
c) Scotch-Irish........	....	....	....	....	....	....
d) Canadian English.....	....	....	....	....	....	....
e) Canadian Scotch......	....	....	....	....	....	....
f) Canadian unspec.....	....	....	....	....	....	....
g) British mixed.......	....	....	....	....	....	....
h) British, others.....	....	....	....	....	....	....
Chinese................	3	....	....	....	3	*
Colored................	9	....	4	....	13	.3
Czech.................	2	....	....	....	2	*
Dutch.................	....	....	5	19	24	.5
Finnish................	2	....	2	....	4	.1
French Canadian.........	1,516	62	321	51	1,950	39.2
French, total all others....	112	17	41	35	205	4.1
a) French, France.......	....	....	....	....	....	....
b) Walloon............	....	....	....	....	....	....
c) Alsatian...........	....	....	....	....	....	....
d) Swiss..............	....	....	....	....	....	....
e) French mixed........	....	....	....	....	....	....
German................	7	4	38	42	91	1.8
Greek.................	21	....	2	....	23	.5
Irish.................	272	47	256	112	687	13.8
Italian................	414	....	29	1	444	8.9
Jewish................	191	....	4	1	196	3.9
Portuguese (white)........	27	1	10	2	40	.8
Roumanian..............	40	....	3	....	43	.9
Scandinavian total........	35	....	21	17	73	1.4
a) Swedish............	34	....	14	14	62	1.2
b) Norwegian...........	....	....	2	3	5	.1
c) Danish.............	1	....	5	....	6	.1
Slavic total.............	838	....	152	....	990	19.9
a) Polish.............	493	....	73	....	566	11.4
b) Ukrainian...........	325	....	57	....	382	7.7
c) Russian............	18	....	17	....	35	.7
d) Lithuanian..........	2	....	5	....	7	.1
e) (Galician)..........	....	....	....	....	....	....
Spanish................	....	....	....	3	3	*
Syrian................	71	....	....	....	71	1.4
Turkish................	....	....	....	....	....	....
Mixed grandparents.......	....	....	1	8	9	.2
Unspecified (n.d.)........	37	17	113	96	263	5.3
Others unspecified........	6	....	9	....	15	.3
GRAND TOTAL........	4,031	214	1,297	552	....	....

* Less than .1 per cent.

one. Table 48 is a summary table indicating how the stocks are actually distributed in this manner. The counts inevitably overlap. The object is always to determine: How many children carry each strain? The end result is this: British stock, representing 12.2 per cent of the total stock,[1] is diffused through 17.5 per cent of the children; French-Canadian stock, representing 34.9 per cent of the total stock, is diffused through 39.2 per cent of the children; Irish stock, constituting 9.3 per cent of the total population, is diffused through 13.8 per cent of the children. Other stocks present similar situations though the extent of diffusion varies.

If there had been no admixture, 12.2 per cent of the British stock would be borne by only 12.2 per cent of the children. The French-Canadian stock amounting to the numerical equivalent 34.9 per cent would be carried by 34.9 per cent of the children, and so on. In that case, each group would have fulfilled its quota 100 per cent. The result for each of the major groups is indicated in Table 47, the index in each case representing the degree to which the specific stock has fulfilled its quota.

The Irish fulfil their quota by 148,[2] the British by 143, while the Jews, among whom there has been but little intermarriage, keep to 100, and the Italians to 103. In general these comparative figures corroborate the various measures of fusion previously established. Yet they do more than measure rates of disintegration. They measure the extent of influence of each stock as it becomes diffused, or, in other words, its spread through the population.

Why is it that the extent of influence is so much larger for some groups than for others? In the first place, there are differences in the number and percentage of persons who marry out of each group. In the second place, the older groups have had a longer time in which to exert their influence and time has allowed free play to these factors; the A index therefore measures the extent of fusion with particular reference to the long-time influence. The results indicated by this index are themselves the product of complex social processes over and above those effected by differential intermarriage rates.

Since the numerical equivalents assigned the stocks were already weighted by the number of children, differential birth-rates do not affect index A. The weight of the stock referred to is always that already present

---

[1] The first figure is in each case derived from Table 48a, col. f, the second figure from Table 48, col. f.

[2] This figure is obtained by dividing 13.8 per cent by 9.3 per cent. See also formula given below.

in the population of children. The differences in the A indices arise only from the manner in which each strain distributes itself.

For example, among the Irish there are almost as many children who are one-half Irish as there are children of homogeneous Irish descent.[1] Among children with British blood, less than one-half are all British. Almost one-third are one-half British, and many are only one-fourth British. In each of these two ethnic groups a large proportion of the children have only one British grandparent, or one Irish grandparent. Both groups are represented by only few children in the column for three grandparents. The manner in which any one group makes its contribution leads to considerable difference in the results as far as composition is concerned. Four grandparents always equal four grandparents in numerical equivalents. But four grandparents of any one stock, let us say Irish, may be represented by one homogeneous child. On the other hand, four other grandparents of this same stock may have married four individuals coming from four different stocks. In that case these four Irish grandparents are represented by at least four children, each one-fourth Irish. The amount of stock is in each case the same when expressed in numerical equivalents, but the actual situations are very different. This is exactly what has happened in the case of the Irish and the British strains. The stocks are distributed over a wide surface. This type of distribution is due largely to the fact that intermarriage has taken place first among grandparents, and then again among the parents.

The high indices for the older groups are determined by initial differences in the rates of intermarriage, the long-time influence, and by the fact that they measure the cumulative effect exerted by successive intermarriage in the history of the family, intermarriage among grandparents, and the consequent secondary fusion through parental matings.

METHODOLOGICAL NOTE ON CHECKING RESULTS
(With Reference to Table 48a, Col. f)

If the procedure has been consistent throughout the study, our present summary dealing with the distribution of stock through children should yield the ethnic elements or numerical equivalents we started with in chapter iii. In weighting children by the number of grandparents of each stock which they represent, we arrive at the same distribution obtained directly by a "count of grandparents" in chapter iii.

As a matter of laboratory practice it is unnecessary to make both these

[1] Table 48.

TABLE 48a

STOCKS: MANNER OF THEIR DIFFUSION THROUGH 4,978 CHILDREN: COUNT OF GRANDPARENTS (19,912) AND NUMERICAL EQUIVALENTS

ETHNIC DERIVATION OF GRANDPARENTS	NUMBER OF GRANDPARENTS OF GIVEN STRAIN DERIVED BY WEIGHTING CHILDREN* BY				TOTAL NUMBER OF GRANDPARENTS OF GIVEN STRAIN IN POPULATION	PER CENT OF TOTAL NUMBER OF GRANDPARENTS (NUM. EQUIV.)
	Four Grandparents	Three Grandparents	Two Grandparents	One Grandparent		
	(a)	(b)	(c)	(d)	(e)	(f)
Albanian...............	4	....	2	....	6	....
Armenian...............	132	....	....	2	134	.7
Austrian...............						
Belgian (Flemish).........	36	12	32	8	88	.4
British total...........	1,540	186	538	155	2,419	12.2
a) English...............						
b) Scotch...............						
c) Scotch-Irish...........						
d) Canadian English......						
e) Canadian Scotch.......						
f) Canadian unspec.....						
g) British mixed...........						
h) British, others........						
Chinese................	12	....			12	.1
Colored................	36	....	8		44	.2
Czech.................	8				8	....
Dutch.................			10	19	29	.2
Finnish...............	8	....	4	....	12	.1
French Canadian........	6,064	186	642	51	6,943	34.9
French, total all others....	448	51	82	35	616	3.1
a) French, France.......						
b) Walloon.............						
c) Alsatian.............						
d) Swiss.............						
e) French mixed.........						
German...............	28	12	76	42	158	.8
Greek.................	84	....	4	....	88	.4
Irish.................	1,088	141	512	112	1,853	9.3
Italian.................	1,656		58	1	1,715	8.6
Jewish................	764	....	8	1	773	3.9
Portuguese (white)........	108	3	20	2	133	.7
Roumanian.............	160	....	6	....	166	.8
Scandinavian total........	140		42	17	199	1.0
a) Swedish.............	*136*		*28*	*14*	*178*	*.9*
b) Norwegian.............			*4*	*3*	*7*	....
c) Danish...............	*4*	....	*10*	....	*14*	*.1*
Slavic total.............	3,352		304	....	3,656	18.3
a) Polish.............	*1,972*		*146*	....	*2,118*	*10.6*
b) Ukrainian.............	*1,300*		*114*	....	*1,414*	*7.1*
c) Russian.............	*72*		*34*	....	*106*	*.5*
d) Lithuanian.............	*8*		*10*	....	*18*	*.1*
e) (Galician).............				*3*	*3*	....
Spanish...............						
Syrian..................	284	....	....	....	284	1.4
Turkish...............						
Mixed grandparents.......			2	8	10	.1
Unspecified (n.d.).........	148	51	226	96	521	2.6
Others unspecified.......	24	....	18	....	42	.2
GRAND TOTAL........	16,124	642	2,594	552	19,912	100.0

* As given in Table 48.

tabulations. The choice of one or the other depends upon the objective of the particular investigation. If the object is merely to obtain ethnic origins, the count of grandparents made in an earlier chapter is a simple and direct expedient for arriving at these. The present chapter serves better, however, to describe the manner in which each of the various stocks is diffused. If this is the purpose of the investigation, and this is more time consuming, the initial count of grandparents is unnecessary, and ethnic origins or numerical equivalents may be derived from the present tabulation.

LIMITATIONS OF THE "A" INDEX

While the A index of racial influence measures the effect of two variables—differential rates of intermarriage and the long-time influence—it fails to take into consideration the influence exerted upon a population because of differential birth-rates, since it begins with data deliberately weighted to wipe out this differential. The items in column a, Table 47, represent the numerical equivalents of the total stock as they already appear in children; column b the per cent of children who carry that stock. There is no information here bearing on the ratio of the present stock or of children to that of parents—a fact which is not to be overlooked.

It is generally supposed that the larger families characteristic of some ethnic groups and the smaller families of the British act as differential causes in determining final composition. The data in chapter xiii dealing with the size of family indicate that such differences and radical ones do exist. Conclusions about racial influences on composition, and certainly all possible attempts at prediction, depend upon the use of a tool which will take into consideration this additional variable. This factor can be measured by the use of a similar device which we shall designate as the "B index of racial influence."

THE "B" INDEX OF RACIAL INFLUENCE
(Tables 49 and 52a)

In the A index the child is the unit of enumeration; the numerical equivalents called into use are those based on the number of grandparents weighted by 4 for 4,978 children, or 19,912. These describe the composition of the child population. The ethnic composition of the child population differs from that of the parental population, owing to changes brought about by admixture, time, and differential rates of increase.

If the numerical equivalent for the parental stock is used as the base instead of the numerical equivalent for children, the result is an index which measures changes due to all three of these variables.

The numerical equivalents for the various strains in the parental generation are indicated in column f of Table 52a. The unit of enumeration is now the sib. The numerical equivalents are those derived from a count of grandparents weighted by 4 for 2,876 sibs, or 11,504. The results are the same as if we weighted 5,752 parents by 2. They represent the numerical equivalents of the racial strains represented in the parental generation.[1] The manner in which the distribution of stocks through families

TABLE 49

B INDICES FOR MAJOR GROUPS

	Numerical Equivalents of Each Stock in Parental Population (a)†	Per Cent of 4,978 Children Carrying Each Strain (b)‡	B Index = 100b/a* (c)
British....................	12.5	17.5	140
French Canadian...........	38.7	39.2	101
Irish.....................	9.0	13.8	153
Italian...................	6.7	8.9	133
Jewish...................	3.5	3.9	111
Slavic...................	16.5	19.9	121

* Or the formula on p. 170 may be used.
† These figures are derived from Table 52a, col. ƒ.
‡ These figures are derived from Table 48, col. ƒ.

or sibs is indicated in Tables 52 and 52a is parallel to that in Tables 48 and 48a where the child is the unit of stock transmission. For example, 12.5 per cent of the parental stock is British as against 12.2 per cent of the school stock. This parental stock measuring 12.5 per cent of the total is distributed through 17.5 per cent of the children. The B index may be used to represent the ratio of children to parental stock. In the case of the British the B index is $17.5/12.5 \times 100$ or 140. The A index was 143. The B indices for the major groups are indicated in Table 49.

THE "A" AND "B" INDICES COMPARED

At first glance the difference between each of these indices seems unimportant. A slightly different method of computation might ignore a decimal place and leave these even closer to each other. At second glance, however, we discover that the changes in the plus or minus direction,

[1] The results are identical with those contained in Table 5, col. c', but they have been arrived at differently. See also note to p. 169.

however small, correspond to processes which have been described else-where[1] and which were clear only after a laborious analysis of much raw material. It would appear, then, that we have a tool for measuring ethnic change which is peculiarly sensitive and yet more expeditious than the methods we have been obliged to use in other analyses.

A comparison of the two symbols for several groups is significant.

The only additional factor which is measured by the B index over those measured by the A index is the differential rate of increase. The estimate of diffusion in the population of children is now based upon numerical equivalents in the parental stock. The foregoing figures corroborate the results described in chapter xiii dealing with the size of family. The B index for the British, for example, is lower than the A index because the B index measures the ratio of child stock to parental stock; the British have small families. The B index for the Irish is higher than the A index;

Index	British	French Canadian	Irish	Italian	Jewish	Slavic
A	143	112	148	103	100	109
B	140	101	153	133	111	121

the Irish have larger families. The Italian and Slavic groups achieve higher B indices for the same reason. A further implication that may be drawn from these figures is that, given time, the Italian and Slavic groups may overtake the British in their influence upon the population, even though the British influence is relatively much stronger now, owing to greater diffusion and to the long-time influence. These indices are measures relative to the group's own numerical strength. The differences in numerical strength are additional factors to be taken into consideration in estimating the actual influence of the group, or in predicting ethnic change in the future.

The French-Canadian index alone seems to fail us. It was to be expected that the B index would be higher than the A index, since the French Canadians, like the Italians, have the largest families. This decrease, however, may be attributed to the fact that so many French-Canadian families have some of their children in parochial schools. The French-Canadian group, therefore, does not get full credit for its progeny when the index takes into consideration size of family. The rate of influence is indicated in the A index when the index measures admixture

[1] See chap. xiii for a discussion of differential rates of increase.

and time only. This exception proves the rule. The French Canadians resemble the Italians in the size of family and the British in length of residence in the community. It is fair to assume that the B index for the French Canadians stands between 135 and 140.

LIMITATIONS AND IMPLICATIONS OF THE "A" AND "B" INDICES OF RACIAL INFLUENCE

There are certain limitations which may be urged against the A and B indices—two in particular. One is concerned with terminology and the other with the method of recording the distribution of stock.

In the first instance, the use of the term "index" may be questioned. The symbol does not truly conform to the rules and regulations laid down for the statistical index; the word "influence" is of doubtful merit here, and we are not dealing with races. Frankly, the author confesses her inability to do better and invites substitute terminology. However, we do have here measures of population change which have actually taken place and which are due to several variables.

In the second place: Is this possibly unfair recording? A child who is one-fourth English and three-fourths French Canadian is counted once with the English group and only once with the French-Canadian group. What biologic significance, if any, has this particular type of inheritance? Is three-fourths necessarily more potent than one-fourth in its influence?

The degree to which there is biologic significance in this type of stock distribution for the individual seems to be a problem in Mendelian inheritance. The tricks played by the possible dominance of any unit character in the minority stock might well outreach the possible contribution of the major ethnic component.

As for the possibility that this is unfair recording of an ethnic contribution which is quantitatively dominant, the answer is as follows: In the analyses seeking ethnic derivations and numerical equivalents, the actual amount of each stock in the population is measured and recorded. The grandparents are counted according to the number of times they are represented by children. Now the children are counted, i.e., the number of children carrying each strain, irrespective of the amount carried. What significance have these figures when compared?

There are those who have quite correctly surmised that the old stocks in this country have exerted a greater influence than is usually indicated in composition data. This fact has been borne out emphatically as we have followed these groups through the various processes which have led to the present situation. Every analysis has given the earlier stocks, more particularly the British and Irish, more prestige. For example, only 5.0 per cent of the children report British regions for their fathers' birthplace. On the other hand, 12.2 per cent of the total stock of children is of British descent.[1] This is distributed among 17.5 per cent of the children,[2] so that the British group fulfils its promise with a quota or index of 143.

Or, to take the Irish, only 1.7 per cent of the children report fathers born in Ireland, but 9.3 per cent of the stock is Irish, and this is distributed among 13.8 per cent of the children. The Irish fulfil their quota by 148.

In some instances the weight assigned older groups has increased several fold in succeeding tabulations.

SUMMARY

Our several analyses have given us various measures of composition and of fusion. No one single measure can be indicative of all the processes at work. This chapter seeks to establish a symbol which will indicate the extent to which each group exerts influence in terms relative to its own initial strength or contribution.

The A index of racial influence is tentatively presented to measure the manner and the extent to which each group has spread its stock through the population. It aims to measure two variables: rates of intermarriage and the long-time influence.

In the A index the computations are based upon the numerical equivalents of stock in the population of children. It is the ratio of children to stock in the same population.

The B index of racial influence is tentatively presented as a measure of three variables: rates of intermarriage, long-time influence, and differential rates of increase.

In each case the index has no reference to the differences in numerical strength existing between groups in the community.

In the B index the computations are based upon the numerical equivalents of each stock in the parental population. In this case the index expresses the ratio of children in the present population to the ethnic contribution in the parental stock.

Both indices are presented tentatively since they need to be tested out in other situations covering a more significant number of cases.

The A indices indicate that the British and Irish project themselves over a wider area with a given amount of stock than do other groups.

---

[1] Table 48a, col. f.   [2] Table 48, col. f.

The *B* indices which take into consideration the ratio of parental stock to child stock are higher for the more recent immigrants, especially for the Italians and the Slavic groups. There is a tendency on the part of these groups to overtake the old groups in contribution to stock, quite aside from the differences which exist in numerical strength.

The *B* index is suggested as a tool for measuring differentials due to diffusion and to natural rates of increase. It corroborates the findings on differentials in composition due to size of family. Its use when tested further would obviate the laborious task of gathering and tabulating data on size of family.

In the preceding pages the A and B indices were computed from tables and percentages which were prepared in connection with this investigation. The formulas given below may be used to compute indices directly from the basic data.

SYMBOLS USED IN CONNECTION WITH FORMULAS FOR COMPUTING THE *A* AND *B* INDICES OF RACIAL INFLUENCE

N = Total number of children in the public-school population (4,978)

M = Total number of sibs in the public-school population (2,876)

$4N$ = Total number of grandparents in the public-school population weighted as to 4,978 children (19,912)

$4M^1$ = Total number of grandparents in the public-school population weighted as to 2,876 sibs (11,504)

C = Number of children carrying specified strain (each child is counted once whether it has 1, 2, 3, or 4 grandparents of the given strain)

S = Number of sibs carrying specified strain (each sib is counted once whether it has 1, 2, 3, or 4 grandparents of the given strain)

Gc = Number of grandparents of given strain for C

Gs = Number of grandparents of given strain for S

---

[1] It is possible to use parents instead of sibs. Let P equal the number of parents (5,752). The parental stock would then be represented by $2P$, or 11,504 grandparents. The figures are the same, $2P = 11,504$ and $4M = 11,504$. Such a procedure would be more logical in an effort to determine parental stock except that computations based on 2,876 sibs, have already been computed and serve this investigation as a whole best. It is simpler to derive the figures from existing tables. They would be identical in any case.

FORMULA FOR COMPUTING THE A INDEX*

$$A \text{ index} = \frac{C/N}{Gc/4N} \times 100 \ .$$

Illustration: BRITISH

$$C = \ \ \ 871$$
$$N = \ 4,978$$
$$Gc = \ 2,419$$
$$4N = 19,912$$

$$\frac{871/4,978}{2,419/19,912} \times 100 = 144 \ .$$

* See Table 50.

FORMULA FOR COMPUTING THE B INDEX*

$$B \text{ index} = \frac{C/N}{Gs/4M} \times 100 \ .$$

Illustration: BRITISH

$$C = \ \ \ 871$$
$$N = \ 4,978$$
$$Gs = \ 1,433$$
$$4M = 11,504$$

$$\frac{871/4,978}{1,433/11,504} \times 100 = 141 \ .$$

* See Table 51.

TABLE 50

Basic Data for Computing the *A* Index

(For Major Groups by Formula)*

	Number of Children Carrying Given Strain† (a)	Number of Grandparents of Given Strain (Numerical Equivalent for 19,912)‡ (b)	*A* Index per Formula (c)
British total................	871	2,419	144
French Canadian...........	1,950	6,943	112
French, total all others	205	616	133
Irish......................	687	1,853	148
Italian....................	444	1,715	103
Jewish....................	196	773	100
Slavic total................	990	3,656	108
a) Polish..................	566	2,118	106
b) Ukrainian..............	382	1,414	108
c) Russian................	35	106	132
d) Lithuanian.............	7	18	§

* It is simpler to derive the index from the percentages as was done in the text, if the percentages are available from some other table without further computation. There is, however, a slight difference in result depending upon the method of calculation.

† This includes the homogeneous children and those in the melting pot who are in part of the given strain, as given in col. *e*, Table 48.

‡ Derived from a count of grandparents weighted for 4,978 children (see col. *e*, Table 48*a*, or Table 1).

§ See statement on "Procedure" (chap. ii, p. 19) in explanation of this grouping. The index is not significant as too few cases are involved.

TABLE 51

Basic Data for Computing the *B* Index

(For Major Groups by Formula)*

	Number of Children Carrying Given Strain† (a)	Number of Grandparents of Given Strain (Numerical Equivalent for 11,504)‡ (b)	*B* Index per Formula (c)
British total................	871	1,433	141
French Canadian...........	1,950	4,452	101
French, total all others	205	398	119
Irish......................	687	1,040	152
Italian....................	444	767	133
Jewish....................	196	401	112
Slavic total................	990	1,900	120
a) Polish..................	566	1,078	121
b) Ukrainian..............	382	750	118
c) Russian................	35	62	140
d) Lithuanian.............	7	10	§

* It is simpler to derive the index from the percentages as was done in the text, if the percentages are available from some other table without further computation. There is, however, a slight difference in result depending upon the method of calculation.

† This includes the homogeneous children and those in the melting pot who are in part of the given strain, as given in col. *e*, Table 48.

‡ Derived from a count of grandparents weighted for 2,876 sibs (see col. *e*, Table 52*a*, or col. *c*, Table 5).

§ See statement on "Procedure" (chap. ii, p. 19) in explanation of this grouping. The index is not significant as too few cases are involved.

TABLE 52*

2,876 Sibs Classified by Number of Grandparents of Given Strain

Ethnic Derivation of Grandparents	Number of Sibs With				Total No. of Sibs Bearing Given Strain	Per Cent of 2,876 Sibs Bearing Given Strain
	Four Grand-parents	Three Grand-parents	Two Grand-parents	One Grand-parent		
	(a)	(b)	(c)	(d)	(e)	(f)
Albanian	1	....	1	....	2	.1
Armenian	14	....	....	2	16	.6
Austrian	....	....	....	....	....	....
Belgian (Flemish)	8	2	16	7	33	1.1
British total	222	43	161	94	520	18.1
a) English	....	....	....	....	....	....
b) Scotch	....	....	....	....	....	....
c) Scotch-Irish	....	....	....	....	....	....
d) Canadian English	....	....	....	....	....	....
e) Canadian Scotch	....	....	....	....	....	....
f) Canadian unspec.	....	....	....	....	....	....
g) British mixed	....	....	....	....	....	....
h) British, others	....	....	....	....	....	....
Chinese	3	....	....	....	3	.1
Colored	3	....	2	....	5	.2
Czech	1	....	....	....	1	†
Dutch	....	....	2	14	16	.6
Finnish	2	....	1	....	3	.1
French Canadian	970	39	191	27	1,227	42.7
French, total all others	80	14	31	20	145	5.0
a) French, France	....	....	....	....	....	....
b) Walloon	....	....	....	....	....	....
c) Alsatian	....	....	....	....	....	....
d) Swiss	....	....	....	....	....	....
e) French mixed	....	....	....	....	....	....
German	5	3	22	23	53	1.8
Greek	10	....	1	....	11	.4
Irish	144	28	158	64	394	13.7
Italian	183	....	17	1	201	7.0
Jewish	99	....	2	1	102	3.5
Portuguese (white)	19	1	4	1	25	.9
Roumanian	23	....	2	....	25	.9
Scandinavian total	21	....	16	10	47	1.6
a) Swedish	*20*	....	*11*	*8*	*39*	*1.4*
b) Norwegian	....	....	*2*	*2*	*4*	*.1*
c) Danish	*1*	....	*3*	....	*4*	*.1*
Slavic total	441	....	68	....	509	17.7
a) Polish	*254*	....	*31*	....	*285*	*9.9*
b) Ukrainian	*175*	....	*25*	....	*200*	*7.0*
c) Russian	*11*	....	*9*	....	*20*	*.7*
d) Lithuanian	*1*	....	*3*	....	*4*	*.1*
e) (Galician)	....	....	....	....	....	....
Spanish	....	....	....	2	2	.1
Syrian	25	....	....	....	25	.9
Turkish	....	....	....	....	....	....
Mixed grandparents	....	....	1	8	9	.3
Unspecified (n.d.)	24	10	63	60	157	5.5
Others unspecified	6	....	8	....	14	.5
GRAND TOTAL	2,304	140	767	334	....	....

* Tables 52 and 52a are analogous to Tables 48 and 48a in which the child is the unit of enumeration, and are included for comparison.

† Less than .1 per cent.

TABLE 52a

STOCKS: MANNER OF THEIR DIFFUSION THROUGH 2,876 SIBS: COUNT OF
GRANDPARENTS (11,504) AND NUMERICAL EQUIVALENTS

ETHNIC DERIVATION OF GRANDPARENTS	NUMBER OF GRANDPARENTS OF GIVEN STRAIN DERIVED BY WEIGHTING SIBS* BY				TOTAL NUMBER OF GRAND-PARENTS OF GIVEN STRAIN IN POPULATION	PER CENT OF TOTAL NUMBER OF GRAND-PARENTS (NUM. EQUIV.)
	Four Grand-parents	Three Grand-parents	Two Grand-parents	One Grand-parent		
	(a)	(b)	(c)	(d)	(e)	(f)
Albanian	4	....	2	....	6	.1
Armenian	56	....	....	2	58	.5
Austrian	....	....	....	....	....	....
Belgian (Flemish)	32	6	32	7	77	.7
British total	888	129	322	94	1,433	12.5
a) English						
b) Scotch						
c) Scotch-Irish						
d) Canadian English						
e) Canadian Scotch						
f) Canadian unspec						
g) British mixed						
h) British, others						
Chinese	12	....	....	....	12	.1
Colored	12	....	4	....	16	.1
Czech	4	....	....	....	4	....
Dutch	....	....	4	14	18	.1
Finnish	8	....	2	....	10	.1
French Canadian	3,880	117	428	27	4,452	38.7
French, total all others	320	42	16	20	398	3.5
a) French, France						
b) Walloon						
c) Alsatian						
d) Swiss						
e) French mixed						
German	20	9	44	23	96	.8
Greek	40	....	2	....	42	.4
Irish	576	84	316	64	1,040	9.0
Italian	732	....	34	1	767	6.7
Jewish	396	....	4	1	401	3.5
Portuguese (white)	76	3	8	1	88	.8
Roumanian	92	....	4	....	96	.8
Scandinavian total	84	....	32	10	126	1.1
a) Swedish	*80*	....	*22*	*8*	*110*	*.9*
b) Norwegian		....	*4*	*2*	*6*	*.1*
c) Danish	*4*	....	*6*	....	*10*	*.1*
Slavic total	1,764	....	136	....	1,900	16.5
a) Polish	*1,016*	....	*62*	....	*1,078*	*9.4*
b) Ukrainian	*700*	....	*50*	....	*750*	*6.5*
c) Russian	*44*	....	*18*	....	*62*	*.5*
d) Lithuanian	*4*	....	*6*	....	*10*	*.1*
e) (Galician)	....	....	....	....	....	....
Spanish	....	....	....	2	2	....
Syrian	100	....	....	....	100	.9
Turkish	....	....	....	....	....	....
Mixed ancestry	....	....	2	8	10	.1
Unspecified (n.d.)	96	30	126	60	312	2.7
Others unspecified	24	....	16	....	40	.3
GRAND TOTAL	9,216	420	1,534	334	11,504	100.0

* As given in Table 52.

TABLE 53

ETHNIC ELEMENTS AND THEIR DIFFUSION THROUGH 2,876 SIBS*

Ethnic Derivation	Numerical Equivalents Per Cent of Total Stock (a)†	Per Cent of Total Stock and Homogeneous (b)‡	Per Cent of Stock and Diffused c = (a−b) (c)	Per Cent of Each Stock in Diffusion d = c/a (d)**
Albanian........................	.1	....	.1	....
Armenian.......................	.5	.5	....	....
Austrian........................	....	....	....	....
Belgian (Flemish)...............	.7	.3	.4	....
British total....................	12.5	7.7	4.8	38.4
a) English.....................	9.3	4.9	4.4	47.3
b) Scotch.....................	....	....	....	....
c) Scotch-Irish...............	....	....	....	....
d) Canadian English..........	....	....	....	....
e) Canadian Scotch...........	....	....	....	....
f) Canadian unspec...........	....	....	....	....
g) British mixed..............	....	....	....	....
h) British, others.............	....	....	....	....
Chinese........................	.1	.1	....	....
Colored........................	.1	.1	....	....
Czech..........................	....	....	....	....
Dutch..........................	.1	....	.1	....
Finnish.........................	.1	.1	....	....
French Canadian................	38.7	33.7	5.0	12.9
French, total all others..........	3.5	2.8	.7	20.0
a) French, France.............	....	....	....	....
b) Walloon...................	....	....	....	....
c) Alsatian...................	....	....	....	....
d) Swiss.....................	....	....	....	....
e) French mixed..............	....	....	....	....
German........................	.8	.2	.6	....
Greek..........................	.4	.4	....	....
Irish...........................	9.0	5.0	4.0	44.4
Italian.........................	6.7	6.4	.3	4.5
Jewish.........................	3.5	3.4	.1	2.9§
Portuguese (white)..............	.8	.7	.1	....
Roumanian.....................	.8	.8	....	....
Scandinavian total..............	1.1	.7	.4	36.4
a) Swedish...................	.9	.7	.2	....
b) Norwegian.................	.1	....	.1	....
c) Danish....................	.1	....	.1	....
Slavic total....................	16.5	15.3	1.2	7.3
a) Polish.....................	9.4	8.8	.6	6.4
b) Ukrainian.................	6.5	6.1	.4	6.2
c) Russian...................	.5	.4	.1	....
d) Lithuanian................	.1	....	.1	....
e) (Galician).................	....	....	....	....
Spanish........................	....	....	....	....
Syrian.........................	.9	.9	....	....
Turkish........................	....	....	....	....
Mixed ancestry.................	.1	....	....	....
Partly unspecified..............	2.7	....	....	....
Other unspecified...............	.3	....	....	....
TOTAL HOMOGENEOUS........	....	79.1	....	....
TOTAL UNSPECIFIED..........	....	3.1	....	....
GRAND TOTAL...............	100.0	81.2‖	17.8	....

* For diffusion of stocks through children see chap. iii, Table 2.

† The figures in this column are derived from Table 5, col. c'.

‡ The figures in this column are derived from Table 16b, col. o.

§ This figure is misleading; there are but few cases involved. There are only 2 intermarriages and 99 Jewish families.

‖ This includes the unspecified group.

** This per cent is computed only for numerically significant groups.

PART III
CULTURAL ASPECTS

CHAPTER XII

THE COMMUNITY AREA[1]

The object of the ethnic survey is primarily to describe a community area, the community area being the region encompassed by a public-school system. This provides also a population which is being welded together, culturally, by the most powerful Americanization force we have in the United States. This survey has limited itself thus far to a description of the population in a given region.

CULTURAL ASPECTS

Obviously, if the ethnic survey proves to be a valid tool for describing ethnic origins and ethnic change, its scope may be extended to cover a wider area—a state, or even the nation. We are not at this point concerned with the implications which any findings on this score may have for census-taking or any bearing they may have on the national-origins situation. The questions are rather: (1) Has the ethnic survey validity as a tool to describe the community, both in its racial and in its cultural aspects? (2) What research leads are pregnant in this basic investigation? (3) What validity has the concept of the community area for the study of cultural adjustment? (4) What pragmatic contribution toward community planning or toward Americanization policy can be made by this mode of approach to the problem?

The first of these researches into ethnic origin by the writer had its inception in the practical needs confronting the social worker in the field of Americanization. In the case of New London, the initial effort was directed toward ascertaining the basic nature of the population at a time, immediately after the World War, when Americanization programs were being reformulated. New London, reputed to be a New England harbor town, New England geographically, traditionally, and racially, echoed the trend of thought and practice throughout the country. During the post-war period following the Armistice this community reverberated all that was finest and all that was crudest in the veritable epidemic of Americanization programs that were current throughout the country.

[1] This is a revision of Part II of an earlier paper which appeared in the *American Journal of Sociology*. See chap. i, p. 7.

Here, as elsewhere, the policy of those fostering such campaigns was predicated upon the desire to maintain a presupposed racial and cultural integrity of the town, upon the assumption of Anglo-Saxon homogeneity, and also upon the assumption of activities on the part of the various culture groups dangerously vitiating community life. We are not now describing or evaluating the programs of the community at large or the activities on the part of various culture groups. The problem which confronted that community, the other communities surveyed, in fact every community which has before it the task of converting diverse ethnic elements into a harmonious unit, is the dearth of factual data regarding the situation with which it deals. It is rarely found that official records truly describe the situation. And yet, as we have seen, certain assumptions regarding racial composition of the American people and a very definite race philosophy underlie our national immigration policy today. Both our restrictive legislation and our policies of incorporation are based upon these assumptions. It is quite obvious, however, that any given program, whether it be national or communal in the narrower sense, requires more careful inquiry into the actual facts of the situation.

There seems to be but little question that the ethnic survey is a tool which truly describes the population in its racial aspects. The problem confronting any community is, on the one hand, what stocks are to be welded together? And, on the other, what cultural traits are dominant among them?

However much this investigation might wish to lay claim to being a cultural survey of an American community, it has of necessity limited itself thus far to the basic problem of disentangling the facts of origin. The attempt to examine purely cultural factors was limited to very few items, to those most closely related to origin, migration, and early adjustment. Inevitably one was drawn into the vortex of French-Canadian theories of Americanization, for one must understand the men who are subjects of study, and the French Canadians constitute a group of especial importance in Woonsocket. In addition, a historical sketch of the community seemed necessary and feasible. These subjects are treated in the subsequent chapters.

RESEARCH LEADS

But the ethnic survey is at best merely an exploratory venture which points the way to numerous other lines of research which are needed before we can speak authoritatively about immigrant adjustment. Studies in ethnic composition are basic to other researches in allied fields on the same unit or in the same area. Research in racial biology, in ethnic psychology, and in the field of sociology all depend upon a more adequate classification of the individuals than we have hitherto been prone to make. These other investigations may have significance only in so far as individuals and groups are carefully classified for ethnic derivation. Groups of children who are themselves racially homogeneous but of different origins constitute separate units of study, while children who are of mixed descent form a new unit for investigation.

If we are dealing with physical norms, it is only after we have thus classified the subjects that any attempt can be made to formulate judgment, for example, on changes in the developmental life of children. Does the physical type of Old American children of French-Canadian descent conform to that of French-Canadian children, or has there been a release from retarding influence which results in a new type?[1]

More significant are the mental and educational problems. The literature on mental levels has had much to say on racial differences. Little research, however, has been conducted on educational adjustment with reference to factors other than "innate capacity" as determined by intelligent quotient. No specialized investigations were conducted in these fields in Woonsocket, but such studies were being conducted in these fields by the Study in Providence, Rhode Island. Miss Margaret Tully in her report[2] deals with the relation between ethnic history and educational adjustment. She not only finds significant differences between the adjustment of racial groups, but differences between the adjustment of individuals of the same group from one school district to another. Even more significant are her findings that the particular field in which children of the same nationality do superior work seems to be linked up with the generation of the family. Thus, immigrant children make better standing in the application subjects, like spelling and arithmetic, while their Americanized confrères fall down in these subjects but achieve superior rank in the comprehension subjects such as reading comprehension and arithmetic fundamentals.

---

[1] On this problem note the findings of Boas, Hrdlička, and others.

[2] *Op. cit.* See chap. i, p. 13. The subsequent illustrations are likewise drawn from reports made by graduate students in a seminar upon ethnic problems, Brown University, 1927–28. As special supervisors in the research department of the Providence public schools, and as school principals, these investigators had first-hand information on the problems under discussion.

Numerous research cues constantly present themselves to one working continuously in the field. For example, why is it that the higher I.Q.'s in one group of Italian children occur quite regularly among children who have some native parentage? To what extent does biculturalism lead to emotional conflict and to what extent may maladjustment be due to such conflict? One investigator reports a definite connection, for example, between stammering among Italian children and just such emotional situations. The psychology of the child who comes from an ethnic background possibly held in contempt by his American playmates, or which he fears may be held in contempt by his teachers, has not yet been explored.[1]

The literatures produced by the folk groups themselves give recognition to these factors and to the problems of social control. Each group has its own theory of adjustment in a new country, its own Americanization theory. The two groups who have been most tenacious of their cultural tradition and who have most definitely enunciated policies of control are perhaps the Jews and the French Canadians. But here the analogy ends.

The Jewish philosophy[2] of Americanization is different; the practice is different. In language usage, in religious ceremonial practice (without reference to belief), in the many "ways of living," Jews become completely and quickly de-Europeanized. Adherence to foreign-language and parochial schools are quite outside the Jewish program; they are on the other hand essential to the cultural integrity of a French-Canadian group in America. And so one might go on and treat of Polish attitudes or Italian attitudes—each group has its own way of life.

But analogies and comparisons are invidious without further inquiry. The views held by immigrant peoples in our midst and the extensive literatures on the subject developed by them are themselves properly the subject of objective analysis.

But these are views from the inside looking out. How do these several theories interplay? What kind of community do we get when numerous

[1] For works recognizing the function of the attitudes produced by cultural settings one turns, of course, to Thomas and Znaniecki, *The Polish Immigrant in Europe and America*, and to Herbert Miller, *Races, Nations, and Classes*.

[2] For a statement of their position the reader may be referred to Isaac Baer Berkson, *Theories of Americanization* (a critical study with special reference to the Jewish group) (New York: New York Teachers College, Columbia University, 1920); Alexander M. Dushkin, "The Profession of Jewish Education," *Menorah*, April, 1917, pp. 90–97; June, 1917, pp. 174–81; Julius Drachsler, "Racial Diversities and Social Progress," *Proceedings of the National Conference of Social Work at the 49th Annual Session* (Chicago: University of Chicago Press, June, 1922).

folk theories are put in practice in the same area? The study of specific groups and of their adjustment represents one aspect of the picture; the study of the interaction of these groups represents another phase, for here Americanization is a process of unification. It is just at this point that the concept of the community area as a unit for the study of ethnic adjustment can make its contribution.

THE CONCEPT OF THE COMMUNITY AREA

Associated with the studies in the specialized fields indicated in the preceding sections, namely, those dealing with physical and educational measurements, or those dealing with the specific approach to Americanization made by each group, might come a study of the cultural pattern of the present community which has resulted from the interaction of all these ethnic factors. This approach will necessarily be historical and analytical in its treatment, and presupposes historical surveys of the various groups within the community. It involves, in the long run, an evaluation of the activities, personal and institutional, of the folk groups in the community: first, as to their function in the life of each group, and, second, as to their function in the community as a whole. This approach follows from the growing realization that sociological studies depend primarily upon techniques borrowed from the field of social psychology and cultural anthropology. These are the sciences which deal especially with the response of individuals and of groups to new social situations and with the development of a new cultural pattern.

The use of the term "area" is in itself a recognition of our indebtedness to the field of anthropology. Reference here is to the concept of the "culture area," although the concept as stated by anthropologists has a somewhat different connotation. There the area is defined geographically by the phenomena which characterize it. Here it is determined by the existing social organization, the school district, the town, or the city. But the analogy does not seem out of place. Much methodology recently refined in anthropology for the study of primitive communities might be applied to the study of ethnic problems in American community life.

Students of social anthropology are familiar with the study of culture areas in primitive communities and with the co-operative attack that is possible only when the techniques of several social sciences are called into use simultaneously. While investigations have been conducted in one phase or another of immigrant life, seldom have the techniques in use by the several social sciences been applied to the same social unit. Seldom, if ever, is the modern population studied carefully for one aspect classified accurately as to its derivation. A study of Americanization inevitably resolves itself into a study of acculturation, and it is quite possible to set up objective standards for the measurement of this process in spite of the difficulties involved in work among subjects who are so vitally interested and concerned in the problems under investigation. These interests on the part of immigrant leaders themselves offer great promise could they be harnessed. Just as the ethnologist is dependent upon his interpreter in reaching his group, even more so is the student of Americanization dependent upon the exponents of the several nationalities in any community for his information about these people.

As has already been indicated, there is much variability in the methods used by specific groups to Americanize themselves, and in the manner in which different communities quite spontaneously incorporate or Americanize these diverse elements. From empirical observation it is obvious that immigrants thrown in contact with one another become more rapidly Americanized in the material aspects of culture than in those representative of social organization. Note the almost immediate changes in housing, dress, food, economic adjustment, etc. Part of this is, to be sure, involuntary, or enforced adaptation, but this adaptation proceeds with less protest than the adaptations to new forms of social organization.

Certain tendencies in Americanization are general and yet variable within limits, differing from community to community. Thus it can be anticipated that Italian behavior in Providence, Rhode Island, differs from that in Berkeley, California. French-Canadian adjustment presents a different front in querulous Woonsocket from what it does in prosperous Worcester, and again from that in Manchester, New Hampshire, and certainly from that in Canada.

So, too, Jewish Americanization is varied in its manifestation. Observation in any community brings to light rapid and far-reaching changes in the cultural life of groups. Thus, for example, within the past two decades there have been changes which are nothing short of revolutionary in the burial habits of the Jews of Providence, Rhode Island. A comparative study of burial habits among Jews would indicate that the Jew inevitably succumbs to a more primitive type of burial in New London than in Providence. As modernized as a Jewish funeral may be in Providence, it is primitive compared to that possible for an observing Jew to obtain for himself in Philadelphia or Boston. The position of the Portuguese and the

Italian immigrant in New London is different from that in Rhode Island. Numerous other illustrations might be invoked.

We might ask, Do the local groups in their ways of life represent variants of the cultures from which they are derived? Or are they variants of American culture? Do they, possibly, represent first one and then the other? How may we measure such change?

The study of Americanization as a process of acculturation involves nothing more nor less than a study of the whole American people and of all the social and cultural processes operating within given areas. When stated in this way the problem is hopeless and amorphous. It calls for the use of all the social-science disciplines and leaves one aghast for want of some tangible and immediate means of study. We are therefore confronted with the need of creating a concrete methodological approach to the problem as a whole. What can be more concrete and definite for analytic purposes than the use of the community area as a unit of investigation within which cultural processes function? The clue to a study of these problems may be found in the anthropological literature of the day. Wissler, for example, in his *Man and Culture* offers a valuable technique for the study of the form and content of culture in any modern community. The student of acculturation as a process in American life would do well to heed the developments in these allied fields of science.[1]

IMPLICATIONS FOR SOCIAL PRACTICE

The ends just described may seem of sufficient interest in themselves, but the investigator in this field of research is constantly confronted with the ubiquitous question, Of what practical use is all this?

It is scarcely necessary to enlarge upon the need for educational practice and social work to be based upon more adequate analysis of those situations which involve ethnic factors. Studies of composition, the classification of children, further inquiry into the rôle which ethnic factors play in achievement, the possibility of an enriched school program utilizing the cultural content of children, social legislation, and Americanization programs, inevitably all depend upon information which social scientists gather in the several fields indicated.

[1] Reference has already been made to *Middletown* as a contribution to this field. Another work of special interest, particularly in its discussion of method, is that by the Mexican anthropologist Manuel Gamio: translation of the Introduction, synthesis, and conclusions of the work, *The Population of the Valley of Teotihuacan*, Mexico: Talleres Gráficos de la Nación, 1922.

Those who are interested in "community" as it is the subject matter of social work and community planning will find necessary these more far-reaching analyses which the ethnic survey projects. The social survey in general has made a valuable contribution whenever it has been employed to throw light on a given area. But the social survey itself must seek explanation of its data in the light of facts revealed by the ethnic survey, irrespective of whether the technique proposed in this investigation or some better and more adequate tool for arriving at these facts is adopted. Community planning, directed toward social ends, can best be formulated in cognizance of the ethnic interrelations which exist, and of the ethnic problems which are inherent in the community to be Americanized.

The Woonsocket survey as a pioneer experiment in this field concentrated upon the basic facts concerning the racial origin of its population. Nevertheless, as we have already indicated, the survey did yield data on certain cultural phases of life in that community, which give us a picture in general of the existing "civilization" in Woonsocket. We now turn to a discussion of these aspects of its life.

CHAPTER XIII

CULTURAL FACTORS

In addition to the historical[1] and racial data contained in this monograph, there was gathered, in the course of the survey, some information relating to the social life of all groups.

Facts that pertain peculiarly to the problem of ethnic change are those bearing upon the date of entry, size of family, age of mother, and language usage. The data collected on this score add considerably to the picture of the behavior of specific groups and to the picture of the community which is affected by this behavior.

In all the summaries so far presented, individuals were classified according to ethnic derivation and generation in America. There was no indication, however, how long first-generation parents have been in this country. But there is a wide range of difference among first-generation parents. Some were brought to this country as infants and have lived in the United States "always." They know no other homeland. Other first-generation parents came within the past few years and, perhaps, brought with them foreign-born children. In each instance such parents have been put in the same category as first-generation parents, and yet it is probable that the former are culturally more nearly allied with second- and third-generation parents than they are with recent immigrants. The only defense such a classification has is that when dealing with large numbers of cases over a long period historically the generation categories are adequate to reconstitute a picture of historical change in the community and of the origins of its population. From the practical standpoint it differentiates those who are citizens of the United States by virtue of nativity from those who are not. But the study of acculturation requires further refinement of data relating to first-generation adjustment within shorter time periods. The basic question here is, How long have first-generation immigrants been in the country?

DATE OF ENTRY

(Tables 54, 54a, and 54b; Fig. 5)

Information reported regarding date of entry to the United States is sufficient to indicate the sequence in the arrival of different groups to this

[1] See historical sketch in chap. xiv.

country. Table 54 and Figure 5 indicate that the data are continuous with those bearing on generation in America.[1] Thus, the old immigrants, those largely comprising the second- and third-generation groups, are represented as being among the earliest comers in the first generation, namely, French Canadians, British, and Irish. Each of these groups is well represented among those who came before 1900. The numbers for the Irish are small, but they came most largely before the new century.

The French Canadians, who have been outnumbering the Irish several fold for some time, reached the period of maximum immigration between 1895 and 1899. The period immediately following, 1905–9, represents the years of maximum immigration alike for British, Jews, and Poles, although the Poles now outnumber other groups several fold.

It has been indicated in the previous chapters that the British constitute a continuous stream of immigration and are well represented among new immigrants as well as among the old. Small as the figures are, the number was actually increasing just before the war.[2] With the French Canadians, on the other hand, there was a steady decline in the two prewar decades, but a rise in the post-war period.

The modal period differs slightly for men and women among the Irish and French Canadians (Tables 54a and 54b). In each case it is later for the women than for the men. This is a feature of immigration generally known to exist. The men precede the women. Its influence is readily detected in analytic studies comparing data about men and women regarding age and length of residence at time of marriage.

In general, then, the years of maximum immigration of first-generation parents in the major groups fall within the fifteen or twenty years previous to 1926, the year of the investigation. Among the recent immigrants the maximum period of migration for Poles and Jews antedate those for Ukrainians and Italians. However, even though the two latter groups reach their own maximum later than the Jews, they outnumber the Jews in the preceding period.

The period of the World War is marked by a radical drop in immigration. The distribution for date of entry of parents is consistent with the fact that 92.7 per cent of the children are native born, all of which means that most of the families have had a decade or more in which to work out some adjustment to the new environment. The length of family residence in this country has significance, too, for the study of language usage and of intermarriage.

[1] Chap. v.

[2] We have previously noted that these came largely from Great Britain. See chap. v, p. 63.

TABLE 54*

Date of Entry of First-Generation Parents

(Fathers and Mothers Combined; Major Groups Only)

	1875–79	1880–84	1885–89	1890–94	1895–99	1900–1904	1905–9	1910–14	1915–19	1920–24	1925	Total No. of Replies Recorded		No. of Rejects	Grand Total
												No.	% of Gr'd Total		
British.........	3	8	22	20	13	17	**39**	37	4	1	1	165	93.8	11	176
French Canadian	60	79	121	120	**132**	108	76	49	44	91	30	910	77.4	266	1,176
Irish..........	2	12	**17**	16	8	9	5	2	0	5	0	76	88.4	10	86
Italian........	0	0	2	7	15	50	88	**148**	22	15	0	347	95.6	16	363
Jewish.........	1	0	6	19	31	41	**51**	23	1	3	2	178	96.7	6	184
Polish.........	1	1	2	11	20	113	**169**	145	5	2	0	469	94.0	30	499
Ukrainians....	0	0	0	0	3	17	87	**212**	9	0	1	329	94.3	20	349

* The mode in each group is indicated in boldface.

TABLE 54a*

Date of Entry of First-Generation Fathers

(Major Groups Only)

	1875–79	1880–84	1885–89	1890–94	1895–99	1900–1904	1905–9	1910–14	1915–19	1920–24	1925	Total No. of Replies Recorded		No. of Rejects	Grand Total
												No.	% of Gr'd Total		
British.........	2	5	12	9	9	7	**19**	17	2	0	0	82	94.3	5	87
French Canadian	40	45	**66**	61	61	46	34	21	23	45	15	457	74.3	158	615
Irish..........	2	8	6	7	3	3	1	1	0	3	0	34	87.2	5	39
Italian........	0	0	1	5	8	34	48	**68**	3	5	0	172	94.5	10	182
Jewish.........	0	0	4	9	16	21	**27**	11	0	1	1	90	94.7	5	95
Polish	0	1	2	8	9	54	**84**	73	1	1	0	233	92.8	18	251
Ukrainian......	0	0	1	5	8	34	48	**68**	3	5	0	172	94.5	10	182

* The mode in each group is indicated in boldface.

TABLE 54b*

Date of Entry of First-Generation Mothers

(Major Groups Only)

	1875–79	1880–84	1885–89	1890–94	1895–99	1900–1904	1905–9	1910–14	1915–19	1920–24	1925	Total No. of Replies Recorded		No. of Rejects	Grand Total
												No.	% of Gr'd Total		
British.........	1	3	10	11	4	10	**20**	20	2	1	1	83	93.3	6	89
French Canadian	20	34	55	59	**71**	62	42	28	21	46	15	453	80.7	108	561
Irish..........	0	4	**11**	9	5	6	4	1	0	2	0	42	89.4	5	47
Italian........	0	0	1	2	7	16	40	**80**	19	10	0	175	96.7	6	181
Jewish	1	0	2	10	15	20	**24**	12	1	2	1	88	98.9	1	89
Polish.........	1	0	0	3	10	59	**85**	72	4	1	0	236	95.2	12	248
Ukrainian......	0	0	0	0	3	5	37	**118**	1	0	1	165	94.8	9	174

* The mode in each group is indicated in boldface.

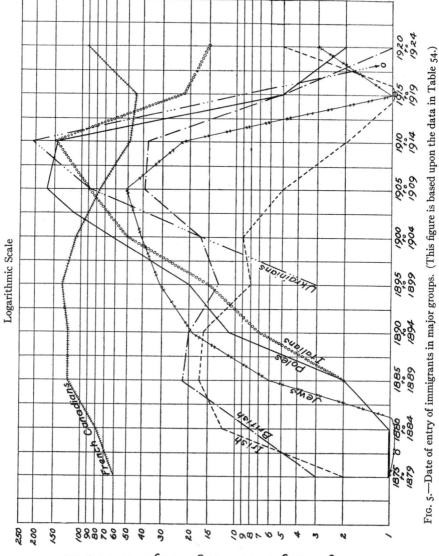

Fig. 5.—Date of entry of immigrants in major groups. (This figure is based upon the data in Table 54.)

(Tables 55, 56)

The age distribution of mothers is another one of the basic facts upon which numerous other adjustments depend, and therefore calls for treatment before problems such as size of family, language usage, and other factors which seem to determine intermarriage. An older mother who has come to this country but recently offers her family a different cultural setting from one who is younger and who migrated at an earlier date.

The condition of the investigation excludes from the unit women who have no children, since every woman in this population is the mother of at least one child. It also excludes the women in Woonsocket all of whose children are beyond school age, and the women all of whose children are of preschool age. In spite of these limitations, the range in the age of mothers is from 20 to 65.[1] The average age of all mothers for whom we have a record of age[2] is 40.5.

Attention should be called to the fact, however, that the data on age are somewhat more limited than one might desire. Confessedly, securing age data was the most difficult task of all.

Information about the date of entry and length of residence in the United States is significant only for first-generation immigrants. On the other hand, the age of mother and size of family constitute information which is equally valuable for all classes in the community, natives and immigrants alike.

But American women will not give their age. No question in the Stamford investigation aroused so much resentment as that referring to age. This inhibition against giving one's age is peculiarly a characteristic of American-born mothers. Resentment on this score is not nearly so pronounced in cases where the mother is foreign born. It therefore seemed the better part of wisdom to respect this sensitivity; the question on age was omitted in the Woonsocket survey. There were substituted, however, two questions: "When did your mother come to this country?" "At what age?"

The present age of mother was derived from this information, but only for foreign-born mothers. This means that the data are fairly complete for the recent immigrant groups, but much less so for French Canadians,

[1] There is only one case in the age group 20–25, an Italian mother of three children, and four mothers are 65 years old or more. In the tables these two classes have been incorporated in each case into a larger age group.

[2] We have record for 85.8 per cent of all first-generation mothers.

TABLE 55

Age Distribution for First-Generation Mothers*

Ethnic Derivation	29 AND UNDER (a)	30–34 (b)	35–39 (c)	40–44 (d)	45–49 (e)	50–54 (f)	55–59 (g)	60 AND OVER (h)	Total No. of Replies Recorded — No. (i)	% of Gr'd Total (j)	REJECTS (k)	GRAND TOTAL (l)
Albanian												
Armenian												
Austrian												
Belgian (Flemish)												
British total	1	9	12	19	17	11	7	1	77	86.5	12	89
a) English												
b) Scotch												
c) Scotch-Irish												
d) Canadian English												
e) Canadian Scotch												
f) Canadian unspec.												
g) British mixed												
h) British, others												
Chinese												
Colored												
Czech												
Dutch												
Finnish												
French Canadian	10	48	75	114	87	67	29	11	441	78.6	120	561
French, total all others	2	9	18	12	12	3	1	2	59	89.4	7	66
a) French, France												
b) Walloon												
c) Alsatian												
d) Swiss												
e) French mixed												
German												
Greek												
Irish		4	5	9	13	7	2	1	41	87.2	6	47
Italian	22	31	48	36	22	3	2	1	165	91.2	16	181
Jewish		13	19	21	14	10	3	2	82	92.1	7	89
Portuguese (white)												
Roumanian												
Scandinavian total												
a) Swedish												
b) Norwegian												
c) Danish												
Slavic total												
a) Polish	18	64	76	39	14	14	1	....	226	91.1	22	248
b) Ukrainian	20	70	40	21	4	3	1	....	159	91.4	15	174
c) Russian												
d) Lithuanian												
e) (Galician)												
Spanish												
Syrian												
Turkish												
All other intras†	4	27	31	30	18	3	2	....	115	85.2	20	135
Unspecified	....	2	1	1	2	2	....	....	8	....	1	9
Total intramarriages†	77	275	324	301	201	121	48	18	1,365	85.8	225	1,590
Total intermarriages†	12	29	29	23	20	17	5	1	136	85.5	23	159
Grand total	89	306	354	325	223	140	53	19	1,509	85.8	249	1,758

* The mode for each group is indicated in boldface.
† The women who intermarried were treated as a separate unit.

British, and Irish who are only in part first-generation immigrants. The question arises whether the age for first-generation mothers is derived from a fair sample for all mothers in these groups. The answer is that the results obtained seem to fit well the interpretations that follow from other analyses, but here again the percentage of replies accepted as complete, even for first-generation mothers, is smaller for these three groups than it is for other and more recent comers. The recent immigrants in each case returned information in over 90 per cent of the cases, the French Canadians in only 78.6 per cent, the British in 86.5 per cent, and the Irish in 87.2 per cent. It is difficult to determine whether the lower percentage of replies from these mothers is due to Americanization and consequent refusal to give age even in this indirect form, or whether it is due to uncertainty about date of migration or age at migration, since they were remote facts in the history of the individual.[1] Answers which require mental arithmetic are not desirable, unless they offer the only alternative. In the present instance this approach seemed the only one feasible.

Since the investigation included all the mothers of public-school children, it might possibly be taken for granted that the age distribution was similar for all nationalities. Such an assumption, however, proved to be unwarranted.

The data on age distribution indicate that there is considerable difference in the average or modal age from one group to another. In some instances this difference amounts to ten or fifteen years. This is a very significant difference and one to be taken into consideration in analyzing data for language usage and size of family. The more recent immigrants fall on the whole in the younger age groups.

The age distributions for the different groups (Table 55) indicate that the mode falls at four different age classes for the groups under discussion. The mode is, in each case, indicated in boldface. The modal age falls in the age group 45–49 for the Irish; for the British, French Canadians, and Jews it is 40–44; for Italians and Poles, 35–39; for Ukrainians, 30–34.

Other methods of computing average age as a comparable unit offered in general the same sequence. The Italian, Polish, and Ukrainian mothers fall in the youngest age groups.

Since the age of mothers is a factor to be considered in determining what differential contributions to stock exist in the community, the arithmetic average may be a better tool to use. This gives due weight to

[1] In the case of French Canadians, the frequent migration back and forth over the boundary line leads to confusion on the date of the initial entry.

classes which appear on either side of the mode, classes which belong practically to the same child-bearing period. The arithmetic average in years for age of mother for each nationality is 44.9 for the Irish, 44.0 for the British, 43.7 for French Canadians, 42.5 for Jews, 37.8 for Italians, 37.3 for Poles, and 34.9 for Ukrainians.[1]

There seems to be no doubt, however, that in general the age data represent a true sample for each nationality. Other refinements bear out this deduction.[2] A glance at the absolute figures in Table 55 indicates that there are very few British and Irish mothers in the early age groups, and that between the ages of 30–39 they are greatly outnumbered by practically every other group.

SIZE OF FAMILY

(Table 56)

There are three possible objects in analyzing data on size of family. These are:

1. What differentials already exist which give one group an advantage over the others in composition?

2. What light do the data throw on trends that may be characteristic of one group or another regarding average size of family?

3. What implications do both these have in predicting population change?

Even a cursory examination of the data on size of family indicates immediately that there are differentials here which affect the composition of the population. The simplest procedure is to estimate the ratio of children to families in public school for each nationality.

The average number of children per family in public school for the whole city is 1.7. The Italians lead with an average of 2.2 children per family in school, and the British are found at the bottom of the list with an average of 1.7 children per family in school (see table 56, col. b). The low figure for French Canadians has no significance, since we know that most of the French-Canadian children who are in public school have brothers and sisters in parochial schools.

The evidence is clear, however, that between the British and other stocks, in particular the Italian, there is a significant difference in the accretions to stock. This is a differential which exists now and which will

---

[1] These averages are derived from Table 55; the midpoint in each case was used for computing the arithmetic mean.

[2] See chap. xi, "Indices of Racial Influence."

of course be manifest when this group reaches maturity as an adult population.

The question may be raised however, To what extent are these figures indicative of differentials in the community at large? Is there some selective factor similar to that operating for the French Canadians which makes this group of mothers not representative for the city? Are these figures sufficient to draw conclusions regarding the tendency in any one group to have smaller or larger families?

Evidence is available on the average size of family irrespective of the number of children actually in school, since information was obtained on

TABLE 56

AVERAGE NUMBER OF CHILDREN PER FAMILY IN MAJOR GROUPS COMPARED*

Ethnic Group	Average Number of Children per Family† (a)	Average Number of Children per Family in Public School‡ (b)	Average Number of Children per Family Not in Public School $c = (a-b)$ (c)
British............	2.9	1.7	1.2
French Canadian..	**4.8**	1.4	3.4
Irish.............	4.3	1.9	2.4
Italian...........	4.1	2.2	1.9
Jewish...........	3.9	1.9	2.0
Polish...........	3.6	1.9	1.7
Ukrainian........	2.9	1.9	1.0

* The group with the largest number of children is in boldface.
† Computed from data in Table 59.
‡ This is in each case a ratio of homogeneous children to homogeneous families derived from data in chaps. vi and vii.

this score. The average number of children per family in each nationality, irrespective of age of mother and irrespective of whether or not the children are in school, shows greater variance than do the school figures. The Italians now take third rank and are preceded in rank by both French Canadians and Irish, the French Canadians ranking first and the Irish second. The British share lowest rank with the Ukrainians for average number of children per family (Table 56).

The average number of children per family, the average number in school, and the average number not in school for each of the major groups are indicated in Table 56.[1]

The average number of children per family is a better indication of the differentials which exist in the population at large than is the average number in school, since it throws more light on folk differences and also offers a better basis for predicting ethnic change. The two groups having

[1] Throughout the discussion the reference is to living children only.

the largest number of children not in public school are French Canadians and Irish. Those having the fewest number of children not in school are British and Ukrainians.

The evidence is sufficiently clear that certain stocks are now effecting changes in composition due to differential increase over and above those due to numerical strength in the community. However, caution must be invoked in interpreting the evidence without further examination of possible selective factors.

SIZE OF FAMILY VERSUS AGE OF MOTHER

(Tables 57, 58, 59, and 59a; Fig. 6)

The most significant factor to be taken into consideration in this respect is the possible difference in the average age of mothers. We have seen that

TABLE 57

SUMMARY: MAJOR GROUPS COMPARED: AVERAGE AGE OF MOTHER,
AVERAGE SIZE OF FAMILY, RANK BY AGE OF MOTHER,
RANK BY SIZE OF FAMILY

Ethnic Group	Average Age of Mother* (a)	Average Size of Family† (b)	Rank by Age of Mother‡ (c)	Rank by Size of Family§ (d)
British..............	44.0	2.9	2	7
French Canadian....	43.7	4.8	3	1
Irish..............	44.9	4.3	1	2
Italian.............	37.8	4.1	5	3
Jewish.............	42.5	3.9	4	4
Polish.............	37.3	3.6	6	5
Ukrainian..........	34.9	2.9	7	6
Major groups combined.....	40.5	4.0	....	....

* Derived from Table 55.   ‡ Highest average = 1.
† See Table 57, col. a.   § Largest families = 1.

there is a marked difference in the average age of mothers in each nationality. It is therefore necessary to modify our conclusions with particular reference to age. The difficulty is that the numbers in some age classes are so small that the nationality groups are not comparable at each age. These facts necessarily determine the mode of presenting the data. The data were therefore given above irrespective of age. The following material is given with reference to the age of mother. It is limited in scope, but in spite of this fact adds to the picture and throws further light on trends characteristic among the different nationalities.

Table 57 indicates the rank of each group according to the average age of mother and according to the average size of family. It appears that the sequence of groups for age of mother does not coincide with that for size of family except in the case of the Jews. French Canadians claim the largest families, but the mothers belong to the third oldest age group; Italians claim third rank for size of family but rank fifth for average age of mother; British mothers who, with the Ukrainians, claim the smallest

TABLE 58

AVERAGE NUMBER OF CHILDREN PER FAMILY IN MAJOR GROUPS
COMPARED BY AGE CLASS OF MOTHER

Age of Mother	No. of Cases in Each Class*	British	French Cana-dian†	Irish	Italian†	Jewish	Polish	Ukrain-ian‡	All Groups Com-bined
		(a)	(b)	(c)	(d)	(e)	(f)	(g)	(h)
29 and under..........	71	1.0	3.5	......	3.4+	......	2.3	1.9−	2.7
30–34.................	239	2.1	3.5+	2.0	3.5+	2.0	2.7	2.8−	2.9
35–39.................	275	2.2	4.5+	4.4	4.0+	1.1	3.8	3.3−	3.8
40–44.................	259	3.3	4.8+	4.1	4.8+	4.5	4.7	3.4−	4.5
45–49.................	171	3.5	5.5+	4.2	4.9+	4.9	4.1	4.8−	4.9
50–54.................	115	2.6	5.0+	5.7	4.7	4.6	4.6	3.0−	4.7
55–59.................	45	3.1	6.1+	5.0	6.0+	6.7	5.0	1.0−	5.5
60–64.................	12	1.0	4.6+	6.0	5.0+	......	......	......	4.4
65–69.................	4	......	6.0+	......	......	4.0	......	......	5.0
Average number of children per mother	......	2.9	4.8	4.3	4.1	3.9	3.6	2.9	4.0
Average age of moth-ers in given group.	1,191*	44.0	43.7	44.9	37.8	42.5	37.3	34.9	40.5

* The number of cases which fall in each age class for each nationality is indicated in Table 55. There are in all 1,590 first-generation mothers (intramarriages). The figure, 1,191, is exclusive of European French, all others, and rejects. The averages given above are computed from unpublished data.

† Plus sign indicates that the specific average is above general average in col. h.

‡ Minus sign indicates that the specific average is below general average in col. h.

families, belong to the higher age classes. Ukrainian mothers, however, belong to the youngest age group.

There is sufficient information to indicate that the trends outlined above are truly characteristic of each nationality. It will be noted (Table 58) that the French Canadians have a higher average than the general one for number of children per family for mothers of each age group. Similarly, the Italians rise above the average in almost every case. The Ukrainians, on the other hand, show a deviation below the normal for average number of children at each age group. This would indicate that the small families among the Ukrainians may not be attributed entirely to the fact that the Ukrainian mothers are a younger age group, but that

TABLE 59

Number of Children per Family by Ethnic-Group
Foreign-Born Mothers (First Generation)

ETHNIC DERIVATION	NUMBER OF CHILDREN IN FAMILY*											
	1	2	3	4	5	6	7	8	9	10	11	Total
Albanian...............	....	....	....	....	....	....	....	....	....	....	....	.....
Armenian...............	....	....	....	....	....	....	....	....	....	....	....	....
Austrian...............	....	....	....	....	....	....	....	....	....	....	....	....
Belgian (Flemish)...........	....	....	....	....	....	....	....	....	....	....	....	....
British total...............	18	22	22	13	7	3	1	1	2	....	....	89
a) English...............												....
b) Scotch..............												
c) Scotch-Irish.........												
d) Canadian English.......												
e) Canadian Scotch........												
f) Canadian unspec........												
g) British mixed..........												
h) British, others..........												
Chinese...............												
Colored...............												
Czech...............												
Dutch...............												
Finnish...............												
French Canadian...........	41	77	**100**	73	74	69	42	32	16	18	19	561
French, total all others......	**23**	18	10	6	3	2	1	1	1	1	....	66
a) French, France...........												
b) Walloon.............												....
c) Alsatian.............												...
d) Swiss.............												.....
e) French mixed...........												
German...............												
Greek...............												...
Irish...................	7	6	**9**	7	4	7	4	1	1	1	....	47
Italian...................	21	31	**33**	21	27	18	16	6	3	1	4	181
Jewish...............	9	14	**21**	13	15	9	5	1	1	1	....	89
Portuguese (white)..........												....
Roumanian..............												
Scandinavian total.........												
a) Swedish.............												
b) Norwegian............												...
c) Danish..............												...
Slavic total..............												
a) Polish..................	24	**55**	54	48	28	22	11	3	2	1	....	248
b) Ukrainian.............	31	44	**51**	22	15	8	2	1	....	....	....	174
c) Russian.............												...
d) Lithuanian............												
e) (Galician).............												
Spanish...............												
Syrian...............												
Turkish...............												
All other intras............	28	23	24	20	18	9	7	3	3	....	....	135
Unspecified	2	4	1	1	....	....	1	....	....	....	....	9
TOTAL INTRAMARRIAGES.	202	290	**324**	223	191	147	89	49	29	23	23	1,590
TOTAL INTERMARRIAGES.	32	**39**	27	22	19	5	10	2	2	1	....	159
GRAND TOTAL.........	236	333	**352**	246	210	152	100	51	31	24	23	1,758

* The mode for each group is indicated in boldface.

TABLE 59a

NUMBER OF CHILDREN PER FAMILY BY ETHNIC-GROUP
NATIVE-BORN MOTHERS (2x GENERATION)

ETHNIC DERIVATION	1	2	3	4	5	6	7	8	9	10	11	Total
Albanian..................	....	....	....	....	....	....	....	....	....	....	....	....
Armenian.................	....	....	....	....	....	....	....	....	....	....	....	....
Austrian..................	....	....	....	....	....	....	....	....	....	....	....	....
Belgian (Flemish)..........	....	....	....	....	....	....	....	....	....	....	....	....
British total..............	31	**34**	30	8	13	7	5	3	....	2	....	133
a) English...............	....	....	....	....	....	....	....	....	....	....	....	....
b) Scotch................	....	....	....	....	....	....	....	....	....	....	....	....
c) Scotch-Irish...........	....	....	....	....	....	....	....	....	....	....	....	....
d) Canadian English.......	....	....	....	....	....	....	....	....	....	....	....	....
e) Canadian Scotch.......	....	....	....	....	....	....	....	....	....	....	....	....
f) Canadian unspec.......	....	....	....	....	....	....	....	....	....	....	....	....
g) British mixed..........	....	....	....	....	....	....	....	....	....	....	....	....
h) British, others.........	....	....	....	....	....	....	....	....	....	....	....	....
Chinese..................	....	....	....	....	....	....	....	....	....	....	....	....
Colored..................	....	....	....	....	....	....	....	....	....	....	....	....
Czech....................	....	....	....	....	....	....	....	....	....	....	....	....
Dutch....................	....	....	....	....	....	....	....	....	....	....	....	....
Finnish..................	....	....	....	....	....	....	....	....	....	....	....	....
French Canadian..........	53	68	**75**	72	57	17	30	23	4	7	3	409
French, total all others.....	....	**4**	2	3	2	1	1	1	....	....	....	14
a) French, France........	....	....	....	....	....	....	....	....	....	....	....	....
b) Walloon..............	....	....	....	....	....	....	....	....	....	....	....	....
c) Alsatian..............	....	....	....	....	....	....	....	....	....	....	....	....
d) Swiss.................	....	....	....	....	....	....	....	....	....	....	....	....
e) French mixed.........	....	....	....	....	....	....	....	....	....	....	....	....
German..................	....	....	....	....	....	....	....	....	....	....	....	....
Greek....................	....	....	....	....	....	....	....	....	....	....	....	....
Irish....................	17	**21**	15	12	14	9	5	1	1	2	....	97
Italian...................	....	1	....	....	1	....	....	....	....	....	....	2
Jewish...................	2	**4**	2	2	....	....	....	....	....	....	....	10
Portuguese (white)........	....	....	....	....	....	....	....	....	....	....	....	....
Roumanian...............	....	....	....	....	....	....	....	....	....	....	....	....
Scandinavian total.........	....	....	....	....	....	....	....	....	....	....	....	....
a) Swedish..............	....	....	....	....	....	....	....	....	....	....	....	....
b) Norwegian...........	....	....	....	....	....	....	....	....	....	....	....	....
c) Danish...............	....	....	....	....	....	....	....	....	....	....	....	....
Slavic total..............	....	....	....	....	....	....	....	....	....	....	....	....
a) Polish................	....	....	1	**4**	....	1	....	....	....	....	....	6
b) Ukrainian............	....	1	....	....	....	....	....	....	....	....	....	1
c) Russian..............	....	....	....	....	....	....	....	....	....	....	....	....
d) Lithuanian...........	....	....	....	....	....	....	....	....	....	....	....	....
e) (Galician)............	....	....	....	....	....	....	....	....	....	....	....	....
Spanish..................	....	....	....	....	....	....	....	....	....	....	....	....
Syrian...................	....	....	....	....	....	....	....	....	....	....	....	....
Turkish..................	....	....	....	....	....	....	....	....	....	....	....	....
All other intras...........	1	5	5	....	....	1	....	....	....	....	....	12
Partly unspecified..........	15	22	15	7	3	1	....	2	1	....	1	67
Unspecified (n.d.)..........	7	3	1	1	1	....	....	....	....	....	....	13
TOTAL UNSPECIFIED.....	22	25	16	8	4	1	....	2	1	....	1	80
TOTAL INTRAMARRIAGES.	104	138	130	101	87	36	41	28	5	11	3	684
TOTAL INTERMARRIAGES.	73	96	73	40	37	17	11	4	2	....	1	354
GRAND TOTAL..........	199	259	219	149	128	54	52	34	8	11	5	1,118

* The mode for each group is indicated in boldface.

there is a tendency for smaller families all along the line, a tendency which manifests itself in the early age groups.

Interestingly enough, the Ukrainians differ from their Slavic kindred, the Poles, the latter showing a tendency to have larger families.

It appears that the tabulations refined for age corroborate the conclusions which were drawn from the tabulations without reference to age. This means that the data bearing upon the number of children per family in each nationality in school are in general indicative of the trends in the population at large. The data are illustrated in Figures 6a, b, and c. Figure 6a, in which the data are plotted without reference to age, corroborates in general the trends indicated in Figure 6b where the data are plotted for the age group 35–39, and in Figure 6c where the data are plotted for the combined age groups 45 and over.

It is manifest that there are already outstanding differences in the contributions to stock made by the different nationalities. In addition, one may safely assume that among the British and Irish the children who are not in school are probably beyond school age. Among the Italians and Slavs they are probably of preschool age. The conclusion must be that the potential increase which may be looked for in this population probably lies with the Italian and Slavic mothers.

There is a difference between the average number of children per mother among the foreign-born and that among the native-born mothers; also between mothers who intramarry and those who intermarry. The mode for foreign-born mothers (who intramarry) is 3; the mode for native-born mothers is 2; the mode for all mothers who intermarry is 2 (Tables 59 and 59a). These statements are without reference to age, except as we know that the mode for first-generation mothers falls in the age group 35–39.

LANGUAGE USAGE

There is perhaps no culture trait that is so generally accepted as a mark of Americanization as is the acquisition of English. The ready acquisition of a new language is in itself the mark of adaptability. It is also an indication of adaptability to other aspects of culture. In many ways it is the very condition of adjustment, while language facility and usage undeniably define the cultural milieu of family or of group.

Several questions on the inquiry sheet dealt with language usage as a possible measure of culture status and culture change. Some questions sought to ascertain what languages parents and children could speak,

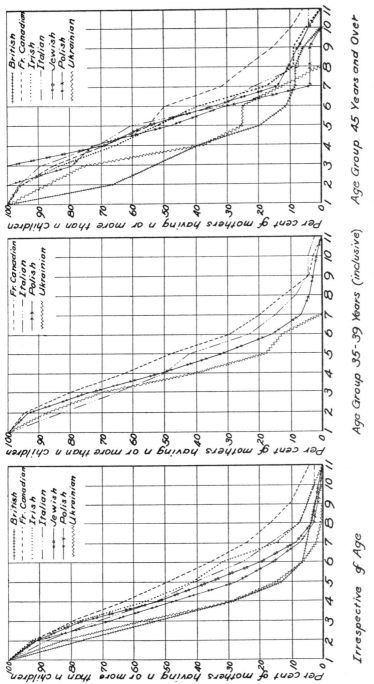

Irrespective of Age   Age Group 35–39 Years (inclusive)   Age Group 45 Years and Over

Fig. 6.—Major groups compared for size of family. (These figures are based upon the data in Tables 58 and 59.)

and others what language or languages were ordinarily spoken in the homes from which these children came.[1]

LANGUAGE FACILITY OF CHILDREN
(Table 60)

All the children included in the unit were in public school. By far the vast majority had been in public school over a period of several years. Ninety-two and seven-tenths per cent were, as we have seen, native born. Though these children come from immigrant homes, they have been subjected to situations which impose the use of English upon them. They are, therefore, all English speaking. If, in addition, they have retained their ancestral language, they are bilingual and probably in other ways bicultural.

The replies indicate that only 28.3 per cent of the children were limited to the use of English only, while, on the other hand, 71.7 per cent can speak in addition one or more foreign languages; 4.2 per cent of all children are multilingual.

The foregoing percentages include children from homes in which English is the ancestral language, and homes of mixed descent where foreign-language usage is diminished. In order to test the hold which the ancestral language has upon the American-born child, the inquiry might well be limited to those children who come from families where English is not the ancestral language. Counting only the children who come from foreign-speaking homes, we find that over 80 per cent have retained their ancestral language.[2]

The groups vary in the tenacity with which they cling to the ancestral language. Thus 98.0 per cent of the French–Canadian children are either bilingual or multilingual, speaking the language of their parents in addition to English. The figure is 97.0 per cent for the Slavs, 88.5 per cent for the Jews, and 93.4 per cent for the Italians. These high percentages are truly remarkable in view of the fact that with the exception of the French Canadians all these groups represent pre-war settlement in the United States, and the children are for the most part native born.

In Woonsocket multilingualism is largely an American product. A newcomer to Woonsocket learns English and French! French was fre-

[1] Languages obviously learnt in high school were not included. For discussion of reliability see Appendix B.

[2] This figure is derived from Table 60 by eliminating from the computation the children derived from English-speaking groups.

TABLE 60

LANGUAGE ABILITY OF 4,978 CHILDREN

ETHNIC DERIVATION	NUMBER				PER CENT			
	Monolingual* (a)	Bilingual† (b)	Multilingual (c)	Total (d)	Monolingual* (a')	Bilingual† (b')	Multilingual (c')	Total (d')
Albanian..............	......	1	....	1	......	100.0	....	100.0
Armenian............	3	23	7	33	9.1	69.7	21.2	100.0
Austrian.............								
Belgian (Flemish)......	......	9	....	9	......	100.0	....	100.0
British total..........	368	17	....	385	95.6	4.4		100.0
a) English.............								
b) Scotch.............								
c) Scotch-Irish........								
d) Canadian English...								
e) Canadian Scotch....								
f) Canadian unspec....								
g) British mixed......								
h) British, others.....								
Chinese..............	......	3	....	3	......	100.0	....	100.0
Colored.............	6	3‡	....	9	66.7	33.3	....	100.0
Czech...............	......	......	2	2	......	......	100.0	100.0
Dutch...............								
Finnish..............	1	1	....	2	50.0	50.0	....	100.0
French Canadian......	30	1,483	3	1,516	2.0	97.8	.2	100.0
French, total all others.	4	101	7	112	3.5	90.2	6.3	100.0
a) French, France.....								
b) Walloon............								
c) Alsatian............								
d) Swiss..............								
e) French mixed.......								
German.............	5	1	1	7	71.4	14.3	14.3	100.0
Greek...............	1	14	6	21	4.8	66.6	28.6	100.0
Irish................	261	11	....	272	96.0	4.0	....	100.0
Italian..............	27	297	90	414	6.5	71.7	21.8	100.0
Jewish..............	22	155	14	191	11.5	81.2	7.3	100.0
Portuguese (white)....	......	27	....	27	......	100.0	....	100.0
Roumanian...........	......	37	3	40	......	92.5	7.5	100.0
Scandinavian total.....	13	22	....	35	37.1	62.9	....	100.0
a) Swedish............								
b) Norwegian..........								
c) Danish.............								
Slavic total..........	25	765	48	838	3.0	91.3	5.7	100.0
a) Polish.............	20	442	31	493	4.0	89.7	6.3	100.0
b) Ukrainian..........	4	304	17	325	1.2	93.6	5.2	100.0
c) Russian............	1	17	....	18	5.6	94.4	....	100.0
d) Lithuanian.........		2		2		100.0		100.0
e) (Galician).........								
Spanish.............								
Syrian...............	2	61	8	71	2.8	85.9	11.3	100.0
Turkish..............								
Partly unspecified (n.d.)	102	29	....	131	77.9	22.1	....	100.0
Unspecified (n.d.)......	35	2	....	37	94.6	5.4	....	100.0
Others unspecified	2	4	....	6	33.3	66.7	....	100.0
Mixed ancestry........	500	296	20	816	61.3	36.2	2.5	100.0
GRAND TOTAL.....	1,407	3,362	209	4,978	28.3	67.5	4.2	100.0

* Monolingual refers to children speaking only English.

† Bilingual refers to children speaking English and their ancestral language.

‡ Portuguese colored.

quently given as a language in use by parents and by children who were
themselves non-French in origin. The Italians contribute the largest
multilingual group of children. Ninety children speak several languages.
Among the Slavs 48 children speak more than one language, a situation
characteristic, however, of Slavs in other cities.

The percentage for children who are monolingual and those who are
bilingual is radically different for the children of mixed ancestry from that
for the population at large. Thus, 61.3 per cent of the children of mixed
descent speak only English as compared with 28.3 per cent for the total
population. By contrast, 36.3 per cent of the mixed children are bilingual
as compared with 67.5 per cent for the whole population. Children of
mixed descent, then, are more largely limited to English than others, but
they are also more largely the children of parents who belong to the second
and third generation, and they are derived in large measure from English-
speaking peoples. In view of these facts, even 36.3 per cent[1] seems an un-
usually high rate of bilingualism. It would seem to indicate that French
holds its own in the melting pot, since the French Canadians are the
predominant non-English-speaking element in the mixed population.
Though the language ability of children varies with different nationalities,
it is significant that of all children in the public schools 71.7 per cent are
either bilingual or multilingual, and that children from foreign homes
show a tendency to adopt more than one new language, if conditions in the
community favor it.

LANGUAGE USAGE IN HOMES
(Table 61)

It may well be asked, By what processes or influences do the immigrant
cultures achieve their hold upon American-born children to such an extent
that over 71.7 per cent[2] of the children should be either bilingual or
multilingual? This is no mean achievement and indicates a form of control to be recognized. The explanation for this situation is readily found
in the fact that the majority of parents are of the first generation, and

[1] Alice M. Towsley reports a much higher percentage of foreign-language usage in homes
of mixed descent, where each parent reports a different foreign language as mother-
tongue (see chap. x). Her findings would seem to indicate that French is used predominantly
in the homes of persons who come from regions in which French is the ordinary language in
use and some Slavic tongue in situations where both parents are derived from different Slavic
groups. The foregoing figures cover all mixed cases. Miss Towsley's figures refer only to 1–1
homes where each parent reports a different foreign language.

[2] The figure, as we have seen, is over 80 per cent if we count only those children whose
ancestral language is other than English.

TABLE 61

LANGUAGE USAGE IN THE HOMES OF 2,298 HOMOGENEOUS FAMILIES

ETHNIC DERIVATION	NUMBER OF FAMILIES SPEAKING					PER CENT SPEAKING				
	Foreign Language Only (a)	English Only (b)	English and Foreign (c)	Total English (d)	Grand Total (e)	Foreign Language Only (a')	English Only (b')	English and Foreign (c')	Total English (d')	Grand Total (e')
Albanian................	1	....	....	....	1	100.0	....	....	....	100.0
Armenian...............	9	2	3	5	14	64.3	14.3	21.4	35.7	100.0
Austrian................										
Belgian (Flemish).........	8	....	....	....	8	100.0	....	....	....	100.0
British total.............	....	222	....	222	222	....	100.0	....	100.0	100.0
a) English..............										
b) Scotch..............										
c) Scotch-Irish.........										
d) Canadian English.....										
e) Canadian Scotch......										
f) Canadian unspec......										
g) British mixed........										
h) British, others.......										
Chinese.................	3	....	....	....	3	100.0	....	....	....	100.0
Colored.................	1*	2	....	2	3	33.3	66.7	....	66.7	100.0
Czech..................	1	....	....	....	1	100.0	....	....	....	100.0
Dutch..................										
Finnish.................	1	1	....	1	2	50.0	50.0	....	50.0	100.0
French Canadian.........	677	78	215	293	970	69.8	8.0	22.2	30.2	100.0
French, total all others.....	54	6	20	26	80	67.5	7.5	25.0	32.5	100.0
a) French, France.......										
b) Walloon.............										
c) Alsatian.............										
d) Swiss...............										
e) French mixed........										
German.................	2	3	....	3	5	40.0	60.0	....	60.0	100.0
Greek..................	6	....	4	4	10	60.0	....	40.0	40.0	100.0
Irish...................	....	144	....	144	144	....	100.0	....	100.0	100.0
Italian.................	136	13	34	47	183	74.3	7.1	18.6	25.7	100.0
Jewish..................	32	38	29	67	99	32.3	38.4	29.3	67.7	100.0
Portuguese (white)........	14	2	3	5	19	73.7	10.5	15.8	26.3	100.0
Roumanian..............	16	....	7	7	23	69.6	....	30.4	30.4	100.0
Scandinavian total........	7	11	3	14	21	33.3	52.4	14.3	66.7	100.0
a) Swedish.............	7	10	3	13	20	35.0	50.0	15.0	65.0	100.0
b) Norwegian...........										
c) Danish..............	....	1	....	1	1	....	100.0	....	100.0	100.0
Slavic total..............	359	18	64	82	441	81.4	4.1	14.5	18.6	100.0
a) Polish..............	199	11	44	55	254	78.4	4.3	17.3	21.6	100.0
b) Ukrainian...........	150	6	19	25	175	85.7	3.4	10.9	14.3	100.0
c) Russian.............	9	1	1	2	11	81.8	9.1	9.1	18.2	100.0
d) Lithuanian..........	1	....	....	....	1	100.0	....	....	....	100.0
e) (Galician)...........										
Spanish.................										
Syrian..................	13	7	5	12	25	52.0	28.0	20.0	48.0	100.0
Turkish.................										
Unspecified (n.)..........	....	24	....	24	24	100.0	100.0	....	100.0	100.0
GRAND TOTAL........	1,340	571	387	958	2,298	58.4	24.8	16.8	41.6	100.0

* Colored Portuguese speaking Portuguese.

that the ancestral languages are so largely the languages usually spoken
in the homes. The families have been here long enough to learn English,
but not long enough to discard the use of the mother-tongue as the
language of common usage in the home.

Table 61 is a summary of the data for language usage in homogeneous
families for all generations. In 58.4 per cent of the homes the ancestral
language is commonly used in the home; in 16.8 per cent of the homes
English and the ancestral language are both in common use; in only 24.8
per cent of the homes is English the only language used. But in this last
group about two-thirds of the cases are drawn from homes in which the
ancestral language is ordinarily English; only 7.8 per cent of the families
whose original tongue is not English now use English alone as the cus-
tomary language.[1]

The groups vary considerably in practice, the Ukrainians rank first in
percentage of families using only the ancestral language with 85.7 per
cent. The Poles report 78.4 per cent; the Italians, 74.3 per cent; the
French Canadians, 69.8 per cent; and the Jews, only 32.3 per cent.

All children speak English as a matter of course, but since the ancestral
language is in common use in 58.4 per cent of the homes and in 16.8 per
cent of the other homes a foreign language is used along with English, it
is not surprising to find that almost a corresponding percentage of the
children in the city, 71.7, report ability to speak a foreign language. They
hear it and use it constantly.

It may seem for a moment that the French Canadians are dropping
their language more quickly than the others. But the groups are not
strictly comparable. The French Canadians represent the only foreign-
speaking nationality in this case which is not entirely a first-generation
group. When we limit the inquiry to French Canadians in the 1–1 class,
the percentage using French only, and the one more strictly comparable
with the other old immigrant groups, rises to 84.7 per cent. They compete
with the Ukrainians in tenacity for their mother-tongue.

When, on the other hand, the data are differentiated for generation,
French Canadians show a steady decrease in the use of French only and
a steady increase in the number of families using French and English, also
in the number using English only (Table 62). Thus, English only is used
in 2.3 per cent of the 1–1 homes. The figure rises to 8.8 per cent[2] in homes

[1] Computed from data contained in Table 61.

[2] This figure is an average for two groups ($2x$–1) and (1–$2x$) combined, and is derived from
Table 62.

where one parent is native born and to 17.8 per cent in homes where both parents are native born.[1] By contrast, bilingualism is characteristic in 13.0 per cent of the homes where both parents are foreign born; in 24.7 per cent of the homes in which one parent[2] is native born; and in 36.5 per cent of the homes in which both parents are native born. There is quite definitely a steady decline in the number of homes which are limited to the use of French. Only 45.7 per cent of the homes in which both parents are native born report French as the common language. This is an exceedingly high figure for bilingualism in families of native parentage, and yet it indicates quite definitely that, given time, even the most tenacious of cultures gives way to the culture pressures of the immediate environ-

TABLE 62

LANGUAGE USAGE IN FRENCH-CANADIAN FAMILIES COMPARED BY GENERATIONS
(Only the 970 Families of Homogeneous Descent Included)

GENERATION OF	NUMBER USING				PER CENT USING			
Fa.–Mo.	French Only	English Only	French and English	Total	French Only	English Only	French and English	Total
1–1..........	359	10	55	424	84.7	2.3	13.0	100.0
2x–1.........	132	14	44	190	69.5	7.4	23.1	100.0
1–2x.........	86	15	37	138	62.3	10.9	26.8	100.0
2–2.........	58	21	42	121	47.9	17.4	34.7	100.0
3–2.........	37	16	34	87	42.5	18.4	39.1	100.0
Rejects.......	5	2	3	10	50.0	20.0	30.0	100.0
GRAND TOTAL	677	78	215	970	69.8	8.0	22.2	100.0

ment. French Canadians may be tenacious of their culture and ardent for its survival; with the lapse of three generations, however, the hold loosens. French Canadians become bilingual in the course of the first generation and long remain a bilingual group. However, norms are relative. English is relatively twice as frequent as the language of common usage in homes among the Jews of the first generation as it is among the French Canadians of the second and third generations.

Language usage in the home is a thing apart from language ability. French may be the language in common use among French Canadians, but there is evidence that they learn English readily and can speak it, even in the first generation. English is the secondary language.

[1] This percentage is derived from Table 62, and is an average for 2–2 and the 3–2 classes combined.

[2] The table indicates in detail the figures for language usage when it is the father who is native born and when it is the mother.

LANGUAGE ABILITY AMONG PARENTS

(Table 63)

The preceding summaries deal more particularly with language usage. They indicate what language or languages are in common use in the homes specified. The second and third questions, however, serve to test

TABLE 63

Language Facility of Parents in Major Groups Compared

(Only Those Parents Included Who Are Foreign Born and Who Have Not Intermarried)

	Per Cent Speaking No English			Per Cent Speaking English				Grand Total
Ancestral Only (a)	Ancestral and Other Foreign (b)	Total Foreign Only (c)	English Only (d)	English and Ancestral (e)	English, Ancestral and Other (f)	Total Using English (g)	$h=c+g$ (h)	
French Canadians (1,176)*:								
Men (615)..........	21.3	....	21.3	....	78.4	.3	78.7	100.0
Women (561)........	44.4	....	44.4	....	55.6	....	55.6	100.0
Italians (363):								
Men (182)..........	14.8	8.2	23.0	.6	53.9	22.5	77.0	100.0
Women (181).......	31.5	9.9	41.4	1.1	45.9	11.6	58.6	100.0
Jews (184):								
Men (95)..........	1.0†	7.4	8.4	3.2	25.3	63.1	91.6	100.0
Women (89)........	3.4	7.9	11.3	2.2	32.6	53.9	88.7	100.0
Poles (499):								
Men (251)..........	16.7	2.0	18.7	....	70.5	10.8	81.3	100.0
Women (248)........	27.4	3.6	31.0	....	64.9	4.1	69.0	100.0
Ukrainians (349):								
Men (175)..........	20.0	8.6	28.6	.5	46.3	24.6	71.4	100.0
Women (174).......	27.6	17.8	45.4	.6	35.6	18.4	54.6	100.0

* The figures in parentheses indicate the total number of cases examined for each nationality. Only the percentages are given across for the subgroups. The absolute number in each class can be readily derived from the total in col. *a*.

† Probably an error as the man was here more than twelve years.

language ability. The question asked in each case is, What other language does the parent speak, i.e., what language in addition to the one commonly used in the home?

It is most enlightening to compare the behavior of different groups in this regard. Except in the case of the French Canadians there have been but few newcomers to these groups since 1915. There has therefore been at least a decade to allow for certain tendencies to establish themselves. What most interests the student of acculturation is the range of language ability, the extent to which English is one of the languages used, and the length of time needed for an adjustment. There are therefore five classes into which the results may be grouped:

PER CENT OF INDIVIDUALS

I. *a*) Speaking only their ancestral language
  b) Speaking their ancestral language and some other foreign tongue
II. *c*) Speaking only English
III. *d*) Speaking English and the ancestral tongue
  e) Speaking English and more than one foreign language

The first classes speak no English; the last three do.

Summary Table 63 throws light upon the practice of various groups in this regard, and upon differences between men and women. Jewish men rank first in language adaptability—they are the least prone to limit themselves to the use of a foreign language. Only 8.4 per cent of the men do not speak English. They also show the highest percentage of men who use English entirely, and the highest percentage who are multilingual; 3.2 per cent use English entirely, and 63.1 per cent are multilingual (Table 63, col. *f*). In language adaptability the Jews have no competitors. The women lag a bit behind the men in this group, but they, too, rank first in language adaptability when compared with the women from other ethnic groups. They also rank higher than the men of all other nationalities.

Polish men take second rank in acquiring English, and French-Canadian men take third rank. Only 21.3 per cent of French-Canadian men are limited to the use of French alone. Practically no French Canadians are multilingual, none use English entirely—78.7 per cent speak both languages. Italian men rank fourth and Ukrainians fifth in the acquisition of English and in sole dependence upon the ancestral language. In all groups the women show a serious lag behind the men in the use of English.

In multilingualism the Jews rank first, 63.1 per cent reporting the use of several languages. The Ukrainians rank second with 24.6 per cent, the Italians third with 22.5 per cent, while the Poles claim only 10.8 per cent. Jews and Slavs in other communities also report a high percentage of multilingualism, both among those who speak English and among those who do not use English. This is characteristic of persons who come from Slavic countries, but the Slavic groups adopt the use of English less quickly than do the Jews, and there are significant differences among the Slavic groups themselves. The Ukrainians are markedly multilingual but are slowest to adopt English. The exact significance of the relative rank held by the Poles and Ukrainians is obscured somewhat by the fact that the Poles as a group have been in the country somewhat longer than the Ukrainians. This may account for the lower percentage of multilingualism among Poles but it does not seem to account entirely for the difference. The peak for Italian immigration falls in the same period as that for the Ukrainians, the French Canadians of the first generation are more recent immigrants, and yet the percentage of men in each of these three groups

TABLE 64

LANGUAGE USAGE OF FRENCH-CANADIAN PARENTS BY LENGTH OF
RESIDENCE IN THE UNITED STATES

(Only Those Parents Included Who Are Foreign Born and Who
Have Not Intermarried)

| | NUMBER OF | | | | | | PER CENT | |
| | Fathers Speaking | | | Mothers Speaking | | | | |
NO. OF YEARS IN THE U.S.	French Only (a)	French and English (b)	Total (c)	French Only (d)	French and English (e)	Total (f)	Bilingual Fathers* (g)	Bilingual Mothers† (h)
Less than 1	10	5	15	14	1	15	33.3	6.7
1–5	28	17	45	32	14	46	37.8	30.4
6–10	9	14	23	13	8	21	60.9	38.1
11–15	8	13	21	16	12	28	61.9	42.9
16–20	13	21	34	30	12	42	61.8	28.6
21–25	5	41	46	18	44	62	89.1	71.0
26–30	8	53	61	32	39	71	86.9	54.9
31–35	4	57	61	15	44	59	93.4	74.6
36 or more	12	139	151	26	83	109	92.1	76.1
TOTAL NUMBER RE-CORDED	97	360	457	196	257	453	78.8	56.7
Rejects	34	124	158	53	55	108	78.5	50.9
GRAND TOTAL	131	484	615	249	312	561	78.7	55.6

* These percentages are derived from the items in col. *b*. The percentage is the ratio of *b*:*c*.
† These percentages are derived from the items in col. *e*. The percentage is the ratio of *e*:*f*.

who use no English is only 21.3 per cent for the French Canadians as against 23.0 per cent for the Italians and 28.6 per cent for the Ukrainians. While correlations based upon the study of individual cases for language usage and length of residence might throw further light on this question, it seems clear from the data we now have that the Ukrainians as a group either show less ability or less eagerness to take on English than other groups who have been in the country the same length of time. Both among those who speak English and among those who do not, the Ukrainians, like others from Slavic countries, show a high proportion of men and of women who are multilingual.

The Italians report a considerable proportion who are multilingual. It would seem that the Italians must be adding French as well as English to their language equipment. Among the Italians 8.2 per cent who do not speak English speak two foreign languages. It is probable that French in this instance is acquired even before English. The greater similarity between the French and Italian tongue, proximity in the mills, common religious practice, multiple community interests, bring these foreign

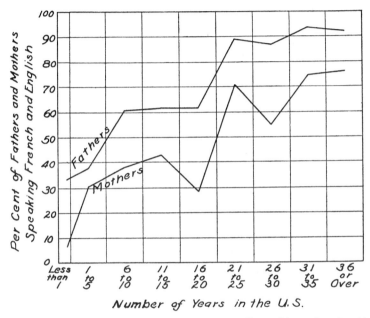

FIG. 7.—Increase of bilingualism among French Canadians with continued residence in the United States. (These figures are based upon the data in Table 64.)

groups closer to each other than to the other groups culturally more distant.

The relation of language usage to length of residence is best shown in the case of the French Canadians where the number of cases is sufficient over a continuous period of years. Table 64 and Figure 7 indicate how steadily French Canadians become bilingual with increased residence in this country. This bilingualism is, as we have seen, carried over into the second and third generation. The tenacity with which the French Canadians cling to their cultural values does not seem to interfere with their ability to take on traits of their new environment—a point of view which they themselves stoutly maintain.

CONCLUSIONS

Perhaps the outstanding feature in the whole cultural situation described above is the fact that there are obvious differences between the adjustments to American life made by specific ethnic groups—differences in size of family, in language usage, and, as the investigators discovered, in policies of Americanization. While the data here presented are not sufficient to warrant dogmatic generalizations about the different nationalities, the trends are surely descriptive of the situation in Woonsocket.

The foregoing chapters give us a picture of the racial and cultural complex of the community as that picture was reconstituted from data gathered directly from school children. It is an interpretation based entirely upon an analytic approach to the problem. In the following chapter the historian contributes a picture reconstructed from the resources usually available to the historian.

CHAPTER XIV

HISTORICAL SKETCH OF WOONSOCKET, RHODE ISLAND

By HENRY W. LAWRENCE

PERIODS IN THE HISTORY OF WOONSOCKET

FIRST PERIOD: Pioneer settlement, 1666–1719
    1666. Arnold and Comstock built the first sawmill
    1719. Quakers built the first meeting-house
SECOND PERIOD: Agricultural economy, 1719–90
    1790. Samuel Slater arrived in the Blackstone Valley
THIRD PERIOD: Transition from agriculture to manufacturing, 1790–1831
    1831. Edward Harris bought his first mill in Woonsocket
FOURTH PERIOD: Industrial economy, 1831 to date:
    a) Large immigration of French Canadians and others
        French Canadians came rapidly after the sixties
        Rise of Roman Catholic influence
    b) Ascendancy of French Canadians and Roman Catholicism

This history deals only with immigrants. The Indian aborigines do not come into the story, except as they affected slightly the fortunes of the white invaders. The purchase (so called) of lands from the natives approximated fairness a little more nearly in this Rhode Island region than in most other parts of New England, thanks to the benevolent intentions of Roger Williams and the unwarlike habits of the Quaker settlers. Possibly this helps to explain why the Indians gave relatively little trouble[1] to that section with which we are here concerned, namely, the northeast corner of the state, particularly the town, later city, of Woonsocket, which, until the last third of the nineteenth century, was included in the older towns of Cumberland and Smithfield.

The patron divinity of this region is the Blackstone River, called also by several other names. It was this stream that invited the earliest settlers, watering their live stock and their crops, and very early beginning to supply them with that superman and superhorse power which, in the nineteenth century, finally induced them to abandon agriculture and turn to manufacturing. When, about the year 1666, two young men, Richard Arnold and Samuel Comstock, passed up this river, they built a sawmill

[1] Richardson, p. 100. (See pp. 228–29 for full citation of references used in this chapter.)

on the site of the present Woonsocket,[1] and were thus the first to harness this serviceable giant in behalf of civilization. Settlement seems to have followed rather slowly, however, for the first house built in this immediate neighborhood dates from 1690,[2] log cabins and other lesser structures having served the inhabitants for the first quarter-century. Real estate promotion was considerably handicapped in those days, nor should we forget that King Philip's War, which occurred in this time and region, tended to make investors slightly hesitant about risking their savings, and their scalps. Moreover, land titles were sometimes disputed, by whites as well as by reds, the original settlers, Arnold and Comstock, not securing the undisputed recognition of theirs until 1707.[3]

Nevertheless, civilization advanced, slowly but irresistibly. In 1712 the river was harnessed a second time, by the erection of a "corn and fulling mill."[4] Seven years later, organized religion put up a visible evidence of its arrival in this half-century-old community, in the erection of a Quaker meeting-house, the only place of public worship maintained here until more than a century later,[5] and a significant testimonial to the fact that Quakers predominated among the early settlers.

Soon after the Quaker meeting-house was well established, the needs of travel and conviviality were served by the opening of a tavern. This first tavern in Woonsocket was kept by one of the numerous and distinguished Arnold family,[6] and was the forerunner of many other taverns, whose fame, or notoriety, has considerably mellowed the atmosphere of Woonsocket history from that day to this. Meanwhile, the Quakers had contributed again to the progress of civilization by erecting an iron mill, in 1720.[7]

Next, the growing needs of transportation were attended to by the building, in 1736, of the first bridge over the Blackstone River at Woonsocket Falls.[8] The financing of this was a joint matter, public funds being supplemented by private subscriptions. In 1741 the first road was built in this frontier settlement, its predecessors having been mere paths, trails, and blazed ways through the forests.[9] This new avenue of traffic was very far indeed from being a macadamized modern highway, but it did constitute a part of the so-called "turnpike" from Providence to Worcester.

[1] Richardson, p. 39; Bayles, II, 299.   [3] Bayles, II, 268.
[2] Steere, p. 139; Richardson, p. 42.   [4] Richardson, p. 55.
[5] Richardson, p. 77; Steere, p. 139; Bayles, II, 336.
[6] Richardson, pp. 69–75; Bayles, II, 286–88.
[7] Richardson, pp. 55, 79; Bayles, II, 299–300.
[8] Richardson, pp. 61–62.   [9] Richardson, pp. 57–58.

At the point where this turnpike was crossed by an equally ancient road, from Boston to Connecticut, stood a little settlement called Woonsocket Crossroads. This was the commercial center of the neighborhood and the real Woonsocket for nearly a century. With the rise of manufactures, however, in the early nineteenth century, most of the population moved to Woonsocket Falls, near the center of the present city, leaving the crossroads community as a suburb, with a new name, Union Village.

It was the civic conscience of the Quakers that launched public education in this northern, backwoods section of Rhode Island. As early as 1771 their uneasiness and pious hopes are expressed thus in their records: "It is thought necessary yt poor children be schooled." Six years later they took action in the matter. A committee was, in 1777, "appointed to draw up a plan for establishing a free school among Friends."[1] This good work, together with the influence of several private academies a little later, gradually pushed the hesitating authorities of the town of Smithfield into assuming support of free schools soon after 1820.[2] The earliest of the academies was that of Elisha Thornton, a Quaker, established near Slatersville, in which its founder's zeal for learning won him grateful admiration from his pupils, and dark suspicions of witchcraft from his neighbors.[3] The Smithfield Academy, in Union Village, influenced more immediately the Woonsocket communities, beginning its work in 1810 and ending about 1850. In providing funds for its housing a lottery was employed.[4]

The use of the lottery in those days was widespread. Apparently the notorious eighteenth-century New England conscience had, at first, a few qualms about employing this gambling device in aid of the Kingdom of God. At any rate, it was outlawed in Rhode Island in 1733.[5] Eleven years later, however, the ban was lifted, and after 1744 the cause of righteousness was often and variously assisted by this questionable method. Three years before the Smithfield Academy had been lotteried into existence, as mentioned above, a lottery had been authorized for building a meeting-house in the town of Smithfield, and in 1828 the records tell of a committee appointed to superintend the drawing of the Free Will Baptist Society's lottery in Smithfield.[6] Funds for the repair of bridges were frequently raised in this fashion.

[1] Richardson, pp. 87–89; Steere, pp. 139–40; Bayles, II, 328–29.

[2] Richardson, p. 88; Bayles, II, 329.

[3] Richardson, pp. 79–80; Bayles, II, 329.   [5] *Know Rhode Island*, p. 16.

[4] Richardson, pp. 91–92; Steere, p. 140.   [6] Steere, p. 66.

Other aspects of enlightenment and finance are illustrated by the establishment at Woonsocket of its first public library, in 1800,[1] and of its first bank, in 1805. The little library continued its service for nearly a generation, and paved the way for more pretentious successors. The "Old Bank," absorbed in 1915 into the Woonsocket Trust Company, illustrated the primitive methods of early banking in northern Rhode Island. "On September 5, 1805," the bank records tell us, "Nabby Wilkinson was paid one dollar and seventy-five cents for washing and ironing the bills." The cashier's salary was at first one dollar a day, but by 1810 it had been raised to $400 a year, and there it stayed until 1864. In recognition of the high cost of living it was then raised to $500. The earliest bank vault consisted of a hole in the ground. The treasures it contained were safeguarded by brick walls from crumbling earth, worms, burglars, and other intrusions. The entrance was at the top, closed by a door so huge that a block-and-tackle arrangement was employed for opening it. It was locked by a key of massive proportions. Following the pathway of progress and population, the "Old Bank" moved over to Woonsocket Falls, i.e., the present Woonsocket, soon after 1850.[2]

This luring of banks and population into the valley of the Blackstone River was due in large measure to the coming of an English immigrant into Rhode Island, bringing with him certain highly important smuggled goods. The immigrant was one Samuel Slater, and the smuggled goods were the plans and specifications for the new English machinery used in the manufacture of textiles. He escaped detection in carrying these priceless things out of England because he carried them safely concealed in his remarkably accurate and retentive memory. When he finally reached Pawtucket, in 1790, the Blackstone River was no longer permitted to loaf leisurely along its course, but must henceforth increasingly spend its strength in turning the wheels of factories, built by Slater and many of his imitators. Slater's hard-wrought success caused many less competent persons to flock into the cotton-manufacturing business in the next twenty years. The period shortly before the War of 1812 is called by a local historian that of "the cotton mania."[3] Mills were erected at Woonsocket, as elsewhere along the Blackstone River, and many of them failed to pay, in the hands of their pioneer operators. After these failures and a period

[1] Bayles, II, 334.

[2] Bayles, II, 292; also information furnished the writer by F. A. Jackson, second vice-president of the Woonsocket Trust Co., prepared from the records of the "Old Bank."

[3] Richardson, pp. 126, 168 ff.; Bayles, II, 300.

of "hard times," the local factory system resumed its rapid growth under conditions more likely to bring success. The second generation of textile manufacturers in Woonsocket is well represented by the locally famous Edward Harris, who bought his first mill there in 1831,[1] and whose conspicuous achievements have been passed on and amplified down to the present generation of his descendants.

Meanwhile, improvements in transportation facilities had again become urgent. By 1820 there was a regular mail-coach service between Providence and Worcester,[2] and six years later a daily stage line, both passing through Woonsocket. By 1843 this town was joined to Boston also, by a daily coach service, in which the journey took seven hours and cost each passenger a dollar and a half.[3] Between the years 1823 and 1828 a canal was constructed from Providence to Worcester, utilizing largely the course of the Blackstone River. This carried some passengers, but was devoted chiefly to freight. It proved unsuccessful financially in less than a score of years, and was abandoned.[4]

At about the time the canal failed the first railroad came to take its place. Chartered by the state legislature in 1844, the Providence and Worcester Railroad was ready for service in 1847.[5] In the promotion of this railway-building enterprise, a survey was made of towns along the proposed line, to ascertain how much of freight and passenger traffic they would be likely to furnish. This survey contained the following statements about Hamlet, Bernon, and Woonsocket, all included in the present city of Woonsocket:[6]

1. HAMLET—population 250, contains two cotton mills, with 5,832 spindles, 120 looms, employing 67 females and 74 males, producing 20,000 yards of cotton cloth per week, and working 650 bales of cotton per annum.

2. BERNON—population 750, contains two cotton mills, with 11,000 spindles, 288 looms, employing 175 females and 75 males, producing 38,500 yards of cotton cloth per week, and working 1,000 bales of cotton per annum.

3. WOONSOCKET—population 4,000, contains 17 cotton mills, with 34,456 spindles, 812 looms, producing 151,039 yards of cotton cloth per week, and working 5,251 bales of cotton per annum; three woolen mills, with ten sets of machinery, producing 4,700 yards of cloth per week, and working 281,500 pounds of wool per annum; six machine shops, an iron foundry, two grist mills, a saw mill, one spool and bobbin shop, one soap manufactory, two wholesale grocery stores. In the mills 413 females and 456 males are employed.

[1] Richardson, p. 131; Bayles, II, 397–400.   [3] Bonier, p. 71.
[2] Bayles, II, 290.   [4] Bonier, p. 70; Richardson, pp. 165–66.
[5] Richardson, pp. 179–82; Bayles, II, 284; Bonier, p. 72.
[6] Quoted in Bayles, II, 284.

These population figures may have been padded a bit. The local census of 1846 shows only 4,856; that of 1841 gives 3,951.[1] The community was growing with feverish rapidity, and calling into its multiplying factories a labor supply which included more than a fourth of the total population, and of these mill-workers there were more women than men. The old attitude of hostility toward strangers[2] was being changed by the employers of labor into one of welcome, such as it was, toward anybody who was willing to work long hours for low wages in the mills. With the building of the canal and the railroad Irish laborers came in gradually.[3] As early as 1815 at least one French-Canadian family was established in Woonsocket,[4] but it was not until after 1830 that these immigrants from the north began to come in considerable numbers. A census of 1846 shows 250 French Canadians out of a total population of 4,856.[5] The most rapid influx of French immigrants from Canada came, however, after the outbreak of the American Civil War, in 1861.[6] At a critical moment in the development of the textile manufactures the war called away a large part of their labor force. How to replenish this was the problem. The management solved it, partially, by sending French-Canadian agents into the province of Quebec to spread glowing accounts of economic opportunity in the factories and mills of Woonsocket and other New England cities. The response was encouraging, almost overwhelming. The French-Canadian population not only became numerous; it showed signs of becoming predominant before the end of the century. By 1873, for instance, it seemed wise to the Roman Catholic authorities to establish a separate parish for their French-Canadian communicants in Woonsocket, and in less than a decade afterward these French-Canadian Catholics had also their separate church edifice.[7] In 1873 the first French newspaper was started. It proved to be a little premature, and died of inadequate support immediately after its first issue. It was followed by several others which did not long survive, but in 1895 *La tribune* began the service which it still continues, as a daily paper printed entirely in French.[8]

[1] Newman, p. 39; Daniels, p. 13.   [2] Steere, p. 31; Bonier, p. 87.

[3] Richardson, pp. 163–65. According to Newman (p. 39) there were 666 persons of Irish birth in Woonsocket in 1846, out of a total population of 4,856.

[4] Bonier, p. 79.

[5] Bonier, p. 80; Newman, p. 39. Newman's total of only 250 does not include persons of French-Canadian birth who had become citizens of the United States.

[6] Bonier, p. 75; Bayles, II, 301. In 1846 the percentage of foreign-born in Woonsocket was 26.8 (Newman); in 1870, it was 51.5 (U.S. Census).

[7] Bayles, II, 343–44; Holland, p. 8.   [8] Bonier, pp. 340–42.

Along with the sudden growth of population and business there went a corresponding development of organized religion and education. As early as 1821 Universalist preaching had begun in Woonsocket, amid much heavy-handed but ineffective opposition. By 1834 the Universalists had a permanent society, and in 1840 they dedicated a church building.[1] The first Roman Catholic mass in Woonsocket was said in 1828: present, ten men and no women. The first Catholic church building came in 1844, and the first resident pastor in 1846. The service was almost wholly to Irish laborers on the canal, who soon afterward became mill-workers.[2] During the thirties several Protestant denominations got their start and built churches in this thriving factory town. These included Episcopalians, Baptists, and Methodists.[3] At least the latter two came to include in their programs a definite missionary effort toward the French Canadians in their neighborhood.[4] The fight against Demon Rum seems to have begun early in the industrial period. A temperance crusade in 1841 lured 825 into signing a total-abstinence pledge, thus leaving only a little more than 3,000 wet or unaccounted for.[5]

The advance of public education was further marked by the establishing of a high school in 1849, which occupied a three-story frame building erected for the purpose at a cost of $13,000;[6] this when the Woonsocket community had a population which probably did not much exceed 6,500.[7] Ten years later, in 1859, the first parochial schoolhouse was erected, at a cost of $3,100, to serve chiefly the 2,300 Irish Catholics then resident in the Woonsocket parish.[8]

Library facilities of a sort had not been wholly lacking since 1800,[9] yet it was not until 1868 that they were offered quite without expense to the public of Woonsocket, as a gift from the locally well-known Edward Harris, who, in the year mentioned, established in connection with the Harris Institute the first free public library in the state of Rhode Island. This library was open twice a week until 1873, and daily thereafter. In the same building with it was housed the Woonsocket Lyceum, whose

[1] Bayles, II, 345; Richardson, pp. 82–83.

[2] Holland, pp. 1–6; Bayles, II, 340 ff.; Richardson, pp. 84–85.

[3] Richardson, pp. 81–86; Steere, p. 66; Bonier, p. 30.

[4] Bayles, II, 339, 355.   [5] Daniels, pp. 13–16.

[6] Richardson, p. 98; Bayles, II, 332.

[7] Newman (p. 39) gives it as 4,856 in the year 1846. The Census of 1850 gives 6,696.

[8] Bayles, II, 341. According to Holland (p. 7), "In 1855, the parish numbered something like 1,600 souls, almost all Irish immigrants."

[9] Richardson, p. 89; Bayles, II, 334.

meetings and lectures still further cleared the intellectual atmosphere of the hustling, roaring mill town.[1] That the atmosphere, both intellectual and moral, needed to be cleared cannot well be doubted.

Whatever efforts may have been exerted on the part of some employers to improve the labor conditions of that day, contemporary accounts confirm the expectation that here as elsewhere the early stages of the factory system were deplorably inhumane.[2] A critical account of the situation may be found in a pamphlet published by a contemporary, Thomas Man, in 1835, entitled *A Picture of Woonsocket*, in which he says, "My principal object in writing is to purge the noxious vapors from the moral atmosphere." He mentions his own residence in Woonsocket, and dedicates the pamphlet to its citizens, "to guide them in the way of all righteousness." In recommending to their favorable consideration the Decalogue, he underlines the seventh commandment. In directing their attention to the Lord's Prayer, he prints it in French. Concerning the factory conditions he says, "And why does not the Government of the United States regulate the time of labor in Cotton Manufactories, which is severely oppressive to children, as has been done in England, by the last Reform Bill?" The same author, in a pamphlet published in 1833, gives what he calls a *Picture of a Factory Village*, presumably descriptive of local conditions. From this such lines as the following voice his criticism:

> For Liberty our fathers fought,
> Which with their blood, they dearly bought,
> The Fact'ry system sets at naught [p. 7]

The workers protest:

> Our life's in danger, exposed to constant harm,
> The wheels tear the hand, picker takes off an arm,
> A handsome girl is caught in a cursed drum,
> Dash'd from things of sense, into the world to come [p. 11].

On factory stores:

> A Factory store is a sponging-place;
> It is the eel-pot of our sorry race;
> We toil all day, fatigu'd with might and main,
> And the next day repeat it o'er again.
> At the year's end—this you, indeed! well know—
> We've not a single paltry cent to show;

[1] Bayles, II, 335; Richardson, p. 99.

[2] Richardson, pp. 171–73; Bayles, II, 305; Bonier, pp. 44–46.

> You grasping owners, put it in your pocket,
> And we, poor vile wretches, can't unlock it.
> Yes! our best blood we lost by sweat,
> And hardly get enough to eat [p. 13].

A footnote says:

The Memory of the Founder of Cotton Factories should be held in contempt by the present generation and execrated to the remotest ages of Posterity.

Twenty years later, in 1853, the findings of a legislative investigation into factory conditions throughout the state were presented in a *Report*[1] made to the General Assembly at its January session, 1853. It seems highly probable that the statements made in this *Report* are as applicable to Woonsocket as to other industrial towns of the state, and there is no reason to doubt their accuracy. The investigator found fewer young children employed than he expected. He says:

In this respect there has been a great change for the better within the last four years. The improvements in machinery render the employment of young children far less desirable than formerly, and there are now few good establishments that care to employ children under 12 years of age. At a much earlier age, they are frequently urged upon the employer against his will, and taken perhaps as a condition to obtaining or retaining others, and more desirable members of the same family.

The hours of labor, and the opportunities for education, are far worse than I anticipated, and such as it seems to me cannot fail to awaken the attention of the public to the subject and to call for legislative action. First the hours of labor. In this there is a great disparity between the different establishments. There are a few Mills that scarcely average to exceed 11 hours' work per day, certainly not to exceed $11\frac{1}{2}$ hours; very many that do not exceed 12 hours, perhaps the majority of them not more than $12\frac{1}{2}$; whilst there are Mills that, from the best data that could be obtained, work 14 hours per day. There are Mills during last winter that commenced work at $5\frac{1}{2}$ A.M., on all days but Saturday, and on that day at $4\frac{1}{2}$ A.M., as they left work earlier in the afternoon of that day—making more than 13 hours of labor in the very shortest days.

The only relaxation that great numbers of children so employed find, is that of occasional stopping of Mills for water, repairs or on an occasional holiday. . . . . It matters not that the labor be light. It generally requires close attention, and constant standing upon the feet, and gives nothing like the requisite amount of time for the recreation and rest that all children require—it must be admitted that the great body of the operatives in the manufacturing establishments of our State are without any adequate advantages for the most common education. It does not, in my mind, improve the matter, or lessen the evil, that large numbers of these operatives are the children of foreigners.

[1] *Report of the Commissioner Appointed To Ascertain the Number, Ages, Hours of Labor, and Opportunities for Education of Children Employed in the Manufacturing Establishments of Rhode Island.*

There are mills in the State where nearly all the small help are of foreign parentage, not one-half of whom know their own ages. To the inquiry addressed to them, did you ever attend school? the answer not unfrequently would be, [not] since I came from Ireland, or [not] since I came to this country. And perhaps such child has resided in the State or country several years. *Went to school in Ireland, but not since he or she came to this land of free schools!* A remedy must be provided such even as shall overcome if possible, any religious prejudices that tend to this result.

It is not improbable that these inhumanities were somewhat intensified by the fact that the labor force consisted very largely of foreigners, immigrants; people whose alien customs, speech, and religion tended to cut them off from understanding and sympathy on the part of the employing group.[1]

Of all the immigrant groups that have given to Woonsocket its present character and reputation, none other has been so numerous or influential as the French Canadian, and the reason for this pre-eminence is not hard to discover. While living in the province of Quebec, before migrating into New England, these French Canadians were neither contented nor prosperous. The farms on which they were living had been cultivated too long and replenished too little. Moreover, these farms were too small to support the large families that tilled them, and neither capital nor enterprise was available for introducing the improved agricultural methods and machinery which might have made the impoverished acres yield an adequate supply. Their well-established dislike of British institutions and British neighbors made the Quebec French disinclined to seek escape from their pinching adversity by migration to other parts of Canada.[2] They were, however, without any such prejudice against their neighbors to the southward, sometime rebellious colonists of Great Britain, now citizens of the free United States of America. When the invitation came, therefore, to migrate into this land of freedom and opportunity, they responded hurriedly, and in constantly increasing numbers. Because of their geographical nearness, the call was very definitely sent to them by the mill-owners of New England, hard pressed by the labor shortage which enlistments for the war occasioned here as elsewhere during the sixties. For the Cana-

[1] In 1885, for instance, the state census shows 44 per cent of the total population of Woonsocket to be foreign born, yet of those employed in the woolen and worsted mills more than 59 per cent were foreign born, and in the cotton mills more than 60 per cent.

[2] Bonier, pp. 74–76.

[This is the interpretation also given by Mlle Marthe Bossavy, staff associate, after numerous interviews with old settlers and with members of their families. For an account of her association with these investigations see Appendix A.—B. B. W.]

dians to accept this invitation was relatively easy. Possible competitors from Europe had to cross the stormy and expensive Atlantic, but immigrants from French Canada had to cross only the frontier. If the first factory town they reached did not offer the opportunities they were seeking, they could continue their overland journey to another, and to yet others. In the course of these journeyings a great many of them came to Woonsocket and settled there.[1]

That they liked this new mill town well enough to advise the home folks back in Canada to follow them is eloquent testimony to the living conditions in Canada. By their predecessors in the Woonsocket mills, English and Irish workers chiefly, they were greeted with epithets and other more tangible evidences of disapproval, in which the jobless Yankee soldiers, returned from the war, joined heartily enough no doubt.[2] To most of the mill-owners they were merely so many Canucks, whom a beneficent Providence had accustomed to plain living and hard labor so that they might do their bit toward making the United States of America the richest country in the world.[3] Even the politicians despised them at first, for most of them had no vote.[4] Amid such cordiality of welcome they felt distinctly encouraged to stand together and be self-sufficing—an attitude toward which they were already predisposed by their experiences under British rule.

Their ancestors in Canada, back in the days when that region was still a possession of France, had enjoyed an administration untainted by Anglo-Saxonism, a régime based on the law, language, and religion of the mother-country, though differing from that in some minor aspects, notably in the larger control in the colony exercised by the Roman Catholic church.[5] But all this seemed likely to be swept away after the British victory in the French and Indian War had driven France out of North America. Interestingly enough, however, this French pattern of life was not swept away. The Treaty of 1763 had promised that Britain would respect the religious liberty and legal customs of the French in Canada, and the Quebec Act of 1774 largely redeemed this promise. Whatever grievances the French Canadian might have against Great Britain, he

[1] Bonier, pp. 86–87; also Bossavy, cited above.

[2] Bonier, pp. 60, 87.   [3] Bonier, pp. 44–46.

[4] In 1846 only about 23 per cent of the French inhabitants of Woonsocket born in Canada had been naturalized (Bonier, p. 80); in 1925 about 39 per cent (Rhode Island state census [1925], unpublished).

[5] Bossavy, cited above.

could hardly claim that she was trying to make an Englishman out of him. The situation, nevertheless, made him sensitively aware of his separate and peculiarly precious cultural heritage. Outside Quebec the struggle for its preservation had been almost completely lost. Within Quebec itself, last oasis of French-Canadian culture in an expanding desert of Anglo-Saxon domination, there were grave fears against further encroachments, and ceaseless anxiety lest the French manner of life might be blotted out altogether from North America. This sense of peril was accompanied by great zeal for the preservation of all forms and symbols of the menaced culture.[1]

The attitudes and practices in defense of their culture have been carried over to the new land. A last will and testament, written entirely in French and presented recently to the recording officer in the city of Woonsocket, illustrates, on the language side at least, the present continuance of this zeal. Other illustrations include the presence of a daily newspaper in that city printed wholly in French (until 1928 there had been for some years two French newspapers), and the alleged urging by persons in authority over the French-speaking group that they patronize preferably those stores which employ French clerks.[2]

On the religious side also many of the French-Canadian group in Woonsocket resisted submergence, offering stubborn opposition alike to the Irish domination in church matters (as they had, indeed, done earlier in Canada) and to the Anglo-Saxon tradition in school life, or at least to the full control of education by the state. In illustration of this opposition in church matters may be cited a recent and widely discussed controversy between the Roman Catholic bishop of this region, himself an "Irishman," and certain French-Canadian leaders, including a vigorously propagandist newspaper, who professed to represent the French-Canadian element in that church in protesting against Irish domination therein.[3]

The alleged resistance to the Anglo-Saxon tradition in school affairs is

---

[1] Bossavy, cited above.

[2] Information furnished to the writer by a lawyer of Woonsocket.

[3] See editorials in *La sentinelle*, a recently discontinued French weekly paper of Woonsocket, in which attacks were made against the Roman Catholic bishop of this diocese, William A. Hickey. A much more moderate and conciliatory attitude, however, is taken by *La tribune*, the French daily of Woonsocket (see its editorial, "The Final Triumph," in the issue of November 12, 1924), and by L'Union St. Jean Baptiste d'Amérique, a widely spread French Catholic organization. The attitude of the latter toward this question is shown in a resolution on the subject adopted in a recent convention at Holyoke, Mass. For further reference to this subject see "Histoire de l'agitation sentinelliste dans la Nouvelle-Angleterre, 1925–1928," *La tribune* (Woonsocket, 1928).

still a matter of lively controversy throughout the state, and it involves other cities besides Woonsocket and other foreign-language groups beside the French Canadian. Yet Woonsocket and in particular the French Canadian group, which constitutes so large a majority of its population, have been outstanding in this alleged resistance to the thorough Americanization of the Rhode Island school system, and to its complete control by the state as well as toward the several legislative measures which have been directed towards these ends during the past decade. The chief point publicly at issue, at least as far as the Woonsocket situation is concerned, has been the extent to which instruction in parochial schools shall be French in both language and subject matter. The Americanization forces, crusading to make Rhode Island "literate in English," secured the passage in 1922 of the so-called Peck Law, under which English was to be the basic language in all schools, and the supervisory and certifying power over private schools was placed in the hands of the state authority rather than the local. To this arrangement the representatives of foreign-language constituencies, Woonsocket among them, objected, ostensibly on the ground that it was a violation of the principle of home rule and local self-government in transferring supervision and control from the local authority to the state. The Americanization crusaders urged, however, that the only real objections to state control were, first, that it made more difficult the evasion of the English-language requirement, which evasion a lax local supervision dominated by a foreign-language group might easily facilitate, and, second, that it limited the Roman Catholic control over parochial schools. Repeated attempts to amend the Peck Law were finally successful, in 1925, when a compromise measure transferred the supervisory and certifying power to the local authorities,[1] but provided also for every private school that

reading, writing, geography, arithmetic, the history of the United States, the history of Rhode Island, and the principles of American government shall be taught in the English language substantially to the same extent as such subjects are required to be taught in the public schools, and that the teaching of the English language and of other subjects indicated herein shall be thorough and efficient; provided, however, that nothing herein contained shall be construed or operate to deny the right to teach in such private schools . . . . any of said subjects or any other subject in any other language in addition to the teaching in English as prescribed herein. . . . .[2]

[1] [At the time of the survey this supervisory power was in the hands of a local priest of Irish descent.—B. B. W.]

[2] C. 678 (H. 745, approved April 29, 1925) of Rhode Island Acts and Resolves, January, 1925.

In considering certain characteristics of the predominant language group in Woonsocket, the French Canadian, we must not overlook the presence and influence of numerous other groups of foreign origin. Woonsocket is a true and typical daughter of Rhode Island, and grand-daughter of New England, in being a great deal more foreign than native American in the stock of which her population is made up. According to the 1920 Federal Census, the foreign white stock[1] stood in the following ratios to the total numbers of inhabitants: in New England, 61 per cent; in Rhode Island, 69.6 per cent; in Woonsocket, 84 per cent. According to the same Census, the foreign-born were 25.5 per cent of the total population in New England as a whole; 29 per cent of that in Rhode Island; and 36.8 per cent of that in Woonsocket (Table 66). Some indication as to how this foreign element has been divided during various periods of the town's history among the several nations of origin is given in accompanying tables. The figures are taken from the earliest and the latest censuses available, which cover these details for Woonsocket. The Census of 1846 was a private and somewhat erratic numbering, by one S. C. Newman, a local contemporary. The subsequent figures were obtained from the interdecennial censuses taken by the state of Rhode Island.[2] The Census of 1846 probably underweights slightly the foreign element, owing to the author's peculiar method in dealing with naturalized persons, but it seems nevertheless to be worthy of consideration. Tables 65, 65a, and 66 indicate the changes in the town's population from decade to decade.

Though less than half of the foreign-born French in Woonsocket had, according to the state census of 1925, taken even the first step toward naturalization,[3] the French element seems to be rather well represented in the city government. A count of the personnel of the city officials elected November 6, 1928, for instance, shows the mayor, 3 of the 5 aldermen, and 8 of the 15 councilmen to be French Canadian. A similar count of bank and trust company officials and directors indicates that nearly one-fourth of them are French Canadian, which would seem to indicate that the overwhelming numerical preponderance of the French in Woonsocket is being felt by their significant influence in the "realm of finance."

[1] The term "foreign white stock" here means the foreign-born plus the natives of foreign parentage plus the natives of mixed parentage, i.e., one parent native and the other foreign born.

[2] The 1915 and 1925 censuses are unpublished.

[3] It should be remembered that they are more recent comers to Woonsocket than other groups.

TABLE 65

REGIONAL DERIVATION OF POPULATION IN WOONSOCKET FROM 1846 TO 1925
(Data Derived from Decennial State Censuses and Other Sources)

Regional Derivation	1846	1875	1885	1895	1905	1915	1925
Armenian............							54
Austrian............				1	42	220	396
Belgian (Flemish)......		12	3	38	149	504	405
British total..........							
a) English...........	349			652	785	755	643
b) Scotch and Welsh ...	29	97	102	157	124	144	105
c) Scotch-Irish.......							
d) Canadian English....		450	450	409	392	302	
e) Canadian Scotch....							
f) Canadian others.....							185
g) British mixed.......							
h) British, others......							
Chinese ⎱ ⎰ Colored ⎰	3						
Czech...............							
Dutch...............							
Finnish..............					82	58	
French Canadian.......	250	3,376	4,366	7,481	8,939	8,484	11,695
French, European total..							
a) French, France......		64	60	108	311	817	826
b) Walloon...........							
c) Alsatian...........							
d) Swiss.............							
e) French mixed.......							
German..............	1	37	33	45	76	170	55
Greek...............							85
Irish................	666	2,218	2,081	2,032	1,369	937	645
Italian...............	1		5	11	158	773	859
Jewish..............							
Portuguese (white).....				5		17	149
Roumanian...........							
Scandinavian total.....							
a) Swedish...........			9	38	67	73	51
b) Norwegian.........							7
c) Danish............							
Slavic total...........							
a) Polish.............			5		793	2,167	909
b) Ukrainian..........							
c) Russian............				132	297	338	330
d) Lithuanian.........							2
e) (Galician)..........							
Spanish..............							
Syrian...............							68
Turkish.............				46	88	183	
All others............		9	9	29	62	244	403
TOTAL FOREIGN-BORN	1,299	6,263	7,123	11,184	13,734	16,186	17,872
TOTAL NATIVE-BORN.	3,557	7,313	9,076	13,284	18,462	23,889	31,809*
GRAND TOTAL.......	4,856	13,576	16,199	24,468	32,196	40,075	49,681

* This includes 38 colored and 33 others, not white.

TABLE 65a

PER CENT DISTRIBUTION OF TABLE 65

(Data Derived from Decennial State Census and Other Sources)

Regional Derivation	1846	1875	1885	1895	1905	1915	1925
Armenian							.1
Austrian				*	.1	.5	.8
Belgian (Flemish)		.1	*	.2	.5	1.3	.8
British total							
a) English	7.2			2.7	2.4	1.9	1.3
b) Scotch	.6	.7	.6	.6	.4	.4	.2
c) Scotch-Irish							
d) Canadian English		3.3	2.8	1.7	1.2	.8	
e) Canadian Scotch							
f) Canadian others							.4
g) British mixed							
h) British, others							
Chinese⎫ Colored⎭	.1						
Czech							
Dutch							
Finnish					.3	.1	
French Canadian	5.1	24.8	27.0	30.6	27.8	21.2	23.6
French, European total							
a) French, France		.5	.4	.4	1.0	2.0	1.7
b) Walloon							
c) Alsatian							
d) Swiss							
e) French mixed							
German	*	.3	.2	.2	.2	.4	.1
Greek							.2
Irish	13.8	16.3	12.8	8.3	4.2	2.3	1.3
Italian	*		*	*	.5	1.9	1.7
Jewish							
Portuguese (white)				*		*	.3
Roumanian							
Scandinavian total							
a) Swedish			.1	.2	.2	.2	.1
b) Norwegian							*
c) Danish							
Slavic total							
a) Polish			*		2.5	5.4	1.8
b) Ukrainian							
c) Russian				.5	.9	.8	.7
d) Lithuanian							*
e) (Galician)							
Spanish							
Syrian							.1
Turkish				.2	.3	.5	
All others		.1	.1	.1	.2	.6	.8
TOTAL FOREIGN-BORN	26.8	46.1	44.0	45.7	42.7	40.3	36.0
TOTAL NATIVE-BORN	73.2	53.9	56.0	54.3	57.3	59.7	64.0
GRAND TOTAL	100.0	100.0	100.0	100.0	100.0	100.0	100.0

* Less than .1 per cent.

TABLE 66

REGIONAL DERIVATION OF POPULATION OF WOONSOCKET, RHODE ISLAND, 1920

(Derived from Data in the Fourteenth Census of the United States, 1920)

	Birthplace	Per Cent	Country of Origin	Per Cent	Rank by Country of Origin
Albanian...............					
Armenian...............	86	.2			
Austrian...............	105	.2	2,662	6.1	3
Belgian (Flemish)...........	409	.9	599	1.4	10
British total...............					
a) English...............	705	1.6	1,579	3.6	4
b) Scotch...............	114	.3	266	.6	12
c) Scotch-Irish...............					
d) Canadian English...........					
e) Canadian Scotch...........					
f) Canadian unspec...........	288	.7	623	1.4	9
g) Welsh...............			4	*	25
h) British, others...........			6	*	24.5
Hungarian...............			9	*	23
Dutch...............			141	.3	14
Finnish...............					
French Canadian.............	9,328	21.4	22,189	51.1	1
French, European total........					
a) French, France.............	802	1.8	862	2.0	7
b) Walloon...............					
c) Alsatian...............					
d) Swiss...............			10	*	22
e) French mixed...............					
German...............	48	.1	235	.5	13
Greek...............	139	.3	117	.3	17
Irish...............	774	1.8	3,273	7.5	2
Italian...............	785	1.8	1,328	3.1	5
Newfoundland...............			126	.3	15
Portuguese (white)...........	63	.2	72	.2	18
Roumanian...............			6	*	24.5
Scandinavian total.............					
a) Swedish...............	53	.1	122	.3	16
b) Norwegian...............	8	*	11	*	21
c) Danish...............			13	*	20
Slavic total...............					
a) Polish...............	1,431	3.3			
b) Ukrainian...............					
c) Russian...............	550	1.3	1,292	3.0	6
d) Lithuanian...............	21	.1			
Spanish...............			3	*	26
Syrian...............	61	.1			
Turkish...............			396	.9	11
Mixed foreign...............			690	1.6	8
All others...............	256	.6	15	.1	19
TOTAL FOREIGN WHITE.....	16,026	36.8	36,649	84.3	
TOTAL NATIVE WHITE......	27,383	63.0	6,847	15.7	
Colored...............	70	.2			
Chinese...............	17	*			
TOTAL NATIVE-BORN.......	27,470	63.2			
GRAND TOTAL.............	43,496	100.0	43,496	100.0	

* Less than .1 per cent.

These and many similar signs are hardly needed, however, to make clear the fact that Woonsocket is, to a degree rarely matched throughout the United States, a foreign city. The Federal Census of 1920 shows its native stock to constitute 15.7 per cent, while its foreign-born stock is 84.3 per cent of the total population. It is a foreign city, predominantly French Canadian, to the extent of more than half the whole number of its inhabitants. In this latter group there is vigorous resistance to that type of Americanization effort which would destroy or disregard the values in culture, convenience, and control which depend upon the preservation of the French language and tradition. The numerical dominance of the Roman Catholic church in this city is very great. Approximately half the school children attend the parochial schools; more than half the public-school children are Catholic; and an overwhelming majority of the church-goers attend the Catholic church.

The dual ascendancy of the French-Canadian element and of the Roman Catholic church—together with the industrial background which the city affords—constitute powerful factors in making Woonsocket a unique "American" community and one peculiarly interesting for the student of cultural change.

LIST OF WORKS CITED IN THIS CHAPTER

1. AMERICAN CHILD HEALTH ASSOCIATION, RESEARCH DIVISION OF THE. *A Health Survey of 86 Cities.* New York, 1925.

2. BAYLES, RICHARD M. *A History of Providence County, Rhode Island,* Vol. II (1891).

3. BONIER, MARIE L. *Débuts de la colonie franco-américaine de Woonsocket, Rhode Island.* 1920.

4. CARPENTER, NILES. *Immigrants and Their Children, 1920: A Study Based on Census Statistics Relative to the Foreign Born and the Native White of Foreign or Mixed Parentage,* "Census Monographs," No. VII. Government Printing Office, Washington, 1927.

5. DANIELS, A. S. *Statistics of the Village of Woonsocket.* 1842.

6. HOLLAND, REV. C. J. *St. Charles'—Old and New: Being a Brief Record of the Origin and Development of Catholic Life in Woonsocket in So Far as That Life Affected and Was Affected by the Origin and Development of St. Charles' Parish.* 1929.
   Father Holland is the pastor of this parish.

7. *Know Rhode Island; Facts Concerning the Land of Roger Williams.* Report of the Rhode Island State Bureau of Information, Office of the Secretary of State, 1927.

8. MAN, THOMAS. *A Picture of Woonsocket; or, The Truth in Its Nudity.* 1835.

9. MAN, THOMAS. *Picture of a Factory Village.* 1833.

10. NEWMAN, S. C. *A Numbering of the Inhabitants, with Statistical and Other Information, Relative to Woonsocket, Rhode Island.* 1846.

11. *Rhode Island Acts and Resolves.* 1925.

12. RHODE ISLAND STATE CENSUSES.

The latest census published is that of 1905. Unpublished sheets of the censuses of 1915 and 1925 are available in the office of the Department of Labor, State Capitol, Providence, R.I.

13. RHODE ISLAND GENERAL ASSEMBLY. *Report of the Commissioner Appointed To Ascertain the Number, Ages, Hours of Labor, and Opportunities for Education of Children Employed in the Manufacturing Establishments of Rhode Island; Made to the General Assembly at its January Session, 1853.* Printed by order of the Senate.

An eight-page pamphlet in the Rider Collection, Box 14, of the John Hay Library, at Brown University. The commissioner reporting was W. B. Sayles.

14. RICHARDSON, ERASTUS. *History of Woonsocket.* 1876.

15. *Sentinelle, La.*

A French weekly of Woonsocket, R.I. (recently discontinued).

16. STEERE, THOMAS. *History of the Town of Smithfield, from Its Organization, in 1730-1, to Its Division, in 1871.* Pp. 139. 1881.

17. *Tribune, La.*

The French daily newspaper of Woonsocket.

18. UNITED STATES BUREAU OF THE CENSUS. *Census of 1920* (and of other years), "Census Monographs."

Grateful acknowledgment is here made to the persons, in Woonsocket and elsewhere, who have freely given valuable aid to the writer in preparing this brief sketch.

APPENDIXES

APPENDIX A

FRANCO-AMERICANS IN WOONSOCKET: BIBLIOGRAPHY

INTRODUCTION

It has been persistently obvious from the previous analyses that Woonsocket is unique in the dominant rôle played by one ethnic group in the racial composition and in the cultural life of the community. Two-thirds of all school children[1] in Woonsocket are of French-Canadian descent. Among the public-school children alone 2,155, or 43.3 per cent of the total number, carry some French or French-Canadian blood.[2] The significant position which French Canadians hold in the community, and the results of a special investigation among them, call for further treatment, however brief.

HISTORICAL RÉSUMÉ

It is not always possible to disassociate various French stocks from one another, since they are so intermixed. French stock of one regional derivation or another has played a part in the history of Rhode Island ever since the early days of settlement. The European predecessors of the more humble folk of the present are classed as aristocratic. These are the Huguenots of yesterday. Inscriptions on the tombstones adjoining Trinity Church in Newport, Rhode Island, remind us not only of the presence of Huguenots in the neighborhood, but of the active part which they played in the life of several Rhode Island towns. Trinity Church in Newport and St. John's Church in Providence both owe their origin in large measure to the activity of early French settlers, men who were prominent

[1] I.e., of all children in public and parochial schools.   [2] Table 48.

in their day and whose names appear frequently in the historical record of the communities. Not a few of the old families in Rhode Island count in their fold descendants of British and French blood. Genealogical records in Providence indicate here and there intermarriage with the French. As a result of an unfortunate squabble involving the legal right to hold land in the colony of Frenchtown,[1] numerous French families were uprooted and became migrants throughout the neighboring territory. In those days they were not, of course, aristocrats, but now the research student is warned to remember that "it is fashionable to boast of Huguenot ancestry."

The date of entry and the fusion tables in this study make record in some measure of the relation of the various French groups to one another and to other groups in Woonsocket. It is fair to assume, however, that internal migration within the towns of Massachusetts and Rhode Island would, however, account for the injection of European French blood to a greater extent than indicated, and that from time to time Woonsocket received and sent out of the community French migrants. Even today many of the French Canadians in the "valley" in Rhode Island, a trip some two hours from Woonsocket by automobile, are persons whose families once lived in Woonsocket or who now have relatives in Woonsocket.

Most of the early French settlers and their descendants must have been incorporated into the community at large through intermarriage. Others have been Americanized in the cultural sense. The loss of identity is brought about in some measure by the anglicizing of names. Mlle Bonier[2] gives a list of names of French and French-Canadian families in the earlier days of Woonsocket's history that were anglicized; the "translations" are unique. The tendency, even as it is with other foreign groups now, was to choose names that were in good standing! Thus Isaï Bérard became James Bell; Brindamour became Brown; Georgianna Bérard, Rosanna Barre; Joseph Dubois, Joseph Wood; Paquin became Perkins; Phaneuf, Farnum; Provencher, Moore. And so the list continues. Potter similarly records changes and corruptions of names which make it difficult to trace family lines.[3]

[1] Now East Greenwich, R.I. See bibliography under Potter. Considerable material on this general subject is to be found in the library of the Rhode Island Historical Society, also in the John Carter Brown Library and the John Hay Library of Brown University, and the Redwood Library of Newport.

[2] See bibliography under Bonier.

[3] "It is with great difficulty that their descendants can now be traced, so great have been the changes and corruptions of the names. Two or three such have already been noted, for

It was not until the middle of the nineteenth century, however, that the French Canadians as a group made their advent in Woonsocket, although Lawrence[1] finds record of a first family in 1815. These more recent French immigrants are, it is true, not regarded with the same esteem as their "pure French" predecessors, yet ethnological judgment would find it difficult to classify these as separate stocks excepting for the differentiation due to three centuries in Canada, let it be remembered, in a distinctly French civilization. The situation is analogous to that of the Canadian British. The French and the French Canadians are intermarried so closely as to make it almost futile at times to keep the groups apart in our composition tables. This marriage between European French stocks and French Canadians is frequent in spite of the superiority feeling on the part of the French. "France French" is the gentle reminder offered the investigator in response to an inquiry as to derivation, much as the North Irelander will emphasize the "North" or make it a point to write in "Protestant" when he designates his derivation to be Irish. When it comes to actual marriage, however, the French stocks like the British will prefer mates from their own specific group—France French, Alsatian, and Walloon each choose their own kind. But this preference does not become aversion to other French stocks as against a distinctly different racial group.

After every possible attempt to classify the individuals according to their specific French group or origin, we find a group remaining as of mixed French origin. The tendency for these groups to attract each other is obviously not a new phenomenon. The data in the monograph have been so presented that the French Canadians and other French stocks may be studied as several units or as one combined unit. But the fact is that French infusion is coterminous with the history of Rhode Island.

The present status of French stocks in Woonsocket may be gleaned from the quantitative data at our disposal. The material immediately following is a summary of the data on French Canadians scattered through the various chapters with interpretations about French Canadians based upon Mlle Bossavy's[2] visits to the homes of those French Canadians whose families were old settlers in the United States. She visited 213 families which were in part of the third generation; she lived for a while in the community and came to know the various leaders and their

instance, Le Moine became Money and still later Mawney; Ganeauz became Gano; Daille became Daily or Daly; Targe became Tourgee! Many others might be shown but these suffice to explain the difficulty in following them" (Potter, *op. cit.*).

[1] Chap. xiv.   [2] See chap. i, p. 7.

points of view. In addition, both she and the author met and discussed the chief issues freely with French priests in other communities and in Canada.[1]

RÉSUMÉ OF QUANTITATIVE DATA ON COMPOSITION

Our statistics on immigration are never at any time discontinuous for the French Canadians. They started to come during the last century when the industrial needs of Woonsocket encouraged such coming, and have been coming steadily since then.

Within the past fifty years, a period included in the life-span of the present generation, the stream of French-Canadian immigration has been again continuous. The peak was reached between 1895 and 1899. There is a steady decline during the recent years—a decline which corresponds to the decline generally noticed for that group in Federal Census statistics, but as was noted previously there has been a rise again since the post-war period. Nor do all French-Canadian immigrants in Woonsocket come directly from Canada. Many come from other communities in the United States where they first tried to work out a settlement. The figures in Table 54, and Figure 4 for the date of entry to the United States, indicate that few French-Canadian families in Woonsocket have been in the country less than a decade. Most of them came during the latter years of the nineteenth century.

The French Canadians now in Woonsocket are in large measure an immigrant group, but not to so great an extent as are the other foreign stocks, and a larger proportion of the former belong to older generations. Of the 2,189 French-Canadian parents in the population 1,260, or 57.5 per cent, belong to the first generation; 555, or 25.4 per cent, belong to the second generation; 40, or 1.8 per cent, belong to the third generation; 353, or 16.1 per cent, belong to the 3/2 and third generations combined.[2]

Most of the parents were married in the United States, their marriages having resulted in the distribution of families and children as indicated in Table 67. The distribution for generation when families or children are the units of enumeration and when they are classed according to the generation of parents is also shown in Table 67.

The large number of families and children represented in the 1–1 generation indicates once again the relatively recent advent of French-

[1] In the summer of 1926 Mlle Bossavy and the writer together took a holiday trip into the Canadian country which is the background of the French-Canadian immigrant, traveling into the forest land as far north as Mistassini and Peribonka.

[2] See Table 13.

Canadian families now present in the population. On the other hand, the French Canadians also represent with the British and the Irish the "old immigration" to Woonsocket. The proportion of the French-Canadian population which is in part Old American is significant. Among the children of French-Canadian descent in the public schools 9.4 per cent are in some degree Old American, by virtue of long-continued residence of their families in Woonsocket. In addition, 57.5 per cent of all French-Canadian children have at least one native-born parent. This last criterion places the French Canadians as an "American" group at a level considerably above the "new immigrants," 90 per cent of whom come from 1–1 homes.

TABLE 67

PER CENT DISTRIBUTION OF HOMOGENEOUS FAMILIES AND
CHILDREN OF FRENCH-CANADIAN DESCENT
(By Generation of Parents)

GEN. OF PARENTS	In 970 Homo-geneous Families*	Of 1,516 Homo-geneous Children†
	%	%
1–1................	43.7	41.5
2x–1‡..............	33.8	35.0
2–2................	12.5	13.1
3–2................	9.0	9.4
Rejects.............	1.0	1.0
Total...........	100.0	100.0

* See Tables 16 and 16a.
† See Tables 21 and 21a.   ‡ Including 1–2x.

It does not place them far below the British and the Irish. The Irish represent the least "foreign" group in the community when "foreign" is defined as a 1–1 generation home. The distribution immediately preceding indicates in general the length of residence of the French element in America. It is interesting to see what proportion the French-Canadian stock is of each generation class in the community.

The distribution for parents, families, and children given below indicates that French Canadians constitute a larger proportion of the second generation than of any other class. French-Canadian children constitute only about one-third of the first-generation class, about one-half of the entire second generation, and about one-sixth of the 3/2 group. Incidentally, these tables indicate again the extent to which French Canadians have married out of their generation, but within their own ethnic group. The ancestral culture dominates over the influence of the adopted culture. (Has it been adopted?)

These ratios, however, are in inverse relation to the absolute numbers. There are over four times as many first-generation French-Canadian children as there are 3–3 and 3–2 children, but in relation to the whole population the proportion of French Canadians is very much smaller in the first generation. The coming of the European immigrant has served to counteract the dominant influence of the French-Canadian element in racial composition of the Woonsocket population.

TABLE 68

Per Cent of French-Canadian Parents, Families, and
Children in Each Generation of Total Population

Gen. of Parents Themselves*	Per Cent of Total Class	Generation of Two Parents		
		Fa.–Mo.	In 970 Homogeneous Families† Per Cent of Total Class	Of 1,516 Homogeneous Children‡ Per Cent of Total Class
1st..........	34.9	1–1	28.3	23.3
		1–2x	55.2	52.9
		2x–1	52.7	53.6
2d..........	64.2	2–2	51.1	50.0
3/2..........	28.4	3–2s	17.0	16.6

* See Table 13*b*.   † See Table 16*b*.   ‡ See Table 21*b*.

FRENCH-CANADIAN STOCK IN DIFFUSION

The discussion thus far has dealt only with French Canadians who belong to family units in themselves homogeneous. In addition to the 970 homogeneous French-Canadian families, there are 257 families who are only in part French Canadian. It is interesting to note the composition of that part of the "melting pot" which is French Canadian in origin. Table 52 gives the distribution for families who are in whole or in part French. From Table 17 it is possible to see which strains unite with French strains in creating the melting pot.

Examination of the data contained in Table 17 indicates that three other strains predominate among the families who are in part French. Of these the Irish is numerically most important. Over one-fourth of all the families who are in part French Canadian are French Canadian×Irish. The French Canadian×British rank next, and there remains a group of French Canadians, mated with Old Americans, further unspecified. There are 64 cases of previous admixture. These last two groups are without question drawn from these same three elements.[1] The number of cases

[1] See chap. iv, p. 48.

which represent marriage between French-Canadian and European French stocks are considerable (23) when we remember that there are relatively few parents of European French descent in the entire population—178 European French parents compared with 472 Irish, and 642 British parents. Among the European French 23 married French Canadians, 41 married into *several* non-French stocks. French Canadians were represented as first choice. There is a distinct feeling of kinship between French peoples, in spite of the sense of superiority which characterizes the European French.

Inquiry into ethnic preference as it is exerted in the United States by men and women in different generation groups may be carried farther by examining the detailed figures in Tables 36 and 45. It will be recalled that these figures deal only with marriages which take place in the United States. When French Canadians marry British the marriages are most largely between individuals both of whom are native born, more particularly individuals who belong to the 3/2 generation. The largest proportion of marriages with the Irish occurs between individuals who are both native born, or between individuals one of whom is native born and one foreign born. In more cases it is the French Canadian who is the first-generation party. This is undoubtedly due to the preponderance of French Canadians in the first generation. Relatively few crossings occur between French Canadians and English-speaking groups in the first generation.

In general, French Canadians are less prone to intermarry than most other stocks. The rates of intermarriage are 7.8 per cent for the first generation, 8.8 per cent for the second generation, and 35.0 per cent for 3/2 and third generations combined. These may be compared with the rates for the same generations respectively in the whole city, of 12.1, 20.9, and 40.4 per cent (Table 30a). Although the French-Canadian "rates" of intermarriage and fusion are relatively low, these rates increase with generation in America. As a consequence of this, the percentage of admixture is greater in the older generation groups. Owing to the large number of French Canadians in the community, the number of families and children in part French is large, quite irrespective of the low rate of fusion.

In the 1–1 class there are 25 marriages which are French Canadian on one side only. In the 2x–1 groups there are 101 such marriages; and in the 2x–2 group, i.e., the group in which both parties to the marriage are native born, there are 122 such matings (Tables 38 and 43, also 45).

The few intermarriages in the 1–1 class are scattered among several nationalities. In the second generation the mixture is most emphatically with the Irish. In the third generation British blood competes closely with Irish blood as the constituent element in a part-French group. Three and one-half times as many French homes are part French in the third generation as in the first, indicating a real tendency to group disintegration with increasing length of residence in the United States, notwithstanding the reputation to the contrary which the group enjoys.

One of the most significant of all developments is that in spite of the important rôle which French Canadians play in the community they are coming in the later generations to be outnumbered by the sibs of mixed descent, a group which they have an important share in creating.

The French stocks of European derivation are, for the most part, represented in the first generation.[1] This corroborates the result of other observation in the community. In the first place, there seems to be a tendency at present for French stocks from European countries to send to Woonsocket persons who fill the positions of importance in the factories. In some instances they are purchasing these establishments from Old American owners. On the other hand, the European French, few in number, are quickly absorbed either by the French-Canadian group or in the melting pot in general. The only French group other than French Canadian that is represented in all generations is that designated as "French mixed." The individuals designated as French mixed are persons descended from two different French stocks. Frequently they are French Canadian and European French.

CULTURAL STATUS

Certain findings dealing more particularly with social and cultural factors characteristic of French life in Woonsocket may describe the cultural status of the group.

MIGRATORY HISTORY

The migration to and from Canada, and from one textile or rural center to another in the United States, is a frequent occurrence in the history of families in Woonsocket. Many families report that they went back to Canada several times. Families who report grandparents born in the United States report parents born or brought up in Canada, or married in Canada. "Sometimes," says Mlle Bossavy,[2] "the grandparents alone returned, leaving their children behind, thus strengthening the bond, however, between old country and new." There are foreign-born

---

[1] See tables in body of text.   [2] In an unpublished report filed with the Study.

children who claim native grandparents.[1] One child reports a father born in the United States of Canadian parents, and a mother born in Canada of American-born parents. Or there is the American-born grandmother who migrated with her French-Canadian parents through New York State, then west, then east, while her daughter moved to Canada only to return to the United States. "Such an Odyssey is not exceptional." Mlle Bossavy continues:

One important aspect of French-Canadian life on the continent which is strikingly illustrated, even in this limited group, is the ease with which French Canadians have migrated across it, from east to west, west to east, and from one side of the boundary line to the other.

The trends are well indicated from the information obtained from the Canadian families who counted among them grandparents born in the United States. The birthplaces of native grandparents are scattered over a wide area. Out of 455 grandparents born in the United States over 30 were born in each of the following states: Massachusetts, Rhode Island, New York, Vermont. From 8 to 12 were born in Connecticut, Maine, or New Hampshire. And from 1 to 5 were born in Washington, D.C., Illinois, Pennsylvania, Minnesota, Wisconsin, Michigan.[2]

The greatest number of cases represent direct immigration from Canada to the textile centers. Others drifted first into New York, Vermont, Michigan, or Maine, into the farms and shops of small rural centers. The migration from Canada to these communities is hardly thought of by the Canadians as an emigration at all. It is a transference from one French center to another.

A smaller number represent the adventure of the West; included among them are those who were for a time lured by Manitoba or Saskatchewan, for there again in the great plain out West where everybody speaks English boundary lines matter little.

French Canadians move West, where the civilization is Anglo-Saxon and different, or they change one French-Canadian community for another in the East. Political boundaries matter as little to the descendants of the discoverers, pioneers, and the *coureurs de bois* as they do to the American business man.

AGE OF MOTHER; SIZE OF FAMILY

In the chapter dealing with the age of mother and size of family we found that the average age of French-Canadian mothers is 43.7 years,

[1] This frankly was a severe test of our classificatory scheme, since a child was defined as Old American if he had native grandparents. Can a foreign-born child having possibly foreign-born parents be Old American because he has some native-born grandparents? Forty-two families presented such inconsistencies in grouping. These cases were treated as "migratory" and the children were classed according to their parents. A similar situation exists when American children are born abroad into missionary families. Five families in New London reported children foreign born in families where the grandparents were native born. These were called Old American children. See also chap. x, p. 152, n. ‡.

[2] To add to the colorful American story of origin, some dozen or more families report Indian blood, and at least one a grandfather who fought in the Civil War.

somewhat less than that for the British and Irish, somewhat more than that for more recent immigrant groups. By comparison with the average age of Italian and of Slavic mothers they probably represent more nearly completed families. This might account in part for the fact that in Woonsocket the largest families occur among the French Canadians. It was noted, however, that the average number of children for each age group among French Canadians is well above that for the same age group in the community at large. The mode for size of family is 3, which is the mode for all 1–1 homes. But more so than for any other group, a large number of families boast of 4, 5, and 6 children, and the number of families with children ranging from 7 to 11 in number is not matched by any other group, though the Italians are close competitors. Empirical observation indicates, and so some of the priests assert, that in general the French-Canadian family is growing smaller, but the tendency is not sufficiently manifest to have made any impression on the present population. Together with the Italians, the French Canadians contribute families in size above the average for the community at large. This definite tendency is marked also among French Canadians who are native born. French-Canadian mothers of the second and third generations represent the only significant group for whom the modal family is 3. The mode for the other classes and for the entire group is definitely at 2. And the number of families with children ranging in number up to 11 is considerable. Americanization has apparently not achieved the sophistication which limits the number of children. Native-born Irish women and native-born British women show no aversion to large families. It is possible that the small family, owing to greater knowledge and more frequent use of contraceptives, is not widely prevalent in any class in Woonsocket. The modal number of children has decreased from 3 to 2 among the native-born, but large families still occur to a surprising degree.

BILINGUALISM AND BICULTURALISM

It is in its bilingualism and in its biculturalism that the French-Canadian group is peculiarly distinctive and assertive. The data on language usage as obtained from the case histories of children corroborate the impressions obtained in home visits by Mlle Bossavy, and confirm the theories asserted by leaders in brochures on the subject and in conversation.

French Canadians even when native born and English speaking assert, with pride, their French-Canadian descent. About 90 per cent of all individuals who are native born can speak both languages; about half claim bilingualism in the home. They assert most emphatically that their tenacity for French culture is not inconsistent with loyalty to America or with full acquaintance with American institutions and the English language. They are French speaking even in the third generation. But they are English speaking, too, and become so in the very first generation. Our previous analysis of language usage indicated that with the exception of the Jews no other group in Woonsocket learns English more readily or uses it more extensively. But they differ from the Jews in one regard: Given time, the Jews drop their ancestral language; the French retain it as the familial and ancestral tongue. With the French the attachment to the French language and to things French amounts to a passion. Devotion to the French language and to French-Canadian ancestry was noted among families when even grandparents were native born. In other families one or more of the grandparents were brought here as babies, or the first member of the family came to the United States sixty, seventy, or even eighty years ago, or "too far back to remember," and yet "these families frankly and even proudly claim their French-Canadian ancestry, and still use the French language."[1]

Mlle Bossavy offers three possible causes in explanation of this tenacity for the French language even among Old Americans. She calls attention to the extensive intramarriage between French Canadians of different generations. Numerous marriages occur between two French-Canadian persons, one of whom is native born and the other foreign born. This was noted in our own investigations, but she finds evidence of the same procedure among grandparents and even among great grandparents. Second, frequent migration back and forth to Canada keeps the contacts and the language alive. Third, internal migration in the United States from one community to another where there are centers of French-Canadian life serves to perpetuate ancestral traditions.

"The West, whether American or Canadian, seems to have a fatal influence on the mother-language. But one does not need to move across the continent. It makes a difference in what New England town one happens to settle. The district of Woonsocket a family lives in may make a difference. One may cease to use French for a few years and adopt it again because one's neighbor uses that and no other." This explanation was offered by some of the mothers and was obviously indicative of the situation in numerous homes.

[1] Mlle Bossavy.

The French Canadians in Rhode Island are essentially a bilingual people. That this is characteristic of the group in other situations has been attested by many writers dealing with the same problem, particularly in Canada.

"It is an outstanding fact," writes Helen C. Munroe in a recent article[1] "that the educated French-Canadian speaks almost flawless English in addition to speaking a French that can be understood anywhere in a French-speaking country."

French Canadians who came under our observation expect their children to be bilingual as a matter of course. Native-born children know English and are being taught French and French tradition.

This biculturalism is not limited to the use of French as a language. There is an ardor for all things French. Nor is this devotion necessarily French Canadian. The Canadian flag is rarely exhibited, but the French flag is seen alongside the flag of the United States. To the French the former is the symbol of his culture; the latter, of his country. Loyalty to Canada as a homeland is seldom heard expressed, but loyalty to French culture and American citizenship is urged in every page of their literature. This is a conscious policy indorsed and fostered by those who represent leadership in the group. Its manifestation in Woonsocket is obviously typical of the situation in other communities.

The dependence upon language is closely related to the religious problem. Indeed, the devotion to one gathers strength from the other. To them the French-Canadian church and the parochial schools are the custodians of culture values. It is here that the dominance of the Irish, and particularly the "Irish theory of Americanization"—which assumes that the use of English as the primary language is an essential characteristic in an Americanization program—evokes resentment.

The French Canadian conceives Americanization as a process which brings into harmonious relation two diverse cultures. It is a plea for diversity in American community life. In this they are not alone among foreign nationalities in this country. But they are probably unique in having promulgated, some thirty years ago, a theory of Americanization which anticipated various theories of Americanization now current, one in particular which is in practice among numerous groups in this country.[2] It is a conflict between different theories of Americanization that constitutes the core of the dissensions in Woonsocket to which

---

[1] "Bilingual Signs in Montreal and Its Environs," *American Speech*, V, No. 3, 228.

[2] See bibliography for works of De Nevers.

reference has been made.[1] Knowledge of these theories of cultural adjustment is significant in comprehending the behavior of immigrant groups and in formulating a general program of Americanization which may integrate several group policies frequently functioning in the same community.

Adequate treatment of the subject deserves a volume in itself. As an outcome of her intimate association with the study Mlle Bossavy was led to write out a statement[2] which summarizes and interprets the tenets of this theory as it is the basis of conscious thought and action for the French-Canadian people in America. It is not possible to enlarge further upon this subject here, except to indicate its importance in interpreting the contact of the group in the community under survey, and to point out its significance as another "research lead."

A fuller statement on the French-Canadian position in general must await more careful and deliberate examination of the French literature on the subject. It is, as the appended bibliography indicates, sufficiently ample, but the fact is that here in Woonsocket there are epitomized in the existence of the group national struggles and aspirations truly characteristic of this people in its Canadian history and in its struggle to put itself at ease in our own environment.

FRANCO-AMERICANS

In Woonsocket no other group, excepting possibly the British, can claim to represent old settlers in greater degree or can claim larger contribution to stock. In their group life here the French Canadians are true to the policies articulated in conventions, in their press, and by their leaders.

The French Canadians insist and our data would corroborate the assertion that their adherence to the French language is not inconsistent with the use of English. The indications are that we have here a people that long remains not only bilingual but bicultural. In general, this "biculturation" is uniquely American. They themselves like to describe it as Franco-American, not French Canadian, and this point is made an issue in the educational programs which they foster. "We want an American-trained French clergy," said one Rhode Island priest, "a clergy that is 'American minded.'" Looking toward the clergy for leadership, the need is expressed for leaders trained in the United States, steeped in Catholic French tradition, and cognizant of the problems arising from migration and settlement

[1] Chaps. i and xiv. [2] As yet unpublished.

in still a new homeland. No other nationality can claim to have enunciated a theory of Americanization more clearly or to have organized its group life more consciously toward a given end than have the French Canadians. It is manifestly a theory of adjustment, of Americanization, and one of frank "resistance" to certain Anglo-Saxon (and Irish) traits in American life. It is with them "a way of life" to be defended against certain encroachments which they fear, and to be harmonized with a political theory which they support.

The professions of those who speak with authority for the group, together with our factual data bearing on Woonsocket, indicate that the habits of French Canadians in that community are truly "national" as they would say, and that the struggles there represent genuine cultural issues in the life of the group.

SELECTED BIBLIOGRAPHY ON FRENCH AND FRENCH CANADIANS ON THE AMERICAN CONTINENT

The literature on French Canadians is for the most part a pamphlet literature. Much of it is controversial and has been published by some organization or journal, or reprinted independently. Even when copies have been actually located by the author, it is frequently the case that the brochure carries no date or publisher. It is therefore difficult to trace the origin or to complete a bibliographic reference in every instance. Every effort was made to complete the references by recourse to publisher's lists, bibliographies, the usual facilities at hand to the librarian,[1] also by correspondence with French-Canadian institutions here and in Canada. A few references still remain incomplete.

Except for the subsequent editing and a few additions, the bibliography is based entirely upon the notes left with the writer by Mlle Marthe L. Bossavy. Since the bibliography is so largely and necessarily in French, it seems logical to leave the list of title headings and subheadings in French as Mlle Bossavy gave them.

ABBREVIATIONS

M.L.B. after an annotation indicates that the annotation is by Marthe Lawrence Bossavy.
(W) after a reference indicates that the pamphlet is in the Wessel collection.

[1] The author is indebted to Miss Lavina Stewart, librarian at Connecticut College Library, for her very helpful assistance in tracing references.

BIBLIOGRAPHIE—CANADIENS-FRANÇAIS

I. LES FRANÇAIS EN AMÉRIQUE
II. HISTOIRE DU CANADA
   1. Etudes générales
   2. Les Canadiens-Français dans l'Ouest (américain et canadien)
   3. Les Canadiens-Français dans le Nord-Ouest
III. LA "RACE" CANADIENNE
IV. LA CULTURE CANADIENNE
   1. Tableaux d'ensemble (société, vie politique, psychologie)
   2. Traditions majeures
   3. Le terroir et les mœurs
   4. Langue, littérature, folk lore
V. LA QUESTION DES LANGUES ET LA QUESTION SCOLAIRE
   1. Droits de la langue française au Canada
   2. Organisation scolaire de la province de Québec (Principes d'éducation—
      Bilinguisme)
   3. Conflits dans les autres provinces—Acadie, Manitoba, Nord-Ouest, Ontario
VI. LE CONFLIT DES RACES ET LA DÉFENSE DE LA CULTURE FRANÇAISE SUR LE
      CONTINENT AMÉRICAIN; LA DÉFINITION DES DROITS ETHNIQUES ET LE PROGRAMME
      D'ACTION FRANÇAISE
VII. RELIGION, LANGUE, NATIONALITÉ AU CANADA ET AUX ETATS-UNIS; LES NA-
      TIONALITÉS DANS L'ÉGLISE
VIII. L'ÉMIGRATION CANADIENNE; LES FRANCO-AMÉRICAINS
   1. Etudes générales
   2. Etudes régionales
IX. JOURNAUX, PAMPHLETS, ETC.

I. LES FRANÇAIS EN AMÉRIQUE

AVERY, ELIZABETH HUNTINGTON. *Influence of the French Immigration on the Political History of the United States.* Redfield, S.D., 1895.
Thesis, University of Minnesota.

BAIRD, CHARLES WASHINGTON. *History of the Huguenot Emigration to America.* New York: Dodd, Mead & Co., 1885.

CHINARD, M. GILBERT. Les réfugiés huguenots en Amérique; introduction sur le mirage américain. Paris: Société d'édition "Les Belles-Lettres," 1925.
See also by the same author, "Le souvenir français aux Etats-Unis," *Bulletin*, issued Dec., 1929, by L'Institut Français de Washington of which he is a member. The author is professor of French literature at Johns Hopkins.

DESROSIERS, ABBÉ ADELARD, et FOURNET, ABBÉ. *La race française en Amérique.* Montreal: Beauchemin, 1911. (W)

DOUGLAS, JAMES. *New England and New France; Contrasts and Parallels in Colonial History.* New York: Putnam, 1913.
Forty-five illustrations and maps.

FINLEY, JOHN HUSTON. *The French in the Heart of America.* New York: Scribner, 1915.
Cours à la Sorbonne: "Les gestes des Français au cœur de l'Amérique."

FISKE, JOHN. *New France and New England.* Boston: Houghton Mifflin Co., 1902.

FOSDICK, LUCIAN JOHN. *French Blood in America.* New York: Baker & Taylor Co., 1911.

HIRSCH, ARTHUR HENRY. *The Huguenots of Colonial South Carolina.* Durham, 1928.
Contains chapter on "Assimilation of the Huguenots."

JONES, ROBERT MUMFORD. *America and French Culture in the United States.* Chapel Hill, N.C.: North Carolina University Press, 1927.
Contains Bibliography.

KENTON, EDNA (ed.). *Jesuits: Letters from Missions (North American).* New York: Boni, 1925.
Reference to Canadian history before 1763.

KERLIDOU, REV. J. *St. Anne of Isle Lamotte in Lake Champlain; Its History, etc.* Burlington: No publisher, 1895.

LÉVY, DANIEL. *Les Français en Californie.* San Francisco: Tanzy & Co., 1884.

MADELIN, LOUIS. *L'expansion française de la Syrie au Rhin,* chap. iii: "La France au Canada"; chap. iv; "Un empire français en Amérique." Paris: Plon-Nourrit, 1919.

Memoirs of French Protestants Settled at Oxford, 1686, "Collections of the Massachusetts Historical Society" (3d ser.), Vol. II.
Contains notes on French families who came to the American colonies; bibliographical notes relating to individuals of French descent "distinguished in the annals of New England" and in other parts of the country. Among these names are Baudoin, later Bowdoin; Bernon, of Rhode Island; Faneuil, of Massachusetts fame; the ancestors of John Jay, and others.

MUNRO, W. BENNETT. *Crusaders of New France; a Chronicle of the Fleurs-de-Lis in the Wilderness,* "Chronicles of America," Vol. IV. New Haven: Yale University Press, 1918.

PARKMAN, FRANCIS. *Pioneers of France in the New World.* 2 vols. Boston: Little, Brown & Co., 1897.

―――. *The Jesuits in North America in the 17th Century.* 2 vols. Boston: Little, Brown & Co., 1897.

―――. *The Old Régime in Canada.* Boston: Little, Brown & Co., 1897.

―――. *A Half Century of Conflict; France and England in North America.* 2 vols. Boston: Little, Brown & Co., 1897.
Has reference to the conflict of races in America.

ROCHELEAU, CORINNE. *Françaises d'Amérique; esquisse historique.* Montréal: Beauchemin, 1924.

II. HISTOIRE DU CANADA[1]

1. ÉTUDES GÉNÉRALES

BOURINOT, SIR JOHN G. *Canada under British Rule, 1760–1905.* Rev. ed. Cambridge: University Press, 1909.

CHAPAIS, THOMAS. *Cours d'histoire du Canada.* Québec: Garneau, 1919.

DESROSIERS, ABBÉ ADELARD, et BERTRAND, CAMILLE. *Histoire du Canada.* Montréal: Granger, 1911. (W)

EASTMAN, MARK. *Church and State in Early Canada.* Edinburgh: Constable, 1915.

GARNEAU, FRANÇOIS XAVIER. *Histoire du Canada, depuis sa découverte jusqu'à nos jours.* 4th ed. 4 vols. Montréal: Beauchemin & Valois, 1882–83.

GOYAU, GEORGES. *Une épopée mystique, les origines religieuses du Canada.* Paris: Grasset, 1924.

GROULX, ABBÉ LIONEL. *Cours d'histoire du Canada: Conférences prononcées à l'Université Laval.* Montréal, n.d.

LAUVRIÈRE, EMILE. *La tragédie d'un peuple; histoire de l'Acadie.* 2 vols. Paris: Henri Goulet, 1924. (W)
Grand prix Gobert de l'Académie Française.

MILLER, EMILE. *Terres et peuples du Canada.* Montréal: Beauchemin, 1912.

Quebec Act, The: A Study in Statesmanship.

SALONE, EMILE. *La colonisation de la Nouvelle-France.* Paris: Guilmoto, rue de Mezières, 189—.

SULTE, BENJAMIN. *Le régiment de Carignan,* "Mélanges historiques," Vol. VIII. Montréal: G. Ducharme, 1922.
Contains criticism of the point of view taken by the Abbé Lionel Groulx.

TAURINES, CHARLES GAILLEY DE. *La nation canadienne; étude historique sur les populations françaises du nord de l'Amérique.* Paris: Plon-Nourrit, 1894.

2. LES CANADIENS-FRANÇAIS DANS L'OUEST (AMÉRICAIN ET CANADIEN)

TASSÉ, JOSEPH. *Les Canadiens de l'Ouest: Recueil de biographies, avec une introduction générale sur les Canadiens-Français pionniers du continent.* Montréal: Compagnie d'Imprimerie Canadienne, 1878.

3. LES CANADIENS-FRANÇAIS DANS LE NORD-OUEST

DUGAS, ABBÉ G. *L'Ouest canadien.* Montréal: Cadieux Derôme, 1896.

———. *Histoire véridique des faits qui ont préparé le mouvement à la Rivière Rouge.* Montréal: Beauchemin, 1905.

GROULX, ABBÉ LIONEL. *Notre maître le passé: Conférence sur Mgr. Taché.* Montréal: L'Action Française, 1919.
Conférences prononcées à l'Université Laval de Montréal, 1918–19.

[1] There is little "objective" history of French Canada. Most French-Canadian work is apologetic and practically all French-Canadian literature has a more or less "militant" character.—M. L. B.

OUIMET, ADOLPHE. *La vérité sur la question métisse au Nord-Ouest.* Montréal: Ducharme, 1889.

Biographie et récit de Gabriel Dumont sur les événements de 1885 par B.A.T. de Montigny.

TACHÉ, MGR. ALEXANDRE A. *Vingt années de missions, dans le Nord-Ouest de l'Amérique.* Montréal: Ducharme, 1886.

III. LA "RACE" CANADIENNE

DAVIDSON, JOHN. "The Growth of the French Canadian Race in America," *Annals of the American Academy of Political and Social Science,* VIII (Sept., 1896), 213–35.

DEJORDY, ABBÉ. *Dictionnaire généalogique des familles de Richelieu et de leurs descendants franco-américains.* St. Hyacinthe, P.Q.: La Tribune Imprimerie, 1919.

GROULX, ABBÉ LIONEL. *La naissance d'une race.* Montréal: Bibliothèque de l'Action Française, 1919. (W)

Conférences prononcées à l'Université Laval, Montréal, 1918–19.
An apologetic but interesting effort to define ethnic characters peculiar to the French-Canadian people as they have developed since the foundation of the colony.—M. L. B.

KUCZYNSKI, R. R. "Fecundity of the Native- and Foreign-born Population of Massachusetts, The," *Quarterly Journal of Economics,* XVI (1901–2), 1–36.

MORICE, ADRIEN GABRIEL (O.M.I.). *Dictionnaire historique des Canadiens et des Métis français de l'Ouest.* Québec: Garneau, 1908.

ROY, RÉGIS, et MALCHELOSSE, GÉRARD. *Le régiment de Carignan.* Montréal: Ducharme, 1925.

SALONE, EMILE. *La colonisation de la Nouvelle-France.* See § II.

SULTE, BENJAMIN. *Le régiment de Carignan.* See § II.

TANGUAY, CYPRIEN. *Dictionnaire généalogique des familles canadiennes depuis la fondation.* 7 vols. Montréal: E. Senécal & Fils, 1871–90.

WOOD, WILLIAM. *The French Canadians:* In "Immigrant Backgrounds," by Henry Pratt Fairchild. New York: Wiley, 1927.

IV. LA CULTURE CANADIENNE

I. TABLEAUX D'ENSEMBLE (SOCIÉTÉ, VIE POLITIQUE, PSYCHOLOGIE)

ARNOULD, LOUIS. *Nos amis les Canadiens.* Préface de M. Etienne Lamy, de l'Académie Française. Paris: G. Oudin et Cie, 1911. (W)

A sympathetic study by one who is himself a French Catholic.—M.L.B.

BRACQ, JEAN CHARLEMAGNE. *The Evolution of French Canada.* New York: Macmillan, 1924.

A statement favorable in its attitude toward French Canadians by one who is himself French Protestant.

GROULX, ABBÉ LIONEL A. *Notre maître le passé.* See § II.

———. *La naissance d'une race.* See § III.

PERRAULT, ANTONIO. *Pour la défense de nos lois: idées larges et idées étroites.* Montréal: Ducharme, 1916.

SIEGFRIED, ANDRÉ. *Le Canada, les deux races.* Paris: Armand Colin, 1905. (W)

To be read critically; contains keen analysis of various problems but out of date on many points. Author is French Protestant.—M. L. B.

2. TRADITIONS MAJEURES

BEAUDÉ, ABBÉ HENRI (pseud. HENRI D'ARLES). *La culture française.* 1920.

BOURASSA, HENRI. See §§ V and VI.

CASGRAIN, ABBÉ HENRI RAYMOND. "Une paroisse canadienne au XVIIᵉ siècle: La Rivière Ouelle," *Œuvres complètes de l'Abbé H. R. Casgrain.* 5 vols. Montréal: Beauchemin & Valois, 1884–88.

CHARBONNEAU, JEAN. *Des influences françaises au Canada.* 3 vols. Montréal: Beauchemin, 1916–20.

CONGRÈS DE LA LANGUE FRANÇAISE AU CANADA, PREMIER (Québec, 24–30 juin, 1912). Discours de l'Abbé Lionel Groulx: *La tradition des lettres françaises au Canada.* 2 vols. Vol. I: *Compte rendu;* Vol. II: *Mémoire.* Québec: L'Action Sociale Limitée, 1913–14. (W)

GÉRIN-LAJOIE, A. *Jean Rivard le défricheur.* Montréal: Beauchemin, 1862. (W)

———. *Jean Rivard l'économiste.* Montréal: Beauchemin, 1864. (W)

Récit de la vie réelle. Pour faire suite à Jean Rivard le défricheur.

GROULX, ABBÉ LIONEL A. *La naissance d'une race.* See § III.

Defines the originality of the French-Canadian culture as a "variant" of the French.—M. L. B.

MONTPETIT, EDOUARD. *Au service de la tradition française.* Montréal: Ducharme, 1920.

———. *Les survivances françaises au Canada.* Paris: Plon-Nourrit, 1914.

Notre avenir politique; enquête de l'Action française. 1922.

A summary presentation of the main characteristics and claims of the French people in behalf of their culture on the American continent.—M.L.B.

PAQUET, MGR. LOUIS ADOLPHE. *Bréviaire du patriote canadien-français: Sermon du 23 juin, 1902.* Montréal: L'Action Française, 1925.

3. LE TERROIR ET LES MŒURS

BOUCHARD, GEORGES. *Vieilles choses, vieilles gens; silhouettes campagnardes.* Montréal: Ducharme, 1926.

CASGRAIN, ABBÉ H. R. *Légendes canadiennes et variétés.* Montréal: Beauchemin et Valois, 1884.

DRUMMOND, WILLIAM HENRY. *The Habitant and Other Canadian Poems.* Introduction by LOUIS FRÉCHETTE, with illustrations by FREDERICK S. COBURN. New York: Putnam, 1897.

DUGRÉ, ADELARD. *La campagne canadienne, croquis et leçons.* Montréal: Ducharme, 1925.

See review in *Le devoir,* Jan. 30, 1926.

FRÉCHETTE, LOUIS H. *La noël au Canada.* Montréal: Ducharme, 1900.

Note other works by same author.

GASPÉ, PH. AUBERT DE. *Les anciens Canadiens.* Originally published in 1863. Montréal: L'Action Française, 1899.

A novel about Canadians at the time of the conquest.

GILLES, FRÈRE (O.F.M.). *Les choses qui s'en vont.* Montréal: La Tempérance, 1918. (W)

Causettes canadiennes.

———. *Mon village.*

GROULX, ABBÉ LIONEL A. *Chez nos ancêtres.* 2ᵉ éd. Montréal: L'Action Française, 1920. (W)

———. *Les rapaillages.* Montréal: L'Action Française, 1916.

HÉMON, LOUIS. *Maria Chapdelaine: Récit du Canada français.* Paris: Bernard Grasset, 1921. (W)

Translated into English by W. H. Blake and published by Macmillan, 1924. The author is France French.

LONGSTRETH, THOMAS MORRIS. *The Laurentians; the Hills of the Habitant: Excursion around Lake St. John.* New York: Century, 1922.

MASSICOTTE, E. Z. *Conteurs canadiens-français au XIXᵉ siècle: Choix de contes.* Montréal: Beauchemin, 1908.

MAY, LÉON PAMPHILLE LE. *Contes vrais.* Québec: No publisher, 1899.

POTVIN, DAMASSE. *Le Français: Roman du pays de Québec.* Montréal: Garand, 1925.

RIVARD, ADJUTOR. *Chez nous, chez nous gens.* Montréal: L'Action Française, 1924. (W)

Translated by W. H. Blake.

ROULEAU, C. E. *Légendes canadiennes.* Québec: Ducharme, 1901.

ST. MAURICE, FAUCHER DE. *A la Brunante; contes et récits.* Montréal: Duvernay, 1874.

4. LANGUE, LITTÉRATURE, FOLK LORE

BARBEAU, C. MARIUS, et SAPIR, EDWARD. *Folk Songs of French Canada.* New Haven: Yale University Press, 1925.

See Massicotte.

BEAUDÉ, ABBÉ HENRI (pseud. HENRI D'ARLES). *Louis Fréchette.* No publisher, n.d.

———. *Estampes.* Montréal: L'Action Française, n.d.

———. *Essais et conférences.* Québec: Laflamme & Proulx, 1910.

———. Nos historiens. Montréal: L'Action Française, n.d.

Contes, croyances, dictons populaires canadiens. Reprinted from the *Journal of American Folk-Lore,* XXXII, No. 123 (Jan.–March, 1919). (W)

DIONNE, NARCISSE EUTROPE. *Le parler populaire des Canadiens-Français.* New York: Stechert, 1909.

———. *Les Canadiens-Français: Origine des familles émigrées de France, d'Espagne, de Suisse, etc., pour venir se fixer au Canada, depuis la fondation de Québec jusqu'à ces derniers temps et signification de leurs noms.* Montréal: Granger, 1914.

GAGNON, ERNEST. *Chansons populaires du Canada.* 2ᵉ éd. Québec: R. Morgan, 1880.

GEOFFRIONS, L. PH. *Zigzags autour de nos parlers.* 2 vols. Québec: Ducharme, 1924.

HALDEN, CHARLES. *Etudes de littérature canadienne française.* 2 vols. Paris: F. R. de Rudeval, 1904.

LAMBERT, ADELARD. *Contes populaires canadiens.* Reprinted from the *Journal of American Folk-Lore,* XXXVI (July–Sept., 1923), 1–67.

MASSICOTTE, E. Z., et BARBEAU, C. MARIUS. *Chants populaires du Canada.* 1ère sér. Reprinted from *ibid.,* XXXII, No. 123 (Jan.–March, 1919).

MAYRAND, ERNEST. *Noëls anciens de la Nouvelle-France.* 3ᵉ éd. Montréal: Beauchemin, 1913.

Refrains de chez nous: Chants canadiens. 1ère sér. Montréal: L'Action Française. (W)

ROY, ABBÉ CAMILLE. *Erables en fleurs; pages de critique littéraires.* Québec: L'Action Sociale, 1923.

———. *Essais sur la littérature canadienne.* Québec: Garneau, 1907.

———. *Nos origines littéraires: La littérature canadienne française de 1760 à 1800.* Québec: Ducharme, 1909.

———. *Tableau de l'histoire de la littérature canadienne française.* Québec: L'Action Sociale, 1907.

WARD, CHARLES FREDERICK. *The récit and chronique of French Canada.* Montréal: Ducharme, 1921. (W)

V. LA QUESTION DES LANGUES ET LA QUESTION SCOLAIRE

1. DROITS DE LA LANGUE FRANÇAISE AU CANADA

Action française, L'. Série, congrès, conférences, discours, "Notre système scolaire." Montréal, 1913.

Voir l'enquête sur le bilinguisme, 192—.

BOURASSA, HENRI. *La langue française au Canada; ses droits, sa nécessité, ses avantages: Discours prononcé au monument national, le 19 mai, 1915, sous les auspices du Comité Régional de Montréal, l'A.C.J.C.* Montréal: Le Devoir, 1915.

———. *Le patriotisme canadien-français; ce qu'il est; ce qu'il doit être.* Montréal: Ducharme, 1902.

CONGRÈS DE LA LANGUE FRANÇAISE AU CANADA, PREMIER (Québec, 1912). *Rapport,* Quebéc: L'Action Sociale, 1913. See § IV.

Voir les discours du Sénateur Belcourt, d'Henri Bourassa, de Mgr. Paquet.

CONSTANTINEAU, JUGE A. *La langue française, en Amérique.* Montréal: Le Devoir, 1911. (W)
Texte du remarquable discours prononcé au banquet de la Société St.-Jean-Baptiste de Montréal, le 24 juin, 1911.

FOISY, J. A. *La langue maternelle.* Montréal: L'Action Française, 1922.

HOMIER, PIERRE. *La langue française au Canada; faits et réflexions.* Préface du DR. JOSEPH GAUVREAU. Montréal: Ligue des Droits Français, 1913. (W)

Langues et les nationalités au Canada, Les, par "UN SAUVAGE." Préface de M. HENRI BOURASSA. Montréal: Le Devoir, 1916. (W)

MOORE, WILLIAM HENRY. *The Clash! A Study in Nationalities.* 9th and rev. ed. London: Dent, 1918.
Strongly supports the French-Canadian point of view.

MORLEY, PERCIVAL FELMAN. *Bridging the Chasm: A Study of the Ontario Question.* Toronto: Dent, 1919.

Notre avenir politique; enquête de l'Action française. See § IV.ʳ

SAINT-MAURICE, FAUCHER DE. *Les états de Jersey et la langue française; exemple offert au Manitoba et au Nord-Ouest.* Montréal: Senecal, 1893.

SKELDON, O. D. "The Language Issue in Canada," *Bulletin Department of History and Political and Economic Science,* Kingston, Ontario: Queen's University, April, 1917.

TRÉMAUDAN, A. H. DE. *Pourquoi nous parlons français.* Winnepeg: La Libre Parole, 1916. (W)

2. ORGANISATION SCOLAIRE DE LA PROVINCE DE QUÉBEC (PRINCIPES D'ÉDUCATION—BILINGUISME)

ASSOCIATION CATHOLIQUE DE LA JEUNESSE FRANÇAISE. *Secouons le joug.*
In defense of the language.

LALANDE, R. L. P. *L'éducation de la justice.* Montréal: L'Action Française, n.d.

MAGNAN, C. J. *A propos d'instruction obligatoire, la situation scolaire dans la province de Québec, suivi d'appendices documentaires.* Québec: L'Action Sociale, 1919.

MILLER, J. N. *Code scolaire de la province de Québec, contenant la loi de l'instruction publique, et les règlements du Comité Catholique du Conseil de l'Instruction Publique.* Québec: Le Soleil, 1919. (W)

O'CONNELL, CARDINAL JAMES. *Des justes limites à l'action de l'Etat.* Montréal: L'Action Française, 1920.

ROSS, MGR. F. X. *Questions scolaires; le nouveau programme primaire.* Montréal: Le Devoir, n.d.
Discussion de la question de l'éducation bilingue.

ROY, EGIDE M. *La formation du régime scolaire canadien français.* Québec: Ducharme, 1924.
Important. Treats of the historic development of the unique school system of Quebec. States forcefully the conditions and principles. Tentative evaluation of results.—M. L. B.

SABOURIN, J. A. *L'éducation mixte dans les écoles du Manitoba*. Winnepeg: No publisher, 1926.
Contre l'éducation "non-sectarian."

3. CONFLITS DAN LES AUTRES PROVINCES—ACADIE, MANITOBA, NORD-OUEST, ONTARIO

BELCOURT, N. A. *Regulation 17 Ultra Vires*. Argument before the Supreme Court of Ontario, Nov. 2, 1914. Ottawa: Le Droit, 1914. (W)
A clear and vigorous statement, in English, of the French-Canadian juridical position in the Ontario problem.

BÉRARD, LUC ET FOISY, J. A. *Plus qu'elle même! Roman canadien*. Québec: No publisher, 1921. (W)
Mauvais roman, mais tableau d'une phase de la lutte ontarienne, suivi des documents essentiels sur la question.—M.L.B.

BOURASSA, HENRI. *Pour la justice: La législation scolaire du Nord-Ouest. Les discours de MM. Monk et Pelletier: Quelques objections*. 1912.

———. *Les écoles du Nord-Ouest: Discours prononcé le 17 avril, 1905, à Montréal*. Montréal: Le Nationaliste, 1905.

CERCLE DE LA LÉGALITÉ, LE. *The Juridical and Pedagogical Position of English-French Schools in Ontario*. Ottawa: Le Droit, 1915. (W)
A discussion of suggestions in settlement of school questions proposed by S. M. Genest, chairman of the S.S. Board (Ottawa, July, 1913).

CHARLEBOIS, R. P. CHARLES (O.M.I.). *Les Canadiens Français d'Ontario et la presse: A la première convention biennale des Canadiens Français d'Ontario*. Ottawa: L'Association Canadienne Française d'Education d'Ontario, 1912. (W)

CHARRON, ALPHONSE T. *La langue française et les petits Canadiens Français de l'Ontario: L'Association Canadienne Française d'Education d'Ontario*, Québec: L'Action Sociale, 1914.

CONSTANTINEAU, JUGE A. *La langue française dans l'Ontario: Mémoire lu à la séance publique de la Société du Parler Français au Canada, 1911*. Québec: L'Action Sociale, 1911.

ERNAULT, GABRIEL. *L'enseignement du français en Acadie, 1604–1926*.
Available at the Collège du Sacré Cœur, Bathurst, N.B., Canada.

LANDRY, PHILIPPE. *La question scolaire de l'Ontario; le désaveu*. Québec: Dussault et Proulx, 1916.

———. *Mémoire sur la question de l'Ontario*. Ottawa: Association Canadienne Française d'Education de l'Ontario, juillet, 1915.

TACHÉ, MGR. ALEXANDRE A. *Une page de l'histoire des écoles de Manitoba; étude des cinq phases d'une période de 75 années*. Montréal: Beauchemin, 1894.

———. *Mémoire de Mgr. Taché sur la question des écoles en réponse au rapport du Comité de l'Honorable Conseil Privé du Canada*. Montréal: Beauchemin, 1894. (W)

TREMBLEY, JULES. *Le français en Ontario; son usage et son enseignement sont définis par le droit provenant de l'occupation première, par le droit des gens, par la coutume, par le droit constitutionnel et même par les statuts provinciaux.* Montréal: Nault, 1913. (W)

A brief summary of the arguments put more forcefully by Bourassa in *La langue française au Canada.*—M. L. B.

VI. LE CONFLIT DES RACES ET LA DÉFENSE DE LA CULTURE FRANÇAISE SUR LE CONTINENT AMÉRICAIN; LA DÉFINITION DES DROITS ETHNIQUES ET LE PROGRAMME D'ACTION FRANÇAISE

BASTIEN, HERMAS. *Les énergies rédemptrices.* Montréal: L'Action Française, n.d.

BOURASSA, HENRI. *La langue française au Canada.* Montréal: Le Devoir, 1915. (W)

————. *Religion, langue, nationalité: Discours prononcé à la séance de clôture du XXIième Congrès Eucharistique, à Montréal, le 10 septembre.* Montréal: Le Devoir, 1910. (W)

Suivi du discours de Mgr. Bourne.

————. *Une mauvaise loi: L'assistance publique.* Montréal: Le Devoir, 1921.

FÉRON, JEAN. *Fierté de race; roman canadien.* Montréal: Edouard Garand, 1924.

GROULX, ABBÉ LIONEL A. *L'amitié française d'Amérique; discours prononcé à Lowell, Etats-Unis, le 7 sept., 1922, au Congrès de la Fédération Catholique des Sociétés Franco-Américaines.* Montréal: Ducharme, 1922.

For a united action of all French groups in America.

————. *Consignes de demain; doctrine et origines de l'Action française.* Montréal: L'Action Française, 1921. (W)

————. *Pour l'Action française: Conférence prononcée au monument national, à Montréal, le 10 avril 1918.* Montréal: L'Action Française, 1918. (W)

Defines the program of action of the group represented by the review, *L'action française.*

LAUVRIÈRE, EMILE. *La tragédie d'un peuple.* See § II.

LESTRE, ALONIE DE. *L'appel de la race; roman.* Montréal: L'Action Française, 1922.

An ardent call in novel form for a new spiritual crusade among the French Canadians. Obviously influenced by the nationalistic works of Maurice Barrès.—M. L. B.

MOORE, WILLIAM HENRY. *The Clash!* See § V.

MORLEY, PERCIVAL F. *Bridging the Chasm.* See § V.

NEVERS, EDMOND DE. *L'âme américaine: Les origines; la vie historique; l'évolution; à travers la vie américaine; vers l'avenir.* 2 vols. Paris: Jouve & Boyer, 1900. (W)

Of essential importance to anyone interested in racial and cultural developments and in cultural conflicts on the North American continent. Anticipates much Americanization theory today current in the United States.—M. L. B.

————. *L'avenir du peuple canadien-français.* Paris: No publisher, 1896.

Où allons-nous? Le nationalisme canadien. Lettres d' "Un Patriote" publiées dans le journal, *La presse.* Augmentées d'une introduction, d'additions, et d'appendices documentaires. Montréal: Société d'Editions Patriotiques, 1916. (W)

States the danger inherent in a too-narrow French-Canadian nationalism, and of any attempt at political independence. Directed against Bourassa's attitude during the war.

OUIMET, ADOLPHE. *La vérité sur la question métisse.* See § II.

PELLETIER, GEORGES. *L'immigration canadienne.* Montréal: Le Devoir, 1923.
Enquêtes du *Devoir.*

PERRAULT, ANTONIO. *Ouvrages cités.* See § IV.

SIEGFRIED, ANDRÉ. *Le Canada; les deux races.* See § IV.

SMITH, GOLDWIN. *Canada and the Canadian Question.* New York: Macmillan, 1891.
Presents the viewpoint of the "anglicizers."—M. L. B.

TARDIVEL, JULES PAUL. *Pour la patrie; roman du XXième siècle.* Montréal: Cadieux
& Derome, 1895.
A curious document expressing the fears of an ardent and uncompromising French-Cana-
dian Catholic at the end of the nineteenth century and the dream of an independent French
Canada.—M. L. B.

———. *La langue française au Canada; conférence lue devant l'Union Catholique de
Montréal, le 10 mars, 1901.* Montreal: Revue Canadienne, 1901. (W)

Voir aussi les œuvres et les publications de:

L'action catholique. Société catholique. JULES DORION, directeur. Québec.

L'action française. Revue publiée à Montréal. ABBÉ LIONEL GROULX, directeur.
This periodical is now known as *L'action canadienne française.*

Le devoir. Newspaper. HENRI BOURASSA, directeur. Montréal.

Le droit. Newspaper. Ottawa, Ontario.

VII. RELIGION, LANGUE, NATIONALITÉ AU CANADA ET AUX ETATS-UNIS; LES
NATIONALITÉS DANS L'ÉGLISE

ANDRÉ, M. A. *Le catholicisme aux Etats-Unis de l'Amérique du Nord.* Paris: Bloud,
1905.

ARNOULD, LOUIS. *Nos amis les Canadiens.* 2 vols. Paris: Oudin, 1913.
Particulièrement Tome II, 3ième partie, "Le péril irlandais," et l'appendice.

BEAUDÉ, ABBÉ HENRI (pseud. HENRI D'ARLES). *Le français dans le New Hampshire.*
Tract No. 5 publié par la Ligue du Ralliement Français en Amérique. (W) n. d.

BOURASSA, HENRI. *Religion, langue, nationalité.* See § VI.

BRUNETIÈRE, FERDINAND. "Le catholicisme aux Etats-Unis," *Revue des deux mondes,*
Nov., 1898.

*Des droits respectifs des parents et de l'église dans l'éducation, de la part des laïques dans
l'administration des biens ecclésiastiques, et de la conservation de la langue maternelle
par rapport à la conservation de la foi.* Sans titre.
L'auteur est de nationalité belge.
This reference appears important but it is regrettably incomplete.

GENIESSE, J. B. *Pour aider à la solution de questions qui s'agitent aux Etats-Unis et
au Canada: Mémoire adressé à Sa Sainteté Pie X.* Rome: Tipografia Pontificia,
Nell Instituta, Pie X, 1912. (W)

GUERTIN, MGR. (évêque de Manchester). *La langue française et le christianisme: Discours prononcé au Congrès de la Langue Française de Québec, 1912*. Republished by La Ligue de Ralliement Français en Amérique, Tract No. 3. (W)

HAMON, E. *Les Canadiens Français de la Nouvelle Angleterre*. Québec, N.S.: Hardy, 1891. (W)

HANOTAUX, GABRIEL. *La France vivante en Amérique du Nord*. Mission Champlain, 1912. Paris: Published for Comité France-Amérique by Hachette, 1913.

Histoire de l'agitation sentinelliste dans la Nouvelle Angleterre, 1915–28. Woonsocket, R.I.: La Tribune, 1918.

Contains a history and summary of the recent conflict within the Catholic church in Woonsocket in which one group of French-Canadian Catholics took issue with the hierarchy on its treatment of French Canadians in the diocese. *La sentinelle*, a Woonsocket publication since suspended by order of Rome, was the organ of protest. *La tribune* held a more conciliatory and conservative view of the situation.

KLEIN, ABBÉ FÉLIX. *Au pays de la vie intense*. Paris: No publisher, 189—.

See also other works by the same author. This is an enthusiastic presentation of the achievement of the Catholic church in America. To be compared with Edmond de Nevers, Louis Arnould, Tardivel, and with other critical works. Contains a statement relating to the danger of "Americanism" in and to the church.—M. L. B.

MAIGNAN, CHARLES. *Nouveau catholicisme et nouveau clergé*. Paris: No publisher, 1902.

MEAUX, MARIE-CAMILLE ALFRED, VICOMTE DE. *L'église et la liberté aux Etats-Unis*. Paris: No publisher, n.d.

NEVERS, EDMOND DE. *L'âme américaine*. See § VI.

Tome II, Partie 5: "Vers l'avenir; les problèmes."

Où allons-nous? See § VI.

PAQUET, MGR. LOUIS ADOLPHE. *Discours: Premier congrès de la langue française au Canada*. See § IV.

PARSONS, REV. RUBEN. *Studies in Church History*, Vol. II. 6 vols. New York: Pustet, 1886–1900.

"Programme de la fête St.-Jean-Baptiste, 24 juin, 1926," *La sentinelle* (Woonsocket, R.I., 1926).

"Question de justice, Une: La langue française au Canada," *Le correspondant*, le 10 juillet, 1911.

Article written for the French Catholic periodical after the Eucharistic Congress of Montreal. See reference to this in Louis Arnould, *Le péril irlandais*, Tome II, Part II.

Réponse au mémoire irlandais. Réponse aux prétendus griefs des catholiques irlandais du Canada contre les catholiques français du même pays, ou réponse à un mémoire irlandais adressé d'Ottawa, le 17 juin 1905, à Son Eminence le Cardinal Merry del Val, secrétaire d'état de Sa Sainteté Pie X, 30 mai 1909.

Sentinelle, La. Files of.

For statement of issues in the recent controversy with Bishop Hickey by the editor who was the spokesman in demands made upon the Bishop.

TARDIVEL, JULES. *Les américanistes.* Paris: Collection Arthur Savaète, 76 rue des Saints Pères, 1900.

――――. *La situation religieuse aux Etats-Unis.* Paris: Collection Arthur Savaète, 1900.

VIII. L'ÉMIGRATION CANADIENNE; LES FRANCO-AMÉRICAINS

I. ÉTUDES GÉNÉRALES

BELISLE, ALEXANDRE. *Histoire de la presse franco-américaine comprenant l'histoire de l'émigration des Canadiens-Français aux Etats-Unis, leur développement, et leurs progrès.* Cet ouvrage contient aussi un historique des journaux publiés depuis 1838 jusqu'à nos jours, les biographies des journalistes, défunts et vivants, et un supplément sur les journaux publiés par des Français à New York en Louisiane et ailleurs; avec une préface par J. G. LE BOUTILLIER. Worcester, Mass.: L'Opinion Publique, 1911. (W)

BILODEAU, ABBÉ GEORGES-MARIE. *Pour rester au pays.* Québec: L'Action Sociale, 1926. (W)

Etude sur l'émigration des Canadiens-Français aux Etats-Unis; causes; remèdes.

CHARPENTIER, FULGENCE. *Le mirage américain: L'exode vers Detroit, gain ou perte?* Montréal: L'Action Française, 1924.

DEXTER, ROBERT E.[1] "Fifty-Fifty Americans," *World's Work*, XLVIII (Aug., 1924), 366–71.

A discussion of the general problem created by the close contact of French Canadians with their homeland and the conflict of loyalties it presents.

――――. "French Canadian Patriotism," *American Journal of Sociology*, XXVIII (May, 1923), 694–710.

Deals with the historic factors and the organizations which have built up a strong racial patriotism among the French Canadians in Canada and the United States.

――――. "Gallic War in Rhode Island," *Nation*, CXVII (Aug. 29, 1923), 215–16.

A discussion of the efforts of the French Canadians to defeat a bill calling for instruction in English in the parochial schools in Rhode Island.

――――. "The French Canadian Immigrant: His Contribution to the Past, Present and Future of the United States," *Clark University Theses Abstracts* (Feb., 1930), pp. 159–63.

――――. "The French Canadian Invasion," *The Alien in Our Midst* (ed. CHARLES S. DAVISON and MADISON CLARK). New York: Gatton, 1930.

A summary of the facts in regard to numbers and distributions of French Canadians together with an estimate of their contribution to American life.

Evolution de la race française en Amérique, L'. 2 vols. Montréal: Beauchemin, 1921. (W)

FAVREAU, J. ARTHUR. *The Chinese of the Eastern States.* 1925.

Reprinted from correspondence originally published in full in *L'avenir national*, Manchester, N.H. Described by the editor as an attempt to "counteract in some small measure the per-

――――
[1] I am indebted to the author himself for these annotations.—B. B. W.

nicious propaganda which appears to have reached its culminating point in the article 'Fifty-Fifty Americans' by Robert C. Dexter." Dexter here revives the term "Chinese of the East," a term applied to French Canadians in an attack upon them contained in the Massachusetts Bureau of Statistics of Labor, 1881. See Dexter.

GATINEAU, FÉLIX. *Historique des conventions générales des Canadiens-Français aux Etats-Unis, 1865–1901.* Compilé par FÉLIX GATINEAU; édité par l'UNION ST.-JEAN-BAPTISTE D'AMÉRIQUE. Woonsocket, R.I., 1927.

HAMON, E. *Les Canadiens Français de la Nouvelle-Angleterre.* Québec: Hardy, 1891.

MAGNAN, ABBÉ D. M. A. *Histoire de la race française aux Etats-Unis.* Paris: No publisher, 1912.

ROULEAU, C. E. *L'émigration: Ses principales causes.* Québec: Léger Brousseau, 1896. (W)

WICKETT, S. MORLEY. "Canadians in the United States," *Annals of the American Academy of Political and Social Science,* XLV (Jan., 1913), 83–98.

2. ÉTUDES RÉGIONALES

Connecticut

Histoire et statistiques des Canadiens-Américains du Connecticut: Minutes des conventions nationales des Canadiens-Américains de l'état du Connecticut, 1885–1889. Worcester: L'Opinion Publique, 1889.

Contains much information on the history of French Canadians in Connecticut and has reference to the situations which gave rise to the series of "national" conventions among French Canadians in the United States. The Editorial Preface contains an interesting enunciation of loyalties current among the group.

Maine

LAPLANTE, ODULE. *Recensements des Franco-Américains de l'état du Maine.* 1908.

Massachusetts

BELANGER, ALBERT A. *Guide officiel des Franco-Américains.* (Etabli 1899.) Fall River, Mass., 1927.
Illustrated handbook now in its seventh edition, rich in information.

GATINEAU, FÉLIX. *Histoire des Franco-Américains de Southbridge.* No publisher, 1919.

IMMIGRATION COMMISSION. *Report: The Problem of Immigration in Massachusetts.* House Doc. 2300. Boston: Printed by the state, 1914.
An excellent survey of the immigration problem in Massachusetts made under the direction of Grace Abbott.

KUCZYNSKI, R. R. "The Fecundity of the Native and Foreign Born Population of Massachusetts; Nov., 1901," *Quarterly Journal of Economics,* XVI (1901–2), 1–36.

Massachusetts Bureau of Labor Statistics, 1882: Annual Report of. Published by the Massachusetts Bureau of Statistics.
In 1907 this name was changed to the *Massachusetts Bureau of Statistics: Annual Report of the Statistics of Labor.*

Michigan

St.-Pierre, T. *Histoire des Canadiens du Michigan et du comté d'Essex, Ontario.* Montréal: La Gazette, 1895. (W)

New Hampshire

Beaudé, Abbé Henri (pseud. Henri d'Arles). *Le français dans le New-Hampshire.* Ligue de Ralliement Français en Amérique, Tract 5.

Tardivel, E. H. *Le guide canadien-français de Manchester, N.H., pour 1894–95.* Manchester: John B. Clark, 1894.

Contenant un almanach complet des adresses, le mouvement de la population canadienne depuis 23 ans, un aperçu historique de la ville de Manchester, des paroisses et des sociétés canadiennes.

Rhode Island

Bonier, Marie-Louise. *Débuts de la colonie franco-américaine de Woonsocket, Rhode Island.* Framingham, Mass.: Lakeview Press, 1920.

North Attleboro. "North Attleboro Families": Chabot—5 generations, 98 members; Precourt—5 generations, 128 members, *Providence Journal* (Rhode Island, March 23, 1924).

Potter, Elisha R. *Memoir Concerning the French Settlement in the Colony of Rhode Island.* "Historical Tracts," No. 5. Providence, R.I.: Rider, 1879.

Contains information on the Frenchtown (East Greenwich) settlement in 1686; on the land controversy which deprived the French settlers of their right to the land they were cultivating, and resulted in their dispersion to other Rhode Island communities. Contains also genealogies of several French families, and numerous references to the history of the French in Rhode Island.

Vermont

McLaughlin, *Histoire de l'église catholique en Vermont.*

IX. JOURNAUX, PAMPHLETS, ETC.[1]

Etats-Unis

Voir les œuvres et les publications de *L'avenir national* (Manchester, N.H.); *L'opinion publique* (Worcester, Mass.); *La sentinelle* (Woonsocket, R.I.; discontinued).

CANADA

Bibliothèque de *L'action française,* Montréal.

Pour autre information consultez aussi les publications des sociétés suivantes:

1. La Bibliothèque Mallet, propriété de l'Union St.-Jean-Baptiste d'Amérique. Voir catalogue publié par l'Union, Woonsocket, R.I.
2. Bibliothèque de l'Association Canado-Américaine, Manchester, N.H.
3. L'Institut Français des Etats-Unis, 2 Jackson Place, Washington, D.C.
4. Wessel collection, Connecticut College, New London, Conn.

[1] Collections de la littérature canadienne-française: imprimeurs et listes des organisations qui distribuent des pamphlets.

The following is an alphabetical list of authors whose works are included in the foregoing bibliography. The Roman numerals refer to the sections and the Arabic numerals to the subsections of the bibliography.

Action française, L', V (1)
André, M. A., VII
Arnould, Louis, IV (1); VII
Association Catholique de la Jeunesse Française, V (2)
Avery, Elizabeth H., I

Baird, Charles Washington, I
Barbeau, C. Marius, IV (4)
Bastien, Hermas, VI
Beaudé, Abbé Henri, IV (2), (4); VII; VIII (2)
Belanger, Albert A., VIII (2)
Belcourt, N. A., V (3)
Belisle, Alexandre, VIII (1)
Bérard, Luc, V (3)
Bilodeau, Abbé Georges-Marie, VIII (1)
Bonier, Marie-Louise, VIII (2)
Bouchard, Georges, IV (3)
Bourassa, Henri, IV (2); V (1), (3); VI; VII
Bourinot, Sir John G., II (1)
Bracq, Jean Charlemagne, IV (1)
Brunetière, Ferdinand, VII

Casgrain, Abbé Henri Raymond, IV (2), (3)
Cercle de la Légalité, V (3)
Chapais, Thomas, II (1)
Charbonneau, Jean, IV (2)
Charlebois, R. P. Charles, V (3)
Charpentier, Fulgence, VIII (1)
Charron, Alphonse T., V (3)
Chinard, M. Gilbert, I
Congrès de la Langue Française au Canada IV (2); V (1)
Congrès Eucharistique à Montréal
Connecticut, VIII (2)
Constantineau, Juge A., V (1), (3)
Contes, croyances, dictons populaires canadiens, IV (4)

Davidson, John, III
Dejordy, Abbé, III
Desrosiers, Abbé Adélard I; II (1)
Dexter, Robert E., VIII (1)
Dionne, Narcisse Eutrope, IV (4)
Douglas, James, I
Droits respectifs des parents, etc., Des, VII
Drummond, William Henry, IV (3)

Dugas, Abbé G., II (3)
Dugré, Adélard, IV (3)

Eastman, Mark, II (1)
Ernault, Gabriel, V (3)
Evolution de la race française en Amérique, VIII (1)

Favreau, J. Arthur, VIII (1)
Féron, Jean, VI
Finley, John Huston, I
Fiske, John, I
Foisy, J. A., V (1), (3)
Fosdick, Lucian John, I
Fréchette, Louis H., IV (3)

Gagnon, Ernest, IV (4)
Garneau, François X., II (1)
Gaspé, Ph. Aubert de., IV (3)
Gatineau, Félix, VIII (1), (2)
Geniesse, J. B., VII
Geoffrions, L. Ph., IV (4)
Gérin-Lajoie, A., IV (2)
Gilles, Frère, IV (3)
Goyau, Georges, II (1)
Groulx, Abbé Lionel, II (1), (3); III; IV (1), (2), (3); VI
Guertin, Mgr., VII

Halden, Charles Abder, IV (4)
Hamon, E., VII; VIII (1)
Hanotaux, Gabriel, VII
Hémon, Louis, IV (3)
Hirsch, Arthur Henry, I
Histoire de l'agitation sentinelliste dans la Nouvelle-Angleterre, VII
Homier, Pierre, V (1)

Jones, Robert Mumford, I

Kenton, Edna, I
Kerlidou, Rev. J., I
Klein, Abbé Félix, VII
Kuczynski, R. R., III; VIII (2)

Lalande, R. L. P., V (2)
Lambert, Adélard, IV (4)
Landry, Philippe, V (3)

APPENDIX B[1]

THE ETHNIC SURVEY: METHOD AND RELIABILITY: BIBLIOGRAPHY

Numerous questions present themselves in the course of an investigation which call for an evaluation or critique of the investigation, both as to findings and as to methodology. To what extent may one depend upon the data as reliable? What basis for prediction does it offer? What further implications does it have over and above those arising from its purely descriptive function? Granted the validity of ethnic surveys, are they feasible? Or is the expenditure of time and effort prohibitive? What snags may one expect in conducting similar experiments? Where and when may credence be withheld, and when do the data need to be "interpreted"?

GENERAL RELIABILITY

The specific results obtained in this survey have been sufficiently enlarged upon and need no further treatment. From time to time we have also called attention to the significant fact that results obtained in other communities quite regularly corroborate the trends established in this survey, even though the communities are different in their ethnic set-up. It may be pointed out, however, that the studies are all in New England and need further testing by investigations in other parts of the country. Certain tests have been applied with satisfactory results to

[1] This chapter is intended more particularly for those interested in ethnic research the technique of the survey. The content matter has been determined almost er inquiries received by the author.

264

investigation as it functions for the given area. The question from the methodological point of view has been throughout: Do the conclusions based upon our quantitative analyses bear out the conclusions reached independently by investigators who use other and more empirical tools? Two such parallel investigations were conducted for this area. Professor Henry W. Lawrence was asked to write the historical sketch[1] of the community from resources available to the historian. Professor Marthe L. Bossavy made a study of French-Canadian adjustment on this continent. As was elsewhere indicated, she studied the French-Canadian problem in Woonsocket more intensively, visiting 213 Franco-American homes and having numerous conferences with men and women who represented the leadership among them.

These investigators came to certain conclusions in their own fields, which were corroborated most emphatically in the statistical findings made independently by the author. Thus the quantitative evidence on language usage[2] and intermarriage bear out closely the results which Professor Bossavy was led to expect from her many conversations with old settlers, group leaders, and priests.

In the historical reconstruction the case was similar. Earlier in this presentation[3] we asked whether it might "not be possible to reconstruct the history of the population within a given area from life-histories of present inhabitants." The historical sketch by Professor Lawrence describes the community in different stages of its existence. If there were no internal migration these two would be identical except for ethnic change due to social conditions within the community. It is difficult to measure these changes. If, however, we compare the ethnic data in the historical sketch with the sequence of immigrants as established by generation distribution (Table 14), we find the pictures to be almost identical. The same ethnic changes in the same order are indicated in each case. The families of second-generation parents came on the whole before 1890, and those of third-generation parents must have come before 1875. In Woonsocket the history of the community during the last century and the history of the population within that area are merely different aspects of the same picture.

Before discussing the reliability of replies to certain questions and the problems to be met in conducting such an inquiry, a word may be said about the survey as a basis for prediction.

[1] Chap. xiv.

[2] See chap. xiii.   [3] Chap. i, p. 6.

THE ETHNIC SURVEY AS A TOOL FOR PREDICTING CHANGE

There is a premium today on any claim to prophetic insight, particularly when such claim is reinforced by quantitative data. In many instances the stability of modern life is largely dependent upon the extent to which prediction of social change is possible. In the case of racial change the rôle of prophecy is no less fascinating but assuredly safer than, let us say, in the corresponding field of economic change. We are dealing with phenomena where the units of time are decades, even generations. The author is seldom there to face the consequences of any error in prophecy, nor is he held to account for sudden catastrophic changes which interfere with his prophecy. Even if it is true that certain folk habits are disclosed by the survey and that certain definite trends in the community are brought to light—wars, legislation, and industrial change may annihilate these tendencies. Nevertheless, there are characteristics in the situation described by a school survey which make it a unique tool for prediction.

Since the subjects of investigation are school children, we are describing a population which inevitably is going to partake in American community life. Assuming a continuous survey[1] in any given school area, it is always possible to forecast, or rather definitely to establish, the racial composition of that group of individuals who will be added to the electorate in any given year. The situation is always a dynamic one; school populations change rapidly; they change as they are being described. In describing any school population we are inevitably forecasting the post-school population of the near future.

In addition, the data we have examined undoubtedly afford a basis for further predicting the composition of the on-coming group.[2] The differential rates of fecundity which were disclosed, the racial indices, the folk habits, give us the right to assume for the present and to predict for the near future the increasing importance of European stocks; and parallel with this, a rapid increase in mixed population which is bound to challenge the dominance of any one group in the community.

On the basis of our findings we may safely forecast the further assimilation of certain stocks, the extent and nature of mixed stock, the wiping-out of those lesser differences which exist between British stocks, French stocks, and Slavic stocks. The next generation in Woonsocket will see

[1] A continuous survey involves the use of an ethnic symbol for each child along with the permanent school record of each child, e.g., English 3–3, or Irish 1 × French Canadian 3, etc.

[2] This is particularly true if we include in our discussion the findings presented in chap. xiii which deal with differential fecundity and other social facts.

kaleidoscopic cultural changes which must follow inevitably from the present situations and which will be governed in large measure by the Americanization[1] policies in practice among the various folk groups in that community.

Granted that data such as the survey affords in our midst have intrinsic interest, are investigations of this kind feasible? What warnings has the pioneer investigator to make?

The results of one survey are themselves like a map which indicates the road for others. Yet certain signposts are needed still. These are of two kinds: (1) those regarding the gathering of data, and (2) those that deal with the final acceptance of data. In addition, a word is necessary about the element of time and cost which conceivably may be a necessary consideration.

The time consumed in organization and in gathering data and the adequacy of the returns vary from community to community. Proper organization of the study depends upon the support of numerous individuals and agencies. Unavoidable delays are bound to occur, absence of important officials from the city, grippe epidemics which demoralize attendance, school holidays, blizzards at inopportune moments. These items are inevitably to be encountered and represent a charge against organization.

ENTRÉE

Entrée into the community and success in obtaining the necessary co-operation of leaders depend in large measure upon the investigator and her ability to evoke good will and co-operation. One does not need to enter here upon the principles which govern the "first interview" or any interview, a problem treated in the literature on social work, except to call attention to the fact that skill in this case includes a wide knowledge of racial backgrounds and ethnic theories.

Nordicist, and anti-Nordicist alike, those who are for immigration, those who are against it, all reserve the right to challenge the purpose of the investigation and the uses to which it will be put. More particularly do the priests (of various national descents) challenge the right of entrée to the parochial schools under their jurisdiction. The priest of Irish descent cross-examines boldly and with sureness; the priest of French descent dreads our ignorance of "Franco-American" objectives; the

[1] See discussion with reference to the French-Canadian theory of Americanization (Appendix A).

Polish sister inquires "Who wants to know?" and "Why?" Public-school officials and teachers, equally, present the entire range of racial philosophy. Also they must see in the investigation pragmatic results in terms of their own needs. There is good reason why an investigation of this kind should be challenged by individuals representing the different schools of thought. But their co-operation is needed and securing it depends upon the investigator's familiarity with these various points of view.

Similarly, the follow-up work in the home depends upon the visitor's familiarity with cultural backgrounds and upon her ability as a case-worker to bring herself *en rapport* with the immigrant mother. There is in addition the problem of organizing the visits in such a manner that they are handled as effectively and as quickly as the problem warrants.[1]

GATHERING AND INTERPRETING DATA

Both the organization and the follow-up work were expeditiously handled in Woonsocket. The initial contacts were made in January, the questionnaires were distributed in March, and, as previously reported, 90 per cent of the returns were made within a week. In Providence the surveys proceeded with even greater expedition. This was due in some measure to the experience which the investigators had obtained in other communities and which they were now putting to use, also to exceedingly favorable conditions in the community.[2]

Once a project is indorsed the procedure may follow that adopted in Woonsocket. The preliminaries need consist of only a conference with the school principal, one meeting with the teachers for a discussion of the questionnaire (preferably on a Friday), distribution of the circulars on a Monday, and one week's time for the return of the histories. Experience indicates that with efficient organization 90 per cent of the questionnaires can be expected to be returned in acceptable form in one week.

[1] This study owes much to the ability of Miss Alice M. Towsley to secure the good will of the many individuals interviewed. French-speaking assistants were Mlle Marthe L. Bossavy and Miss Marie Boisvert. Miss S. Etta Sadow, on the basis of her experience as supervisor in social case work, organized the field work most effectively. In the later period a car was always employed and two visitors concentrated upon a given district at the same time. In all, about 2,000 home visits were made by the field-workers in connection with the several investigations.

[2] The investigator had had previous contact with the Providence schools in her capacity as social worker in the community several years before. Entrée therefore did not need to be established anew. Furthermore, she was sufficiently familiar with the different districts and with the families in certain districts to recognize immediately the points at which the investigation was inadequate and to what extent returns needed to be "edited."

When the teacher is especially co-operative or when an experienced member of the staff remains on duty at the school, the number of incomplete returns is practically nil, since unclear points are checked as the children return the schedule.[1]

The returns vary from school district to school district, according to the attitude of the teacher and principal. The principal in Stamford who made the questionnaire an object lesson in geography with the geography books before the children (this was a ten-year-old group) got a response from that class which gave the room an almost complete score in a very few minutes.[2] The children were cognizant of their ancestry, and they were eager to talk about it. In the few instances where principals expressed antagonism[3] toward the immigrant groups represented in their schools or toward the investigation, the schools returned the largest number of incomplete histories and the follow-up load was heavy.

On the whole, teachers are co-operative and they can be depended upon to evoke the proper response from children, but they are less sure about ethnic classification.[4] This interferes with the proper gathering of data, since they are likely to give children unnecessary caution here and there. Our training schools have proved inadequate at the very point where the educational problem demands special knowledge. Teachers have had little training in immigrant backgrounds and for the most part no training in anthropology or ethnology. Their training in "citizenship" makes them especially fond of a wider use of the word "American." To many of them the word "American" designates those born in America (the Constitution bears witness to this); to others "American" refers only to those who are naturalized; and again to others it means those who feel themselves American. Children are encouraged to call themselves American on any score.[5]

There is even some disdain for the ethnic concept of nationality; and it is difficult to make clear the anthropological problems involved. Neces-

---

[1] See chap. ii, p. 16, n. 1.

[2] The histories were then taken home to parents to be checked.

[3] No outspoken antagonism was encountered in any public school in Woonsocket.

[4] This subject was partly discussed in chap. ii.

[5] A school principal who is herself an expert on Americanization in her community and is thoroughly familiar with the ethnic backgrounds of her immigrant children said upon reading this passage: "This is a conscious drive; we want them to feel a part of this great land." Upon discussing the matter further she pointed out the difference between the psychology of the situation to be dealt with and the objective in education.

sary emphasis must be placed upon the fact that it is information on descent which is being sought.

The reactions above indicated are sufficiently widespread to justify warning at this point. The instructions to teachers[1] need to be very specific or the objectives are misconstrued and children are misinformed even while they are being assisted. On the other hand, every survey depends largely upon the intelligence and good will of the teachers. In every community they have shown active interest and have given of themselves freely to meet the needs of the investigation.

Another caution concerning the interpretation of the replies should be made in reference to the questions regarding nationality. The general problem was previously discussed,[2] but the caution here relates specifically to Jews and Irish. There are different concepts of nationality current among Jews and also among Irish. Thus a Jew from a Slavic country usually claims Jewish "nationality." The Reform Jew, especially one whose regional origin is Germany, will invariably give his nationality as American. One of the tenets of Reform Judaism is that Judaism is a creed, and that Jews are not a nationality. Reform Jews make no reference to Jewish affiliation unless the question bears on religion. It therefore becomes necessary to estimate the number of Reform Jews in a given community and to take this item into consideration in any situation covering a wide area. School records usually have this information and provision is made for the teacher to check.[3] The high holy days among Jews, on which days practically all Jewish children are absent from school, serve as an additional check.[4]

The "colored" also offer a group which the present schedule may not reach. Surprisingly enough, the children usually answer in some manner which describes their racial affiliation. "American colored" is a frequent reply. But here again an opportunity is given the teacher to add her checkmark. When the first tabulations for Woonsocket were made, there seemed to be some occasion for questioning the returns on this score since only nine colored children were reported for the entire city. It seemed logical to infer that other colored children had been counted with "Old Americans." An inquiry directed to the school department indicated, however, that there were only nine colored children in the public schools of Woon-

---

[1] See chap. ii, p. 14.   [2] Chap. ii.

[3] See par. 6 of "Instructions to Principals and Teachers," chap. ii, p. 14.

[4] Jewish research agencies have developed methods for estimating the number of Jewish children in a given area.

socket. The questionnaire and the check required of the teacher seem to yield the correct results.

PROVIDENCE SCHOOLS

PUT NO WRITING HERE
M.   T.

School _John Howland_ ... Grade _9A_ Age _9_
(Last birthday)

Name _____ Address _Orchard Ave_
(First)   (Last)   (Number)   (Street)
Providence
Where were you born? ....
(Country)   (Province or State)   (City, if in Rhode Island)

If foreign born, at what age did you come to this country? ....

What language other than English do you speak? _I speak only English_

What is your mother's nationality or racial descent? _Irish._
(Example: English, French Canadian Irish, etc.)

Where was your mother born? _Providence   City_
(Country)   (Province or State)   (City, if in Rhode Island)

If foreign born, how long ago did she come to this country? ...... At what age? ......

Where was your mother's mother born? _Paterson N. J._

Where was your mother's father born? _Ireland._

How long ago did the first member of your mother's family come to Providence? _50 yrs_ To R.I. _50 yrs_ To U.S.A.? _60 yrs._

What is your father's nationality or racial descent? _Irish._

Where was your father born? _Worcester._
(Country)   (Province or State)   (City, if in Rhode Island)

If foreign born, how long ago did he come to this country? ...... At what age? ......

Where was your father's mother born? _New York._

Where was your father's father born? _Worcester._

How long ago did the first member of your father's family come to Providence? _2 yrs_ To R.I. _2 yrs_ To U.S.A. _2 yrs._

In what country were your mother and father married? _Providence R.I._ In what year? _1916._

What language is _usually_ spoken in your home? _English_

What other languages does your mother speak? _" " No other._

What other languages does your father speak? _" "   "   "_

How many persons are there in your family? _There are six (6) in family._

Have you any brothers or sisters in this school? _Yes one (1)._

If so, name them, and give grade _Ursula_ _____

Have you any brothers or sisters in any other school, or in college? _" No. Yes._

If so, name them and give school they are in _Ursula_ _____ _Slater Ave._

Have you any brothers or sisters not in school? _Yes._

If so, name them and give age _Marguerite & Mary_ _____

(Schedule used in population studies in Connecticut and Rhode Island)

C.   J.

The Irish present a different problem. They are sensitive to any appellation which may seem to question their loyalty as American citizens. They use the term "American" in reply to questions about nationality more

frequently than others, but the origin of grandparents always serves as a
check. Parents are on guard against the use of the term "Irish" to define

PROVIDENCE SCHOOLS

School _John Horland_ ...... Grade _4 a_ ... Age _9_ ......
(Last birthday)

Name _____ Address. _~ Upton Ave_ ......
(First)   (Last)   (Number)   (Street)

Where were you born?_U. S. a_ ...... _R. I._ ...... _Warren_ ......
(Country)   (Province or State)   (City, if in Rhode Island)

If foreign born, at what age did you come to this country? ....

What language other than English do you speak?..

What is your mother's nationality or racial descent?_Jewish_ ....
(Example: English, French, Canadian, Irish, etc.)

Where was your mother born?_England_ ....
(Country)   (Province or State)   (City, if in Rhode Island)

If foreign born, how long ago did she come to this country?_28 years ago_ At what age?_6_

Where was your mother's mother born?_Russia_ ....

Where was your mother's father born?_Russia_ ....

How long ago did the first member of your mother's family come to Providence?............To R. I.?............To U. S. A.?............

What is your father's nationality or racial descent?_Jewish_ ....

Where was your father born?_R. I._ ...... _Prov._ ....
(Country)   (Province or State)   (City, if in Rhode Island)

If foreign born, how long ago did he come to this country?............At what age?............

Where was your father's mother born?_Russia_ ....

Where was your father's father born?_Russia_ ....

How long ago did the first member of your father's family come to Providence?............To R. I.?............To U. S. A.?............

In what country were your mother and father married?_U. S._ ......In what year?_1915_

What language is _usually_ spoken in your home?_English_ ....

What other languages does your mother speak?_Jewish_ ....

What other languages does your father speak?_Jewish_ ....

How many persons are there in your family?_4_ ....

Have you any brothers or sisters in this school?_No_ ....

If so, name them, and give grade............

Have you any brothers or sisters in any other school, or in college? _No_ ....

If so, name them and give school they are in............

Have you any brothers or sisters not in school?_Yes - One sister_ ....

If so, name them and give age._Barbara_ _____ _- age 4_ ....

C.   J.

(Schedule used in population studies in Connecticut and Rhode Island)

their own nationality if they claim American citizenship but frankly state
that their own parents were all Irish. "My parents were Irish, I am
American," is a typical reply. The ethnic connotation which the word

carries for other groups, French Canadians, Italians, Slavs, and Slavic Jews, is foreign to the Irish (and to the Reform Jew),[1] and it varies some-

---

PROVIDENCE SCHOOLS

PUT NO
WRITING HERE

M. T.

School _John Howland_ Grade _3 A_ Age _8_
(Last birthday)

Name _____ Address _East George St._
(First)   (Last)   (Number)   (Street)
Providence R. I.
(City, if in Rhode Island)

Where were you born? ....
(Country)   (Province or State)   (City, if in Rhode Island)

If foreign born, at what age did you come to this country? ....

What language other than English do you speak? ....

- -

What is your mother's nationality or racial descent? _American Negro_
(Example: English, French Canadian, Irish, etc.)

Where was your mother born? _Providence R. I._
(Country)   (Province or State)   (City, if in Rhode Island)

If foreign born, how long ago did she come to this country? .... At what age? ....

Where was your mother's mother born? _Seekonk Mass_

Where was your mother's father born? _Washington D. C._

How long ago did the first member of your mother's family come to Providence? .... To R. I.? .... To U. S. A.? ....

What is your father's nationality or racial descent? _American Negro_

Where was your father born? _Virginia_
(Country)   (Province or State)   (City, if in Rhode Island)

If foreign born, how long ago did you come to this country? .... At what age? ....

Where was your father's mother born? _Virginia_

Where was your father's father born? _Virginia_

How long ago did the first member of your father's family come to Providence? .... To R. I.? .... To U. S. A.? ....

In what country were your mother and father married? .... In what year? ....

What language is _usually_ spoken in your home? _English_

What other languages does your mother speak? ....

What other languages does your father speak? ....

How many persons are there in your family? _Three_

Have you any brothers or sisters in this school? _no_

If so, name them, and give grade ....

Have you any brothers or sisters in any other school, or in college? _no_

If so, name them and give school they are in ....

Have you any brothers or sisters not in school? _no_

If so, name them and give age ....

C. J.

(Schedule used in population studies in Connecticut and Rhode Island)

---

[1] It would be difficult to know to what an extent the reactions attributed previously to teachers on p. 269 are characteristic of them as teachers or as members of the Irish group. Not all the teachers who took this stand were Irish, but most of them were; some of them were Old American. On the other hand, the principal referred to in the note on p. 269 is herself Jewish and ardent in her affiliation with that group.

what from group to group. The investigator must be familiar with these differing concepts in interpreting replies.

In general, Italians and Jews returned more complete records than any other group. There is little that is complicated in Italian histories; also, Italians quite readily claim Italian "nationality." Jewish histories are complicated, but the subjects are cognizant of their complex backgrounds and usually take pains to give the facts in comprehensive manner. All immigrant groups have developed an unusual acumen for describing their ethnic relationships. The histories appended are typical for their groups.[1]

VARIABILITY[2] IN REPLIES

(Table 69)

The significance of replies varies from nationality to nationality. Nationalities differ in their willingness or ability to answer certain questions. Questions vary in their strength to evoke replies. They vary in their meaning to different groups.

It must also be recognized that a certain number of histories inevitably are fictitious—there are circumstances of birth, of family history, of entry into the country, which belong to the family closet. Also there are certain situations which inhibit children and parents from confessing descent from some group whose prestige is possibly in question by the dominant element in the community. To the extent that these situations exist there is a margin of error here.

On the other hand, there were several questions on the blank which were included primarily as a check upon replies. Familiarity with the typical reaction of different groups in this respect serves as a guide in interpreting replies. Experience based upon handling 168,000 cases, in checking histories for consistency, comparing histories returned by several children in the same family, visiting 2,000 homes for the purpose of testing the reliability of replies, gives assurance that the margin of error cannot be serious enough to vitiate the conclusions presented. Family visitors were instructed to be particularly careful to locate possible sources of error in replies. The replies dealing with ethnic descent and birthplace always "score higher" than any others.

Table 69 is a summary presentation indicating the number of replies accepted by the investigators as being probably reliable for each question

[1] These particular histories are from the Providence survey.

[2] This word is not used with any statistical connotation here.

TABLE 69

Per Cent of Replies Accepted for Each Question and for Different Nationalities

	British	French-Canadians	Irish	Italians	Jews	Slavs	All Other Homogeneous	Mixed Ancestry	Descent in Part Unspecified	Number of Rejects	Total Number of Replies Possible	Per Cent of Total Replies Rejected	Per Cent of Total Replies Accepted
Pupil: Sec. I													
Key	100.0	100.0	100.0	100.0	100.0	100.0	100.0	100.0	100.0	0	2,876	.0	100.0
Sex and language	100.0	100.0	100.0	100.0	100.0	100.0	100.0	100.0	100.0	0	2,876	.0	100.0
School	100.0	100.0	100.0	100.0	100.0	100.0	100.0	100.0	100.0	0	2,876	.0	100.0
Grade	99.5	99.9	99.3	100.0	99.0	100.0	98.6	99.8	100.0	8	2,876	.3	99.7
Age	99.5	99.2	100.0	98.9	100.0	99.3	98.6	99.0	100.0	22	2,876	.8	99.2
Birthplace	100.0	100.0	100.0	100.0	100.0	100.0	100.0	100.0	100.0	0	2,876	.0	100.0
Age of entry to U.S.	100.0	87.5	66.7	91.7	100.0	90.9	100.0	93.3	50.0	23	253	9.1	90.9
Mother: Sec. II													
Nationality	100.0	100.0	100.0	100.0	100.0	100.0	100.0	100.0	48.3* / 89.9	46* / 9	2,876	1.6* / .3	98.4* / 99.7
Birthplace	100.0	100.0	100.0	100.0	100.0	99.8	100.0	100.0	92.1	8	2,876	.3	99.7
Year of entry to U.S.	93.3	80.7	89.4	96.7	98.9	94.7	93.2	89.3	22.2	186	1,758	10.6	89.4
Age of entry to U.S.	86.5	78.6	87.2	91.2	92.1	91.0	86.8	85.5	22.2	255	1,758	14.5	85.5
Mother's mother's birthplace	100.0	99.8	100.0	100.0	100.0	99.8	100.0	100.0	89.9	12	2,876	.4	99.6
Mother's father's birthplace	100.0	99.8	100.0	100.0	100.0	99.8	100.0	100.0	88.8	13	2,876	.5	99.5
Family entry to Woonsocket	60.8	64.8	60.4	71.0	71.7	59.0	63.5	63.5	51.7	1,050	2,876	36.5	63.5
Family entry to U.S.	47.7	43.3	44.4	60.7	66.7	46.9	41.7	41.7	20.2	1,566	2,876	54.4	45.6
Father: Sec. III													
Nationality	100.0	100.0	100.0	100.0	100.0	100.0	100.0	100.0	20.2* / 87.6	71* / 11	2,876	2.5* / .4	97.5* / 99.6
Birthplace	100.0	100.0	100.0	100.0	100.0	99.8	100.0	100.0	87.6	12	2,876	.4	99.6
Year of entry to U.S.	94.3	74.3	87.2	94.5	94.7	93.1	86.7	88.6	50.0	264	1,844	14.3	85.7
Age of entry to U.S.	88.5	70.6	79.5	88.5	87.4	87.0	81.6	81.1	50.0	364	1,844	19.7	80.3
Father's mother's birthplace	99.5	99.1	100.0	100.0	100.0	99.8	99.5	100.0	85.4	25	2,876	.9	99.1
Father's father's birthplace	99.1	99.4	100.0	99.5	100.0	99.8	99.5	100.0	85.4	23	2,876	.8	99.2
Family entry to Woonsocket	56.3	58.9	47.9	68.3	68.7	55.8	61.4	56.7	40.5	1,213	2,876	42.2	57.8
Family entry to U.S.	43.7	38.8	39.6	56.3	63.6	44.2	43.7	35.9	14.6	1,694	2,876	58.9	41.1
Sec. IV													
Place of marriage	98.6	97.5	98.6	99.5	99.0	96.6	95.3	98.6	88.8	73	2,876	2.5	97.5
Date of marriage	91.9	88.9	93.7	91.8	96.0	93.7	88.8	91.4	79.8	268	2,876	9.3	90.7
Language of home	100.0	100.0	100.0	100.0	100.0	100.0	100.0	100.0	93.3	6	2,876	.2	99.8
Language of parents	100.0	100.0	100.0	99.5	100.0	100.0	100.0	100.0	93.3	7	2,876	.2	99.8
Number in family	100.0	100.0	100.0	100.0	100.0	100.0	100.0	100.0	100.0	0	2,876	.0	100.0
Type stock	99.5	99.0	100.0	100.0	100.0	99.8	100.0	100.0	88.8	22	2,876	.8	99.2
Generation	99.5	99.0	100.0	100.0	100.0	99.8	100.0	100.0	89.9	21	2,876	.7	99.3
Per cent of all replies accepted or rejected	91.8	90.1	91.1	93.7	94.4	91.7	91.4	91.2	76.8	7,272	79,357	9.1	90.9

* These are of native descent but unspecified for ethnic origin; the figure below represents cases which are entirely unspecified.

and for each nationality. A word of caution is needed in interpreting the high scores specified in most instances in the last column of the table. In the first place, this record was attained only after 922 follow-up visits were made to homes of these children in Woonsocket alone, in the course of which visits numerous incomplete or obviously inconsistent replies were made complete.

In the second place, attention should be called to the fact that the titles are those used on the punch card and the high scores indicated in numerous situations could not possibly be anything else, as, for example, those referring to children in Section I and some of those in Section IV. These are for the most part laboratory tools for classifying the cases. Similarly, every nationality must score 100 per cent in its returns for nationality for the simple reason that only those cases which were definitely known to belong in that nationality were placed there; others were placed in the class designated in part unspecified.

Only nine histories in the entire community were completely lacking in information about ethnic descent of mothers, and eleven histories were completely lacking in information about nationality of fathers. For the entire city and after follow-up work 2.9 per cent of the fathers and 1.9 per cent of the mothers, in all 4.8 per cent of the parents, were still incomplete for ethnic descent.[1] Of these, 3.1 per cent were of native descent whose ethnic origin was not otherwise specified.

The lowest scores are recorded against the questions which deal with family entry to the United States. This low record is due in large part to the fact that the form of question was inadequate. The reply was frequently discarded, because it was obvious that the family misunderstood the question. No follow-up visits were made to families whose histories were incomplete only on this score.

Reference has already been made to the inadequacy of the replies from which age is computed. Data on age (derived from data on year of entry and age at entry) were incomplete for 14.2 per cent of the cases, but the score varied greatly from one group to another. As previously indicated,[2] age data were accepted from more than 90 per cent of the new immigrants; the number of answers accepted for the British mothers was 86.5 per cent, for the Irish, 87.2 per cent, and for the French Canadians, 78.6 per cent.

Certain other data require further interpretation. It is fair to assume that specific measures of change indicate trends rather than an actual

[1] See Tables 14b and 15b.   [2] See chap. xiii.

record of all that has transpired in this population. For example, the amount of admixture indicated in any family line is a minimum amount. If there have been four, five, or six strains known to the family, the tendency is to make record only of the outstanding strains; the other is included under a note, "some Scotch," "some Indian."[1]

The data dealing with the number of children similarly refer to living children. In using the data on language ability, languages obviously learned in school were not included in the report. Language ability or facility does not include any test of actual ability or facility. In some instances it probably means only ability to understand another language rather than ability to speak it fluently.

On the whole, the data warrant the conclusion that, with the exceptions noted, they give a true picture of the situations which exist and the changes which are taking place in Woonsocket.

FEASIBILITY

TIME BUDGET

One of the most vital problems in planning a survey is the time element, since both the gathering and handling of data are so time consuming as to make the use of the survey in many cases prohibitive. It took ten months for two able young women to sort the cards by hand[2] for this presentation and to prepare the first tables, and this after all the experimental work of devising classificatory schemes, symbols, and definitions had been done. These women worked with the results of one survey before them which served, so to speak, as a map. This expenditure of time is over and above the time element involved in securing entrée, gathering data, examining histories, coding, and punching. The Woonsocket material was handled along with other materials, but a fair estimate of time consumed in this preliminary work is at least one year for two assistants. This assumes trained supervision and a mapped territory, but it also allows for the extremely costly element of time consumed in experimental classification and in integrating the several independent analyses we have made here.

It should be noted that this presentation involved four complete and extensive tabulations. The data for all factors were tabulated for 2,876 families; they were also tabulated for 4,978 children. All tabulations were made on a geographic basis; again all were made on an ethnic basis. The

[1] A dozen or more families reported some Indian blood.

[2] The experimental nature of the project required a hand count.

summaries selected for presentation were based upon the study of more than 22,000[1] individuals.

In view of this heavy tax upon time, one may well raise the question of feasibility. Can these time-consuming elements be reduced and how? The following aids may be invoked:

TABULATING DATA

1. *Careful selection of those items which serve the ends of any immediate study.*—Certain items were included in this report for purposes of disclosing method, testing schemes, and for comparison. Much of this can be omitted in subsequent surveys. Again, this survey is general; it involves tabulations which may serve several ends—securing data on "national" origins, on intermarriage, on ethnic composition of school population, on ethnic indices of children, and so on. These may be independent objectives and are not necessary for each other except in a situation where a complete ethnic survey is the object. Any one of these objectives may be reached independently and quickly. The presentation of the data on intermarriage (Part II) is the most time-consuming element in the study, and the most costly in presentation. They are least necessary for securing ethnic origins or for making an ethnic inventory of individuals in any population. They deal solely with intermarriage.

2. *"Building the study" may help.*—Numerous tables may be derived from other tables, or the order of counting may be such that one table checks the previous one. The sequence required in presenting data is usually a logical or a chronological one. This is not likely to be the most effective procedure in making tabulations. In this case, the tables presented in the later chapters are those which should be made first. Some of the inventories may be derived from intermarriage tables. If the most complete tables are made first the difficult cases are brought to light in the first handling, cases which are likely to distort several tables because they fall at one time in one class and at some other time in another class.

3. *Use of mechanical devices.*—The use of tabulating machines may facilitate and economize counting processes. They can be used most effectively when the classes are sufficiently large. When the number of cases is limited or when the data fall into numerous small classes, a count by hand is better, particularly if discrimination is necessary in handling each individual case. On the basis of these preliminary tabulations numerous

[1] There were 5,752 parents, 4,978 children, 11,504 grandparents, altogether 22,234 individuals, who had to be tabulated. This does not include the 2,876 families and the 19,912 theoretical grandparents who were counted as units in some of the classifications.

short-cuts may be invoked for massing the data. The experience in these early investigations points the way to the larger groupings to be used in more extensive surveys. The material could be coded immediately with this end in view. Our material has been coded always so that the punch cards carry all possible information which may desirably be extracted by students or other investigators. An ethnic history for an individual child must be concrete and detailed. For the mass study many of these details need not be carried and the tabulation of them could be omitted. Only those items should be assigned to the machine which can be massed.

With its equipment the office of the United States Bureau of the Census probably could prepare in ten or twelve days, and at a cost of from $1,000 to $1,500, the same material which it would take a small staff working independently at least one year, and the cost in the latter case would be several fold. This latter statement applies only to the tabulation of data which have already been prepared for the machines and assumes in either case the same trained supervision in the initial preparation of material. There is no reason why such mechanical equipment cannot be utilized for ethnic surveys.[1] This would bring independent surveys of any regional area within a cost commensurate with the results obtained for that community. It would in addition offer the opportunity of accumulating data from parallel studies of other regional areas.

CONTINUOUS SCHOOL SURVEYS

The foregoing suggestions all refer to situations where the object is either to obtain ethnic origins or to make a complete ethnic survey over an extended area, that is, where the data are secured on a large scale and could be massed.

Educators whose assistance or advice has been sought in these investigations have invariably shown a deep interest in the survey as a tool which might render a service in planning educational work. In such instances the object must be to describe each school district, since the problem differs from neighborhood to neighborhood and racial composition varies greatly from one school district to another. Thus, a rural school is found to be entirely Old American, the teacher has lived in the district all her life and knows every family; another school is 80 per cent Italian; while a third is composed largely of Slavic elements. The needs of this study required a report for the city as a whole; the need of the

[1] Attention should also be directed to the recent organization of the Columbia University Statistical Bureau and to the services which such an agency may render in mechanizing and handling data of this kind.

school administration is served best for a survey of each school district. In Woonsocket this would mean twenty-one school surveys instead of the one community survey we have presented here.

This very condition facilitates the procedure involved in making a continuous school survey. The number of cases in any one school district are never so large but that the basic tabulations can be made in a few days. No coding or punching, or mechanical tabulations, need be employed since simple tabulations may be made directly from records. The instructions are readily communicable by one familiar with racial problems and with the technical problems involved, and the procedure can be readily standardized. Moreover, the data need to be gathered only once for each incoming class to any school.

Assuming a continuous survey for each district to be in progress, an ethnic inventory of children[1] may be made complete for a city in a few weeks, by drawing upon existing data. It should also be recalled that the needs of the individual school do not include the tabulation of the data with the family as a unit, or any of the analyses in Part II of this volume.

Such a school survey not only offers a picture of composition, but it provides an ethnic index for each child who is the subject of education. A continuous survey serves also to record those changes in a city which are due to the shifting of population from one district to another, and thus points the way for changes in educational practice in so far as that practice is determined by ethnic composition of the given unit.

CONCLUSIONS

In general, then, ethnic surveys need not be prohibitive. The cost of independent investigations will vary with the situation. The experimental investigation needs to create its own laboratories, its own methods, and to train anew a staff for each community. The heavy tax upon funds and time due to these elements is, however, almost entirely a charge against the pioneer project. If the end in view is to obtain ethnic origins, the tabulation for an entire area need take only a few days. If the object is to make a complete survey, the time required for the tabulation of the data, assuming the availability of mechanical resources and of expert assistance, is a matter running into months. A continuous school survey once inagurated would require little additional work on the part of school principals; and tabulations for a school system could be made from data

[1] As presented in Table 21 of this volume.

gathered in the district units. The cost of any research or report would depend in each case upon the problems chosen for further investigation, since children's histories invariably present numerous research cues as to the possible relation of ethnic factors to educational adjustment.[1]

SELECTED BIBLIOGRAPHY

The following is a selected list of references which constitutes a minimum workshelf for investigators in this general field.

CLASSIFICATION OF PEOPLES

BOWMAN, ISAIAH. *The New World: Problems in Political Geography.* 4th ed. Yonkers: World Book Co., 1928.

This valuable text deals with ethnographic situations in various countries of the world and with the international problems they create. Contains maps and extensive bibliographies on major problems and on each of the important countries.

Dictionary of Races or Peoples, "Reports of the U.S. Immigration Commission," Vol. V. Washington: Government Printing Office, 1911.

A statement prepared for the United States Immigration Commission as "to the ethnical status of immigrant races or peoples, their languages, their numbers, and the countries from which they come."

KROEBER, A. L. *Anthropology.* New York: Harcourt, Brace & Co., 1923.

A well-known general text in anthropology containing information bearing upon racial problems.

New International Encyclopedia, The.

A standard work of reference.

PITTARD, EUGENE. *Race and History: An Ethnological Introduction to History.* Translated by V. C. C. COLLUM. "The History of Civilization Series." New York: Knopf, 1926.

Contains anthropological history and classification of races for the continents of the world.

The references dealing with specific ethnic groups are too numerous to list. In addition to the standard atlases published in the United States see:

DOMINIAN, LEON. "The Nationality Map of Europe," *A League of Nations,* Vol. I, No. 2 (Dec., 1917). Boston: World Peace Foundation, 1917.

Contains supplement, "Language Map of Europe and Selected List of Books."

GABRYS, J. *Carte ethnographique de l'Europe.* Lausanne: Librairie Centrale des Nationalités, 1918.

M. Gabrys is *secrétaire-général* of the Union des Nationalités. The pamphlet contains a Preface, a Bibliography (of European publications), and an ethnic map.

[1] See reference to Margaret Tully, *op. cit.,* in chap. i, p. 8.

STATISTICAL AND OTHER SOURCES OF INFORMATION ON IMMIGRATION
PROBLEMS IN THIS COUNTRY

Publications of the United States Bureau of the Census.

See especially Census monographs referred to in text of this monograph.

Reports of the United States Immigration Commission. Washington: Government
Printing Office, 1911.

See Vols. I and II for abstracts of the reports of the Commission which were issued in
forty-one volumes.

JEROME, HARRY. *Migration and Business Cycles.* New York: National Bureau of
Economic Research, 1926.

A scientific investigation dealing with the relation of fluctuations in migration to fluctuations in employment and with the effect of quota restriction upon the seasonal movement in
immigration.

LAUGHLIN, HARRY H. *Analysis of America's Modern Melting Pot.* Washington: Government Printing Office, 1923. Hearings of the U.S. Congress, third session of the
Sixty-seventh Congress, November 21, 1922, Serial 7C.

————. *Europe as an Emigrant-exporting Continent and the United States as an Immi-
grant-receiving Nation.* Hearings before the Committee on Immigration and
Naturalization, House of Representatives, Sixty-eighth Congress, first session,
March 8, 1924, Serial 5A. Washington: Government Printing Office, 1923.

"A preliminary report of field investigations concerning present-day human migrations,
with particular reference to racial and national fortunes, statistically and biologically considered."

In support of immigration restriction on a eugenic basis, with particular reference to
present quota legislation. Table 5 in the second report gives the approximate annual quotas
admissible, under each of twenty-five different formulas. The appendixes include text of the
Immigration Act of 1924 and other pertinent statements.

TREVOR, JOHN B. *An Analysis of the American Immigration Act of 1924. International
Conciliation Bull. 202,* September, 1924. New York: Carnegie Endowment for
International Peace, 1924.

Contains the text of the Immigration Act of 1924 and of other official documents. A study
of the population of the United States.

CURRENT SOURCES OF INFORMATION

Files of the *United States Daily.*

Contain adequate news presentation of legislation on national-origins and other immigration problems.

FOREIGN LANGUAGE INFORMATION SERVICE. *The Interpreter Releases.* Directed by
MARIAN SCHIBSBY. New York City.

Constitutes the best current source of information on immigrant problems.

INTERMARRIAGE

DRACHSLER, JULIUS. *Democracy and Assimilation: The Blending of Immigrant Heritages in America.* New York: Macmillan Co., 1920.

A more general treatment of the quantitative data presented in volume noted below.

———. *Intermarriage in New York City: A Statistical Study of the Amalgamation of European Peoples.* "Studies in History, Economics and Public Law," Vol. XCIV, No. 2 (Whole No. 213). New York: Columbia University, 1921.

A statistical monograph based upon an examination of 100,000 cases of intermarriage in New York City, from 1908 to 1912. The outstanding work on Intermarriage in the United States.

PROBLEMS OF METHOD

The works listed here may be considered type studies, each in a specific field, but all contributing to the general problem of procedure in the study of acculturation.

BOAS, FRANZ. *The Mind of Primitive Man.* New York: Macmillan Co., 1921.

A well-known text stating the position of an important school of thought in the field of race study.

DAY, EDMUND E. *Statistical Analysis.* New York: Macmillan Co., 1927.

A valuable text on statistical procedure for use of staff members.

FISCHER, EUGEN. *Die Rehobother Bastards, und das Bastardierungs-Problem beim Menschen.* Jena: Verlag von Gustav Fischer, 1913.

The anthropological study of an isolated mulatto group and of its civilization in Southwest Africa.

GAMIO, MANUEL. Translation of the Introduction, synthesis, and conclusions of the work, *The Population of the Valley of Teotihuacan.* Mexico: Talleres Gráficos de la Nación, 1922.

See note in chap. xii, p. 183.

HRDLIČKA, ALES. *The Old Americans.* Baltimore: Williams & Wilkins Co., 1925.

An anthropometric study of some nineteen hundred subjects whose ancestry in this country dates back at least two generations, namely, parents and grandparents are native born.

LYND, ROBERT S., and LYND, HELEN MERREL, *Middletown: A Study in Contemporary American Culture.* New York: Harcourt, Brace & Co., 1929.

See chap. i, p. 6.

PALMER, VIVIEN. *Field Studies in Sociology: A Student's Manual.* Chicago: University of Chicago Press, 1928.

A text dealing with the scientific investigation of modern society, containing type-study outlines and a discussion of techniques.

PEARL, RAYMOND. *Modes of Research in Genetics.* New York: Macmillan Co., 1915.

A discussion of procedure in attacking a biologic problem of interest to the student of society. See also other works by the same author.

WISSLER, CLARK. *The American Indian: An Introduction to the Anthropology of the New World.* New York: McMurtie, 1917.

———. *Man and Culture.* New York: Crowell, 1923.

———. *Relation of Nature to Man in Aboriginal America.* New York: Oxford Press, 1926.

See chap. xii, p. 183.

AMERICANIZATION THEORY

BERKSON, ISAAC BAER. *Theories of Americanization: A Critical Study with Special Reference to the Jewish Group.* New York: New York Teachers College, Columbia University, 1920.

Contains selected references.

FRENCH CANADIANS. See bibliography of Appendix A.

INDEX

INDEX

A index; *see* Indices
Abbreviations:
  list of, 25
Admixture; *see* Fusion
Age:
  at intermarriage, 145
  first-generation mothers, 189–90, 194–98
Americanization:
  of French Canadians, 244
  programs of, in New London, 177–78
  study of theories of, 178–83
Americans, Old:
  defined, 21
  derivation of children of, 90–92
  descent of, 74–79
  partly, defined, 21
    descent of, 90–92
  use of term, 92
  visits to, 17
Arnold, Richard, 211, 212

B index; *see* Indices
Berkson, Isaac B., 180
Bernon, 215
Bibliography:
  ethnic survey, 281–84
  French and French Canadians, 247–63
  history of Woonsocket, 227–29
Bilingualism; *see* Language
Boas, Franz, 18, 33, 179
Boisvert, Marie, 268
Bossavy, Marthe L., 7, 8, 17, 220, 222, 235–36, 240–43, 245, 246, 268
Bowman, Isaiah, 5, 21
British:
  ethnic preference in mating, 51, 116–18, 129–37; *see* Ethnic preference
  fusion, rates of, 158–62
  in melting pot, 38–42, 48–51; *see* Melting pot *and* Numerical equivalents
  intermarriage, rates for, 109; *see* Intermarriage
  kindred strains, marriage with, 116; *see* Kindred strains
Brown University, 7, 179
Buffalo, 8, 9
  University of, 8, 9

Carpenter, Niles, 4, 8, 9, 56
Carter, Isabel G., 8
Catholic schools, 10–11, 12
  French-Canadian, 216
  see Schools
Census Bureau:
  statistics of, 4, 23, 29
Children:
  colored, 270

derivation of all, 81–100; *see* Ethnic and Regional
generation of all, 85–89; *see* Generation
language facility of, 200–202
number of, in family, 193–98; *see* Size of family
of mixed descent, 92–97
of repeated admixture, 93–95
Classification, 18–19
Columbia University:
  statistical bureau of, 279
Community:
  entrée to, 10, 11, 13, 267, 268
Community area, 177–84
  concept of, 181
  cultural aspects, 177
  research leads to study of, 178–80
Composition; *see* Ethnic
Comstock, Samuel, 211, 212
Country of origin:
  defined, 22
  use of, 29
Cultural aspects of survey, 177
Cultural factors of area discussed, 185–210

Davenport, Charles B., 118
Derivation:
  ethnic, geographic, and regional, defined, 22
  see also Children, Families, Fathers, Mothers, Parents, Grandparents, Numerical equivalents, Intermarriage
Derivations:
  list of, 20
  tests of classification of, 55–56
Descent; *see* Sibs, Children, Fathers, Parents, Ethnic, etc.
Diffusion:
  manner of, 159–70
  of ethnic elements, 29–42, 159–71
  of stocks through sibs, 173–74
  see also Sibs, Children
Drachsler, Julius, 5, 6, 118, 180
Dushkin, Alexander M., 180

Entrée, to community; *see* Community
Entry, to United States; *see* United States
Ethnic:
  composition, methods to ascertain, 29; *see* Derivation
  descent, 6, 16
    of parents, 47
      by generation, 63
    of sibs, 71–79
  fusion, defined, 22; *see also* Diffusion, Marriage, Intermarriage

287